Writing Culture

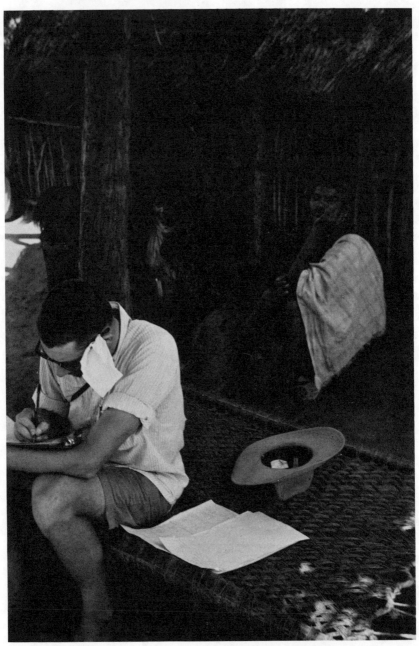

Stephen Tyler in the Field. Photography by Martha G. Tyler.

Writing Culture

The Poetics and Politics of Ethnography

EDITED BY JAMES CLIFFORD
AND GEORGE E. MARCUS

A School of American Research
Advanced Seminar

University of California Press
BERKELEY   LOS ANGELES   LONDON

University of California Press
Berkeley and Los Angeles, California
University of California Press, Ltd.
London, England
© 1986 by
The Regents of the University of California
Printed in the United States of America
     2   3   4   5   6   7   8   9

Library of Congress Cataloging-in-Publication Data
Main entry under title:
Writing Culture.
   Seminar held in Santa Fe, N.M., April 1984.
   Bibliography: p.
   Includes index.
   1. Ethnology—Authorship—Congresses.
2. Ethnology—Methodology—Congresses.   I. Clifford, James,
1945–   II. Marcus, George E.   III. School of American
Research (Santa Fe, N.M.)
GN307.7.W75   1986   306'.01'8   85-14860
ISBN 0-520-05729-5 (alk. paper)

Contents

Preface   vii

JAMES CLIFFORD
Introduction: Partial Truths   1

MARY LOUISE PRATT
Fieldwork in Common Places   27

VINCENT CRAPANZANO
Hermes' Dilemma: The Masking of
Subversion in Ethnographic Description   51

RENATO ROSALDO
From the Door of His Tent:
The Fieldworker and the Inquisitor   77

JAMES CLIFFORD
On Ethnographic Allegory   98

STEPHEN A. TYLER
Post-Modern Ethnography:
From Document of the Occult
to Occult Document   122

TALAL ASAD
The Concept of Cultural Translation
in British Social Anthropology   141

GEORGE E. MARCUS
Contemporary Problems of Ethnography
in the Modern World System   165

MICHAEL M. J. FISCHER
Ethnicity and the Post-Modern Arts
of Memory   194

PAUL RABINOW
Representations Are Social Facts:
Modernity and Post-Modernity in
Anthropology   234

GEORGE E. MARCUS
Afterword: Ethnographic Writing and
Anthropological Careers   262

Bibliography   267

Notes on Contributors   295

Index   297

Preface

These essays are the product of intensive discussions held at the School of American Research in Santa Fe, New Mexico, during April 1984. Following the school's format for "advanced seminars," conversations continued over a week, and the number of participants was strictly limited to ten. The group discussed papers circulated in advance and explored a wide range of topics relevant to the seminar's focus on "the making of ethnographic texts." Some of the participants had been recent innovators in the writing of ethnography (Paul Rabinow, Vincent Crapanzano, Renato Rosaldo, Michael Fischer); others had been systematically developing critiques of its history, rhetoric, and current prospects (Mary Louise Pratt, Robert Thornton, Stephen Tyler, Talal Asad, George Marcus, James Clifford). All were involved with advanced, ongoing work in textual criticism and cultural theory. Eight of the ten participants had backgrounds in anthropology, one in history, one in literary studies. The group's center of gravity in one field, cultural anthropology, ensured a common language and range of reference, thus allowing the exchanges to take place at an advanced level. But the seminar's scope was interdisciplinary. All the participants had questioned disciplines and genres in their recent work, drawing as needed from historical, literary, anthropological, political, and philosophical sources. More information is contained in the "Notes on Contributors" (pp. 295–96 below), and the volume's common Bibliography gives full citations of relevant works by each individual. Of the ten essays presented at the seminar, nine are included here. (For contingent reasons, Robert Thornton could not revise his in time to meet the deadline.)

By looking critically at one of the principal things ethnographers *do*—that is, write—the seminar sought both to reinterpret cultural anthropology's recent past and to open up its future possibilities. But while pursuing textual and literary analyses, the seminar also considered the limitations of such approaches. Several papers stressed, and the discussions repeatedly returned to, larger contexts of systematic

power inequality, world-systems constraints, and institutional formations that could only partly be accounted for by a focus on textual production. The seminar thus pursued a limited set of emphases self-
critically in an attempt to come to terms with the politics and poetics
of cultural representation. For a fuller account of the Santa Fe discussions (including topics that have not found their way into this volume),
see the report published in *Current Anthropology* 26 (April 1985):
267–71. Some of the more blatant exclusions produced by the organization and focus of the seminar are discussed there, as well as in the
Introduction that immediately follows this Preface.

The essays in this volume are all revised versions of the working
papers presented at the seminar. Some are now quite different. As
editors we have not prodded them toward thematic unity or tried to
contrive artificial "conversations" between them. Readers will doubtless find friction as well as agreement. Nor have we tried to impose a
uniformity of style on the essays; on the contrary, we have encouraged
diversity. The sequential ordering of the volume's parts does not hold
any great significance. There is a general progression from studies
with a literary bent toward those that question this emphasis—for example, Rabinow's critical framing of the entire "textualist" approach.
The essays tend, also, to move from retrospective critiques of ethnographic conventions to discussions of current possibilities for experimental work. By this logic, Tyler's evocation of a "post-modern ethnography" might have been placed at the end. But in fact his essay
looks to pre-modern sources for the post-modern and is generally un-
classifiable. We did not wish to leave the impression that the volume as
a whole points in any utopian or prophetic direction.

As editors, we would particularly like to thank the seminar participants for their cooperation and good humor; the School of American
Research (notably its president, Douglas Schwartz, and its director of
publications, Jane Kepp) for hospitality and encouragement; the Hu-
manities Division at the University of California, Santa Cruz; and especially Barbara Podratz, with the help of Margi Wald, at Rice University, for assistance in preparing the manuscript. At the University
of California Press, Naomi Schneider and James Clark offered editorial help and encouragement. We are grateful, also, to more than a
few press and nonpress readers of the manuscript, not only for their
specific suggestions, but especially for their general enthusiasm. They
confirmed our hope that the book would strike an important, controversial chord in all those fields where ethnography and cultural criticism are becoming important. Many of these readers are fully as qualified to contribute to a volume on this topic as are the ten individuals
who gathered at Santa Fe. The questions raised in the pages that fol-

low are being widely debated; we did not invent them. We trust that those who have already contributed to the debate will find themselves appropriately thanked, or at least engaged.

Finally, as an Invocation, we offer the following verses composed in mock despair by our first editorial reader, Jane Kepp, dictionary in hand.

The Hermeneut's Dilemma, or, A Jargon Poem

Twas prelapsarian, and the hermeneut
Sat huddled with his faithful trope,
Sunk in thaumasmus, idly strumming his lute,
Lost in subversion with nary a hope.

Then with heartfelt apoplanesis he cried,
O come, interlocutor, give me your ear!
In my pathopoeia I've slandered and lied;
Now of my grim project this discourse you'll hear.

I've dabbled in vile phenomenological rites,
And joined in a secret synecdoche,
Squandered my received knowledge in bibulous nights,
And embraced epistemological heresy.

O, but now my metonymy is too great to bear!
This ecphonesis has become too deictic to hide!
I've lost all the poesis I once held so dear . . .
And, with typical hypotyposis, he died.

James Clifford
University of California, Santa Cruz

George E. Marcus
Rice University

JAMES CLIFFORD

Introduction: Partial Truths

Interdisciplinary work, so much discussed these days, is not about confronting already constituted disciplines (none of which, in fact, is willing to let itself go). To do something interdisciplinary it's not enough to choose a "subject" (a theme) and gather around it two or three sciences. Interdisciplinarity consists in creating a new object that belongs to no one.

ROLAND BARTHES, "Jeunes Chercheurs"

You'll need more tables than you think.

ELENORE SMITH BOWEN, advice for fieldworkers, in *Return to Laughter*

Our frontispiece shows Stephen Tyler, one of this volume's contributors, at work in India in 1963. The ethnographer is absorbed in writing—taking dictation? fleshing out an interpretation? recording an important observation? dashing off a poem? Hunched over in the heat, he has draped a wet cloth over his glasses. His expression is obscured. An interlocutor looks over his shoulder—with boredom? patience? amusement? In this image the ethnographer hovers at the edge of the frame—faceless, almost extraterrestrial, a hand that writes. It is not the usual portrait of anthropological fieldwork. We are more accustomed to pictures of Margaret Mead exuberantly playing with children in Manus or questioning villagers in Bali. Participant-observation, the classic formula for ethnographic work, leaves little room for texts. But still, somewhere lost in his account of fieldwork among the Mbuti pygmies—running along jungle paths, sitting up at night singing, sleeping in a crowded leaf hut—Colin Turnbull mentions that he lugged around a typewriter.

In Bronislaw Malinowski's *Argonauts of the Western Pacific*, where a photograph of the ethnographer's tent among Kiriwinan dwellings is prominently displayed, there is no revelation of the tent's interior. But in another photo, carefully posed, Malinowski recorded himself writing at a table. (The tent flaps are pulled back; he sits in profile, and some Trobrianders stand outside, observing the curious rite.) This remarkable picture was only published two years ago—a sign of our times, not his.[1] We begin, not with participant-observation or with cultural texts (suitable for interpretation), but with writing, the making of texts. No longer a marginal, or occulted, dimension, writing has emerged as central to what anthropologists do both in the field and thereafter. The fact that it has not until recently been portrayed or seriously discussed reflects the persistence of an ideology claiming transparency of representation and immediacy of experience. Writing reduced to method: keeping good field notes, making accurate maps, "writing up" results.

The essays collected here assert that this ideology has crumbled. They see culture as composed of seriously contested codes and representations; they assume that the poetic and the political are inseparable, that science is in, not above, historical and linguistic processes. They assume that academic and literary genres interpenetrate and that the writing of cultural descriptions is properly experimental and ethical. Their focus on text making and rhetoric serves to highlight the constructed, artificial nature of cultural accounts. It undermines overly transparent modes of authority, and it draws attention to the historical predicament of ethnography, the fact that it is always caught up in the invention, not the representation, of cultures (Wagner 1975). As will soon be apparent, the range of issues raised is not literary in any traditional sense. Most of the essays, while focusing on textual practices, reach beyond texts to contexts of power, resistance, institutional constraint, and innovation.

Ethnography's tradition is that of Herodotus and of Montesquieu's Persian. It looks obliquely at all collective arrangements, distant or nearby. It makes the familiar strange, the exotic quotidian. Ethnography cultivates an engaged clarity like that urged by Virginia Woolf: "Let us never cease from thinking—what is this 'civilization' in which we find ourselves? What are these ceremonies and why should we take part in them? What are these professions and why should we make money out of them? Where in short is it leading us, the procession of the sons of educated men?" (1936: 62–63). Ethnography is actively situated *between* powerful systems of meaning. It poses its questions at the boundaries of civilizations, cultures, classes, races, and genders. Ethnography decodes and recodes, telling the grounds of collective order and diversity, inclusion and exclusion. It describes processes of

1. Malinowski 1961 : 17. The photograph inside the tent was published in 1983 by George Stocking in *History of Anthropology* 1 : 101. This volume contains other telling scenes of ethnographic writing.

innovation and structuration, and is itself part of these processes.

Ethnography is an emergent interdisciplinary phenomenon. Its authority and rhetoric have spread to many fields where "culture" is a newly problematic object of description and critique. The present book, though beginning with fieldwork and its texts, opens onto the wider practice of writing about, against, and among cultures. This blurred purview includes, to name only a few developing perspectives, historical ethnography (Emmanuel Le Roy Ladurie, Natalie Davis, Carlo Ginzburg), cultural poetics (Stephen Greenblatt), cultural criticism (Hayden White, Edward Said, Fredric Jameson), the analysis of implicit knowledge and everyday practices (Pierre Bourdieu, Michel de Certeau), the critique of hegemonic structures of feeling (Raymond Williams), the study of scientific communities (following Thomas Kuhn), the semiotics of exotic worlds and fantastic spaces (Tzvetan Todorov, Louis Marin), and all those studies that focus on meaning systems, disputed traditions, or cultural artifacts.

This complex interdisciplinary area, approached here from the starting point of a crisis in anthropology, is changing and diverse. Thus I do not want to impose a false unity on the exploratory essays that follow. Though sharing a general sympathy for approaches combining poetics, politics, and history, they frequently disagree. Many of the contributions fuse literary theory and ethnography. Some probe the limits of such approaches, stressing the dangers of estheticism and the constraints of institutional power. Others enthusiastically advocate experimental forms of writing. But in their different ways they all analyze past and present practices out of a commitment to future possibilities. They see ethnographic writing as changing, inventive: "History," in William Carlos Williams's words, "that should be a left hand to us, as of a violinist."

∿∿∿

"Literary" approaches have recently enjoyed some popularity in the human sciences. In anthropology influential writers such as Clifford Geertz, Victor Turner, Mary Douglas, Claude Lévi-Strauss, Jean Duvignaud, and Edmund Leach, to mention only a few, have shown an interest in literary theory and practice. In their quite different ways they have blurred the boundary separating art from science. Nor is theirs a new attraction. Malinowski's authorial identifications (Conrad, Frazer) are well known. Margaret Mead, Edward Sapir, and Ruth Benedict saw themselves as both anthropologists and literary artists. In Paris surrealism and professional ethnography regularly exchanged both ideas and personnel. But until recently literary influences have been held at a distance from the "rigorous" core of the discipline. Sapir and Benedict had, after all, to hide their poetry from the scientific gaze of Franz Boas. And though ethnographers have often been called novelists manqué (especially those who write a little too well), the notion that literary procedures pervade any work of cultural representation is a recent idea in the discipline. To a growing number, however, the "literariness" of anthropology—and especially of ethnography—appears as much more than a matter of good writing or distinctive style.[2] Literary processes—metaphor, figuration, narrative—affect the ways cultural phenomena are registered, from the first jotted "observations," to the completed book, to the ways these configurations "make sense" in determined acts of reading.[3]

It has long been asserted that scientific anthropology is also an "art," that ethnographies have literary qualities. We often hear that an author writes with style, that certain descriptions are vivid or convincing (should not every accurate description be convincing?). A work is deemed evocative or artfully composed in addition to being factual; expressive, rhetorical functions are conceived as decorative or merely as ways to present an objective analysis or description more effectively. Thus the facts of the matter may be kept separate, at least in principle, from their means of communication. But the literary or rhetorical dimensions of ethnography can no longer be so easily compartmentalized. They are active at every level of cultural science. Indeed, the very notion of a "literary" approach to a discipline, "anthropology," is seriously misleading.

The present essays do not represent a tendency or perspective within a coherent "anthropology" (pace Wolf 1980). The "four-field" definition of the discipline, of which Boas was perhaps the last virtuoso, included physical (or biological) anthropology, archaeology, cultural (or social) anthropology, and linguistics. Few today can seriously claim that these fields share a unified approach or object, though the dream persists, thanks largely to institutional arrangements. The essays in this volume occupy a new space opened up by the disintegration of "Man" as telos for a whole discipline, and they draw on recent developments in the fields of textual criticism, cultural history, semiotics, hermeneutic philosophy, and psychoanalysis. Some years ago, in

2. A partial list of works exploring this expanded field of the "literary" in anthropology includes (not mentioning contributors to the present volume): Boon 1972, 1977, 1982; Geertz 1973, 1983; Turner 1974, 1975; Fernandez 1974; Diamond 1974; Duvignaud 1970, 1973; Favret-Saada 1980; Favret-Saada and Contreras 1981; Dumont 1978; Tedlock 1983; Jamin 1979, 1980, 1985; Webster 1982; Thornton 1983, 1984.

3. See the work of Hayden White (1973, 1978) for a tropological theory of "prefigured" realities; also Latour and Woolgar (1979) for a view of scientific activity as "inscription."

a trenchant essay, Rodney Needham surveyed the theoretical incoherence, tangled roots, impossible bedfellows, and divergent specializations that seemed to be leading to academic anthropology's intellectual disintegration. He suggested with ironic equanimity that the field might soon be redistributed among a variety of neighboring disciplines. Anthropology in its present form would undergo "an iridescent metamorphosis" (1970:46). The present essays are part of the metamorphosis.

But if they are post-anthropological, they are also post-literary. Michel Foucault (1973), Michel de Certeau (1983), and Terry Eagleton (1983) have recently argued that "literature" itself is a transient category. Since the seventeenth century, they suggest, Western science has excluded certain expressive modes from its legitimate repertoire: rhetoric (in the name of "plain," transparent signification), fiction (in the name of fact), and subjectivity (in the name of objectivity). The qualities eliminated from science were localized in the category of "literature." Literary texts were deemed to be metaphoric and allegorical, composed of inventions rather than observed facts; they allowed a wide latitude to the emotions, speculations, and subjective "genius" of their authors. De Certeau notes that the fictions of literary language were scientifically condemned (and esthetically appreciated) for lacking "univocity," the purportedly unambiguous accounting of natural science and professional history. In this schema, the discourse of literature and fiction is inherently unstable; it "plays on the stratification of meaning; it narrates one thing in order to tell something else; it delineates itself in a language from which it continuously draws effects of meaning that cannot be circumscribed or checked" (1983:128). This discourse, repeatedly banished from science, but with uneven success, is incurably figurative and polysemous. (Whenever its effects begin to be felt too openly, a scientific text will appear "literary"; it will seem to be using too many metaphors, to be relying on style, evocation, and so on.)[4]

By the nineteenth century, literature had emerged as a bourgeois institution closely allied with "culture" and "art." Raymond Williams (1966) shows how this special, refined sensibility functioned as a kind of court of appeals in response to the perceived dislocations and vulgarity of industrial, class society. Literature and art were, in effect, cir-

4. "It might be objected that *figurative style* is not the only style, or even the only poetic style, and that rhetoric also takes cognizance of what is called *simple* style. But in fact this is merely a less decorated style, or rather, a style decorated more simply, and it, too, like the lyric and the epic, has its own special figures. A style in which figure is strictly absent does not exist," writes Gérard Genette (1982:47).

cumscribed zones in which nonutilitarian, "higher" values were maintained. At the same time they were domains for the playing out of
experimental, avant-garde transgressions. Seen in this light, the ideological formations of art and culture have no essential or eternal status. They are changing and contestable, like the special rhetoric of
"literature." The essays that follow do not, in fact, appeal to a literary
practice marked off in an esthetic, creative, or humanizing domain.
They struggle, in their different ways, against the received definitions
of art, literature, science, and history. And if they sometimes suggest
that ethnography is an "art," they return the word to an older usage—
before it had become associated with a higher or rebellious sensibility—to the eighteenth-century meaning Williams recalls: art as the
skillful fashioning of useful artifacts. The making of ethnography is
artisanal, tied to the worldly work of writing.

Ethnographic writing is determined in at least six ways: (1) con-
textually (it draws from and creates meaningful social milieux); (2)
rhetorically (it uses and is used by expressive conventions); (3) institutionally (one writes within, and against, specific traditions, disciplines,
audiences); (4) generically (an ethnography is usually distinguishable
from a novel or a travel account); (5) politically (the authority to represent cultural realities is unequally shared and at times contested);
(6) historically (all the above conventions and constraints are changing). These determinations govern the inscription of coherent ethnographic fictions.

To call ethnographies fictions may raise empiricist hackles. But
the word as commonly used in recent textual theory has lost its connotation of falsehood, of something merely opposed to truth. It suggests the partiality of cultural and historical truths, the ways they are
systematic and exclusive. Ethnographic writings can properly be
called fictions in the sense of "something made or fashioned," the
principal burden of the word's Latin root, *fingere*. But it is important
to preserve the meaning not merely of making, but also of making up,
of inventing things not actually real. (*Fingere*, in some of its uses, implied a degree of falsehood.) Interpretive social scientists have recently come to view good ethnographies as "true fictions," but usually
at the cost of weakening the oxymoron, reducing it to the banal claim
that all truths are constructed. The essays collected here keep the oxymoron sharp. For example, Vincent Crapanzano portrays ethnographers as tricksters, promising, like Hermes, not to lie, but never undertaking to tell the whole truth either. Their rhetoric empowers *and*
subverts their message. Other essays reinforce the point by stressing
that cultural fictions are based on systematic, and contestable, exclusions. These may involve silencing incongruent voices ("Two Crows

denies it!") or deploying a consistent manner of quoting, "speaking for," translating the reality of others. Purportedly irrelevant personal or historical circumstances will also be excluded (one cannot tell all). Moreover, the maker (but why only one?) of ethnographic texts cannot avoid expressive tropes, figures, and allegories that select and impose meaning as they translate it. In this view, more Nietzschean than realist or hermeneutic, all constructed truths are made possible by powerful "lies" of exclusion and rhetoric. Even the best ethnographic texts—serious, true fictions—are systems, or economies, of truth. Power and history work through them, in ways their authors cannot fully control.

Ethnographic truths are thus inherently *partial*—committed and incomplete. This point is now widely asserted—and resisted at strategic points by those who fear the collapse of clear standards of verification. But once accepted and built into ethnographic art, a rigorous sense of partiality can be a source of representational tact. A recent work by Richard Price, *First-Time: The Historical Vision of an Afro-American People* (1983), offers a good example of self-conscious, serious partiality. Price recounts the specific conditions of his fieldwork among the Saramakas, a Maroon society of Suriname. We learn about external and self-imposed limits to the research, about individual informants, and about the construction of the final written artifact. (The book avoids a smoothed-over, monological form, presenting itself as literally pieced-together, full of holes.) *First-Time* is evidence of the fact that acute political and epistemological self-consciousness need not lead to ethnographic self-absorption, or to the conclusion that it is impossible to know anything certain about other people. Rather, it leads to a concrete sense of why a Saramaka folktale, featured by Price, teaches that "knowledge is power, and that one must never reveal all of what one knows" (1983 : 14).

A complex technique of revelation and secrecy governs the communication (reinvention) of "First-Time" knowledge, lore about the society's crucial struggles for survival in the eighteenth century. Using techniques of deliberate frustration, digression, and incompleteness, old men impart their historical knowledge to younger kinsmen, preferably at cock's crow, the hour before dawn. These strategies of ellipsis, concealment, and partial disclosure determine ethnographic relations as much as they do the transmission of stories between generations. Price has to accept the paradoxical fact that "any Saramaka narrative (including those told at cock's crow with the ostensible intent of communicating knowledge) will leave out most of what the teller knows about the incident in question. A person's knowledge is supposed to grow only in small increments, and in any aspect of life people are deliberately told only a little bit more than the speaker thinks they already know" (10).

It soon becomes apparent that there is no "complete" corpus of First-Time knowledge, that no one—least of all the visiting ethnographer—can know this lore except through an open-ended series of contingent, power-laden encounters. "It is accepted that different Saramaka historians will have different versions, and it is up to the listener to piece together for himself the version of an event that he, for the time being, accepts" (28). Though Price, the scrupulous field-worker and historian, armed with writing, has gathered a text that surpasses in extent what individuals know or tell, it still "represents only the tip of the iceberg that Saramakas *collectively* preserve about First-Time" (25).

The ethical questions raised by forming a written archive of secret, oral lore are considerable, and Price wrestles with them openly. Part of his solution has been to undermine the completeness of his own account (but not its seriousness) by publishing a book that is a series of fragments. The aim is not to indicate unfortunate gaps remaining in our knowledge of eighteenth-century Saramaka life, but rather to present an inherently imperfect mode of knowledge, which produces gaps as it fills them. Though Price himself is not free of the desire to write a complete ethnography or history, to portray a "whole way of life" (24), the message of partiality resonates throughout *First-Time*.

Ethnographers are more and more like the Cree hunter who (the story goes) came to Montreal to testify in court concerning the fate of his hunting lands in the new James Bay hydroelectric scheme. He would describe his way of life. But when administered the oath he hesitated: "I'm not sure I can tell the truth. . . . I can only tell what I know."

∿

It is useful to recall that the witness was speaking artfully, in a determining context of power. Since Michel Leiris's early essay of 1950, "L'Ethnographe devant le colonialisme" (but why so late?), anthropology has had to reckon with historical determination and political conflict in its midst. A rapid decade, from 1950 to 1960, saw the end of empire become a widely accepted project, if not an accomplished fact. Georges Balandier's *"situation coloniale"* was suddenly visible (1955). Imperial relations, formal and informal, were no longer the accepted rule of the game—to be reformed piecemeal, or ironically distanced in various ways. Enduring power inequalities had clearly constrained ethnographic practice. This "situation" was felt earliest in

France, largely because of the Vietnamese and Algerian conflicts and through the writings of an ethnographically aware group of black intellectuals and poets, the *négritude* movement of Aimé Césaire, Léopold Senghor, René Ménil, and Léon Damas. The pages of *Présence Africaine* in the early fifties offered an unusual forum for collaboration between these writers and social scientists like Balandier, Leiris, Marcel Griaule, Edmond Ortigues, and Paul Rivet. In other countries the *crise de conscience* came somewhat later. One thinks of Jacques Maquet's influential essay "Objectivity in Anthropology" (1964), Dell Hymes's *Reinventing Anthropology* (1973), the work of Stanley Diamond (1974), Bob Scholte (1971, 1972, 1978), Gérard Leclerc (1972), and particularly of Talal Asad's collection *Anthropology and the Colonial Encounter* (1973), which has stimulated much clarifying debate (Firth et al. 1977).

In popular imagery the ethnographer has shifted from a sympathetic, authoritative observer (best incarnated, perhaps, by Margaret Mead) to the unflattering figure portrayed by Vine Deloria in *Custer Died for Your Sins* (1969). Indeed, the negative portrait has sometimes hardened into caricature—the ambitious social scientist making off with tribal lore and giving nothing in return, imposing crude portraits on subtle peoples, or (most recently) serving as dupe for sophisticated informants. Such portraits are about as realistic as the earlier heroic versions of participant-observation. Ethnographic work has indeed been enmeshed in a world of enduring and changing power inequalities, and it continues to be implicated. It enacts power relations. But its function within these relations is complex, often ambivalent, potentially counter-hegemonic.

Different rules of the game for ethnography are now emerging in many parts of the world. An outsider studying Native American cultures may expect, perhaps as a requirement for continuing research, to testify in support of land claim litigation. And a variety of formal restrictions are now placed on fieldwork by indigenous governments at national and local levels. These condition in new ways what can, and especially cannot, be said about particular peoples. A new figure has entered the scene, the "indigenous ethnographer" (Fahim, ed. 1982; Ohnuki-Tierney 1984). Insiders studying their own cultures offer new angles of vision and depths of understanding. Their accounts are empowered and restricted in unique ways. The diverse post- and neo-colonial rules for ethnographic practice do not necessarily encourage "better" cultural accounts. The criteria for judging a good account have never been settled and are changing. But what has emerged from all these ideological shifts, rule changes, and new compromises is the fact that a series of historical pressures have begun to reposition anthropology with respect to its "objects" of study. Anthropology no longer speaks with automatic authority for others defined as unable to speak for themselves ("primitive," "pre-literate," "without history"). Other groups can less easily be distanced in special, almost always past or passing, times—represented as if they were not involved in the present world systems that implicate ethnographers along with the peoples they study. "Cultures" do not hold still for their portraits. Attempts to make them do so always involve simplification and exclusion, selection of a temporal focus, the construction of a particular self-other relationship, and the imposition or negotiation of a power relationship.

The critique of colonialism in the postwar period—an undermining of "The West's" ability to represent other societies—has been reinforced by an important process of theorizing about the limits of representation itself. There is no way adequately to survey this multifarious critique of what Vico called the "serious poem" of cultural history. Positions proliferate: "hermeneutics," "structuralism," "history of mentalities," "neo-Marxism," "genealogy," "post-structuralism," "post-modernism," "pragmatism"; also a spate of "alternate epistemologies"—feminist, ethnic, and non-Western. What is at stake, but not always recognized, is an ongoing critique of the West's most confident, characteristic discourses. Diverse philosophies may implicitly have this critical stance in common. For example, Jacques Derrida's unraveling of logocentrism, from the Greeks to Freud, and Walter J. Ong's quite different diagnosis of the consequences of literacy share an overarching rejection of the institutionalized ways one large group of humanity has for millennia construed its world. New historical studies of hegemonic patterns of thought (Marxist, Annaliste, Foucaultian) have in common with recent styles of textual criticism (semiotic, reader-response, post-structural) the conviction that what appears as "real" in history, the social sciences, the arts, even in common sense, is always analyzable as a restrictive and expressive set of social codes and conventions. Hermeneutic philosophy in its varying styles, from Wilhelm Dilthey and Paul Ricoeur to Heidegger, reminds us that the simplest cultural accounts are intentional creations, that interpreters constantly construct themselves through the others they study. The twentieth-century sciences of "language," from Ferdinand de Saussure and Roman Jacobson to Benjamin Lee Whorf, Sapir, and Wittgenstein, have made inescapable the systematic and situational verbal structures that determine all representations of reality. Finally, the return of rhetoric to an important place in many fields of study (it had for millennia been at the core of Western education) has made possible a detailed anatomy of conventional expressive modes. Allied with semiotics and discourse analysis, the new rhetoric is concerned with what Kenneth Burke called "strategies for the encompassing of situations" (1969:3). It is less about how to speak well than about how to speak at all, and to act meaningfully, in the world of public cultural symbols.

The impact of these critiques is beginning to be felt in ethnography's sense of its own development. Noncelebratory histories are becoming common. The new histories try to avoid charting the discovery of some current wisdom (origins of the culture concept, and so forth); and they are suspicious of promoting and demoting intellectual precursors in order to confirm a particular paradigm. (For the latter approach, see Harris 1968 and Evans-Pritchard 1981). Rather, the new histories treat anthropological ideas as enmeshed in local practices and institutional constraints, as contingent and often "political" solutions to cultural problems. They construe science as a social process. They stress the historical discontinuities, as well as continuities, of past and present practices, as often as not making present knowledge seem temporary, in motion. The authority of a scientific discipline, in this kind of historical account, will always be mediated by the claims of rhetoric and power.[5]

Another major impact of the accumulating political/theoretical critique of anthropology may be briefly summarized as a rejection of "visualism." Ong (1967, 1977), among others, has studied ways in which the senses are hierarchically ordered in different cultures and epochs. He argues that the truth of vision in Western, literate cultures has predominated over the evidences of sound and interlocution, of touch, smell, and taste. (Mary Pratt has observed that references to odor, very prominent in travel writing, are virtually absent from ethnographies.)[6] The predominant metaphors in anthropological research have been participant-observation, data collection, and cultural description, all of which presuppose a standpoint outside—looking at, objectifying, or, somewhat closer, "reading," a given reality. Ong's

5. I exclude from this category the various histories of "anthropological" ideas, which must always have a Whiggish cast. I include the strong historicism of George Stocking, which often has the effect of questioning disciplinary genealogies (for example, 1968:69–90). The work of Terry Clark on the institutionalization of social science (1973) and of Foucault on the sociopolitical constitution of "discursive formations" (1973) points in the direction I am indicating. See also: Hartog (1980), Duchet (1971), many works by De Certeau (e.g., 1980), Boon (1982), Rupp-Eisenreich (1984), and the yearly volume *History of Anthropology*, edited by Stocking, whose approach goes well beyond the history of ideas or theory. An allied approach can be found in recent social studies of science research: e.g., Knorr-Cetina (1981), Latour (1984), Knorr-Cetina and Mulkay (1983).

6. An observation by Pratt at the Santa Fe seminar. The relative inattention to sound is beginning to be corrected in recent ethnographic writing (e.g., Feld 1982). For examples of work unusually attentive to the sensorium, see Stoller (1984a, b).

work has been mobilized as a critique of ethnography by Johannes
Fabian (1983), who explores the consequences of positing cultural
facts as things observed, rather than, for example, heard, invented in
dialogue, or transcribed. Following Frances Yates (1966), he argues
that the taxonomic imagination in the West is strongly visualist in
nature, constituting cultures as if they were theaters of memory, or
spatialized arrays.

In a related polemic against "Orientalism" Edward Said (1978)
identifies persistent tropes by which Europeans and Americans have
visualized Eastern and Arab cultures. The Orient functions as a theater, a stage on which a performance is repeated, to be seen from a
privileged standpoint. (Barthes [1977] locates a similar "perspective"
in the emerging bourgeois esthetics of Diderot.) For Said, the Orient
is "textualized"; its multiple, divergent stories and existential predicaments are coherently woven as a body of signs susceptible of virtuoso
reading. This Orient, occulted and fragile, is brought lovingly to light,
salvaged in the work of the outside scholar. The effect of domination
in such spatial/temporal deployments (not limited, of course, to Orientalism proper) is that they confer on the other a discrete identity,
while also providing the knowing observer with a standpoint from
which to see without being seen, to read without interruption.

Once cultures are no longer prefigured visually—as objects, theaters, texts—it becomes possible to think of a cultural poetics that is
an interplay of voices, of positioned utterances. In a discursive rather
than a visual paradigm, the dominant metaphors for ethnography
shift away from the observing eye and toward expressive speech (and
gesture). The writer's "voice" pervades and situates the analysis, and
objective, distancing rhetoric is renounced. Renato Rosaldo has recently argued, and exemplified, these points (1984, 1985). Other
changes of textual enactment are urged by Stephen Tyler in this volume. (See also Tedlock 1983.) The evocative, performative elements
of ethnography are legitimated. And the crucial poetic problem for
a discursive ethnography becomes how "to achieve by written means
what speech creates, and to do it without simply imitating speech"
(Tyler 1984c:25). From another angle we notice how much has been
said, in criticism and praise, of the ethnographic gaze. But what of the
ethnographic ear? This is what Nathaniel Tarn is getting at in an interview, speaking of his experience as a tricultural French/Englishman
endlessly becoming an American.

It may be the ethnographer or the anthropologist again having his ears wider
open to what he considers the exotic as opposed to the familiar, but I still feel
I'm discovering something new in the use of language here almost every day.

I'm getting new expressions almost every day, as if the language were growing from every conceivable shoot. (1975:9)

∧∧∧

        An interest in the discursive aspects of cultural representation draws attention not to the interpretation of cultural "texts" but to their relations of production. Divergent styles of writing are, with varying degrees of success, grappling with these new orders of complexity—different rules and possibilities within the horizon of a historical moment. The main experimental trends have been reviewed in detail elsewhere (Marcus and Cushman 1982; Clifford 1983a). It is enough to mention here the general trend toward a *specification of discourses* in ethnography: who speaks? who writes? when and where? with or to whom? under what institutional and historical constraints?

        Since Malinowski's time, the "method" of participant-observation has enacted a delicate balance of subjectivity and objectivity. The ethnographer's personal experiences, especially those of participation and empathy, are recognized as central to the research process, but they are firmly restrained by the impersonal standards of observation and "objective" distance. In classical ethnographies the voice of the author was always manifest, but the conventions of textual presentation and reading forbade too close a connection between authorial style and the reality represented. Though we discern immediately the distinctive accent of Margaret Mead, Raymond Firth, or Paul Radin, we still cannot refer to Samoans as "Meadian" or call Tikopia a "Firthian" culture as freely as we speak of Dickensian or Flaubertian worlds. The subjectivity of the author is separated from the objective referent of the text. At best, the author's personal voice is seen as a style in the weak sense: a tone, or embellishment of the facts. Moreover, the actual field experience of the ethnographer is presented only in very stylized ways (the "arrival stories" discussed below by Mary Pratt, for example). States of serious confusion, violent feelings or acts, censorships, important failures, changes of course, and excessive pleasures are excluded from the published account.

        In the sixties this set of expository conventions cracked. Ethnographers began to write about their field experience in ways that disturbed the prevailing subjective/objective balance. There had been earlier disturbances, but they were kept marginal: Leiris's aberrant *L'Afrique fantôme* (1934); *Tristes Tropiques* (whose strongest impact outside France came only after 1960); and Elenore Smith Bowen's important *Return to Laughter* (1954). That Laura Bohannan in the early sixties had to disguise herself as Bowen, and her fieldwork narrative as a "novel," is symptomatic. But things were changing rapidly,

and others—Georges Balandier (*L'Afrique ambiguë* 1957), David
Maybury-Lewis (*The Savage and the Innocent* 1965), Jean Briggs (*Never
in Anger* 1970), Jean-Paul Dumont (*The Headman and I* 1978), and Paul
Rabinow (*Reflections on Fieldwork in Morocco* 1977)—were soon writing
"factually" under their own names. The publication of Malinowski's
Mailu and Trobriand diaries (1967) publicly upset the applecart.
Henceforth an implicit mark of interrogation was placed beside any
overly confident and consistent ethnographic voice. What desires and
confusions was it smoothing over? How was its "objectivity" textually
constructed? [7]

A subgenre of ethnographic writing emerged, the self-reflexive
"fieldwork account." Variously sophisticated and naive, confessional
and analytic, these accounts provide an important forum for the discussion of a wide range of issues, epistemological, existential, and political. The discourse of the cultural analyst can no longer be simply
that of the "experienced" observer, describing and interpreting custom. Ethnographic experience and the participant-observation ideal
are shown to be problematic. Different textual strategies are attempted. For example, the first person singular (never banned from
ethnographies, which were always personal in stylized ways) is deployed according to new conventions. With the "fieldwork account"
the rhetoric of experienced objectivity yields to that of the autobiography and the ironic self-portrait. (See Beaujour 1980, Lejeune 1975.)
The ethnographer, a character in a fiction, is at center stage. He or
she can speak of previously "irrelevant" topics: violence and desire,
confusions, struggles and economic transactions with informants.
These matters (long discussed informally within the discipline) have
moved away from the margins of ethnography, to be seen as constitutive, inescapable (Honigman 1976).

Some reflexive accounts have worked to specify the discourse of
informants, as well as that of the ethnographer, by staging dialogues
or narrating interpersonal confrontations (Lacoste-Dujardin 1977,
Crapanzano 1980, Dwyer 1982, Shostak 1981, Mernissi 1984). These
fictions of dialogue have the effect of transforming the "cultural" text
(a ritual, an institution, a life history, or any unit of typical behavior to
be described or interpreted) into a speaking subject, who sees as well
as is seen, who evades, argues, probes back. In this view of ethnography the proper referent of any account is not a represented "world";
now it is specific instances of discourse. But the principle of dialogical
textual production goes well beyond the more or less artful presenta-

7. I have explored the relation of personal subjectivity and authoritative cultural
accounts, seen as mutually reinforcing fictions, in an essay on Malinowski and Conrad
(Clifford 1985a).

tion of "actual" encounters. It locates cultural interpretations in many sorts of reciprocal contexts, and it obliges writers to find diverse ways of rendering negotiated realities as multisubjective, power-laden, and incongruent. In this view, "culture" is always relational, an inscription of communicative processes that exist, historically, *between* subjects in relations of power (Dwyer 1977, Tedlock 1979).

Dialogical modes are not, in principle, autobiographical; they need not lead to hyper self-consciousness or self-absorption. As Bakhtin (1981) has shown, dialogical processes proliferate in any complexly represented discursive space (that of an ethnography, or, in his case, a realist novel). Many voices clamor for expression. Polyvocality was restrained and orchestrated in traditional ethnographies by giving to one voice a pervasive authorial function and to others the role of sources, "informants," to be quoted or paraphrased. Once dialogism and polyphony are recognized as modes of textual production, monophonic authority is questioned, revealed to be characteristic of a science that has claimed to *represent* cultures. The tendency to specify discourses—historically and intersubjectively—recasts this authority, and in the process alters the questions we put to cultural descriptions. Two recent examples must suffice. The first involves the voices and readings of Native Americans, the second those of women.

James Walker is widely known for his classic monograph *The Sun Dance and Other Ceremonies of the Oglala Division of the Teton Sioux* (1917). It is a carefully observed and documented work of interpretation. But our reading of it must now be complemented—and altered—by an extraordinary glimpse of its "makings." Three titles have now appeared in a four-volume edition of documents he collected while a physician and ethnographer on the Pine Ridge Sioux Reservation between 1896 and 1914. The first (Walker, *Lakota Belief and Ritual* 1982a, edited by Raymond DeMallie and Elaine Jahner) is a collage of notes, interviews, texts, and essay fragments written or spoken by Walker and numerous Oglala collaborators. This volume lists more than thirty "authorities," and wherever possible each contribution is marked with the name of its enunciator, writer, or transcriber. These individuals are not ethnographic "informants." *Lakota Belief* is a collaborative work of documentation, edited in a manner that gives equal rhetorical weight to diverse renditions of tradition. Walker's own descriptions and glosses are fragments among fragments.

The ethnographer worked closely with interpreters Charles and Richard Nines, and with Thomas Tyon and George Sword, both of whom composed extended essays in Old Lakota. These have now been translated and published for the first time. In a long section of *Lakota Belief* Tyon presents explanations he obtained from a number of Pine Ridge shamans; and it is revealing to see questions of belief (for example the crucial and elusive quality of *"wakan"*) interpreted in differing, idiosyncratic styles. The result is a version of culture in process that resists any final summation. In *Lakota Belief* the editors provide biographical details on Walker, with hints about the individual sources of the writings in his collection, brought together from the Colorado Historical Society, the American Museum of Natural History, and the American Philosophical Society.

The second volume to have appeared is *Lakota Society* (1982b), which assembles documents roughly relating to aspects of social organization, as well as concepts of time and history. The inclusion of extensive Winter Counts (Lakota annals) and personal recollections of historical events confirms recent tendencies to question overly clear distinctions between peoples "with" and "without" history (Rosaldo 1980; Price 1983). Volume three is *Lakota Myth* (1983). And the last will contain the translated writings of George Sword. Sword was an Oglala warrior, later a judge of the Court of Indian Offenses at Pine Ridge. With Walker's encouragement, he wrote a detailed vernacular record of customary life, covering myth, ritual, warfare and games, complemented by an autobiography.

Taken together, these works offer an unusual, multiply articulated record of Lakota life at a crucial moment in its history—a three-volume anthology of ad hoc interpretations and transcriptions by more than a score of individuals occupying a spectrum of positions with respect to "tradition," plus an elaborated view of the ensemble by a well-placed Oglala writer. It becomes possible to assess critically the synthesis Walker made of these diverse materials. When complete, the five volumes (including *The Sun Dance*) will constitute an expanded (dispersed, not total) text representing a particular *moment* of ethnographic production (not "Lakota culture"). It is this expanded text, rather than Walker's monograph, that we must now learn to read.

Such an ensemble opens up new meanings and desires in an ongoing cultural *poesis*. The decision to publish these texts was provoked by requests to the Colorado Historical Society from community members at Pine Ridge, where copies were needed in Oglala history classes. For other readers the "Walker Collection" offers different lessons, providing, among other things, a mock-up for an ethnopoetics with history (and individuals) in it. One has difficulty giving these materials (many of which are very beautiful) the timeless, impersonal identity of, say, "Sioux myth." Moreover, the question of *who writes* (performs? transcribes? translates? edits?) cultural statements is inescapable in an expanded text of this sort. Here the ethnographer no longer holds unquestioned rights of salvage: the authority long associated with bringing elusive, "disappearing" oral lore into legible textual form. It is unclear whether James Walker (or anyone) can appear as author of these writings. Such lack of clarity is a sign of the times.

Western texts conventionally come with authors attached. Thus it is perhaps inevitable that *Lakota Belief*, *Lakota Society*, and *Lakota Myth* should be published under Walker's name. But as ethnography's complex, plural *poesis* becomes more apparent—and politically charged— conventions begin, in small ways, to slip. Walker's work may be an unusual case of textual collaboration. But it helps us see behind the scenes. Once "informants" begin to be considered as co-authors, and the ethnographer as scribe and archivist as well as interpreting observer, we can ask new, critical questions of all ethnographies. However monological, dialogical, or polyphonic their form, they are hierarchical arrangements of discourses.

A second example of the specification of discourses concerns gender. I shall first touch on ways in which it can impinge on the reading of ethnographic texts and then explore how the exclusion of feminist perspectives from the present volume limits and focuses its discursive standpoint. My first example, of the many possible, is Godfrey Lienhardt's *Divinity and Experience: The Religion of the Dinka* (1961), surely among the most finely argued ethnographies in recent anthropological literature. Its phenomenological rendition of Dinka senses of the self, of time, space, and "the Powers" is unparalleled. Thus it comes as a shock to recognize that Lienhardt's portrayal concerns, almost exclusively, the experience of Dinka men. When speaking of "the Dinka" he may or may not be extending the point to women. We often cannot know from the published text. The examples he chooses are, in any case, overwhelmingly centered on males. A rapid perusal of the book's introductory chapter on Dinka and their cattle confirms the point. Only once is a woman's view mentioned, and it is in affirmation of men's relation to cows, saying nothing of how women experience cattle. This observation introduces an equivocation in passages such as "Dinka often interpret accidents or coincidences as acts of Divinity distinguishing truth from falsehood by signs which appear to men" (p. 47). The intended sense of the word "men" is certainly generic, yet surrounded exclusively by examples from male experience it slides toward a gendered meaning. (Do signs appear to women? in significantly different ways?) Terms such as "the Dinka," or "Dinka," used throughout the book, become similarly equivocal.

The point is not to convict Lienhardt of duplicity; his book specifies gender to an unusual extent. What emerges, instead, are the history and politics that intervene in our reading. British academics of a certain caste and era say "men" when they mean "people" more often than do other groups, a cultural and historical context that is now less invisible than it once was. The partiality of gender in question here was not at issue when the book was published in 1961. If it were, Lienhardt would have directly addressed the problem, as more recent ethnographers now feel obliged to (for example, Meigs 1984:xix). One did not read "The Religion of the Dinka" then as one now must, as the religion of Dinka men and only perhaps Dinka women. Our task is to think historically about Lienhardt's text and its possible readings, including our own, as we read.

Systematic doubts about gender in cultural representation have become widespread only in the past decade or so, in certain milieux, under pressure of feminism. A great many portrayals of "cultural" truths now appear to reflect male domains of experience. (And there are, of course, inverse, though much less common cases: for example, Mead's work, which often focused on female domains and generalized on this basis about the culture as a whole.) In recognizing such biases, however, it is well to recall that our own "full" versions will themselves inevitably appear partial; and if many cultural portrayals now seem more limited than they once did, this is an index of the contingency and historical movement of all readings. No one reads from a neutral or final position. This rather obvious caution is often violated in new accounts that purport to set the record straight or to fill a gap in "our" knowledge.

When is a gap in knowledge perceived, and by whom? Where do "problems" come from?[8] It is obviously more than a simple matter of noticing an error, bias, or omission. I have chosen examples (Walker and Lienhardt) that underline the role of political and historical factors in the discovery of discursive partiality. The epistemology this implies cannot be reconciled with a notion of cumulative scientific progress, and the partiality at stake is stronger than the normal scientific dictates that we study problems piecemeal, that we must not overgeneralize, that the best picture is built up by an accretion of rigorous evidence. Cultures are not scientific "objects" (assuming such things exist, even in the natural sciences). Culture, and our views of "it," are produced historically, and are actively contested. There is no whole picture that can be "filled in," since the perception and filling of a gap lead to the awareness of other gaps. If women's experience has been significantly excluded from ethnographic accounts, the recognition of this absence, and its correction in many recent studies, now highlights

---

8. "The stork didn't bring them!" (David Schneider, in conversation). Foucault described his approach as a "history of problematics" (1984).

the fact that men's experience (as gendered subjects, not cultural types—"Dinka" or "Trobrianders") is itself largely unstudied. As canonical topics like "kinship" come under critical scrutiny (Needham 1974; Schneider 1972, 1984), new problems concerning "sexuality" are made visible. And so forth without end. It is evident that we know more about the Trobriand Islanders than was known in 1900. But the "we" requires historical identification. (Talal Asad argues in this volume that the fact that this knowledge is routinely inscribed in certain "strong" languages is not scientifically neutral.) If "culture" is not an object to be described, neither is it a unified corpus of symbols and meanings that can be definitively interpreted. Culture is contested, temporal, and emergent. Representation and explanation—both by insiders and outsiders—is implicated in this emergence. The specification of discourses I have been tracing is thus more than a matter of making carefully limited claims. It is thoroughly historicist and self-reflexive.

In this spirit, let me turn to the present volume. Everyone will be able to think of individuals or perspectives that should have been included. The volume's focus limits it in ways its authors and editors can only begin to make apparent. Readers may note that its anthropological bias neglects photography, film, performance theory, documentary art, the nonfiction novel, "the new journalism," oral history, and various forms of sociology. The book gives relatively little attention to new ethnographic possibilities emerging from non-Western experience and from feminist theory and politics. Let me dwell on this last exclusion, for it concerns an especially strong intellectual and moral influence in the university milieux from which these essays have sprung. Thus its absence cries out for comment. (But by addressing this one exclusion I do not mean to imply that it offers any privileged standpoint from which to perceive the partiality of the book.) Feminist theorizing is obviously of great potential significance for rethinking ethnographic writing. It debates the historical, political construction of identities and self/other relations, and it probes the gendered positions that make all accounts of, or by, other people inescapably partial.[9] Why, then, are there no essays in this book written from primarily feminist standpoints?

9. Many of the themes I have been stressing above are supported by recent feminist work. Some theorists have problematized all totalizing, Archimedian perspectives (Jehlen 1981). Many have seriously rethought the social construction of relationship and difference (Chodorow 1978, Rich 1976, Keller 1985). Much feminist practice questions the strict separation of subjective and objective, emphasizing processual modes of knowledge, closely connecting personal, political, and representational processes. Other strands deepen the critique of visually based modes of surveillance and portrayal, linking them to domination and masculine desire (Mulvey 1975, Kuhn

The volume was planned as the publication of a seminar limited by its sponsoring body to ten participants. It was institutionally defined as an "advanced seminar," and its organizers, George Marcus and myself, accepted this format without serious question. We decided to invite people doing "advanced" work on our topic, by which we understood people who had already contributed significantly to the analysis of ethnographic textual form. For the sake of coherence, we located the seminar within, and at the boundaries of, the discipline of anthropology. We invited participants well known for their recent contributions to the opening up of ethnographic writing possibilities, or whom we knew to be well along on research relevant to our focus. The seminar was small and its formation ad hoc, reflecting our specific personal and intellectual networks, our limited knowledge of appropriate work in progress. (I shall not go into individual personalities, friendships, and so forth, though they are clearly relevant.)

Planning the seminar, we were confronted by what seemed to us an obvious—important and regrettable—fact. Feminism had not contributed much to the theoretical analysis of ethnographies as texts. Where women had made textual innovations (Bowen 1954, Briggs 1970, Favret-Saada 1980, 1981) they had not done so on feminist grounds. A few quite recent works (Shostak 1981, Cesara 1982, Mernissi 1984) had reflected in their form feminist claims about subjectivity, relationality, and female experience, but these same textual forms were shared by other, nonfeminist, experimental works. Moreover, their authors did not seem conversant with the rhetorical and textual theory that we wanted to bring to bear on ethnography. Our focus was thus on textual theory as well as on textual form: a defensible, productive focus.

Within this focus we could not draw on any developed debates generated by feminism on ethnographic textual practices. A few very initial indications (for example, Atkinson 1982; Roberts, ed. 1981) were all that had been published. And the situation has not changed dramatically since. Feminism clearly has contributed to anthropological theory. And various female ethnographers, like Annette Weiner (1976), are actively rewriting the masculinist canon. But feminist eth-

---

1982). Narrative forms of representation are analyzed with regard to the gendered positions they reenact (de Lauretis 1984). Some feminist writing has worked to politicize and subvert all natural essences and identities, including "femininity" and "woman" (Wittig 1975, Irigaray 1977, Russ 1975, Haraway 1985). "Anthropological" categories such as nature and culture, public and private, sex and gender have been brought into question (Ortner 1974, MacCormack and Strathern 1980, Rosaldo and Lamphere 1974, Rosaldo 1980, Rubin 1975).

nography has focused either on setting the record straight about women or on revising anthropological categories (for example, the nature/culture opposition). It has not produced either unconventional forms of writing or a developed reflection on ethnographic textuality as such.

The reasons for this general situation need careful exploration, and this is not the place for it.[10] In the case of our seminar and volume, by stressing textual form and by privileging textual theory, we focused the topic in ways that excluded certain forms of ethnographic innovation. This fact emerged in the seminar discussions, during which it became clear that concrete institutional forces—tenure patterns, canons, the influence of disciplinary authorities, global inequalities of power—could not be evaded. From this perspective, issues of content in ethnography (the exclusion and inclusion of different experiences in the anthropological archive, the rewriting of established traditions) became directly relevant. And this is where feminist and non-Western writings have made their greatest impact.[11] Clearly our sharp separation of form from content—and our fetishizing of form—was, and is, contestable. It is a bias that may well be implicit in modernist "textualism." (Most of us at the seminar, excluding Stephen Tyler, were not yet thoroughly "post-modern"!)

We see these things better, of course, now that the deed is done, the book finished. But even early on, in Santa Fe, intense discussions turned on the exclusion of several important perspectives and what to do about them. As editors, we decided not to try and "fill out" the volume by seeking additional essays. This seemed to be tokenism and to reflect an aspiration to false completeness. Our response to the problem of excluded standpoints has been to leave them blatant. The present volume remains a limited intervention, with no aspiration to be comprehensive or to cover the territory. It sheds a strong, partial light.

10. Marilyn Strathern's unpublished essay "Dislodging a World View" (1984), also discussed by Paul Rabinow in this volume, begins the investigation. A fuller analysis is being worked out by Deborah Gordon in a dissertation for the History of Consciousness program, University of California, Santa Cruz. I am indebted to conversations with her.

11. It may generally be true that groups long excluded from positions of institutional power, like women or people of color, have less concrete freedom to indulge in textual experimentations. To write in an unorthodox way, Paul Rabinow suggests in this volume, one must first have tenure. In specific contexts a preoccupation with self-reflexivity and style may be an index of privileged estheticism. For if one does not have to worry about the exclusion or true representation of one's experience, one is freer to undermine ways of telling, to focus on form over content. But I am uneasy with a general notion that privileged discourse indulges in esthetic or epistemological subtleties, whereas marginal discourse "tells it like it is." The reverse is too often the case. (See Michael Fischer's essay in this volume.)

∿∿

A major consequence of the historical and theoretical movements traced in this Introduction has been to dislodge the ground
from which persons and groups securely represent others. A conceptual shift, "tectonic" in its implications, has taken place. We ground
things, now, on a moving earth. There is no longer any place of overview (mountaintop) from which to map human ways of life, no Archimedian point from which to represent the world. Mountains are in
constant motion. So are islands: for one cannot occupy, unambigu-
ously, a bounded cultural world from which to journey out and analyze other cultures. Human ways of life increasingly influence, dominate, parody, translate, and subvert one another. Cultural analysis is
always enmeshed in global movements of difference and power. However one defines it, and the phrase is here used loosely, a "world system" now links the planet's societies in a common historical process.[12]

A number of the essays that follow grapple with this predicament.
Their emphases differ. How, George Marcus asks, can ethnography—
at home or abroad—define its object of study in ways that permit detailed, local, contextual analysis and simultaneously the portrayal of
global implicating forces? Accepted textual strategies for defining cultural domains, separating micro and macro levels, are no longer adequate to the challenge. He explores new writing possibilities that blur
the distinction between anthropology and sociology, subverting an un-
productive division of labor. Talal Asad also confronts the systematic
interconnection of the planet's societies. But he finds persistent, gla-
cial inequalities imposing all-too-coherent forms on the world's diversity and firmly positioning any ethnographic practice. "Translations"
of culture, however subtle or inventive in textual form, take place
within relations of "weak" and "strong" languages that govern the international flow of knowledge. Ethnography is still very much a one-
way street. Michael Fischer's essay suggests that notions of global
hegemony may miss the reflexive, inventive dimensions of ethnicity
and cultural contact. (And in a similar vein, my own contribution
treats all narratives of lost authenticity and vanishing diversity as self-
confirming allegories, until proven otherwise.) Fischer locates ethnographic writing in a syncretic world of ethnicity rather than a world of
discrete cultures and traditions. Post-modernism, in his analysis, is
more than a literary, philosophical, or artistic trend. It is a general

12. The term is, of course, Wallerstein's (1976). I find, however, his strong sense of
a unitary direction to the global historical process problematic, and agree with Ortner's
reservations (1984:142–43).

condition of multicultural life demanding new forms of inventiveness and subtlety from a fully reflexive ethnography.

Ethnography in the service of anthropology once looked out at clearly defined others, defined as primitive, or tribal, or non-Western, or pre-literate, or nonhistorical—the list, if extended, soon becomes incoherent. Now ethnography encounters others in relation to itself, while seeing itself as other. Thus an "ethnographic" perspective is being deployed in diverse and novel circumstances. Renato Rosaldo probes the way its rhetoric has been appropriated by social history and how this makes visible certain disturbing assumptions that have empowered fieldwork. The ethnographer's distinctively intimate, inquisitive perspective turns up in history, literature, advertising, and many other unlikely places. The science of the exotic is being "repatriated" (Fischer and Marcus 1986).

Ethnography's traditional vocation of cultural criticism (Montaigne's "On Cannibals," Montesquieu's *Persian Letters*) has reemerged with new explicitness and vigor. Anthropological fieldworkers can now realign their work with pioneers like Henry Mayhew in the nineteenth century and, more recently, with the Chicago school of urban sociology (Lloyd Warner, William F. Whyte, Robert Park). Sociological description of everyday practices has recently been complicated by ethnomethodology (Leiter 1980): the work of Harold Garfinkel, Harvey Sacks, and Aaron Cicourel (also neglected in the present volume) reflects a crisis in sociology similar to that in anthropology. Meanwhile a different rapprochement between anthropological and sociological ethnography has been taking place under the influence of Marxist cultural theory at the Birmingham Centre for Contemporary Cultural Studies (Stuart Hall, Paul Willis). In America fieldworkers are turning their attention to laboratory biologists and physicists (Latour and Woolgar 1979, Traweek 1982), to American "kinship" (Schneider 1980), to the dynastic rich (Marcus 1983), to truckers (Agar 1985), to psychiatric clients (Estroff 1985), to new urban communities (Krieger 1983), to problematic traditional identities (Blu 1980). This is only the beginning of a growing list.

What is at stake is more than anthropological methods being deployed at home, or studying new groups (Nader 1969). Ethnography is moving into areas long occupied by sociology, the novel, or avant-garde cultural critique (Clifford 1981), rediscovering otherness and difference within the cultures of the West. It has become clear that every version of an "other," wherever found, is also the construction of a "self," and the making of ethnographic texts, as Michael Fischer, Vincent Crapanzano, and others in this volume show, has always in-

volved a process of "self-fashioning" (Greenblatt 1980). Cultural
poesis—and politics—is the constant reconstitution of selves and
others through specific exclusions, conventions, and discursive practices. The essays that follow provide tools for the analysis of these processes, at home and abroad.

These essays do not prophesy. Taken as a whole, they portray historical constraints on the making of ethnographies, as well as areas of
textual experiment and emergence. Talal Asad's tone is sober, pre-
occupied (like Paul Rabinow) with institutional limits on interpretive freedom. George Marcus and Michael Fischer explore concrete
examples of alternative writing. Stephen Tyler evokes what does
not (cannot?) yet exist, but must be imagined—or, better, sounded.
Many of the essays (especially those of Renato Rosaldo, Vincent
Crapanzano, Mary Pratt, and Talal Asad) are occupied with critical
ground clearing—dislodging canons to make space for alternatives.
Rabinow identifies a new canon, post-modernism. Other essays (Tyler
on oral and performative modes, my own treatment of allegory) recapture old rhetorics and projects for use now. "For use now!" Charles
Olson's poetic rule should guide the reading of these essays: they are
responses to a current, changing situation, interventions rather than
positions. To place this volume in a historical conjuncture, as I have
tried to do here, is to reveal the moving ground on which it stands,
and to do so without benefit of a master narrative of historical development that can offer a coherent direction, or future, for ethnography.[13]

One launches a controversial collection like this with some trepi-
dation, hoping it will be seriously engaged—not simply rejected, for
example, as another attack on science or an incitement to relativism.
Rejections of this kind should at least make clear why close analysis of
one of the principal things ethnographers do—that is, write—should
not be central to evaluation of the results of scientific research. The
authors in this volume do not suggest that one cultural account is as
good as any other. If they espoused so trivial and self-refuting a relativism, they would not have gone to the trouble of writing detailed,
committed, critical studies.

Other, more subtle, objections have recently been raised to the literary, theoretical reflexivity represented here. Textual, epistemo-

13. My notion of historicism owes a great deal to the recent work of Fredric
Jameson (1980, 1981, 1984a, b). I am not, however, persuaded by the master narrative
(a global sequence of modes of production) he invokes from time to time as an alternative to post-modern fragmentation (the sense that history is composed of various
local narratives). The partiality I have been urging in this introduction always presupposes a local historical predicament. This historicist partiality is not the unsituated "partiality and flux" with which Rabinow (see p. 252) taxes a somewhat rigidly defined
"post-modernism."

logical questions are sometimes thought to be paralyzing, abstract, dangerously solipsistic—in short, a barrier to the task of writing "grounded" or "unified" cultural and historical studies.[14] In practice, however, such questions do not necessarily inhibit those who entertain them from producing truthful, realistic accounts. All of the essays collected here point toward new, better modes of writing. One need not agree with their particular standards to take seriously the fact that in ethnography, as in literary and historical studies, what counts as "realist" is now a matter of both theoretical debate and practical experimentation.

The writing and reading of ethnography are overdetermined by forces ultimately beyond the control of either an author or an interpretive community. These contingencies—of language, rhetoric, power, and history—must now be openly confronted in the process of writing. They can no longer be evaded. But the confrontation raises thorny problems of verification: how are the truths of cultural accounts evaluated? Who has the authority to separate science from art? realism from fantasy? knowledge from ideology? Of course such separations will continue to be maintained, and redrawn; but their changing poetic and political grounds will be less easily ignored. In cultural studies at least, we can no longer know the whole truth, or even claim to approach it. The rigorous partiality I have been stressing here may be a source of pessimism for some readers. But is there not a liberation, too, in recognizing that no one can write about others any longer as if they were discrete objects or texts? And may not the vision of a complex, problematic, partial ethnography lead, not to its abandonment, but to more subtle, concrete ways of writing and reading, to new conceptions of culture as interactive and historical? Most of the essays in this volume, for all their trenchant critiques, are optimistic about ethnographic writing. The problems they raise are incitements, not barriers.

These essays will be accused of having gone too far: poetry will again be banned from the city, power from the halls of science. And extreme self-consciousness certainly has its dangers—of irony, of elitism, of solipsism, of putting the whole world in quotation marks. But I trust that readers who signal these dangers will do so (like some of the essays below) *after* they have confronted the changing history, rhetoric, and politics of established representational forms. In the wake of semiotics, post-structuralism, hermeneutics, and deconstruction there has been considerable talk about a return to plain speaking and to realism. But to return to realism one must first have left it! Moreover, to

14. The response is frequently expressed informally. It appears in different forms in Randall (1984), Rosen (1984), Ortner (1984:143), Pullum (1984), and Darnton (1985).

recognize the poetic dimensions of ethnography does not require that one give up facts and accurate accounting for the supposed free play of poetry. "Poetry" is not limited to romantic or modernist subjectivism: it can be historical, precise, objective. And of course it is just as conventional and institutionally determined as "prose." Ethnography is hybrid textual activity: it traverses genres and disciplines. The essays in this volume do not claim ethnography is "only literature." They do insist it is always writing.

I would like to thank the members of the Santa Fe seminar for their many suggestions incorporated in, or left out of, this Introduction. (I have certainly not tried to represent the "native point of view" of that small group.) In graduate seminars co-taught with Paul Rabinow at the University of California at Berkeley and Santa Cruz, many of my ideas on these topics have been agreeably assaulted. My special thanks to him and to the students in those classes. At Santa Cruz, Deborah Gordon, Donna Haraway, and Ruth Frankenberg have helped me with this essay, and I have had important encouragement and stimulus from Hayden White and the members of the Research Group on Colonial Discourse. Various press readers made important suggestions, particularly Barbara Babcock. George Marcus, who got the whole project rolling, has been an inestimable ally and friend.

MARY LOUISE PRATT

Fieldwork in Common Places

In his introduction to *Argonauts of the Western Pacific* (1922) Bronislaw Malinowski celebrates the advent of professional, scientific ethnography: "The time when we could tolerate accounts presenting us the native as a distorted, childish caricature of a human being are gone," he declares. "This picture is false, and like many other false-hoods, it has been killed by Science" (Malinowski 1961 : 11). The statement is symptomatic of a well-established habit among ethnographers of defining ethnographic writing over and against older, less special-ized genres, such as travel books, personal memoirs, journalism, and accounts by missionaries, settlers, colonial officials, and the like. Al-though it will not supplant these genres altogether, professional eth-nography, it is understood, will usurp their authority and correct their abuses. In almost any ethnography dull-looking figures called "mere travelers" or "casual observers" show up from time to time, only to have their superficial perceptions either corrected or corroborated by the serious scientist.

This strategy of defining itself by contrast to adjacent and ante-cedent discourses limits ethnography's ability to explain or examine itself as a kind of writing. To the extent that it legitimates itself by op-position to other kinds of writing, ethnography blinds itself to the fact that its own discursive practices were often inherited from these other genres and are still shared with them today. At times one still hears expressed as an ideal for ethnography a neutral, tropeless discourse that would render other realities "exactly as they are," not filtered through our own values and interpretive schema. For the most part, however, that wild goose is no longer being chased, and it is possible to suggest that ethnographic writing is as trope-governed as any other discursive formation. This recognition is obviously fundamental for those who are interested in changing or enriching ethnographic writ-ing or simply in increasing the discipline's self-understanding. In this essay I propose to examine how some tropes of ethnographic writing are deployed and how they derive from earlier discursive traditions. In particular, I propose to focus on the vexed but important relation-

ship between personal narrative and impersonal description in ethnographic writing and to look at some of the history of this discursive
configuration, notably its history in travel writing.

A recent controversy in the *American Anthropologist* underscores
the difficulties ethnography has had in establishing its relations to adjacent discourses. The controversy surrounded Florinda Donner's
*Shabono: A True Adventure in the Remote and Magical Heart of the South
American Jungle* (1982). The book is a personal account of the experience of a graduate student in anthropology who, while doing fieldwork in Venezuela, is chosen by members of a remote group of Yanomamo to live with them and learn their lifeways. The book has been a
great success. On the cover of the paperback Carlos Castaneda hails it
as "at once art, magic and superb social science"; a Queens College
anthropologist calls it "a rare and beautiful book . . . [that] illuminates
the world of the Yanomamo Indians [and] conveys a sense of the mystery and power still to be found in ritual"; *Newsweek* praises it for
going "way beyond anthropological questions and categories into the
far reaches of a fascinating alien culture."

Controversy about *Shabono* broke out when the September 1983
issue of the *American Anthropologist* published a comment accusing
Donner of plagiarism and fraud. "Frankly," says Rebecca B. DeHolmes,
"I find it hard to believe that Donner spent any length of time with the
Yanomamo" (DeHolmes 1983:665). Donner's ethnographic data, she
suggests, were "rather expertly borrowed from other sources and as-
sembled in a kind of melange of fact and fantasy for which Castaneda
is so famous" (ibid.). DeHolmes's most serious accusation is that much
of Donner's borrowing was outright plagiarism from another extraordinary book, a contemporary captivity narrative called *Yanoama: The
Narrative of a White Girl Kidnapped by Amazonian Indians*, which appeared in Italian in 1965 and in English translation in 1969. This
book, whose authenticity no one has questioned, presents the life
story of a Brazilian, Helena Valero, who lived from childhood to
adulthood with a group of Yanomamo who kept her following an attack on her family.[1]

DeHolmes's accusation of plagiarism is supported by a series of
sample passages from the two books and a sizeable list of what she calls
"parallel accounts of the same events, plus similar or identical time

1. This book, incidentally, should have generated a scandal of its own, for its
editor-transcriber, Ettore Biocca, claims it as his own and inexcusably fails to credit
Valero adequately for her own story. Her name appears nowhere on the cover, and one
hopes that, in addition to getting editorial credit, Biocca is not also collecting the royalties. At story's end, Valero is on her own in a Brazilian city, struggling to get her children
through school.

sequences." The anthropologists with whom I spoke had found this evidence immediately convincing. They had agreed with DeHolmes that Donner's whole book must be a fabrication and that Donner had probably never lived with the Yanomamo.

I was surprised both by how quickly people rushed to this extreme conclusion and by how schematic the terms in which the issue was discussed were. Donner's book was either true or false, meaning, apparently, that she had either lived with the Yanomamo or had not, and nothing more was at issue. I was also suspicious, especially at the eagerness to settle the matter quickly and at Donner's expense, despite the fact that many anthropologists had apparently read and appreciated Donner's book, and found it believable. *Shabono*, it looked to me, was being "killed by science," in Malinowski's words, and without much in the way of a trial. The case obviously threatened some delicate disciplinary boundaries. Most pointedly, it brought to the surface the anguished and messy tangle of contradictions and uncertainties surrounding the interrelations of personal experience, personal narrative, scientism, and professionalism in ethnographic writing. By way of explanation, let me push the example a little further.

To an outsider, one of the most interesting puzzles in the singularly impoverished debate on *Shabono* was that the book's factual accuracy did not seem to be at issue. DeHolmes's meticulous scrutiny had produced only a single ethnographic error in 300 pages (a reference to running between *rows* of manioc). Implicitly it was accepted that given a certain quantity of secondary material, one in fact could construct a convincing, vivid, ethnographically accurate account of life in another culture *without personal experience in the field*. Why, I wondered, would ethnographers be so willing to concede such a thing? If it were so, exactly what sort of public threat would Donner's (alleged) deception be?

What was at issue was not ethnographic accuracy, but a set of problematic links between ethnographic authority, personal experience, scientism, and originality of expression. If Donner really did live with the Yanomamo, why would her text so resemble Valero's? But by the standards of ethnography, the opposite question also arises: How could her account *not* resemble Valero's? The allegedly plagiarized passages DeHolmes cites are indeed very similar to Valero's text, though never exact repetitions. The first five cases listed include: (a) Nabrushi club fight between men, (b) women's fishing techniques, (c) girl's coming-of-age confinement and subsequent presentation to group as a woman, (d) preparation of curare and testing on a monkey, (e) invitation to a feast (DeHolmes 1983:665). Of these, one describes a generalized practice or custom (fishing techniques), the other four are rituals—events anthropologists have always specialized in treating as codifiable, repeatable forms, rather than unique events. If Donner's account of these rituals had *not* coincided in detail with Valero's, fraud by anthropology's own lights would have been certain. But what was being argued was the exact opposite.

In the end, for DeHolmes, the authority of the ethnographic text is directly constituted by the writer's personal experience, in turn attested by originality of expression: "If Donner's *Shabono* is to be called 'superb social science,' as Castaneda claims, it must be shown that the ethnographic data on which she bases her story were actually gathered personally by her while living among the Yanomama and not rewritten from previously published works."

By contrast, for Debra Picchi, who reviewed the book in the same journal, *Shabono*'s failure to be science arises rather from its "narcissistic focus" on Donner's "personal growth in the field." "To confine anthropology to the personal experiences of specific anthropologists is to deny its status as a social science" and "renders the discipline trivial and inconsequential" (Picchi 1983:674). Donner fails to display what for Picchi is the distinguishing characteristic of anthropology's project, namely a "commitment to the documentation of relationships between behavioral variables on a cross-cultural basis." For Picchi, the idea of borrowing and rewriting is not a problem. Since Donner rejected formal field methods, destroying her notebooks early in the game, "one assumes," Picchi says, "that the standard anthropological information included in the book is the result of the reconstruction from memory or research of the now extensive literature on the Yanomamo Indians" (ibid.). Picchi takes the book to be a bona fide "ethnography of the Yanomamo Indians . . . based on 12 months of fieldwork" and recommends it to teachers of introductory anthropology.

Why are Donner's fairly explicit claims NOT to be writing a work of anthropology or social science irrelevant to this discussion? Though it is not written in the standard idiom of ethnographic description, what places her personal narrative within anthropology's purview? Once there, why is there such confusion about how it should be evaluated?

For some reason, it all made me think of a teenager hanging around outside a strip joint who gets dragged inside in order to be turned over to the police and kicked out again—that'll teach him. So "disciplining" is often done, if not at strip joints, then certainly in academies. What Donner clearly did was write an infuriatingly ambiguous book, which may or may not be "true," is and is not ethnography, is and is not autobiography, does and does not claim professional and academic authority, is and is not based on fieldwork, and so on. An ungrateful apprentice can do no worse than this. For if Florinda Donner did fabricate much of her story (as she may have), she has disgraced the profession by lying, and lying so well no one could tell. If she did not fabricate her story, she scored one of the anthropological scoops of the century. For her experience, as she recounts it, is in many respects an ethnographer's dream. She is *invited* by the group to study their lifeways; instead of sessions in which she interviews them, it is they who sit down to teach her. She is spared the anguish and guilt of paying her way by distributing Western goods; the group has chosen to stay so remote that it is a near first encounter. To realize this ethnographer's dream, and then to refuse to convert it into the currency of the discipline that made it all possible, this is indeed a monumental betrayal.

I have dwelt on the case of *Shabono* because it illustrates some of the confusion and ambiguity that personal narrative, not having been killed by science, raises in the "discursive space" of ethnography. Personal narratives like Donner's are not unknown within academic anthropology. Indeed, personal accounts of field experiences are a recognizable anthropological subgenre, but they always come accompanied—usually preceded—by a formal ethnography, the book Donner has not (yet?) written. One thinks of such paired books as David Maybury-Lewis's *Savage and the Innocent* and *Akwe-Shavante Society*; Jean-Paul Dumont's *Under the Rainbow* and *The Headman and I*; Napoleon Chagnon's *Yanomamo: The Fierce People* and *Studying the Yanomamo*; Paul Rabinow's *Symbolic Domination* and *Reflections on Fieldwork in Morocco*. Earlier examples include the writings of Clyde Kluckhohn and Roy-Franklin Barton; this personal subgenre is also the conventional textual space into which Malinowski's diaries were published.

Of these pairs of books, the formal ethnography is the one that counts as professional capital and as an authoritative representation; the personal narratives are often deemed self-indulgent, trivial, or heretical in other ways. But despite such "disciplining," they have kept appearing, kept being read, and above all kept being taught within the borders of the discipline, for what one must assume are powerful reasons.

Even in the absence of a separate autobiographical volume, personal narrative is a conventional component of ethnographies. It turns up almost invariably in introductions or first chapters, where opening narratives commonly recount the writer's arrival at the field site, for instance, the initial reception by the inhabitants, the slow, agonizing process of learning the language and overcoming rejection, the anguish and loss at leaving. Though they exist only on the margins of the formal ethnographic description, these conventional opening narratives are not trivial. They play the crucial role of anchoring that description in the intense and authority-giving personal experience of fieldwork. Symbolically and ideologically rich, they often turn out to be the most memorable segments of an ethnographic work—nobody forgets the frustration-ridden introduction to Evans-Pritchards's *The Nuer*. Always they are responsible for setting up the initial positionings of the subjects of the ethnographic text: the ethnographer, the native, and the reader.

I find it quite significant that this kind of personal narrative, in the form both of books and opening anecdotes, has in fact not been "killed by science," that it persists as a conventional form in ethnographic writing. This fact is particularly noteworthy given the multiple pressures on ethnography that militate against narrative ("mere anecdote") and devalue it as a vehicle of usable knowledge. Against these pressures operates an urgent sense that ethnographic description is somehow not enough on its own. The fact that personal narrative has this conventional place in ethnographic discourse suggests why *Shabono*, regardless of its author's own wishes, does fall within anthropology's purview and must be reckoned with. The fact that personal narrative is marginal and stigmatized explains why a book like *Shabono* has to be recognized only to be rejected.

I think it is fairly clear that personal narrative persists alongside objectifying description in ethnographic writing because it mediates a contradiction within the discipline between personal and scientific authority, a contradiction that has become especially acute since the advent of fieldwork as a methodological norm. James Clifford speaks of it as "the discipline's impossible attempt to fuse objective and subjective practices" (see p. 109 below). Fieldwork produces a kind of authority that is anchored to a large extent in subjective, sensuous experience. One experiences the indigenous environment and lifeways for oneself, sees with one's own eyes, even plays some roles, albeit contrived ones, in the daily life of the community. But the professional text to result from such an encounter is supposed to conform to the norms of a scientific discourse whose authority resides in the absolute effacement of the speaking and experiencing subject.

In terms of its own metaphors, the scientific position of speech is that of an observer fixed on the edge of a space, looking in and/or down upon what is other. Subjective experience, on the other hand, is spoken from a moving position already within or down in the middle of things, looking and being looked at, talking and being talked at. To convert fieldwork, via field notes, into formal ethnography requires a tremendously difficult shift from the latter discursive position (face to face with the other) to the former. Much must be left behind in the process. Johannes Fabian characterizes the temporal aspect of this contradiction when he speaks of "an aporetic split between recognition of coevalness in some ethnographic research and denial of coevalness in most anthropological theorizing and writing" (Fabian 1983 : 36). In other words, the famous "ethnographic present" locates the other in a time order different from that of the speaking subject; field research on the other hand locates both self and other in the same temporal order. There are strong reasons why field ethnographers so often lament that their ethnographic writings leave out or hopelessly impoverish some of the most important knowledge they have achieved, including the self-knowledge. For the lay person, such as myself, the main evidence of a problem is the simple fact that ethnographic writing tends to be surprisingly boring. How, one asks constantly, could such interesting people doing such interesting things produce such dull books? What did they have to do to themselves?

Personal narrative mediates this contradiction between the engagement called for in fieldwork and the self-effacement called for in formal ethnographic description, or at least mitigates some of its anguish, by inserting into the ethnographic text the authority of the personal experience out of which the ethnography is made. It thus recuperates at least a few shreds of what was exorcised in the conversion from the face-to-face field encounter to objectified science. That is why such narratives have not been killed by science, and why they are worth looking at, especially to people interested in countering the tendency toward alienation and dehumanization in much conventional ethnographic description.

The practice of combining personal narrative and objectified description is hardly the invention of modern ethnography, however. It has a long history in those kinds of writing from which ethnography has traditionally distinguished itself. By the early sixteenth century in Europe, it was conventional for travel accounts to consist of a combination of first-person narration, recounting one's trip, and description of the flora and fauna of regions passed through and the manners and customs of the inhabitants. These two discourses were quite clearly distinguished in travel books, narrative predominating over description. The descriptive portions were sometimes seen as dumping grounds for the "surplus data" that could not be fitted into the narrative.

To give a representative example, a book called *The Captivity of Hans Stade of Hesse in A.D. 1547–1555 among the Wild Tribes of Eastern Brazil* achieved a wide readership in the sixteenth and seventeenth centuries. Stade's account was divided into two such parts, the first some 100 pages long, recounting his captivity among the Tupi Nambas, and the second some 50 pages long, giving a "veritable and short account of all the by me experienced manners and customs of the Tuppin-Imbas, whose prisoner I was" (Stade 1874:117). In this latter section, Stade's descriptive agenda has much in common with that of modern ethnography, including chapters on "what their dwellings are like," "how they make fire," "the places wherein they sleep," "how skilful they are in shooting wild animals and fish with arrows," "how they cook their food," "what kind of regimen and order they have in government and laws," "what they believe in," "how many wives each of them has, and how he manages them," "how they are betrothed," "how they make their beverages wherewith they drink themselves drunk, and how they order their drinking," and so forth. Moreover Stade's descriptions resemble those of modern ethnography in their specificity, their search for neutrality and evenhandedness, their linkage of social and material orders, as in this description of a house, where spatial organization is seen as determined by social relations:

> They prefer erecting their dwellings in spots where they are not far from wood and water, nor from game and fish. After they have destroyed all in one district, they migrate to other places; and when they want to build their huts, a chief among them assembles a party of men and women (some forty couples), or as many as he can get, and these live together as friends and relations.
>
> They build a kind of hut, which is about fourteen feet wide, and perhaps a hundred and fifty feet long, according to their number. The tenements are about two fathoms high, and round at the top like a vaulted cellar; they thatch them thickly with palm leaves, so that it may not rain therein, and the hut is all open inside. No one has his specially-prepared chamber; each couple, man and woman, has a space of twelve feet on one side; whilst on the other, in the same manner, lives another pair. Thus their huts are full, and each couple has its own fire. The chief of the huts has also his lodging within the dwelling. They all have commonly three entrances, one on each side, and one in the middle; these are low, so that they must stoop when they go in and out. Few of their villages have more than seven huts. (ibid.: 125)

I use the example of Hans Stade deliberately to underscore the point that this discursive configuration I am talking about is the product neither of an erudite tradition nor of the rise of modern science, despite its similarities with contemporary ethnography. Hans Stade was a ship's gunner with little formal education; his book was a very popular one, and it predates the rise of "natural history" in the eighteenth century.

In some cases, in travel writing, the descriptive discourse is found enmeshed in the narrative, as illustrated by this excerpt from Mungo Park's *Travels in the Interior Districts of Africa* (1799):

We stopped a little at a village called Dangali; and in the evening arrived at Dalli. We saw upon the road two large herds of camels feeding. When the Moors turn their camels to feed, they tie up one of their fore legs, to prevent their straying. . . . The people were dancing before the Dooty's house. But when they were informed that a white man was come into the town, they left off dancing and came to the place where I lodged, walking in regular order, two and two, with the music before them. They play upon a sort of flute; but instead of blowing into a hole in the side, they blow obliquely over the end. (Park 1860:46)

Though interwoven, particularized narrative and generalized description remain distinguishable here, and shifts from one to the other are clear, the most conspicuous signs being, of course, the shift from past tense to present tense and from specific persons to tribal labels. (As I shall be illustrating below, this is the configuration that turns up in the work of Malinowski and Raymond Firth.)

In its various guises the narration-description duality has remained remarkably stable in travel writing right down to the present, as has the conventional ordering—narration first, description second; or narration superordinate, description subordinate. By the late nineteenth century, however, the two modes often had about equal weight in travel books, and it was common for a trip to result in two separate volumes, such as Mary Kingsley's masterpiece *Travels in West Africa* (1897) and *West African Studies* (1899). Richard Burton's *The Lake Regions of Central Africa* (1868) alternates chapters of narration with chapters describing the "geography and ethnology" of each region passed through.

Modern ethnography obviously lies in direct continuity with this tradition, despite the disciplinary boundary by which it separates itself off from travel writing. Ethnographic writing as a rule subordinates narrative to description, but personal narrative is still conventionally found, either in the separate personal volumes or in vestigial form at the beginning of the book, setting the stage for what follows.

It is no surprise, then, to find that the opening narratives in ethnographies display clear continuities with travel writing. For instance, Firth in *We, the Tikopia* (1936) introduces himself via the classic Polynesian arrival scene. This scene became a commonplace in the literature of the South Sea explorations of Cook, Bougainville and others in the 1760s and 70s. It is a memorable passage, to which Clifford Geertz has also recently turned his attention (Geertz 1983c).

In the cool of the early morning, just before sunrise, the bow of the Southern Cross headed towards the eastern horizon, on which a tiny dark blue outline was faintly visible. Slowly it grew into a rugged mountain mass, standing up sheer from the ocean. . . . In an hour or so we were close inshore, and could see canoes coming round from the south, outside the reef, on which the tide was low. The outrigger-fitted craft drew near, the men in them bare to the waist, girdled with bark-cloth, large fans stuck in the backs of their belts, tortoise-shell rings or rolls of leaf in the ear-lobes and nose, bearded, and with long hair flowing loosely over their shoulders. Some plied the rough heavy paddles, some had finely plaited pandanus-leaf mats resting on the thwarts beside them, some had large clubs or spears in their hands. The ship anchored on a short cable in the open bay off the coral reef. Almost before the chain was down the natives began to scramble aboard, coming over the side by any means that offered, shouting fiercely to each other and to us in a tongue of which not a word was understood by the Mota-speaking folk of the mission vessel. I wondered how such turbulent human material could ever be induced to submit to scientific study. . . .

We slipped overboard on to the coral rock and began to wade ashore hand in hand with our hosts, like children at a party, exchanging smiles in lieu of anything more intelligible or tangible at the moment. We were surrounded by crowds of naked chattering youngsters. . . . At last the long wade ended, we climbed up the steeply shelving beach, crossed the soft, dry sand strewn with the brown needles of the Casuarina trees—a home-like touch; it was like a pine avenue—and were led to an old chief clad with great dignity in a white coat and a loin-cloth, who awaited us on his stool under a large shady tree. (Firth 1936:1–2)

Firth reproduces in a remarkably straightforward way a utopian scene of first contact that acquired mythic status in the eighteenth century, and continues with us today in the popular mythology of the South Sea paradise (alias Club Méditerranée/Fantasy Island). Far from being taken for a suspicious alien, the European visitor is welcomed like a messiah by a trusting populace ready to do his or her bidding. For comparison, consider Louis de Bougainville's arrival in Tahiti in 1767:

We run with all sails set towards the land, standing to windward of this bay, when we perceived a pariagua coming from the offing, and standing for the land, and making use of her sail and paddles. She passed athwart us, and joined a number of others, which sailed ahead of us, from all parts of the island. One of them went before all the rest; it was manned by twelve naked men, who presented us with branches of bananas; and their demonstrations signified that this was their olive branch. We answered them with all the signs of friendship we could imagine; and they then came along side of our ship; and one of them, remarkable for his prodigious growth of hair, which stood like bristles divergent on his head, offered us, together with his branch of peace, a little pig, and a cluster of bananas. . . .

The two ships were soon surrounded with more than an hundred per-
iaguas of different sizes, all which had outriggers. They were laden with
cocoa-nuts, bananas, and other fruits of the country. The exchange of these
fruits, which were delicious to us, was made very honestly for all sorts of tri-
fles. (Bougainville 1967 : 213)

Bougainville has a lot more trouble than Firth in getting his ship anchored, but once he does, the same drama resumes:

When we were moored, I went on shore with several officers, to survey the
watering-place. An immense crowd of men and women received us there, and
could not be tired with looking at us; the boldest came to touch us; they even
pushed aside our clothes with their hands, in order to see whether we were
made exactly like them: none of them wore any arms, not so much as a stick.
They sufficiently expressed their joy at our arrival. The chief of this district
conducted and introduced us into his house, in which we found five or six
women, and a venerable old man. (ibid. : 220)

The similarities between the two scenes are obvious. There are some
interesting differences too. Bougainville's version of the scene uses
one trope Firth does not reproduce, the sentimental commonplace
whereby the natives try to undress the foreigners to determine their
humanity and, symbolically, level the difference between them. Firth
stays dressed, like the king he is to meet. Bougainville also carefully
mentions the material relationship that is immediately established
between Europeans and natives, an exchange whose spontaneous
equality he stresses. In Firth this opening exchange is present, but de-
materialized, an exchange of "smiles, in lieu of anything more intelligible or tangible at the moment" and leaving unclear what his material relation to these people is going to be. At the same time, Firth
demystifies the egalitarianism of the conventional vision with his note
of irony about how all this human material "could be made to submit
to scientific study." Indeed, his irony here lightly marks the royal-
arrival trope as a trope, and as part of a language of conquest. The
fact that his own project is also an assertion of power is tacitly acknowledged. Firth's opening presentation of self suggests the story of
Tikopia's becoming "his little island," as Malinowski was later to call it
(Firth 1937 : 1).

Malinowski in *Argonauts* introduces a quite different self-image,
also from the annals of travel writing. His "brief outline of an Ethnographer's tribulations" opens with the now famous line: "Imagine
yourself suddenly set down surrounded by your gear, alone on a
tropical beach close to a native village while the launch or dinghy
which has brought you sails away out of sight" (Malinowski 1961 : 4).

This is unmistakably the image of an old-fashioned castaway. That it turns up here is especially apt, since it corresponds to Malinowski's own situation at the time. An Austrian citizen living in Australia, he had been sent to sit out the war in the Trobriand Islands rather than risk reprisals or deportation.

There are other reasons why the image of the castaway is an evocative and utopian self-image for the ethnographer. For as the figures of Helena Valero, Florinda Donner, and Hans Stade suggest, castaways and captives in many ways realize the ideal of the participant-observer. The authority of the ethnographer over the "mere traveler" rests chiefly on the idea that the traveler just passes through, whereas the ethnographer lives with the group under study. But of course this is what captives and castaways often do too, living in another culture in every capacity from prince to slave, learning indigenous languages and lifeways with a proficiency any ethnographer would envy, and often producing accounts that are indeed full, rich, and accurate by ethnography's own standards. At the same time, the experience of captivity resonates a lot with aspects of the experience of fieldwork— the sense of dependency, lack of control, the vulnerability to being either isolated completely or never left alone.

Then again, the image of the castaway mystifies the ethnographer's situation in ways mentioned earlier. Castaway and ethnographer differ fundamentally in their material relation to the indigenous group. Castaways take up a place within the indigenous social and economic organization; that is how they survive—if, indeed, they do survive, for captivity is a rather higher-risk business than fieldwork. Anthropologists customarily establish a relationship of exchange with the group based on Western commodities. That is how they survive and try to make their relations with informants nonexploitive. But of course this strategy is enormously contradictory, for it makes anthropologists constant contributors to what they themselves see as the destruction of their object of study. The status of the captive or castaway, by contrast, is innocent, and one can see why it would be a compelling image to the contradiction-ridden ethnographer (though actually going native, as captives often did, is taboo for anthropologists).

Firth and Malinowski, then, both invoke well-established images from travel literature in their opening view of the ethnographer. The bodies of their ethnographies are also similar, at least in their deployment of narrative and descriptive discourse. Both writers move freely and fluidly between the two, introducing anecdote constantly to illustrate or elaborate on the ethnographic generalizations, in a way somewhat reminiscent of the text from Mungo Park cited above (p. 35). Firth is full of complex passages like this one, where his ethnographic generalizations, his eyewitness anecdotes, and his personal irony interweave:

Relatives by marriage do occasionally get in sly digs at each other without absolutely transgressing the bounds of good manners. Pa Ranifuri told me with great glee of how the Ariki Taumako spoke to him of his classificatory son-in-law Pa-Panisi as "*Matua i te sosipani*"—*sosipani* being the native pronunciation of *saucepan*, of which sooty vessel this man was as far as I recollect the only possessor in the island. As a dark-skinned foreigner he was slightly sneered at (behind his back) by the Tikopia. Scolding, I was told, though not permitted by convention directly, may take place at a distance. (Firth 1936:274)

What Firth and Malinowski (his teacher) seem to be after is a kind of *summa*, a highly textured, totalizing picture anchored in themselves, where "self" is understood not as a monolithic scientist-observer, but as a multifaceted entity who participates, observes, and writes from multiple, constantly shifting positions. Such are the reflective capacities of this versatile, larger-than-life subject that it can absorb and transmit the richness of a whole culture.[2] In this subject is also anchored the heady optimism both Firth and Malinowski convey about the ethnographic enterprise. There is a significant irony in the fact that the speaking subject in the work of these founders of "scientific ethnography," as Malinowski called it, is anything but the self-effaced, passive subject of scientific discourse.

The richly perceptive, but terribly unsystematic, textual being that is the ethnographer in Malinowski and Firth contrasts sharply with the frustrated and depressed figure that appears in some subsequent classic ethnographies, such as those of Evans-Pritchard and Maybury-Lewis. If Firth shows up as a benevolent eighteenth-century scientist-king, Evans-Pritchard comes on stage in the later guise of the gruff Victorian explorer-adventurer who exposes himself to all sorts of dangers and discomforts in the name of a higher (national) mission. In his famed opening description of field conditions in *The Nuer* (1940), Evans-Pritchard joins a century-long line of African travelers who lose their supplies and cannot control their bearers. His initial self-representation reads thus:

I arrived in Nuerland early in 1930. Stormy weather prevented my luggage from joining me at Marseilles, and owing to errors, for which I was not responsible, my food stores were not forwarded from Malakal and my Zande servants were not instructed to meet me. I proceeded to Nuerland (Leek country) with my tent, some equipment, and a few stores bought at Malakal,

2. James Clifford has made similar observations about Malinowski, and I am indebted to his work here (see Clifford 1985a).

and two servants, an Atwot and a Bellanda, picked up hastily at the same place.

    When I landed at Yoahuang on the Bahr el Ghazal the catholic missionaries there showed me much kindness. I waited for nine days on the river bank for the carriers I had been promised. By the tenth day only four of them had arrived. . . . On the following morning I set out for the neighbouring village of Pakur, where my carriers dropped tent and stores in the centre of a treeless plain, near some homesteads, and refused to bear them to the shade about half a mile further. Next day was devoted to erecting my tent and trying to persuade the Nuer . . . to remove my abode to the vicinity of shade and water, which they refused to do. (Evans-Pritchard 1940:5)

Such episodes are a commonplace of the African travel and exploration writers of the last century. Here for instance is the eternally cranky Sir Richard Burton, whose expedition recounted in *The Lake Regions of Central Africa* (1868) is given much the same inauspicious beginning:

We were delayed ten days off Wale Point by various preliminaries to departure. Said bin Salim, a half-caste Arab of Zanzibar, who, sorely against his will, was ordered by the prince to act as Ras Kafilah, or caravan-guide, had, after ceaseless and fruitless prayers for delay, preceded us about a fortnight, for the purpose of collecting porters. . . . He had crossed over, on the 1st of June, to the mainland, and had hired a gang of porters, who, however, hearing that their employer was a Muzungu, "white man", at once dispersed, forgetting to return their hire. About one hundred and seventy men were required; only thirty-six were procurable. . . . It was necessary to leave behind, till a full gang of porters could be engaged, the greater part of the ammunition, the iron boat which had proved so useful on the coasting voyage to Mombasah, and the reserve supply of cloth, wire and beads, valued at 359 dollars. The Hindus promised faithfully to forward these articles. . . . Nearly eleven months, however, elapsed before they appeared. (Burton 1961:12)

And so it goes, over and over, till Burton's narrative, like Evans-Pritchard's introduction, reads like one long, frustrating master-servant feud. Evans-Pritchard's choice of this particular self-representation is not haphazard. Clifford Geertz's recent analysis of an old military memoir of Evans-Pritchard's (Geertz 1983a) connects Evans-Pritchard directly with the tradition of African colonial exploration and writing.

    With respect to discursive conventions, Evans-Pritchard must also be thought of as producing a hugely degraded version of the utopian arrival scene exemplified in Bougainville and Firth. This is first contact in a fallen world where European colonialism is a given and native and white man approach each other with joyless suspicion. Maybury-Lewis gives a similarly degraded version of the scene in *Akwe-Shavante*

Society. He does find help with his luggage, but the chief who awaits him is not recognizably regal, the opening exchange of goods not reciprocal:

A number of Shavante from the village had come to the airstrip when our plane landed and helped to carry our baggage to the post. They set it down at the feet of an elderly man, who we discovered was the chief of the village. He clearly expected us to open the trunks then and there and distribute their contents. (Maybury-Lewis 1967 : xxiii)

The problem here, it turns out, is contamination from outside. The Shavante have been spoiled by Brazilian army officers who fly in to see them as a curiosity and bring "elaborate gifts." Like Evans-Pritchard (his teacher), Maybury-Lewis complains at length about his informants' hostility and uncooperativeness, their refusal to talk to him in private, their refusal to leave him alone, his problems with the language, and so on.

In both these anti-utopian instances, the opening narrative is given by way of explaining the limitations on the ethnographer's ability to carry out his scientific mission. Paradoxically enough, the conditions of fieldwork are expressed as an impediment to the task of doing fieldwork, rather than as part of what is to be accounted for in fieldwork. The contrast with the tone of Firth and Malinowski is obvious. Evans-Pritchard and Maybury-Lewis are the heirs of the scientific, professional ethnography Malinowski invented. The scientific ideal seems to press on them acutely, calling for codified field methodology, professional detachment, a systematic write-up. Whatever about the other culture impedes these tasks is an ethnographic obstacle, as well as an ethnographic fact. Both writers complain, for instance, about the impossibility of having private conversations with informants, as if private conversation, once baptized as a field method, ought to be culturally possible everywhere. As methodology gets increasingly codified, the clash between "objective and subjective practices" becomes increasingly acute.

In Evans-Pritchard's case, the difficulties translate into a rigid separation between personal narrative (his long and vivid introduction) and impersonal description (the rest of his account). Gone is the constantly shifting position of speech of Firth or Malinowski, and gone is the sense of authority, the possibility of reliable totalizing. Evans-Pritchard strives for a totalizing picture of the Nuer, centered on cattle, but feels he must be emphatic, both at the beginning and the end of his book, about the limitations on his capacities and his achievement. Maybury-Lewis's response, on the other hand, is to try to reaffirm the authority and legitimacy of personal narrative, and to make it explicit as a subgenre. He publishes his personal account first (*The Savage and the Innocent* 1965), fills his ethnographic book with personal narrative, and suggests that "it is time we abandoned the mystique which surrounds field-work and made it conventional to describe in some detail the circumstances of data-collecting" (Maybury-Lewis 1967 : xx).

Each of these opening narrative self-portraits (Malinowski, Firth, Evans-Pritchard, Maybury-Lewis) comes straight out of the tropology of travel writing. Intriguingly, they often come out of the specific tradition of writing on the region in which the ethnographer is working (Central Africa, the South Pacific). At the same time, each expresses in an only slightly mediated fashion some specifics of the particular situation in which each ethnographer finds himself. They are emblematic self-portraits, which operate as a prelude to, and commentary on, what follows. In this respect they are not trivial, for one of their tasks is to position the reader with respect to the formal description. As often as not in modern ethnographies such passages undertake to problematize the reader's position, as they do in Evans-Pritchard and Maybury-Lewis. The ethnographer's trials in working to know another people now become the reader's trials in making sense of the text.

In all the cases I have discussed, much is mystified in the ethnographer's self-portrait. Much is ironized, indirectly questioned, but never named—notably the sheer inexplicability and unjustifiability of the ethnographer's presence from the standpoint of the other. Evans-Pritchard's dogged misreading of a conversation with an informant in his preface could provide no clearer example. Equally mystified is the larger agenda of European expansion in which the ethnographer, regardless of his or her own attitudes to it, is caught up, and that determines the ethnographer's own material relationship to the group under study. This relationship is one of the great silences in the midst of ethnographic description itself. It is the silence that shapes the traditional ethnographic project of trying to describe the culture as it was before Western intervention.

I have been making a loose generational argument in this essay, and propose to end up with one final example from a yet more recent generation of ethnographers. Marjorie Shostak's *Nisa: The Life and Words of a !Kung Woman* (1981) is widely regarded as one of the more successful recent experiments in rehumanizing ethnographic writing. The arrival trope is only one of many conventions of ethnographic writing that get remolded in her text. The introduction to *Nisa* contains two versions of the conventional arrival scene. Here is the first:

Walking into a traditional !Kung village, a visitor would be struck by how fragile it seemed beneath the expanse of sky and how unobtrusively it stood amid
the tall grass and sparse tree growth of the surrounding bush. . . . A visitor
who arrived in the middle of the cold season—June and July—and just at
sunrise would see mounds of blankets and animal skins in front of the huts,
covering people still asleep beside their fires. Those who had already awakened would be stoking the coals, rebuilding the fire, and warming themselves
in the chilly morning air. . . . A visitor on another morning, in the hot, dry
months of October and November, would find people moving about, even at
dawn, up early to do a few hours of gathering or hunting before the midday
heat would force them to rest in the thickest shade. (Shostak 1981 : 7–8)

As in Firth, this hypothetical arrival is at dawn—new day, new place.
And, in a slightly different way, it presents an ethnographic utopia:
here is a traditional society doing its traditional thing, oblivious to the
alien observing presence. Unlike the other arrival scenes considered
above, this one is hypothetical and normalized. It represents what
"a visitor (not an anthropologist) would experience if. . . ." The status
of this fantasy is made apparent several pages later when Shostak
recounts at great length her own arrival experience, the night she
meets Nisa:

By the time we arrived at Gausha, from Goshi, where we had our main camp,
it had long since been dark. We drove the Land Rover past one !Kung village
and stopped at a deserted village site farther down the road. The full moon,
high in the sky, appeared small and gave off a cold light. . . . Kxoma and
Tuma, two !Kung men traveling with us, suggested we make our camp at this
site where Richard Lee and Nancy Howell, other anthropologists, had set their
camp four years earlier. Living where someone had lived before was right,
they said: it connected you to the past. The slender stick shell of Richard and
Nancy's hut was still there. It stood out in the moonlight, a bizarre skeleton set
apart from the surrounding bush . . . a traditional !Kung frame. The grass
had long since been taken and used in Nisa's village. As it stood, the hut
offered no protection from the weather, nor any privacy. (Shostak 1981 : 23)

To begin with, this is a nocturnal arrival, relatively rare in both travel
writing and ethnography. For the anthropologists, this is the land of
the dead—the moon is small and cold, and inexplicably they take
themselves past the village of the living, to a deserted one, and set
themselves up in the skeleton of a hut. Shostak's own symbolism contrasts sharply with the !Kung's understanding of what they are doing.
For them, the link with the past is a haven, a comfort. Shostak and
her companion are haunted by the ghosts of their anthropological
predecessors.

  There is no spontaneous native welcome in Shostak's account, but unlike both Firth and Evans-Pritchard, these anthropologists do not want or need one: "It was too late for visiting. They knew us by then; we would still be there in the morning." They unpack by themselves ("I thought of the time Nancy had found a puff adder in her sleeping bag"). What is biting the dust here, of course, is even the pretense or fantasy of a first encounter. Far from being the first European on the scene, Shostak is even a long way from being the first anthropologist. And this point gets woefully dramatized when the indigenous wel- comers, themselves unwelcome, belatedly appear after the luggage work is done and the party is ready for bed: "Nisa wore an old blanket loosely draped over the remnants of a faded, flower-print dress, sizes too big. Bo was wearing a pair of shorts, even the patches of which were worn through in places." There they are, in European clothes they have obviously been wearing for a long time. And instead of a song of welcome to Shostak and her partner, what Nisa sings is a praise song for their predecessors. "Richard and Nancy! I really liked them! They liked us too—they gave us beautiful presents and took us everywhere with them. Bo and I worked hard for them. . . . Oh how I wish they were here!"

It is an awful scene, a real return of the repressed. These others are fallen, corrupted not only as non-Europeans, but specifically as ethnographic informants. Bo and Nisa arrive praising the guilty rela- tionship of exchange based on Western commodities, the point at which the anthropologist preserver-of-the-culture is the intervention- ist corrupter-of-the-culture. It is the naive informant turned hustler. In short, this arrival scene contemplates, reluctantly and in the dark of night, the aftermath of the ethnographic episode: the indigenous people who, specifically through the ethnographic contact, have ac- quired a vested interest in westernization and a concrete day-to-day link with the larger structures of exploitation. It is like a bad dream, and Shostak's reaction, as she describes it, is to try to pretend it is not happening and wait for a more standard arrival scene in the morning, complete with the ritual exchange of goods: "That was when we would give [tobacco] to the rest of the !Kung with whom we planned to work" (Shostak 1981:25).

After long resistance, Shostak ultimately capitulates to this de- graded anthropological world, consents to be hustled/seduced by Nisa, and then and only then finds a fieldwork relationship that is in fact enormously productive for ethnographic purposes. For Nisa is advertising a genuine talent for story telling and for reflecting on her own culture and experience.

Out of that encounter, Shostak produces a text that, in a way very different from Malinowski and Firth, again seeks to recognize the authority of personal narrative within the ethnographic description. Shostak's own story is concentrated at the beginning and end of the book. In between, Nisa's narrative predominates, edited into a life story by Shostak, who introduces each section with a few pages of ethnographic generalizing and commentary. So this book tries to mediate the contradiction between objectifying ethnographic representation, in which all natives are equivalent and equal, and the subjective experience of fieldwork, in which all informants are not equivalent or equal. What is sought here as an alternative is not, however, a totality or a synthesis anchored in the multifaceted subjectivity of the fieldworker/traveler/scientist, but something less unified and more polyphonous.[3]

A utopian element persists, however, for the polyphony Shostak creates is strikingly harmonious. One finds little evidence of struggle among the various voices, despite Shostak's awareness of the intolerable contradictoriness of her position. Current Western conceptions of female solidarity and intimacy seem to be part of what produces this cross-cultural harmony: she and Nisa are bound together in ways that perhaps transcend culture. It is to Shostak's credit that the last lines of the book challenge that harmony. Nisa's final words in the text are: "My niece . . . my niece . . . you are someone who truly thinks about me." Shostak's are: "I will always think of her and I hope she will think of me, as a distant sister." Each assigns the other a different honorary kinship.

In the darkness that shrouds Shostak's arrival scene, Western readers will recognize the symbolism of guilt. In part there is guilt linked to the particularities of Shostak's situation as the last in a series of anthropologists working among the !Kung. And in part it is guilt that comes down to her from much farther in the past. For as with the other examples I have discussed, Shostak's text, and those of her fellow participants in the Harvard Kalahari Project, displays direct continuities with a long tradition of writing about the !Kung—three centuries of it in fact. It is a nonprofessional "lay" tradition from which the Harvard anthropologists energetically dissociate themselves (most explicitly by replacing the earlier European name for the group, the Bushmen). What that tradition documents is a long and violent history of persecution, enslavement, and extermination. The contemporary !Kung are the survivors of that history; the contemporary anthropologists the heirs to its guilt. A few details will clarify this point.

3. See also James Clifford's review of *Nisa* in *The Times Literary Supplement* (London), September 17, 1982, 994–95.

It is at the end of the eighteenth century that the Bushmen start turning up in European accounts as objects of (a) ethnographic interest and (b) pathos and guilt. Not surprisingly, this was also the point at which the Bushmen definitively lost their struggle against European encroachment on their land and lifeways. For the previous century, they had existed in European writings as hordes of wild, bloodthirsty marauders fiercely resisting the advancing colonists, raiding their farms at night, turning loose or stealing cattle, and sometimes murdering colonists or laborers. Given a free hand by colonial authorities, the settlers embarked on a war of extermination. Commandos descended on Bushman kraals, often at night, killing men and either killing or enslaving women and children. Gradually the settlers won this war, so that by the 1790s "the Bushmen were still numerous along the interior mountain range, but in other parts of the colony there were hardly any left" (Theal 1897: I, 198–201).[4]

It is at this point that the discourse on the Bushmen changes. Late eighteenth-century travelers, like the Swede Anders Sparrman (*Voyage to the Cape of Good Hope* 1785) and Englishman John Barrow (*Travels in the Interior of Southern Africa* 1801), vociferously deplore the brutality of the colonists and the injustice of the extermination campaign. The same writers construct a new ethnographic portrait of the Bushmen. No longer seen as militant warriors or bloodthirsty marauders, they acquire the characteristics that the powerful commonly find in those they have subjugated: meekness, innocence, passivity, indolence coupled with physical strength and stamina, cheerfulness, absence of greed or indeed desires of any kind, internal egalitarianism, a penchant for living in the present, inability to take initiatives on their own behalf. Thus Sparrman describes the Bushmen as "free from many wants and desires, that torment the rest of mankind," "detesting all manner of labour," yet easily induced into slavery by a little meat and tobacco (Sparrman 1975: 198–201). Barrow finds they are "mild and manageable in the highest degree, and by gentle usage may be moulded into any shape." "In his disposition," says Barrow, "[the Bushman] is lively and cheerful; in his person active. His talents are far above mediocrity." Their constitutions are "much stronger and their lives of longer duration, than those of the Hottentots"; "universal equality prevails in his horde . . . they take no thought for the morrow. They have no sort of management or economy with regard to provisions" (Barrow 1801: 287).

Presented as objectified ethnographic description of the (eternal)

---

4. My remarks here on the history of Bushman-European contact are based mainly on Theal's *History of South Africa* (1892–1919).

Bushman and his (natural) disposition, this is a portrait of a conquered people, simultaneously acknowledging the innocence and pathos of their condition, evaluating their potential as a labor pool, and legitimating their domination on the grounds that they do not know how to manage themselves.

Caught between celebrating and deploring, historicizing and naturalizing the Bushmen's condition, Barrow expresses the guilt and anguish of his position in a nocturnal arrival scene that has numerous points in common with Shostak's, despite being written 180 years earlier. In Barrow's account, too, the all-important personal contact with the other is achieved only through a kind of descent into hell. Though his motives are entirely benevolent, the only way Barrow can make contact with the terrified Bushmen is by hiring a group of Boer farmers to help him ambush a group at night. As with Shostak, the result is a nightmare of contradiction, one of the few episodes of personal narrative in Barrow's book. Barrow describes the raiding party descending from the hillsides down onto the sleeping camp: "Our ears were stunned with a horrid scream like the war-hoop of savages; the shrieking of women and the cries of children proceeded from every side" (Barrow 1801:272). Despite Barrow's instructions, his Boer guides begin shooting down the fleeing people; Barrow's protests are ignored. "'Good God!' [the Boer farmer] exclaimed, 'Have you not seen a shower of arrows falling among us?' I certainly had seen neither arrows or people, but had heard enough to pierce the hardest heart" (272). Later Barrow remarks in shame that "nothing could be more unwarrantable . . . than the attack made by our party upon the kraal" (291).

This scene that disrupts Barrow's highly impersonal account is an explicit reversal not only of the utopian arrival scene a la Bougainville, but also of the traditional image of the Bushman horde descending on European ranches. Its symbolism and position in Barrow's text are similar to those in Shostak's, and the two share the same discursive history. (Interestingly, Shostak's predecessor and colleague Richard Lee also uses a nocturnal arrival scene to introduce his third visit to the !Kung [Lee 1979:xvii].)

But it is not only arrival scenes that contemporary anthropologists share with earlier writers on the Bushmen. Their ethnographic descriptions likewise reproduce the discursive legacy, even as they openly repudiate it. One is struck by the extent to which twentieth-century anthropological and journalistic writers have continued to celebrate and naturalize in the Bushmen many of the same characteristics singled out by Barrow, Sparrman, and the rest. Cheerfulness, humor, egalitarianism, nonviolence, disinterest in material goods, longevity, and stamina are all underscored with admiration and affection in both journalistic writings like those of Laurens van der Post (*The Lost World of the Kalahari* 1958) and ethnographic work from Elizabeth Marshall Thomas's *The Harmless People* (1959) to the writers of the Harvard Kalahari Project (1963–70). What turns up throughout this literature is the same blazing contradiction between a tendency on the one hand to historicize the !Kung as survivor-victims of European imperialism, and a tendency on the other to naturalize and objectify them as primal beings virtually untouched by history. (In both cases, they stand doomed to extinction.) Detailed discussion of the extensive contemporary literature on the !Kung/Bushmen is impossible here, but Shostak's own text can exemplify the ambivalence I am talking about.

By introducing Nisa to us clad in a dress and selling her talents on the anthropological free market, Shostak repudiates the image of the pure primitive so often associated with the !Kung. Yet it is ultimately that image of the primitive that motivates Shostak's inquiry. For her, as for the Harvard Kalahari group as a whole, the !Kung are of interest as evidence concerning our human and prehuman ancestors. Shostak hopes !Kung women will be able to "clarify some of the issues raised by the American women's movement," especially because, she says,

their culture, unlike ours, was not being continuously disrupted by social and political factions telling them first that women were one way, then another. Although the !Kung were experiencing cultural change, it was still quite recent and subtle and had thus far left their traditional value system mostly intact. A study revealing what !Kung women's lives were like today might reflect what their lives had been like for generations, possibly even for thousands of years. (Shostak 1981:6)

"Recent" and "subtle" are not the adjectives that come to mind when one ponders the grim history of the Bushman conquest. This is a history of which Shostak and her colleagues seem at times deeply aware, at times totally oblivious. Repeatedly, Richard Lee and others warn that the !Kung are not to be treated as "living fossils" or "missing links" (Lee 1979:xvii), that their colonial past and changing present must be given full recognition to avoid dehumanization and distortion. Yet the inquiry the group proposes is explicitly an evolutionary one (initiated by primatologists) in which the !Kung are important as "evidence which will help in understanding human history" (S. Washburn in Lee and Devore 1976:xv) as examples of an ecological adaptation "that was until ten thousand years ago, a human universal" (Lee 1979:1). Focusing heavily on physical and biological issues like diet, physiology, use of time, settlement patterns, spacing of births, use of food resources, disease, aging, and so on, this literature naturalizes current !Kung lifeways with a vengeance. The researchers' sincere desire to be sensitive to the !Kung's situation in present historical circumstances is simply incompatible with their project of viewing the !Kung as a complex adaptation to the ecology of the Kalahari desert, and an example of how our ancestors lived. The use of primarily quantitative methods (producing tables like "Average number of child-caring acts by a subject per child per hour of observation" [P. Draper in Lee and Devore 1976 : 214]) intensifies the reification.

An outsider, on reading the history of European contact with the !Kung/Bushmen, inevitably questions this image of them as representatives of hunting-gathering life as it was lived 10,000 years ago. Is it not worth even asking the question whether 300 years of warfare and persecution at the hands of white settlers (to say nothing of the competition with indigenous pastoralists) have had an impact on the lifeways, the consciousness, the social organization, even the physiology of the group undergoing these traumas? Did the long-term practice of massacring men and enslaving women have no impact on "what women's lives were like" or how women saw themselves? What picture of the !Kung would one draw if instead of defining them as survivors of the stone age and a delicate and complex adaptation to the Kalahari desert, one looked at them as survivors of capitalist expansion, and a delicate and complex adaptation to three centuries of violence and intimidation? There are times when such a perspective does seem to be implied, ever-so-indirectly, as in Shostak's characterization of a !Kung village as looking "fragile" and "unobtrusive" (see quotation on p. 43 above).

To make sense of the conflicting concerns of the Harvard group, one must locate them on the one hand in the context of the American counterculture of the 1960s, many of whose social ideals seem to realize themselves in the !Kung, and on the other hand, in the context of the expansion of the biological, "hard science" sector of anthropology that has made Harvard the center for sociobiology in the 1980s. At the same time, one must also recognize their continuities with the discursive history coming down from Sparrman, Barrow, and the rest, a discursive history they sometimes wish to "kill by science."

As I have been arguing throughout this paper, anthropologists stand to gain from looking at themselves as writing inside as well as outside the discursive traditions that precede them; inside as well as outside the histories of contact on which they follow. Such a perspective is particularly valuable for people who would like to change or enrich the discursive repertoire of ethnographic writing—especially that "impossible attempt to fuse objective and subjective practices."

Surely a first step toward such change is to recognize that one's tropes are neither natural nor, in many cases, native to the discipline. Then it becomes possible, if one wishes, to liberate oneself from them, not by doing away with tropes (which is not possible) but by appropriating and inventing new ones (which is).

VINCENT CRAPANZANO

Hermes' Dilemma:
The Masking of Subversion
in Ethnographic Description

"All translation," Walter Benjamin (1969:75) wrote, "is only a somewhat provisional way of coming to terms with the foreignness of languages." Like translation, ethnography is also a somewhat provisional way of coming to terms with the foreignness of languages—of cultures and societies. The ethnographer does not, however, translate texts the way the translator does. He must first produce them. Text metaphors for culture and society notwithstanding, the ethnographer has no primary and independent text that can be read and translated by others. No text survives him other than his own. Despite its frequent ahistorical—its synchronic—pretense, ethnography is historically determined by the moment of the ethnographer's encounter with whomever he is studying.

The ethnographer is a little like Hermes: a messenger who, given methodologies for uncovering the masked, the latent, the unconscious, may even obtain his message through stealth. He presents languages, cultures, and societies in all their opacity, their foreignness, their meaninglessness; then like the magician, the hermeneut, Hermes himself, he clarifies the opaque, renders the foreign familiar, and gives meaning to the meaningless. He decodes the message. He interprets.

The ethnographer conventionally acknowledges the provisional nature of his interpretations. Yet he assumes a final interpretation—a definitive reading. "I have finally cracked the Kariera section system," we hear him say. "I finally got to the root of all their fuss about the *mudyi* tree." He resents the literary critic's assertion that there is never a final reading. He simply has not got to it yet.

The ethnographer does not recognize the provisional nature of his presentations. They are definitive. He does not accept as a paradox that his "provisional interpretations" support his "definitive presentations." (It is perhaps for this reason that he insists on a final reading.) Embedded in interpretation, his presentations limit re-interpretation. Ethnography closes in on itself. It is even possible that the more general theories the ethnologist generates from ethnography are only refractions, distorted repetitions in another register, of the provisional interpretations that support the presentation of data. The possibility must be entertained. Hermes was the tutelary god of speech and writing, and speech and writing, we know, are themselves interpretations.

Hermes, etymologically "he of the stone heap," was associated with boundary stones (Nilsson 1949; Brown 1969). The herm, a head and a phallus on a pillar, later replaced the stone heap. The eth-nographer, if I may continue my conceit, also marks a boundary: his ethnography declares the limits of his and his readers' culture. It also attests to his—and his culture's—interpretive power. Hermes was a phallic god and a god of fertility. Interpretation has been understood as a phallic, a phallic-aggressive, a cruel and violent, a destructive act, and as a fertile, a fertilizing, a fruitful, and a creative one. We say a text, a culture even, is pregnant with meaning. Do the ethnographer's presentations become pregnant with meaning because of his inter-pretive, his phallic fertilizations? (I have insisted here on using the masculine pronoun to refer to the ethnographer, despite his or her sexual identity, for I am writing of a stance and not of the person.)

The ethnographer is caught in a second paradox. He has to make sense of the foreign. Like Benjamin's translator, he aims at a solution to the problem of foreignness, and like the translator (a point missed by Benjamin) he must also communicate the very foreignness that his interpretations (the translator's translations) deny, at least in their claim to universality. He must render the foreign familiar and pre-serve its very foreignness at one and the same time. The translator accomplishes this through style, the ethnographer through the coup-ling of a presentation that asserts the foreign and an interpretation that makes it all familiar.

Hermes was a trickster: a god of cunning and tricks. The eth-nographer is no trickster. He, so he says, has no cunning and no tricks. But he shares a problem with Hermes. *He must make his message convincing.* It treats of the foreign, the strange, the unfamiliar, the ex-otic, the unknown—that, in short, which challenges belief. The eth-nographer must make use of all the persuasive devices at his disposal to convince his readers of *the* truth of his message, but, as though these rhetorical strategies were cunning tricks, he gives them scant recog-nition. His texts assume a truth that speaks for itself—a whole truth that needs no rhetorical support. His words are transparent. He does

not share Hermes' confidence. When Hermes took the post of messenger of the gods, he promised Zeus not to lie. He did not promise to
tell the whole truth. Zeus understood. The ethnographer has not.

In this paper I shall present a reading of three ethnographic
texts, only one of which was written by an anthropologist, to look at
some of the ways the ethnographer tries to make his message convincing. They are George Catlin's (1841; 1867) account of the Mandan Indians' O-Kee-Pa ceremony, Johann Wolfgang von Goethe's (1976a;
1982) description of the Roman carnival in his *Italienische Reise* of
1789, and Clifford Geertz's (1973) study of the Balinese cockfight.
The events described in the three texts are explosive, teasing if not the
performers' then the authors' assumptions of meaning and order.
The authors are challenged, and all make use of many different rhetorical strategies for convincing the reader, and presumably themselves, of the accuracy of their descriptions (see Marcus 1980).
Foremost among these strategies is the constitution of the ethnographer's authority: his presence at the events described, his perceptual ability, his "disinterested" perspective, his objectivity, and his
sincerity (see Clifford 1983a). In all three cases, the ethnographer's
place in his text is purely rhetorical. It is deictically, or better perhaps,
pseudo-deictically, constructed. It is impossible to fix his vantage point.
His is a roving perspective, necessitated by his "totalistic" presentation
of the events he is describing. His presence does not alter the way
things happen or, for that matter, the way they are observed or interpreted. He assumes an invisibility that, unlike Hermes, a god, he cannot, of course, have. His "disinterest," his objectivity, his neutrality are
in fact undercut by his self-interest—his need to constitute his authority, to establish a bond with his readers, or, more accurately, his interlocutors, and to create an appropriate distance between himself and
the "foreign" events he witnesses.
Aside from the devices the ethnographer uses to constitute his authority, he uses others to establish the validity of his ethnographic presentations directly. I single out three of these, which are used to various extents and with variable success by Catlin, Goethe, and Geertz.
In Catlin it is a hypotyposis that predominates. In Goethe it is an external (nonmetaphorical) theatrical narrativity. Geertz depends primarily on interpretive virtuosity. In all three cases, as we shall see, the
very figures the authors use to convince their readers—and themselves—of their descriptions in fact render them suspect, and in all
three cases this failure to convince is covered by an institutionally legitimated concern for "meaning." Catlin and Goethe give the ceremonies they describe an allegorical (moral) significance. Geertz claims

a phenomenological-hermeneutical perspective on meaning that is, at least rhetorically, insufficient. His essay becomes exemplary, and the cockfight itself takes on not only metaphorical but methodological significance. The O-Kee-Pa, the carnival, and the cockfight all become figures of disorder—of arbitrary violence, unruliness, and meaninglessness—in a transcending story in which precisely this disorder, this violence, unruliness, and meaninglessness are overcome. The ceremonies are shown to have, if not order and meaning, then at least significance. But, ironically, as figures that mask an initial rhetorical subversion—a failure to convince—the descriptions are again subverted. The O-Kee-Pa, the Roman carnival, and the Balinese cockfight become the "O-Kee-Pa," the "Roman carnival," and the "Balinese cockfight."

"With this very honourable degree which had just been conferred upon me, I was standing in front of the medicine-lodge early in the morning, with my companions by my side, endeavouring to get a peep, if possible, into its sacred interior; when the *master of ceremonies*, guarding and conducting its secrets, as I before described, came out of the door and taking me with a firm *professional* affection by the arm, led me into this *sanctum sanctorum*, which was strictly guarded from, even a peep or a gaze from the vulgar, by a vestibule of eight or ten feet in length, guarded with a double screen or door, and two or three dark and frowning centinels with spears or war clubs in their hands. I gave the wink to my companions as I was passing in, and the potency of my *medicine* was such as to gain them quiet admission, and all of us were comfortably placed on elevated seats, which our conductor soon prepared for us."

With these words, George Catlin (1841:161–62), the romantic-realist painter of the American Indians, describes his entrance into a medicine lodge in which he was to witness what is surely one of the most sanguinary rites in the annals of ethnography, the Mandan O-Kee-Pa—"an ordeal of privation and torture" in which young Mandan men, "emaciated with fasting, and thirsting, and waking, for nearly four days and nights," were hung by rawhide passed through the skewered flesh of their shoulders and breasts from the lodge's roof until they were "lifeless." The O-Kee-Pa was celebrated annually, according to Catlin, to commemorate the subsiding of a great flood that the Mandan believed once covered the world, to ensure the coming of the buffalo, and to initiate the young men of the tribe into manhood through an ordeal "which, while it is supposed to harden their muscles and prepare them for extreme endurance, enables the chiefs who are spectators to the scene to decide upon their comparative bodily strength and ability to endure the extreme privations and sufferings that often fall to the lots of Indian warriors" (1841 : 157).

It was the summer of 1832—six years before the Mandan were decimated by an epidemic of smallpox. Catlin had spent several weeks with them. He found that "they are a people of decidedly a different origin from that of any other tribe in these regions," and later he argued that they were descendents of Welsh sailors who under the direction of Prince Madoc had set sail in the fourteenth century (actually in the twelfth century) and were thought to have settled somewhere in North America (Catlin 1867; Ewers 1967). The day before his admission to the medicine lodge, Catlin painted the master of ceremonies, and so pleased was this great magician with his portrait—"he could see its eyes move"—that he and the other "doctors" unanimously elevated Catlin to a "respectable rank in the craft" of magic and mysteries and gave him the name "White Medicine Painter." It was this honor that allowed him to enter the lodge, and it was his reputed medicine that enabled his companions—J. Kipp, an agent of the American Fur Trade who had long been familiar with the Mandan and spoke their language; L. Crawford, Kipp's clerk; and Abraham Bogard, whose identity I have not been able to determine—to accompany him. They were apparently the first white men to witness the O-Kee-Pa, and Catlin was the first to describe it: on January 10, 1833 (though written on August 12, 1832), in the *New-York Commercial Advertiser*; then in 1841 in his *Manners, Customs, and Conditions of the North American Indians*; and, finally, in 1867 in a little book (with a *Folium Reservatum* for scholars) entirely devoted to the ceremony.

Catlin asserts melodramatically that he shudders and even shrinks from the task of reciting what he has seen. "I entered the *medicine-house* of these scenes," he writes

as I would have entered a church, and expected to see something extraordinary and strange, but yet in the form of worship or devotion; but, alas! little did I expect to see the interior of their holy temple turned into a *slaughter-house*, and its floor strewed with the blood of its fanatic devotees. Little did I think that I was entering a house of God, where His blinded worshippers were to pollute its sacred interior with their blood, and propitiatory suffering and tortures—surpassing, if possible, the cruelty of the rack or the inquisition; but such the scene has been, and as such I will endeavour to describe it. (1841 : 156)

Despite all of Catlin's shuddering and shrinking, he and his companions managed to watch the spectacle from the seats they were assigned. "We were then in full view of everything that transpired in the lodge, having before us the scene exactly, which is represented in the first of the four pictures [that Catlin painted of the ceremony and that illustrated his second and third accounts]. To this seat we returned every morning until sun-down for four days, the whole time which these strange scenes occupied" (1841 : 162). They were not even permitted to move from their assigned places. Once when Catlin got up to take a closer look at what he calls the central mystery of the rite— "the *sanctissimus sanctorum*, from which seemed to emanate all the sanctity of their proceedings"—he was sent back to his seat.

I started several times from my seat to approach it, but all eyes were instantly upon me, and every mouth in the assembly sent forth a hush—sh—! which brought me back to my seat again; and I at length quieted my stifled curiosity as well as I could, upon learning the fact, that so sacred was that object, and so important its secrets or mysteries, that not *I* alone, but even the young men, who were passing the ordeal, and all the village, save the conductor of the mysteries, were stopped from approaching it, or knowing what it was. (1841 : 162)

Like an artist standing before his easel, Catlin's vantage point is fixed. So at least he asserts. *And yet*, he is in fact no objectivist, no Robbe-Grillet, describing the ceremony laboriously, metonymous step by metonymous step, from the fixed position of his consciousness. His vision is larger, constructed, exaggerated, uneven—metaphorical. His eye constantly betrays itself. He describes the arrival of the evil one, O-kee-hee-de.

But alas! in the last of these dances, on the fourth day, in the midst of all their mirth and joy, and about noon, and in the height of all these exultations, an instant scream burst forth from the tops of the lodges!—men, women, dogs and all, seemed actually to howl and shudder with alarm, as they fixed their glaring eyeballs upon the prairie bluff, about a mile in the west, down the side of which a man was seen descending at full speed toward the village. This strange character darted about in a zig-zag course in all directions on the prairie, like a boy in pursuit of a butterfly, until he approached the piquets of the village, when it was discovered that his body was entirely naked, and painted as black as a negro, with pounded charcoal and bear's grease. . . . (1841 : 166)

Catlin rambles, repeats, generalizes, simplifies, exaggerates, and embellishes. He refers indiscriminately to what he has seen before or learned afterward. Amidst a purportedly realistic description, masked here as elsewhere in *Manners, Customs, and Conditions* by measurement ("about a mile in the west," "a vestibule of eight or ten feet"), are metaphorical turns of phrase, similes in the above example ("like a boy in pursuit of a butterfly," "painted as black as a negro") that seem as inappropriate to the event he describes as the colors—Baudelaire

(1846) called them terrifying, mysterious—of his Indian paintings.[1] They ring true neither to his presumed experience of the event nor to that of the Mandan participants. The two experiences are stylistically blurred—sacrificed ultimately to the experience Catlin wishes to engender in his readers. This pathopoetic sacrifice of the participant's subjectivity to that of his readers occurs even when Catlin claims to take the participant's point of view. He describes, for example, one of the hanging victims of torture, a condensation apparently of several.

Surrounded by imps and demons as they appear, a dozen or more, who seem to be concerting and devising means for his exquisite agony, gather around him, when one of the number advances toward him in a sneering manner, and commences turning him around with a pole which he brings in his hand for the purpose. This is done in a gentle manner at first; but gradually increased, when the brave fellow, whose proud spirit can control its anger no longer, burst out in the most lamentable and heart rendering cries that the human voice is capable of producing, crying forth a prayer to the Great Spirit to support and protect him in this dreadful trial; and continually repeating his confidence in his protection. In this condition he is continued to be turned, faster and faster—and there is no hope of escape from it, nor chance for the slightest relief, until by fainting, his voice falters, and his struggling ceases, and he hangs, apparently, a still and lifeless corpse! (1841 : 171)

Here Catlin moves from his (objectifying) metaphorical perspective to that of the tortured; despite this move, his intention is not phenomenological, but rhetorical: He does not describe either the Indian's or his own experience of the torture. The "imps and demons as they appear" (to whom? to Catlin? to the Mandan?) is stylistically equivalent to "there is no hope of escape from it." They are directed to the reader, and it is the reader's reaction that will guarantee Catlin's perceptions.

In these passages and throughout his *Manners, Customs, and Conditions of the North American Indians*, Catlin's principal stylistic figure is hypotyposis. His aim is to impress his experience of what he has *seen* so strongly, so vividly, on his readers that they cannot doubt its veracity. It is the visual that gives authority. The realistic tradition, Alexander Gelley (1979 : 420) observes, "sought to reenforce the description of things and places by making the object of the description coincide

1. In his commentaries on the Salon of 1846, Baudelaire (1846:634), who admired Catlin's work, wrote: "Le rouge, la couleur de la vie, abondait tellement dans ce sombre musée, que c'était une ivresse; quant aux paysages,—montagnes boisées, savanes immenses, rivières désertes,—ils étaient monotonement, éternellement verts; le rouge, cette couleur si obscure, si épaisse, plus difficile à pénétrer que les yeux d'un serpent— le vert, cette couleur calme et gaie et souriante de la nature, je les retrouve chantant leur antithèse mélodique." There is of course something of this melodic antithesis in Catlin's prose.

with the object of a specular act, image, or process." Catlin's assertion of a fixed vantage point, of an assigned seat—there are similar assertions elsewhere in *Manners, Customs, and Conditions*—must be understood rhetorically. It attests deictically to his presence. It gives him the authority of the painter before his easel. It enables him to lead his readers into the visualized scene and to convince them (and himself) of its truth.[2]

Catlin's vision is not, however, secure. Unlike today's social scientists whose theories (regardless of their merit) serve their ethnographic credibility, Catlin's credibility has ultimately to rest on the power of his descriptions. Just as his painting is not particularly believable, nor is his prose. It undermines itself. His intention is realistic, but his style is romantic. Through metaphor, often extravagant metaphor, ecphonesis, the promiscuous use of the vocative, hyperbole, pathopoeia, apoplanesis, interruption, suspense, subjectivism—to name only a few of his stylistic strategies—Catlin tries to give to his descriptions a compelling veracity, but it is precisely these strategies that subvert his intention. Realism demands stylistic sobriety. For Catlin such sobriety precludes the hypotyposis upon which his credibility rests.

In *Manners, Customs, and Conditions* he begins the letter in which he describes the O-Kee-Pa ceremony with these words:

Oh! "*horrible visu—et mirabile dictu!*" Thank God, it is over, that I have seen it, and am able to tell it to the world. (1841:155)

But why see it? Why tell it to the world? Catlin has no framework for his experience—no justification for his reportage. His intention is documentary, but does this intention justify witnessing and describing a "shocking and disgusting custom" that "sickens the heart and even the stomach of a traveller in the country" (182–83) and yet that fills such a traveler with pity?

Catlin rationalizes his description in a confused manner. (He was never a systematic thinker.) He writes that the ceremony "will be new to the civilized world, and therefore worth knowing" (157). He suggests that parts of the ceremony are grotesque and amusing and others, having to do with the deluge, are "harmless and full of interest" (177). He has no theoretical justification. Native exegesis is not satisfactory. The ceremony cannot be historically situated. He argues that even if he had time to elaborate a disquisition on the ceremony,

2. Gelley (1979:420) argues that ways of seeing in the realist novel can be understood "as a type of deictic at a phenomenological level, a sign important not so much on account of its content but because it is capable of identifying the instance of observation and tracing its modifications."

he would probably fail because simple people like the Mandan "have no history to save facts and systems from falling into the most absurd and disjointed fable and ignorant fiction" (177).

Catlin shares here the distinctly nineteenth-century conviction that explanation is embedded in origin. In *Manners, Customs, and Conditions* he relates Mandan beliefs and tales to biblical stories of the flood, Eve's transgression, and the birth and death of Christ. (Such an equation puts a stop fundamentalistically to the quest for both origins and meaning.) Noting the Mandans' distinctive ("white") appearance, noting too that their culture hero is white, Catlin assumes Christian contact, and, as we have seen, twenty-six years later, he argued that the Mandan were descended from the Welsh. But to acknowledge Christian influence or, for that matter, Welsh descent hardly explains the O-Kee-Pa tortures. Catlin shifts abruptly—his informal letter style permits this[3]—and he discusses the Mandans' potential for salvation. "I deem it not folly nor idle to say that these people *can be saved*," he concludes his letter,

nor officious to suggest to some of the very many excellent and pious men, who are almost throwing away the best energies of their lives along the debased frontier, that if they would introduce the ploughshare and their prayers amongst these people, who are so far separated from the taints and contaminating vices of the frontier, they would soon see their most ardent desires accomplished and be able to solve to the world the perplexing enigma, by presenting a nation of savages, civilized and Christianized (and consequently *saved*), in the heart of the American wilderness. (1841:184)

Catlin's ultimate justification—a justification that runs through American anthropology—is pragmatic; applied, as we say; evangelical in the case in point. The pragmatic, the applied, and the evangelical must also be understood rhetorically.

Despite his figurative language, his speculations about meaning, and his concern for the Indians' salvation, Catlin was in fact haunted by this problem of credibility. "I took my sketch-book with me," he writes toward the beginning of his description of the O-Kee-Pa ceremony,

and have made many and faithful drawings of what we saw, and full notes of everything as translated to me by the interpreter; and since the close of that horrid and frightful scene, which was a week ago or more, I have been closely ensconced in an earthcovered wigwam, with a fine sky-light over my head, with my pallette and brushes, endeavouring faithfully to put the whole of

3. There is a revealing parallel between Catlin's disjunctive style and his jumpy speculations about the meaning of the ceremony.

what we saw upon canvas, which my companions all agree to be critically correct, and of the fidelity of which they have attached their certificates to the
backs of the paintings. (1841 : 155)

As if prophetically, Catlin also had Kipp, Crawford, and Bogard attach a certificate of authenticity to his account of the ceremony in
Manners, Customs, and Conditions; for his report was to be questioned
by no less a figure in American ethnology than Henry Rowe Schoolcraft. In the third volume of his *Historical and Statistical Information Re-
specting the History, Condition and Prospects of the Indian Tribes of the
United States*, Schoolcraft (1851–57) included a two-page article on the
Mandan by David D. Mitchell, then superintendent of Indian affairs
in St. Louis, who had been in the Indian trade in Mandan territory in
upper Missouri in the 1830s. Mitchell's article concluded: "Information about their [the Mandans'] peculiar customs can be found in the
Journal of Lewis and Clark. The scenes described by Catlin, existed
almost entirely in the fertile imagination of that gentleman" (254).
When he was in South America, Catlin learned of Schoolcraft's and
Mitchell's repudiation of his work in a letter from Alexander von
Humboldt, who urged him to write to Prince Maximilian of Neuwied,
who had also spent a winter among the Mandan. Before Catlin was
able to obtain a letter of vindication from the prince—he eventually
did in 1866—both Schoolcraft and Mitchell died. Although Catlin's
description is now more or less accepted as an accurate portrayal
of the O-Kee-Pa ceremony (Bowers 1950; see also Matthews 1873),
Catlin himself was plagued by the doubt cast on the accuracy of his
accounts for the rest of his life.

On February 20, 1787, Ash Wednesday, Goethe wrote:

At last the foolishness is over. The innumerable lights last night were another
mad spectacle. One has only to see the Roman carnival to lose all desire ever
to see it again. It is not worth writing about. If need be, it might make an
amusing conversation piece.

(Nun ist der Narrheit ein Ende. Die unzähligen Lichter gestern abend waren
noch ein toller Spektakel. Das Karneval in Rom muss man gesehen haben, um
den Wunsch völlig loszuwerden, es je wieder zu sehen. Zu schreiben ist davon
gar nichts, bei einer mündlichen Darstellung möchte es allenfalls unter-
haltend sein.)[4]

Ironically, a year later Goethe saw the carnival again, and in 1789,
upon his return to Weimar, he published an account of it with colored

---

    4. 1976a:228. All translations are my own. The Auden and Mayer translation
(Goethe 1982) is often very inaccurate.

engravings. He later incorporated this little book, *Das Römische Karneval*, into his *Italienische Reise*, which is essentially an arrangement of letters and diary entries the poet edited twenty-five years after his Italian trip.[5]

Goethe only loosely follows the chronological order of the Roman carnival, which begins, gradually, with the opening of the theaters in Rome after the New Year and culminates on Ash Wednesday. He stresses the fact that the carnival fits in naturally with the Roman lifestyle. It is really not *that* different from Sunday and holiday merriment in Rome.[6] Even the costumes and masks are familiar sights, Goethe argues, citing the hooded monks who accompany funerals throughout the year. He carefully locates the carnival, at least the parts he thinks worthy of describing, on the Corso. (Like Catlin, he is careful to give precise measurements of the location of the ceremony.)

The Corso becomes the carnival's theater. The stage is the street itself. The audience stand or are seated along its sides, on the sidewalk, on balconies, or in front of windows. Goethe describes the costumes, masks, carriages, horses (for the race with which the carnival ends each evening), as though he were describing costumes and props for a theatrical production. The characters—guards, Pulcinelle, *quaccheri* ("Quakers") in old-fashioned, richly embroidered clothes, *sbirri*, Neapolitan boatmen, peasants, women from Frascati, German baker apprentices, who have a reputation for drunkenness—are like characters from the *commedia dell'arte*. (The *quacchero*, Goethe himself remarks, is like the *buffo caricato* of the comic opera; he plays either a vulgar fop or the silly, infatuated, and betrayed old fool.) The characters have no depth. They are emblematic, as are their skits. The overall movement—the action—of the carnival leads each day to a mad, riderless horse race, and the carnival itself ends dramatically on the evening before Ash Wednesday. Everyone carries a lighted candle. Everyone tries to blow out other people's candles, shouting, *Sia ammazzato chi non porta moccola* ("Death to anyone who is not carrying a candle"). Everyone tries to protect his or her own candle.

No one can move much from the spot where he is standing or sitting; the heat of so many human beings and so many lights, the smoke from so many candles, blown out again and again, the noise of so many people, who only yell all the louder, the less they can move a limb, make the sanest head swim. It seems

5. See Michel (1976) for publication details.
6. It "fits in naturally with the Roman life style." (Das Karneval ist, wie wir bald bemerken können, eigentlich nur eine Fortsetzung oder vielmehr der Gipfel jener gewöhnlichen sonn- und festtägigen Freuden; es ist nichts Neues, nichts Fremdes, nichts Einziges, sondern es schliesst sich nur an die römische Lebensweise ganz natürlich an [1976a:642]).

impossible that no accident will occur, that the carriage horses will not go wild, that many will not be bruised, crushed, or otherwise injured.

(Niemand vermag sich mehr von dem Platze, wo er steht oder sitzt, zu rühren; die Wärme so vieler Menschen, so vieler Lichter, der Dampf so vieler immer wieder ausgeblasenen Kerzen, das Geschrei so vieler Menschen, die nur um desto heftiger brüllen, je weniger sie ein Glied rühren können, machen zuletzt selbst den gesundesten Sinn schwindeln; es scheint unmöglich, dass nicht manches Unglück geschehen, dass die Kutschpferde nicht wild, nicht manche gequetscht, gedrückt oder sonst beschädigt werden sollten.) (1976a:675)

The crowd finally disperses, the common people to relish their last meat dish before Lent, the fashionable to the last performance of the theater. The "madness" ends on Ash Wednesday. "How happy I shall be when the fools are silenced next Tuesday," Goethe writes in a letter on February 1, 1778. "It is terribly annoying to watch others go mad when one has not caught the infection oneself" ("Wie froh will ich sein, wenn die Narren künftigen Dienstag abend zur Ruhe gebracht werden. Es ist eine entsetzliche Sekkatur, andere toll zu sehen, wenn man nicht selbst angesteckt ist" [1976a:681]). As we shall see, Ash Wednesday gave Goethe occasion to contemplate the meaning of this folly, this Saturnalian merriment, with its role reversals, its vulgar gestures, its transvestitism, its libertinism, and what offended him most, its disorder.

In contrast to Catlin's account of the O-Kee-Pa ceremony, with its subjectivism, its metaphors and hyperboles, and indeed in contrast to Goethe's own *Sturm und Drang* writings, with their exuberant subjectivism and insistent concern with *Innerlichkeit*, innerness, the *Italian Journey*, including *The Roman Carnival*, treats the external, *das Aussere*, with an emotional calm that must surely have been disappointing to the readers of *Werther*. (There are in fact few "extravagant" metaphors in Goethe's text, and the few there are do not subvert his "realism" as Catlin's do.) On November 10, 1786, Goethe wrote from Rome:

I live here now with a clarity and calm that I have not felt for a long time. My habit of looking at and reading all things as they are, my conscientious [effort] to keep my eyes open, my complete renunciation of all pretension again stand me in good stead and make me privately very happy. Each day a new remarkable object; daily, vast singular new pictures—a whole that, however long one thinks and dreams, is never accessible through the imagination.

(Ich lebe nun hier mit Klarheit und Ruhe, von der ich lange kein Gefühl hatte. Meine Übung, alle Dinge, wie sie sind, zu sehen und abzulesen, meine Treue, das Auge licht sein zu lassen, meine völlige Entäusserung von aller Prätention kommen mir einmal wieder recht zustatten und machen mich im stillen höchst glücklich. Alle Tage ein neuer merkwürdiger Gegenstand, täglich frische, grosse, seltsame Bilder und ein Ganzes, das man sich lange denkt und träumt, nie mit der Einbildungskraft erreicht.) (1976a: 178–79)

There is something salubrious in Goethe's "new" approach to reality. It should be remembered that his Italian trip had a therapeutic intention, to reanimate him, and that he often spoke of it as a rebirth (Fairley 1947). "In this place," he writes on the same day, "whoever looks seriously about him and has eyes to see must become strong; he is bound to acquire an idea of strength that was never so alive for him" ("Wer sich mit Ernst hier umsieht und Augen hat zu sehen, muss solid werden, er muss einen Begriff von Solidität fassen, der ihm nie so lebendig ward" [1976a: 179]). He insists on seeing again and again to avoid the mixture of truth and lies that makes up first impressions (Goethe 1976b: 86; Staiger 1956: 14). Under the tutelage of Angelika Kauffmann he draws to deepen his perception of the objects around him. As Emil Staiger (1956: 15–16) shows, it is the idea ("Begriffe," "anschauender Begriff," "lebendiges Begriff" in Goethe's writing) that unites the changing and the unchanging, the multiple perceptions of an object. Goethe's objectivity remains always the objectivity of a subject. His "objective" is not the opposite of the "subjective." According to Staiger (1956: 18), the contrast is between inner comprehension of the thing ("ein 'innerliches' Erfassen der Dinge") and its objective (*sachlich*) comprehension. Distance, understood both literally and figuratively, is necessary for this "objectivity," but as Staiger (1956: 18) notes, Goethe is less concerned with a specific perspective than with showing an eternal truth.[7]

Although Goethe, like Catlin, occasionally situates himself as if before an easel in his descriptions in the *Italian Journey* (e.g., 1982: 30), he does not assume a fixed perspective in *The Roman Carnival*. Indeed, in the very first paragraph of his work he writes conventionally of the impossibility of describing the carnival and thereby turns the carnival itself into a figure of madness and disorder.

In undertaking to write a description of the Roman Carnival, we must fear the objection that such a festivity cannot really be described. A huge, lively

7. Auch wer nur die Dinge will und sonst nichts, erfasst sie in einer bestimmten Hinsicht, von einem bestimmten Gesichtspunkt aus. Dessen wird Goethe sich nicht bewusst. Er ist überzeugt, *die* ewig gültige Wahrheit entdeckt und begriffen zu haben, und traut sich zu, sie jedem, der Augen hat und sehen will, zeigen zu können. Da es sich um objektive Erkenntnisse handelt, gelingt das auch. Was Goethe darlegt, ist tatsächlich den wechselvollen Launen, der Stimmung, der Willkür der einzelnen Menschen entrückt und insofern zeitlos und überall gültig. Es fragt sich aber, ob jedermann sich für diese Wahrheit interessiert, ob nicht mancher es vorzieht, die Dinge von einem andern Gesichtspunkt aus, in anderer Hinsicht wahrzunehmen. Darüber haben wir nicht zu rechten und ist ein Streit überhaupt nicht möglich (Staiger 1956: 17–18).

mass of sensuous beings moves immediately before one's eyes and will be seen and grasped by everyone in his own way. The objection is still more serious when we admit that the Roman carnival gives neither a whole nor pleasing impression neither particularly delights the eyes nor gratifies the mind of the foreign spectator who sees it for the first time and wants only to watch, indeed can only watch. There is no overview of the long and narrow street in which innumerable people move about; one hardly distinguishes in the midst of the tumult anything the eye can grasp. The movement is monotonous, the noise is deafening, the end of each day unsatisfactory. These doubts alone are soon raised when we examine the matter more closely; and above all the question will be whether or not any description is warranted.

(Indem wir eine Beschreibung des Römischen Karnevals unternehmen, müssen wir den Einwurf befürchten, dass eine solche Feierlichkeit eigentlich nicht beschrieben werden könne. Eine so grosse lebendige Masse sinnlicher Gegenstände sollte sich unmittelbar vor dem Auge bewegen und von einem jeden nach seiner Art angeschaut und gefasst werden. Noch bedenklicher wird diese Einwendung, wenn wir selbst gestehen müssen, dass das Römische Karneval einem fremden Zuschauer, der es zum erstenmal sieht und nur sehen will und kann, weder einen ganzen noch ein erfreulichen Eindruck gebe, weder das Auge sonderlich ergötze, noch das Gemüt befriedige. Die lange und schmale Strasse, in welcher sich unzählige Menschen hin und wider wälzen, ist nicht zu übersehen; kaum unterscheidet man etwas in dem Bezirk des Getümmels, den das Auge fassen kann. Die Bewegung ist einförmig, der Lärm betäubend, das Ende der Tage unbefriedigend. Allein diese Bedenklichkeiten sind bald gehoben, wenn wir uns näher erklären; und vorzüglich wird die Frage sein, ob uns die Beschreibung selbst rechtfertigt.) (1976a:639)

The absence of a single perspective over the carnival is associated with tumult (*Getümmel*), deafening sound (*der Lärm betäubend*), masses of sensuous beings, undifferentiated movement, ultimately with an unpleasant and unsatisfactory experience—at least for the foreign observer. (Throughout the *Italian Journey*, Goethe refers to the foreigner, the foreign observer, as though there were a single "foreign" vantage point on Italy and its carnival.)[8] It will be Goethe's task to bring order to this disorder through his description—a description, he says, that will convey the enjoyment and tumult (*Freude und Taumel*) of the occasion to the reader's imagination.

Goethe himself does not take a specific spatial vantage point—always a possibility even when there is no overview, no *Übersicht*, no cathedral tower, which played such an important role in his student days

---

8. If there is no difference between actors and spectators in the carnival—a point made by Bakhtin (1970)—then any vantage point on the carnival would have to be "foreign"—outside the carnival itself. I doubt, however, that there is no differentiation between actors and spectators—Goethe's "theatrical" description suggests there is—and I would argue that the absence of differentiation is, in fact, ideological—an expression of a defining alterity.

in Strasbourg (Lewes 1949:67). He moves indifferently up and down the Corso. He moves as indifferently through time. With the exception of the lighting of candles on the evening before Ash Wednesday, the only nonrepetitive event in Goethe's carnival, he does not specify the time of the events he describes. He writes in the "present" tense— a tenseless tense, if you will, which serves at once to give a feeling of timeless flow and to permit generalizations. Like Catlin, Goethe conflates—and generalizes—characters and events, and only rarely, to add life and authenticity to his descriptions, does he specify his relationship to particular events and characters.

We remember among others one young man who played perfectly the part of a passionate, quarrelsome, and in no way to be calmed woman. He argued the length of the Corso, grabbing everyone while his companions appeared to be taking great pains to calm him down.

(Wir erinnern uns unter andern eines jungen Menschen, der die Rolle einer leidenschaftlichen, zanksüchtigen und auf keine Weise zu beruhigenden Frau vortrefflich spielte und so den ganzen Corso hinab zankte, jedem etwas anhängte, indes seine Begleiter sich alle Mühe zu geben schienen, ihn zu besänftigen.) (1976a:647)

Or, describing a battle of confetti, he writes:

We ourselves saw one such battle at close quarters. When the combatants ran out of ammunition, they threw the little gilded baskets at one another's heads.

(Wir haben selbst einen solchen Streit in der Nähe gesehn, wo zuletzt die Streitenden aus Mangel an Munition, sich die vergoldeten Körbchen an die Köpfe warfen.) (1976a:660)

More often, however, Goethe does not indicate his relationship to the event through the first person pronoun ("stands out in *my* memory"; "*we* ourselves saw") but by means of various spatial and temporal deictic locutions that give the event and characters an illusory specificity. In a section in which he describes the masks and fancy dresses of the carnival generally, he writes, for example:

Here a Pulcinella comes running along with a large horn dangling from colored strings around his waist. . . . And *here* comes another of his kind, . . . more modest and more satisfied.

(*Hier* kommt ein Pulcinell gelaufen, dem ein grosses Horn an bunten Schnüren um die Hüften gaukelt. . . . *Hier* kommt ein anderer seinesgleichen . . . bescheidner und zufriedner.) (1976a: 647; emphasis added)

Despite the "here's," we have no coordinates other than our general knowledge that we are "with Goethe" somewhere along the Corso during the carnival. Goethe in fact begins this part of his description

with the ringing of the noonday bells on the Capitol, which announces
the period of license, but we do not know which day of the carnival it
is. In other sections he uses temporal deixis. He begins a description
of evening, before the races: "Now as evening approaches" ("Nun
geht es nach dem Abend zu" [1976a: 664]). Again we have no idea
which evening. And at still other times, in the midst of a generalized,
spatially and temporally decontextualized description of an event, he
will suddenly make use of a "meanwhile," an *inzwischen*, that has no
coordinates. As I have said, the function of these deictics is purely
rhetorical, to add life to his descriptions and make them more convincing. They attest to Goethe's presence, and they appeal to the
reader to "join" him. There is an appellative dimension to Goethe's
deictics, perhaps to all deictics. He draws his readers into a seemingly
real moment of observation that is in fact only an artifice of his text.
He offers them the security of his presence as they witness the tan-
talizing disorder of the events that take place in the Corso.

Goethe becomes the reader's mediator—a sort of tour guide to
the carnival. He stands outside it, though, particularly outside the tumultuous crowd—the common people—milling up and down the
Corso. He is aloof, a foreigner, at times condescending. He sees little
joy in the carnival and, like Hawthorne and Henry James after him,
he does not share in any of its merriment. He preserves his distance,
an order-bestowing theatrical distance, and only occasionally does he
identify with the spectators—not with the huge lively mass of sensuous beings, but with an elite who watch the crowd from their benches
and chairs. He describes the homey feeling produced by the rugs
hanging from balconies and windows, by the embroidered tapestries
draped over the stands, and by the chairs brought out from inside the
houses and palaces along the Corso. When you leave the house, you
do not believe you are outside, among strangers, but in a room full of
acquaintances ("Indem man aus dem Hause tritt, glaubt man nicht im
Freien und unter Fremden, sondern in einem Saale unter Bekannten
zu sein" [1976a: 646]). He does not abandon his class. He does not
phenomenologically or rhetorically assume the subjectivity of the participants. Indeed, in his first mention of the carnival the year before,
he was more sensitive to the participants' experience.

What one finds unpleasant about it is the absence of inner gaiety in the
people, who lack the money to gratify the few desires they may still have. . . .
On the last days the noise was incredible, but there was no heartfelt joy.

(Was man dabei unangenehm empfindet, dass die innere Fröhlichkeit den
Menschen fehlt und es ihnen an Gelde mangelt, das bisschen Lust, was sie
noch haben mögen, auszulassen. . . . An den letzten Tagen war ein unglaub-
licher Lärm, aber keine Herzensfreude.) (1976a: 228–29)

In the *Roman Carnival*, Goethe is interested in display, the external, *das Aussere*, in what he can see—and not in the *Innerlichkeit* of the participants.

And yet it is precisely with the "inner meaning" of the carnival that Goethe concludes his essay. It passes like a dream or a fairytale, he says, leaving perhaps fewer traces on the soul of the participant (*Teilnehmer*) than on Goethe's readers. He has brought to their imagination and understanding a coherent whole ("vor deren Einbildungskraft und Verstand wir das Ganze in seinem Zusammenhange gebracht haben"). Is Goethe suggesting that for an experience to be more than ephemeral it must be described—given coherence and order? He goes on to observe that "the course of these follies" draws our attention to the most important stages of human life

when a vulgar Pulcinella indecently reminds us of the pleasures of love to which we owe our existence, when a Baubo profanes the mysteries of birth in public places, when so many lighted candles at night remind us of the ultimate ceremony.

(wenn uns . . . der rohe Pulcinell ungebührlich an die Freuden der Liebe erinnert, denen wir unser Dasein zu danken haben, wenn eine Baubo auf öffentlichem Platze die Geheimnisse der Gebärerin entweiht, wenn so viele nächtlich angezündete Kerzen uns an die letzte Feierlichkeit erinnern.) (1976a:676)

He sees the Corso itself as the road of earthly life where one is both spectator and actor and where one has little room to move freely because of external forces. The horses racing past are like fleeting delights "that leave only a trace on our soul." Carried away by the force of his imagery, Goethe remarks

that freedom and equality can only be enjoyed in the intoxication of madness and that the greatest desire rises to its highest pitch when it approaches close to danger and relishes in voluptuous, sweet-anxious sensations.

(dass Freiheit und Gleichheit nur in dem Taumel des Wahnsinns genossen werden können, und dass die grösste Lust nur dann am höchsten reizt, wenn sie sich ganz nahe an die Gefahr drängt und lüstern ängstlich-süsse Empfindungen in ihrer Nähe geniesset.) (1976a:677)

Reminiscent of his unrestrained *Sturm und Drang* period, these last observations seem removed from any specific referent in the carnival. The carnival is an excuse for Goethe's meditation. His concern is with its meaning not for the participants, but for himself and his readers. Ignoring the historical and the collective, the link, as Bakhtin (1965) stresses, between popular destiny, penetrated by the comic principle, and the earth, Goethe reduces the carnival to a conventional allegory of individual destiny. Its meaning lies in a transcendent story—the kind Catlin sought for the O-Kee-Pa ceremony but could never really find. Through Goethe's allegory, the individual is, so to speak, resurrected from the milling, seething, tumultuous—the unindividuated—crowd.[9] Goethe, a kind of trickster, a magician of words, a Hermes reporting the carnival to those up north, across the border, restores order at this reflective level to an event that, despite the expository, the theatricalized order he has already given it in his description, must rhetorically remain a symbol of madness and disorder. Like Catlin, Goethe seeks moral significance (albeit trivial) in ceremony—in the carnival.

And so without even thinking about it, we have also concluded with an Ash Wednesday meditation, which we trust has not saddened our readers. Rather, since life as a whole remains like the Roman Carnival, without an overview, unsavory, and precarious, we wish that through this carefree crowd of maskers everyone will be reminded with us of the importance of every one of the momentary and often seemingly trivial pleasures of life.

(Und so hätten wir, ohne selbst daran zu denken, auch unser Karneval mit einer Aschermittwochsbetrachtung geschlossen, wodurch wir keinen unsrer Leser traurig zu machen fürchten. Vielmehr wünschen wir, dass jeder mit uns, da das Leben im ganzen wie das Römische Karneval unübersehlich, ungeniessbar, ja bedenklich bleibt, durch diese unbekümmerte Maskengesellschaft an die Wichtigkeit jedes augenblicklichen, oft gering scheinenden Lebensgenusses erinnert werden möge.) (1976a:677)

A conventional Ash Wednesday meditation, perhaps, Goethe's conclusion marks a return to contemplation, introspection, and concern for the meaning of what we do.[10] His "return" parallels a return in the ceremony he describes. During the carnival there is no reflection, just play, masquerading, and, as we say nowadays, acting out. With Ash Wednesday begins a period of penitence, and, we must presume, a return to introspection, order, and individuality.

The title of Clifford Geertz's essay "Deep Play: Notes on a Balinese Cockfight," written about the time the film *Deep Throat* was all the

---

9. It is interesting to note that Henry James (1873:139 et seq.) also includes an Ash Wednesday meditation, "a Lenten peroration," in his description of the carnival in 1873. It is inspired by the view of a young priest praying by himself in a little church on the Palatine hill and continues as James, alone, keeps carnival "by strolling perversely along the silent circumference of Rome."

10. By his addressing the reader, the reader's function becomes, as Michael André Bernstein (1983) remarks, "akin to the function of the next day in a 'real' Saturnalia, the instant when everyone resumes his conventional roles, with the important distinction, however, that the reader's position represents a *continuously* present source of authority which even the most anarchic moments of the festival day do not succeed in suspending." Though I acknowledge the authoritative role of the reader in Goethe's *Römische Karneval*, Goethe's own authoritative position, far stronger than Catlin's, seems to be quite independent of his reader's.

rage, announces a series of erotic puns—puns, Geertz maintains, the Balinese themselves would understand—used throughout his essay. Puns are frequent in ethnography. They position the ethnographer between his world of primary orientation, his reader's world, and the world of those others, the people he has studied, whom at some level, I believe, he is also addressing (Crapanzano 1977a). Through the pun he appeals collusively to the members of one or the other world, usually the world of his readership, thereby creating a hierarchical relationship between them. He himself, the punster, mediates between these worlds.

Geertz's essay is divided into seven sections, and the titles of these sections—"The Raid," "Of Cocks and Men," "The Fight," "Odds and Even Money," "Playing with Fire," "Feathers, Blood, Crowds, and Money," and "Saying Something of Something"—are all suggestive of a distinctly urban environment, of a sex-and-violence whodunit, something out of Mickey Spillane, perhaps, which, unlike Geertz's erotic puns, the villagers could not possibly have understood, at least in 1958. The titles do little to characterize the ethos of a Balinese village or cockfight, but, like puns, they create a collusive relationship between the ethnographer and, in this case, his readers. They also attest to the ethnographer's stylistic virtuosity. He and his readers come out on top of the hierarchy of understanding.

Geertz's essay begins with a humorous tale of entry—by now, in its own right, a genre or subgenre of ethnography. The hero, the anthropologist, is cast stereotypically as a *naïf*, an awkward simpleton, not at all sure of his identity, often suffering from some sort of exotic malady, who is caught in a betwixt and between world. We could see him at Goethe's Roman Carnival. He is no longer in his own world, and he has not yet mastered his new world—the world he will constitute through his ethnography.

Early in April of 1958, my wife and I arrived, malarial and diffident, in a Balinese village we intended, as anthropologists, to study. A small place, about five hundred people, and relatively remote, it was its own world. We were intruders, professional ones, and the villagers dealt with us as Balinese seem always to deal with people not part of their life who yet press themselves upon them: as though we were not there. For them, and to a degree for ourselves, we were nonpersons, specters, invisible men. (1973:412)

Here in the first paragraph of "Deep Play," Geertz establishes an opposition between himself and his wife and the Balinese who live in their own remote little world. Geertz and his wife are "anthropologists," "professionals," and "intruders." The tale of entry is, as I have noted, called "The Raid," referring manifestly to a police raid of a village cockfight. It may also reflect Geertz's attitude toward his and his wife's presence, their mission, in the village. He claims dramatically that he and his wife were "nonpersons, specters, invisible men" for the villagers and "to a degree for ourselves"—that is, until like the other villagers attending the cockfight, they fled the police. Then they were recognized. Geertz offers no evidence for this contention, and in the very next paragraph he contradicts himself.

> But except for our landlord and the village chief, whose cousin and brother-in-law he was, everyone ignored us only as the Balinese can do. As we wandered around, uncertain, wistful, eager to please, people seemed to look right through us with a gaze focused several yards behind us on some more actual stone or tree. Almost nobody greeted us; but nobody scowled or said anything unpleasant to us either which would have been almost as satisfactory. . . . The indifference, of course, was studied; the villagers were watching every move we made, and they had an enormous amount of quite accurate information about who we were and what we were going to be doing. But they acted as if we simply did not exist, which, in fact, as this behavior was designed to inform us, we did not, or anyway not yet. (412–13)

There is of course a difference between being a nonperson, a specter, an invisible man—a collection of nonequivalent statuses in any case— and being treated with "studied indifference." The Geertzes may have been treated as though they were not there, but they were surely there. How else could they be informed of their "nonexistence"?

I call attention here to what might simply be dismissed as a not altogether successful storytelling ruse, were it not indicative of a more serious problem that flaws Geertz's essay. Here, at a descriptive level, he blurs his own subjectivity—his experience of himself in those early Balinese days—with the subjectivity and the intentionality of the villagers. (His wife's experience presents still another problem as well as something of a conceptual embarrassment: she is dismissed from this tale of men and cocks—a dismissal already heralded in the first paragraph by the use of "men" in the phrase "invisible men.") Later, at the level of interpretation, we discover the same confusion (see Crapanzano 1981a; Lieberson 1984). We must ask whether this interpretive confusion is facilitated by Geertz's particular descriptive tack.

Through puns, titles, subtitles, and simple declarations, the "anthropologist" and his "Balinese" are separated from one another. In the opening section of "Deep Play" Geertz and his wife are cast, however conventionally, as individuals. The Balinese are not. They are generalized. Turns of phrase like "as Balinese always do," reminiscent if not of superficial travel accounts, then of national character studies, run through "Deep Play": "in a way only a Balinese can do" (412); "the deep psychological identification of Balinese men with their cocks" (417); "the Balinese never do anything in a simple way when they can contrive to do it in a complicated way" (425); "the Balinese are shy to the point of obsessiveness of open conflict" (446). The "Balinese"—surely not the Balinese—becomes a foil for Geertz's describing, interpreting, and theorizing—for his self-presenting.

Geertz likens his nonpersonhood to being "a cloud or a gust of wind": "My wife and I were still very much in the gust of wind stage, a most frustrating, and even, as you begin to doubt whether you are really real after all, unnerving one when . . ." (413). And he goes on to describe the police raid through which he achieved his "personhood." This passage is significant not so much because of what Geertz has to say about himself and his wife as because of a pronoun switch from "I/we," or more accurately from "I + noun" ("my wife and I") to "you." This switch anticipates his disappearance in the sections to come. The "you" serves as more, I suggest, than an appeal to the reader to empathize with him. It decenters the narrator in the space of intersubjective understanding. He engages in dialogue with his reader in a way, at least in his presentation, that he does not engage with the Balinese. *They* remain cardboard figures.

Despite popular grammatical understanding that a pronoun is simply a noun substitute, there is, as Emile Benveniste (1966) and others have observed, a fundamental difference between first and second person personal pronouns ("I" and "you" and their plurals) and third person pronouns ("he," "she," "it," "they"). The first and second are properly indexical: they "relate" to the context of utterance. The third person pronouns refer back anaphorically to an antecedent, a noun, often enough a proper noun, in the text. They are liberated, so to speak, from the context of utterance, but they are embedded in the textual context. They are intratextual and derive their meaning from their textually described antecedents. Thus, in Geertz's essay, and in most ethnography, the "I/you" of the ethnographer and the "I/you" of the ethnographer's interlocutors in the field are converted asymmetrically into an anaphorically free "I" and an anaphoric—a cumulative "they." Indeed, in most ethnographic texts, including Geertz's, the "I" itself disappears except in conventional tales of entry or in text-evaluation shifters and becomes simply a stylistically borne "invisible" voice.[11] Symptomatically, "we" seldom occurs in ethnography.

"The Raid" represents a delicate, unstable moment. Geertz, the

11. I am simplifying here. The ethnographer's "I" must be carefully examined in its specific occurrences, for it can serve multiple functions, even simultaneously. It may, for example, be descriptive, referring to a grammatically distorted interlocution ("I said"/"he said" or "I observed") or it may in fact refer to the context of writing. There is also, as I have argued elsewhere (1981b), an anaphoric potential to first and second person indexicals, particularly in "authored" texts.

author/narrator, is an "I." The Balinese are referentially described: a "they." Just as the Balinese recognize Geertz after his flight from the police, he, at least as an I, flees from the text in a section revealingly entitled "Of Cocks and Men." Does the lingering "I" of "The Raid" compensate for Geertz's nonpersonhood in those first days of field-work he is describing?

Throughout the remainder of "Deep Play" there is a continual blurring of Geertz's understanding and the understanding of the Bali-nese as he describes them. Without any evidence he attributes to the Balinese all sorts of experiences, meanings, intentions, motivations, dispositions, and understandings. He writes, for example:

In the cockfight man and beast, good and evil, ego and id, the creative power of aroused masculinity and the destructive power of loosened animality fuse in a bloody drama of hatred, cruelty, violence, and death. It is little wonder that when, as is the invariable rule, the owner of the winning cock takes the carcass of the loser—often torn limb from limb by its enraged owner—home to eat, he does so with a mixture of social embarrassment, moral satisfaction, aesthetic disgust, and cannibal joy. (430–21)

We must not be carried away by Geertz's Grand Guignol sensibility. We must ask: on what grounds does he attribute "social embarrassment," "moral satisfaction," "aesthetic disgust" (whatever that means), and "cannibal joy" to the Balinese? to all Balinese men? to any Balinese man in particular? Clearly Geertz's aim, like Catlin's, is to render the moment vivid, but unlike Catlin, who makes no pretense of uncover-ing the subjective meaning—the experience—of the O-Kee-Pa cere-mony for the Mandan, Geertz does make such a claim of the Balinese.

Toward the end of his essay, as though pulling a rabbit out of a hat, Geertz suddenly declares the cockfight to be an art form, which he understands in a very Western way: "As any art form—for that, finally, is what we are dealing with—the cockfight renders ordinary, everyday experience comprehensible by presenting it in terms of acts and objects which have had their practical consequences removed and been reduced (or, if you prefer, raised) to the level of sheer appear-ance, where their meaning can be more powerfully articulated and more exactly perceived" (443). We must ask: for whom does the cock-fight articulate everyday experience—the experience of status hierar-chy—and render it more perceptible? After likening the cockfight to *King Lear* and *Crime and Punishment*, Geertz goes on to assert that it

catches up these themes—death, masculinity, rage, pride, loss, beneficence, change—and ordering them into an encompassing structure, presents them in such a way as to throw into relief a particular view of their essential nature. It puts a construction on them, makes them, to those historically positioned to appreciate the construction, meaningful—visible, tangible, graspable—"real" in an ideational sense. An image, fiction, a model, a metaphor, the cockfight is a means of expression; its function is neither to assuage social passions nor to heighten them (though, in its playing-with-fire way it does a bit of both), but, in a medium of feathers, blood, crowds, and money, to display them. (443–44)

We must ask: who is historically positioned to appreciate the construction? Geertz completely ignores the fact that *King Lear* and *Crime and Punishment* are culturally and linguistically marked as a tragedy and a novel; as representations of a particular order; as fictions to be read in a special way—indeed, to be read. He offers no proof anywhere that the cockfight is so marked for his Balinese. Piling image on image— "image," "fiction," and "metaphor"—may assuage Geertz's own theoretical anxiety, but it hardly gets rid of the problem. (Image, fiction, model, and metaphor are of course no more equivalent than nonperson, specter, and invisible man.) Cockfights are surely cockfights for the Balinese—and not images, fictions, models, and metaphors. They are not marked as such, though they may be read as such by a foreigner for whom "images, fictions, models, and metaphors" have interpretive value.[12] It is perhaps no accident that in a following paragraph Geertz describes the cockfight as "disquietful": "The reason it is disquietful is that, joining pride to selfhood, selfhood to cocks, and cocks to destruction, it brings to imaginative realization a dimension of Balinese experience normally well-obscured from view" (444). We must ask yet again: for whom is the cockfight disquietful?

In the final pages of "Deep Play" Geertz likens the cockfight to a text. He also refers to it as "a Balinese reading of Balinese experience," "a story they tell the natives about themselves," a "metacommentary." "It is a means of saying something about something." It requires the anthropologist to "penetrate" it, just as a critic "penetrates" a text. For Geertz the interpreted text, the cockfight, is a drama of status hierarchy, and in blatantly intentional language he suggests that is why Balinese go to cockfights: "Balinese go to cockfights to find out what a man, usually composed, aloof, almost obsessively self-absorbed, a kind of moral autocosm, feels like when attacked, tormented, challenged, insulted, and driven in result to the extremes of fury, he has totally triumphed or been brought low" (450).

Elsewhere, he asserts Balinese subjectivity at cockfights.

Enacted and re-enacted, so far without end the cockfight enables the Balinese, as, read and reread, *Macbeth* enables us, to see a dimension of his own

12. One would ultimately have to consider the ontological status of Balinese equivalents (if there are any) of these Western categories.

subjectivity. As he watches fight after fight, with the active watching of an owner and a bettor (for cockfighting has no more interest as a pure spectator sport than does croquet or dog-racing), he grows familiar with it and what it has to say to him much as the attentive listener to a string quartet or the absorbed viewer of still life grows slowly more familiar with them in a way which opens his objectivity to himself. (450–51)

Who told Geertz? How can a whole people share a single subjectivity? Are there not differences between texts, commentaries, metacommentaries, dramas, sports, string quartets, and still lifes? Has Professor Geertz abandoned all of the analytic distinctions that have characterized the success (and the failure) of his civilization? Like Catlin's colorful, concrete metaphors, Geertz's colorless, abstract metaphors subvert both his description and his interpretation. Indeed, they subvert his authority. His message is simply not convincing.

Despite his phenomenological-hermeneutical pretensions, there is in fact in "Deep Play" no understanding of the native from the native's point of view. There is only the constructed understanding of the constructed native's constructed point of view. Geertz offers no specifiable evidence for his attributions of intention, his assertions of subjectivity, his declarations of experience. His constructions of constructions of constructions appear to be little more than projections, or at least blurrings, of his point of view, his subjectivity, with that of the native, or, more accurately, of the constructed native.

Finally, as if to give his, or any anthropologist's, constructions a certain, if you will, substantialized authority, Geertz refers in "Deep Play" to culture "as an ensemble of texts, themselves ensembles, which the anthropologist strains to read over the shoulder of those to whom they properly belong" (452–53).[13] The image is striking: sharing and not sharing a text. It represents a sort of asymmetrical we-relationship with the anthropologist behind and above the native, hidden but at the top of the hierarchy of understanding. It reflects, I believe, the indexical drama of "The Raid" in which the parties to the ethnographic encounter are brought together in the narration as they are separated through style. There is never an I-you relationship, a dialogue, two people next to each other reading the same text and discussing it face-to-face, but only an I-they relationship. And, as we have seen, even the I disappears—replaced by an invisible voice of authority who declares what the you-transformed-to-a-they experience.

13. See my discussion (Crapanzano 1981c) of text and text metaphors. I argue that despite a certain literary critical penchant to view texts abstractly, their rhetorical force rests on the concreteness, the tangible existence, of the text.

In traditional ethnography the ethnographer's encounter with the people he has studied is rarely described. Often, as in the case of Geertz's "Deep Play," hardly a traditional ethnography, even the activity that is described and interpreted—a cockfight, a carnival, a test of prowess, or, for that matter, the weaving of a basket or the preparation of a meal—is not presented in its particularity as a single, and in some ways unique, performance. We are usually given a general picture. Presumably many observations, taken from many vantage points, are conflated into a single, constructed performance, which becomes a sort of ideal, a Platonic performance. Catlin and Goethe describe a single performance, but, despite deictic and other particularizing locutions, they do it in a generalizing way. Geertz, who apparently attended many cockfights, never describes a specific cockfight. He constructs the Balinese cockfight and interprets his construction: "the Balinese cockfight." His conventional tale of entry serves a deictic function not that different from Catlin's assigned place or Goethe's "here's" and "now's." It gives the illusion of specificity when there is no specific temporal or spatial vantage point. It attests to the ethnographer's having been there and gives him whatever authority arises from that presence.

In "Deep Play" the problem of the ethnographer's authoritative constructions is further complicated by the author's phenomenological and hermeneutical pretentions. Neither Catlin nor Goethe make any sustained effort to describe the experience for the participants of the ceremonies they observed. Catlin assumes the perspective of the Mandan only rhetorically. For him, the O-Kee-Pa was a "shocker" ("This part of the ceremony [the torture], as I have just witnessed it, is truly shocking to behold, and will stagger the belief of the world when they read of it" [1857 : 157]); and he struggled unsuccessfully to give it meaning. He could find no familiar story in which to fit it in more than a fragmented way. The Roman carnival became for Goethe an allegory of individual destiny. It was of course not *that* unfamiliar. He was able to organize it along familiar theatrical—*commedia dell'arte*—lines and to synchronize his descriptive rhythm with the carnival's rhythm. We may find Goethe's allegory arch, moribund even, but it is subsuming. For Geertz, the cockfight itself becomes a grand metaphor for Balinese social organization, and, as such, closes in on itself. Despite Geertz's ostensible concern for the understanding of the native's point of view, his essay is less a disquisition on Balinese cockfighting, subjectively or objectively understood, than on interpreting—reading—cultural data. His analysis is exemplary, and this exemplary quality, Geertz's interpretive virtuosity, helps render it ethnographi-

cally convincing. Its ultimate significance is not moral but methodological. Catlin makes a plea for the salvation of the Mandan; Goethe
for the full appreciation of fleeting moments of joy; Geertz for hermeneutics. In all three instances the events described are subverted by
the transcending stories in which they are cast. They are sacrificed to
their rhetorical function in a literary discourse that is far removed
from the indigenous discourse of their occurrence. The sacrifice, the
subversion of the event described, is in the final analysis masked neither by rhetoric, hypotyposis, theatricality, and interpretive virtuosity
nor by their metaphorization—salvation, life, society—but by the authority of the author, who, at least in much ethnography, stands above
and behind those whose experience he purports to describe. All
too often, the ethnographer forgets that the native, like Eduard in
Goethe's *Elective Affinities*, cannot abide someone reading over his
shoulder. If he does not close his book, he will cast his shadow over it.
Of course, the ethnographer will also cast his shadow over it. It is perhaps for this reason, if I may conclude with the conceit of my own tale
of entry into this paper, that Zeus understood when Hermes promised to tell no lies but did not promise to tell the whole truth.

RENATO ROSALDO

From the Door of His Tent:
The Fieldworker
and the Inquisitor

This paper attempts to develop an anatomy of ethnographic rhetoric by exploring modes of authority and representation in two deservedly classic books: E. E. Evans-Pritchard's *The Nuer* and Emmanuel Le Roy Ladurie's *Montaillou*. The former, published in 1940, has long been recognized, along with two other books and various articles on the same people, as an exemplary ethnographic work. The latter, published in 1975 by a noted French social historian, has received wide acclaim for its innovative use of an inquisition register to construct an "ethnographic" analysis of a fourteenth-century French village. Le Roy Ladurie's intervention, among other experimental works of history and anthropology, has been hailed as opening the possibility of a more ethnographic history and a more historical ethnography.[1]

Yet in certain respects Le Roy Ladurie's experiment redeploys an artifact already old-fashioned in its homeland—as so often happens with borrowings both intercultural and interdisciplinary. An anthropological work that aimed at such a total ethnographic analysis as is found in *Montaillou* could be called classic in style, but more outmoded than innovative. From this perspective Le Roy Ladurie's work has a distinctive value. It provides a mirror for critical reflection on modes of authority and descriptive rhetorics in ethnography, particularly in the influential writing of Evans-Pritchard. The latter's work should be understood in this context as a representative example of the discipline's rhetorical conventions. A close reading of these two books, rather than a more superficial review of a wider range of cases,

1. This doubling of history and anthropology has a genealogy that extends back to Herodotus and Thucydides. Evans-Pritchard himself wrote on history and anthropology, and Le Roy Ladurie has taught a course at the Collège de France called Ethnographic History. This reemerging field of inquiry has recently been reviewed in essays by Bernard Cohn (1980, 1981) and Natalie Davis (1981).

enables the development of a general argument that can be appraised by studying extended narrative passages in circumstantial detail. What the argument loses in scope, it gains in intensity.

By looking at *The Nuer* from the distinctive angle of vision offered by *Montaillou*, we discover that the figure of the ethnographic field-worker in troubling ways resembles the fourteenth-century inquisitor who created the document used by Le Roy Ladurie. The historian's work appropriates ways of establishing authority and constructing objective descriptions already developed in the ethnographic literature. Indeed, the historian at times nearly caricatures his ethnographic models. Yet in the manner of an illuminating objectification, precisely this element of exaggeration at once makes strange and reveals an array of discursive practices that in their anthropological homeland have been taken for granted. They have appeared, not peculiar, but normative for writing in the discipline. In making a detour through Le Roy Ladurie's work, I hope to develop a critical perspective on ethnography, both as fieldwork and as descriptive rhetoric.

My reading of Evans-Pritchard's ethnographic writing is guided both by Santayana's dictum that those who forget their past are condemned to repeat it and by the notion that critical reappraisals, the active reappropriation of past works, should play a significant role in shaping future analyses. Such historical critiques, as tales both inspirational and cautionary, can direct future changes in ethnographic discourse.

The Use and Abuse of Ethnographic Authority

Emmanuel Le Roy Ladurie's work borrows ethnography's disciplinary authority to transform fourteenth-century peasants' "direct testimony" (as recorded in the inquisition register of Jacques Fournier) into a documentary account of village life in southern France at the time.[2] The book is divided into two parts, an ecology and an archeology. The former delineates structures that remain unchanged over the long timespan (*longue durée*) and the latter discusses cultural forms (*mentalités*) that often show comparable longevity.

The ecology begins with the physical environment and structures of domination (chapter 1), moves on to the household as the foundation of village life (chapters 2 and 3), and concludes with an extended portrait of transhumant pastoralism (chapters 4, 5, 6, and 7). Le Roy Ladurie opposes village life in households, exemplified by the Clergues,

2. The problem of ethnographic authority has been delineated in a fine essay by James Clifford (1983a).

to shepherd life in the hills, epitomized in the person of Pierre Maury. (The latter, in an anomalous manner discussed below, receives both more extensive and more idealized treatment than the former.) The more loosely organized archeology begins with body language and ends with myth. In between Le Roy Ladurie discusses, often in titillating tones, sex, libido, the life cycle (marriage, childhood, death), time and space, magic, religion, morality, and the other world. Throughout, the narrator punctuates his text with italicized citations, the purportedly free direct speech of the peasants, verbally presented as if one were eavesdropping in the village itself.

Le Roy Ladurie begins by describing his documentary source in these terms:

> Though there are extensive historical studies concerning peasant communities there is very little material available that can be considered the direct testimony of the peasants themselves. It is for this reason that the Inquisition Register of Jacques Fournier, Bishop of Pamiers in Ariège in the Comté de Foix (now southern France) from 1318 to 1325, is of such exceptional interest. (vii)

This beginning makes it clear that the reader will learn, in a remarkably evocative way, about the texture of fourteenth-century peasant life. The rich, vivid descriptions, quite unlike those in other historical works concerned with medieval villagers, do indeed make compelling "ethnographic" reading. The peasants have been textualized in ways that characterize the speakers as articulate and insightful about the conditions of their own existence. Yet the historian's trope of making late medieval peasant voices directly audible to readers in the present arouses more skepticism than appreciation among ethnographers accustomed to pondering difficulties in the translation of cultures.

From the outset the historian's innocent tone gives reason to pause. How can his data ("the direct testimony of the peasants themselves") have remained untainted by the context of domination ("the Inquisition Register")? After all, the inquisitor extracted the testimonies as confessions; he did not overhear them as conversations in everyday life. What could motivate the historian to separate the data from the instrument through which they were collected?

Le Roy Ladurie goes on to buttress the authority of his document through the strategy of novelistic realism carried to extremes.[3] He names names, provides titles, cites specific places, and refers to exact dates. He even goes on to give an impressive sketch of Jacques Four-

3. For a characterization of realism, see Culler 1975: 131–60. For an insightful review of *Montaillou* that, among other things, highlights its conventions of realism, see Clifford 1979.

nier's career, from humble birth through positions as bishop and cardinal to his election in 1334 as Benedict XII, pope at Avignon. Fournier, in Le Roy Ladurie's account, appears ambitious, industrious, and
talented. The reader is supposed to believe that the inquisitor produced a detailed reliable document for the historian's confident, at
times uncritical, use over six centuries later.

Consider, for example, the following passage in which Le Roy
Ladurie portrays Fournier as a tireless inquisitorial seeker of information:

A few details will suggest how our dossier was built up. The inquisition court
at Pamiers worked for 370 days between 1318 and 1325. These 370 days included 578 interrogations. Of these, 418 were examinations of the accused
and 160 examinations of witnesses. In all these hundreds of sessions dealt
with ninety-eight cases. The court set a record for hard work in 1320, with
106 days; it worked ninety-three days in 1321, fifty-five in 1323, forty-three in
1322, forty-two in 1324, and twenty-two in 1325. (xiv)

The imposing numbers, heaped one upon the other in a manner familiar to sports fans, attempt to persuade readers that they constitute
an authoritative exact measure of the inquisition's degree of thorough-
ness. The quantified summary concludes with a year-by-year count of
the inquisition court's working days ordered by rank from the record
high of 106 on down. Le Roy Ladurie's piling up of statistics rhetorically makes it appear that Fournier's investigation was exhaustive and
definitive. The inquisitor, according to the historian, was more an instrument for gathering information than a man bent on making the
guilty confess their heresies.

Le Roy Ladurie ends his introduction, however, by frankly affirming the fundamental inequality of the interchanges between the inquisitor Fournier and his subjects, as follows: "The accused's appearance before the Bishop's tribunal began with an oath sworn on the
Gospels. It continued in the form of an unequal dialogue" (xv). He no
sooner admits to the "unequal dialogue" than he denies it, as if by saying "sorry" he could go on to other things. He simply closes this opening to the interplay of power and knowledge by stressing, more
emphatically than before, the scrupulous will to truth that drove Fournier in his interrogations, as follows:

In all the other cases which provide the material of this book, the Bishop con-
fined himself to tracking down real deviants (often minor from our point of
view). The confessions are rounded out by the accuseds' descriptions of their
own daily lives. They usually corroborated each other, but when they contra-
dicted, Fournier tried to reduce the discrepancies, asking the various pris-
oners for more details. What drove him on was the desire (hateful though it
was in this form) to know the truth. (xv)

The document, taken at face value, purportedly provides reliable depictions of everyday life among fourteenth-century peasants. In this context Le Roy Ladurie uses a half-serious, half-ironic phrase and makes the inquisitor into a fellow scholar by describing him as someone who is as "pedantic as a schoolman" (xv).[4] Deploying a tactic made familiar by Michel Foucault, the narrator invokes the will to truth in order to suppress the document's equally present will to power. His characterization of Fournier's meticulous scholarly close attention to daily life serves the ideological purpose of entitling him to remove the context of interrogation from the "documentary" findings thereby extracted.

Le Roy Ladurie has neatly liberated the document from the historical context that produced it. His introduction thus makes the inquisitor's investigation authoritative and removes the document from the politics of domination. The inquisition register's truth thus becomes more a matter of objective reporting than a series of statements made by certain people (peasant villagers) to a particular person (Fournier) in a specific situation (the inquisition). The historian's document has rhetorically been treated as if it were the creation of a disinterested science. Not unlike his documentary record, the historian himself has achieved the detached observer's innocence. Needless to say, the introduction's central figure, the inquisitor Jacques Fournier, does not again make a significant appearance in the rest of the book.

The Use and Abuse of Descriptive Rhetoric

In the body of his book Le Roy Ladurie cloaks himself with the borrowed authority of ethnographic science. Indeed (as will be seen below) he even follows the ethnographer's tactic of confining to an introduction discussion of the politics of domination that shaped the investigator's knowledge about the people under study. Thus the historian's main text never returns to the opening discussion about how his document was produced. In creating his authority, Le Roy Ladurie covers over the introductory revelation of *Montaillou*'s origins in a document of religious repression. The following, for example, stands as an extreme instance of representing the inquisitorial record as if it were a neutral ethnographic report:

4. Le Roy Ladurie's view of inquisition truth probably emerges from the views of legal historians who see the inquisition as a step forward in the development of rational inquiry. For an incisive critique of the historians' views, see Asad 1983b. My views on this subject, like those of Asad, have been shaped by the work of Michel Foucault (1977, 1978a).

In very rare cases the record does speak of young women who married according to the dictates of their heart. The Register, however, speaks of quite a number of young men who did so. But in the institution of marriage as it then was, the woman was regarded as an object—an object loved or an object beaten, as the case might be. The historian finds himself faced with an area of cultural silence on this subject. (189)

The historian, it seems, has been trapped by the ethnographic myth of his own appropriation. Neither the inquisitor Fournier nor, for that matter, an actual ethnographer could possibly be such an idealized, neutral, omniscient instrument for collecting information. What the inquisition record reveals is that peasant women in Montaillou did not tell their interrogators much about their passions in courtship. Whether the issue was skirted because of the women's reluctance to talk about possibly heretical love magic, out of mutual reticence between women and their male inquisitors, or owing to the historian's imputed "cultural silence," simply cannot be decided on the basis of available evidence. Nonetheless, Le Roy Ladurie simply declares that the things women fail to tell their inquisitor represent areas of cultural silence.

The historian adopts ethnographic authority to enable him to apprehend, in unmediated fashion, late medieval peasant forms of life. His sense of entitlement allows the direct apprehension of historically distant institutions and cultural meanings. Rather than worrying over problems of translation, Le Roy Ladurie deploys the false ethnographic authority of polyphony, his voice and peasant voices equally heard, by citing in italics passages that represent direct quotations transmitted directly from the past (though the peasants—who were, it must be kept in mind, confessing before an inquisition court—usually spoke Occitan, which scribes then translated into Latin, which the historian has translated into modern French). The relationship between the historian and his subjects can only strike the ethnographic reader as peculiarly insensitive to power relations and cultural differences.

Implicit in the *Annales* paradigm is a notion, analogous to the ethnographer's term *social structure*, as will be seen below, that enables the historian to assert that his subjects resemble him because of demonstrable structural continuities that endure over a long timespan (*longue durée*). In the following description of Montaillou, for example, one can see how Le Roy Ladurie evokes in his readers a sense of continuity between the medieval and the modern village on that site:

The village of Montaillou, looking out over the plateau, was built in tiers. . . . In more recent times the village has moved away from the shadow of the chateau and is now situated lower down the slope. In the fourteenth century, as today, the curving village street led down to the parish church, built below the village itself. . . . In the time of Jacques Fournier, as today, Montaillou was too high and too cold for vine-growing. (3–4)

In a passage that thematizes continuity more than change, Le Roy Ladurie spatializes the then and the now. He sees continuity in a curving street and, more peculiarly, in the altitude and the climate. Could the village's elevation and weather have changed much since the early fourteenth century?

Yet this very sense of long-term continuity tempts the historian into committing his discipline's cardinal sin: anachronism. Le Roy Ladurie, for example, finds the following social structural foundation for his analysis:

This basic cell was none other than the peasant family, embodied in the permanence of a house and in the daily life of a group co-resident under the same roof. In local language this entity was called an *ostal*; and in the Latin of the Inquisition files it was called a *hospicium* or, more often, a *domus*. It should be noted that the words, *ostal*, *domus* and *hospicium* all and inextricably mean both family and house. (24)

Doubtless the material substantiality of the house encourages the historian to make it the basic building block of the village. He feels free to collapse the household and the family, as if both were a single entity, simply because native terms refer to both.[5] In a particularly striking instance he even recoils when one of his texts shows, as he puts it, a man "using the term *domus* in a derived and somewhat distorted sense, that of relationships (*parentela*)" (25). How can the modern narrator presume, without providing evidence from fourteenth-century sources, to distinguish correct from distorted usages? In attempting to follow the lead of ethnographic discourse by getting into the natives' heads and allowing them to speak, the historian nonetheless cannot contain a schoolmasterly impulse to correct their speech. He thereby violates the ethnographer's deep sense (consider, for example, Evans-Pritchard's subtle explications of the Nuer word *cieng*) that indigenous usage is always correct in its own setting.

In a similar vein the peasants at times seem peculiarly modern, even urban, particularly in their sexuality (as Natalie Davis [1979] has pointed out). The following passage is representative of the narrator's modernization of medieval homosexual acts: "To save bedding, Master Pons slept with two of his pupils. No one now made any attempt on young Verniolles's virtue. But the harm was done. A latent tendency was awakened, and Arnaud de Verniolles was doomed to become a homosexual" (145). The medieval peasant voices represented in the

5. The problem of conflating household and family has been lucidly discussed in Yanagisako 1979.

italicized texts speak not of homosexual character, however, but of
acts regarded as "sinning." Thus when Arnaud de Verniolles tells the
inquisitor about his former practices he describes telling one of his
partners "in perfectly good faith, that the sin of sodomy and those of
fornication and deliberate masturbation were, in point of gravity, just
the same" (146). The narrator nonetheless has seized upon one act
taken from a bundle of sins—sodomy, fornication, and deliberate
masturbation—and conflated it with modern psychoanalytic notions
of latent tendencies and psychosexual character formation. This is
precisely the point at which ethnographic discourse, in contrast with
the historian's, invokes difference, as it describes (culturally constructed) sexuality and personal identity.

The historian further reinforces his sense, based on the continuity of the long timespan, that he and his subjects inhabit similar psychological worlds by invoking the tacit notion that Montaillou is an ancestral national community. Apparently, by virtue of their nationality,
French readers culturally share enough with fourteenth-century peasants to grasp directly what they mean by what they say. Consider, for
example, the following passages spread over but five pages of text:

We have no statistics on the subject, but it may be that the people of Montaillou wept slightly more easily than we do, both in happiness and in
sorrow. (139)

The joys of revenge were accompanied by the lifting of both arms up to
heaven, a gesture of thanksgiving with different connotations from those it
has today. (139)

The Montaillou documents show in passing that certain gestures of politeness
still used today are very ancient and to a certain extent of peasant origin.
People like the inhabitants of Montaillou used to raise their hoods and stand
up, even more automatically than people do today. (140)

In order to mock some apocalyptic prophecy heard on the bridge at Tarascon,
Arnaud de Savignan, a stonemason and bold thinker, gave a flick of the wrist
such as we still make today. (144)

Le Roy Ladurie's readers are thus encouraged to know the peasants of
Montaillou with the privileged intimacy by which they know their own
ancestors. In this context, by virtue of putatively shared blood and
cultural inheritance, national ancestry symbolically neutralizes the
distance separating "us" from "them."

The symbol of national ancestry, however, implies difference as
well as sameness. In the text, descendents reckon the national ancestral community as a double reference point. It stands along a continuous straight line of sameness and a progressive upwardly sloping
curve of difference. The straight line entitles readers, as members of
the same larger community, to know the peasants directly. The curved

line enables readers, as people who have developed further along the same trajectory, to know better than the peasants.

In a similar vein, the historian dwells more on what the villagers of Montaillou lack (usually relative to lowland villages or centers of feudal hierarchy) than on what they possess. This peculiar descriptive rhetoric, depicting through empty negatives rather than positive features, appears frequently in ethnographic discourse, as will be seen in the work of Evans-Pritchard. The following passages indicate how Le Roy Ladurie characterizes his subjects, not by defining their form of life, but by highlighting absences, the technology and forms of social stratification they have failed to develop:

Despite the presence of the shoemaker, Montaillou was underdeveloped as far as the crafts were concerned, compared with the lowland villages. (6)

It should be remembered that there was no absolute distinction between artisan and peasant or artisan and ordinary citizen, or even between artisan and noble. In this part of the world, everybody worked with his hands, and often very skilfully too. (6)

It would be wrong to try to explain this comparative absence of class struggle by weakness pure and simple on the part of the nobility. (18)

In these circumstances, history was absent or almost absent from Montaillou culture. (281)

The relative absences of technology and differentiated social forms make these worlds and the people who inhabit them appear less developed, less fully formed, less well defined than their lowland neighbors, not to mention modern Frenchmen.

When Le Roy Ladurie deftly characterizes the complex double-dealing and shifting alliances that enliven local politics in Montaillou under the inquisition, it appears that the absence of social distinctions leaves only the vendetta as a means of settling differences. The historian's constructed world resembles a miniature village opera with all its absurdities. It breaks down in parts, and it invokes individuality more than patterns and laws. In this context the descriptions of medieval peasant character appear consistent with the accounts of technology, class, politics, and history in the village. With a strong disposition to believe that human nature, including its capacities for good and evil and degrees of impulsiveness and maturity, shows little variation through history and across cultures, the ethnographer cannot help but be skeptical when Le Roy Ladurie asserts that the peasants (not unlike the nobility in Huizinga's waning Middle Ages) were more violent and impulsive than modern Frenchmen.

The historian's claim that the peasants took savage delight in what he calls the "joys of revenge" seems simply unconvincing. In attempting to marshal evidence supporting his generalization about peasant

character, the narrator cites verbatim the testimony of Guillaume
Maurs as he confesses to the inquisitor about how he told a woman
that the priest Pierre Clergue had been arrested for heresy (139). The
woman, according to Maurs's testimony, heard his story and "lifted up
her hands to heaven, saying 'Deo gratias'" (139–40). Much earlier in
his book, however, the narrator provided the context for understanding why Guillaume Maurs and his friends could so exuberantly celebrate the priest's arrest. Guillaume Maurs, his father, and his brother
were arrested in 1308, owing to the priest's denunciations; later Maurs's
mother's tongue was cut out, because the priest urged his brother the
bayle (bailiff) to do so (50). Even this fragment, from a longer story of
the grievances he suffered, suffices to indicate that good reasons,
rather than impulsive "joys of revenge," might have led Guillaume
Maurs to act as he did.

Le Roy Ladurie, however, constructs another, more Utopian
domain beyond the confines of sordid, deceitful village life under the
inquisition (described in a manner that evokes French resistance, collaboration, and double-dealing under the Vichy regime). Though in
general he undermines typifications, for this purpose the historian
creates a social type: Pierre Maury the freedom-loving independent
shepherd. The shepherd figure grows so elevated, particularly in contrast to the peasants, that the narrator confidently asserts that, "For
Pierre Maury, poverty was not only a frequent fact and a cheerfully
accepted companion, but also an ideal and a system of values" (120).

Le Roy Ladurie so identifies with his pastoral figure that he does
not hesitate to exaggerate his own notion of the long timespan by
placing shepherd lifeways on a continuum that derives from the Neolithic, finds its fundamental forms long before the medieval period,
and in its household organization reaches into the nineteenth century,
as in the following:

Though there is no need to talk of modernity (we must not forget that this
pastoral world derived from the early Neolithic age, and its basic principles
were laid down well before the fourteenth century). . . . (124)

So far we have been dealing with long-term tendencies, transhistorical trends,
during which, from the fourteenth to the nineteenth century, the *cabane*
[shepherd's hut] remained unmoved, a living institution. (110)

In so vividly evoking shepherd lifeways, the historian follows the practices of ethnographic discourse by verbally endowing his subjects with
a pristine, relatively unchanging form of life.

The characterization of proud, freedom-loving shepherds, as opposed to rapacious, oppressed peasants, appears in the following
passages:

The shepherd from Ariège or Cerdagne in the fourteenth century was as free as the mountain air he breathed, at least as far as feudalism was concerned. (114)

Here we are chiefly concerned with the itinerant shepherds who moved about the country. They formed a rural nomad semi-proletariat, without hearth or home but with their own traditions, their own pride and their own special conceptions of mountain liberty and fate. (69)

As far as one could be in the fourteenth century, Pierre Maury was a democrat through and through. . . . This egalitarian ideal is a hundred miles away from the rapacity of people like Pierre Clergue or Arnaud Sicre, men who wanted to promote or to recover their *domus* at any price. Pierre Maury laughed at such greed: he had no house, he lived anywhere, detached from the goods of this world. . . . We can guess one of the reasons for the shepherds' attitude to poverty, acquired through experience and accepted quite simply. This reason lay in the fact that they were nomads. . . . Basically the shepherds carried their fortunes on their own backs. (121)

The shepherds' democratic, freedom-loving character thus derives from, as it is determined by, their nomadic mode of subsistence. The historian in this manner endows his subjects with a character to be revered. The shepherds reside within a purely masculine pastoral world, where they are proud, free, unencumbered by worldly goods, and without attachments to women or households. Though linked to the market as a "rural nomad semi-proletariat," these men purportedly move at liberty beyond the reach of feudal oppression. The historian encapsulates his utopian vision by saying, without qualification: "Pierre Maury was a happy shepherd" (135).

Le Roy Ladurie so idealizes his portrait of the poor but "happy shepherd" that an explanation seems in order. Yet I shall defer explanation because comparison with the work of Evans-Pritchard can best clarify this and other issues that have surfaced in the historian's text. The comparison moves in both directions by showing how the inquisitorial record can become ethnographic, and the reverse. The defamiliarization involved in making evident the discomforting resemblances between Evans-Pritchard and the inquisitor has the critical purpose of questioning norms that often guide the construction of authoritative descriptions in ethnography.

Ethnographic Authority Reviewed

Evans-Pritchard's book *The Nuer* roughly falls into two parts, the first dealing with ecology and the second with social structure. The discussion of ecology begins with a vivid, detailed description of

cattle and their relations to the human population that adjusts to
bovine lifeways in its transhumant pastoral economy. The next chapter, a study in human geography, analyzes the habitat and its seasonal
variations. A third transitional chapter depicts notions of time and
space as the interplay of ecology and socially organized activities. The
last three chapters in the book consider in turn the political, the lineage, and the age-set systems. Throughout the latter discussion the
dominant image of social structure is that of segmentary opposition
where two groups can be opposed in certain contexts and stand
united at a higher level in their opposition to yet other groups. This
notion of structural relativity guides a subtle discussion of Nuer political order. Through this lucid, yet supple, analysis the reader gains a
vivid sense of Nuer lifeways.

Both *The Nuer* and *Montaillou* begin with introductions that reveal
their investigators' close links to contexts of domination, and simultaneously attempt to deny the connections between power and knowledge. Their ultimately unconvincing opening project is to bracket the
purity of their data ("My study of the Nuer" and "the direct testimony
of the peasants themselves") from the contaminating contexts through
which they were extracted.

In exploring the power/knowledge interplay it is useful to distinguish tripartite author functions separating (a) the individual who
wrote the work, (b) the textualized persona of the narrator, and (c) the
textualized persona of the field investigator. In *The Nuer* the "narrator" portrayed doing the analysis is distinct from the "fieldworker"
depicted doing participant-observation. In *Montaillou* the "historian"
Le Roy Ladurie is more literally distinct from the "inquisitor" Jacques
Fournier, just visible doing his investigation. In what follows I compare Evans-Pritchard, in his two textualized personae, at times with
Le Roy Ladurie (the narrator) and at times with Fournier (the investigator) with a view to anatomizing aspects of discourse in the classic
Nuer ethnography.

In *The Nuer* the narrator immediately announces the connection
between the fieldworker's research and the colonial regime by saying,
in the book's initial sentence: "My study of the Nuer was undertaken
at the request of, and was mainly financed by, the Government of the
Anglo-Egyptian Sudan, which also contributed generously toward the
publication of its results" (vii). Evans-Pritchard disarms his readers
with his studied casualness. Why did the government of the Anglo-
Egyptian Sudan request his report? How much did it pay for the research and the publication of its results? These questions are offset by
the confidence the narrator's calm lucidity inspires in his reader.

Evans-Pritchard's authority initially is constructed in his fieldwork

narrative, a story of how the fieldworker suffered as he crossed cultural boundaries. In contrast with the historian's portrait of Fournier,
Evans-Pritchard comments on his memorable introductory fieldwork
account by making the following modest claim for his knowledge of
the Nuer: "My total residence among the Nuer was thus about a year.
I do not consider a year adequate time in which to make a sociological
study of a people, especially of a difficult people in adverse circumstances, but serious sickness on both the 1935 and 1936 expeditions
closed investigations prematurely" (14). Rather than parade his suc-
cesses, Evans-Pritchard punctuates his fieldwork narrative by flatly
describing repeatedly ruined bucolic interludes. Studied modesty,
executed with tongue-in-cheek understatement, thus sets the tone of
the narrator's tale. His posture resembles what Paul Fussell, in *The
Great War and Modern Memory*, has called British phlegm: "The trick
here is to affect to be entirely unflappable; one speaks as if the war
were entirely normal and matter-of-fact" (1975:181).

The fieldworker initially reaches Nuerland in 1930 and on arrival
loses first his luggage, then his servants. In time he reaches Muot dit,
where he finds himself happily making friends and regaining his confidence. He describes this interlude's interruption in these terms:

A government force surrounded our camp one morning at sunrise, searched
for two prophets who had been leaders in a recent revolt, took hostages, and
threatened to take many more if the prophets were not handed over. I felt
that I was in an equivocal position, since such incidents might recur, and
shortly afterwards returned to my home in Zandeland, having accomplished
only three and a half months' work among the Nuer. (11)

In 1931 Evans-Pritchard tries again and finds people even more hostile than before. He nonetheless again enjoys a period of acceptance:
"I at last began to feel myself a member of the community and to be
accepted as such" (13). Once again his pastoral interlude ends abruptly
when he falls to an attack of malaria. His 1935 and 1936 expeditions
each last about seven weeks, and both draw to a halt because of serious
illness.

Evans-Pritchard the narrator depicts himself the fieldworker as a
man endowed with calm presence of mind under the most arduous
conditions. He speaks without presumption and pokes fun at the
fieldworker. The reader trusts him as a man who never says more
(and usually says less) than he knows: one who delivers more than he
promises. Moreover, the reader tends to accept Evans-Pritchard's
story of adversities more endured than overcome, a version of the heroic cast in a low mimetic mode rather than in the grander epic mode
of great deeds. The narrator suggests to his reader that he, the field-

worker, lived through physical and psychological conditions most people could not have survived. Evans-Pritchard pointedly begins his fieldwork narrative in this manner:

I, unlike most readers, know the Nuer, and must judge my work more severely than they, and I can say that if this book reveals many insufficiencies I am amazed that it has ever appeared at all. A man must judge his labours by the obstacles he has overcome and the hardships he has endured, and by these standards I am not ashamed of the results. (9)

Evans-Pritchard's mode verges on the comic, for the reader knows that, despite all his trials and tribulations, the fieldworker lived to tell, and even write up, the tale. Put bluntly, Evans-Pritchard was there and his reader was not; he alone can describe Nuer lifeways. Ironic and understated, Evans-Pritchard has presented his fieldworker's credentials in a manner as authoritative as Le Roy Ladurie's was for Fournier.

The narrator further buttresses his authority by claiming that the fieldworker and his human subjects enjoyed a certain intimacy, perhaps comparable to the historian's sense of entitlement gained through the symbol of national ancestry. Evans-Pritchard bases his claim of intimacy on the way the Nuer forced an egalitarian relationship on him (especially as contrasted with his earlier field experience among the Azande), described as follows:

Because I had to live in such close contact with the Nuer I knew them more intimately than the Azande, about whom I am able to write a much more detailed account. Azande would not allow me to live as one of themselves; Nuer would not allow me to live otherwise. Among Azande I was compelled to live outside the community; among Nuer I was compelled to be a member of it. Azande treated me as a superior; Nuer as an equal. (15)

Once again, the reader can justifiably maintain a certain skepticism, rather than taking Evans-Pritchard's modesty as the plain literal truth.[6] Although the narrator may genuinely have felt he could write a more detailed account about the Azande than the Nuer, he did, in the end, write not only *The Nuer* but also *Nuer Kinship and Marriage* and *Nuer Religion*.

The narrator's assertions about the fieldworker's relations of intimacy and equality stand in uneasy tension with the ways in which the Nuer often treated him as a stranger and an enemy. In the text the Nuer appear characterized, variously, as unusually hostile, refusing to

---

6. In the appendix to an abridged edition of *Witchcraft, Oracles, and Magic among the Azande*, Evans-Pritchard (1976:240–54) characterizes his Zande fieldwork much more in terms of participant-observation. Probably he overstated the case to highlight the contrast with his Nuer research.

answer greetings and even turning away when addressed, expert at sabotaging an inquiry, stultifying all efforts to elicit the simplest facts, blocking questions about their customs, and unwilling to discuss serious matters or even to receive the fieldworker in their windscreens (11–12). That the fieldworker should have been treated with suspicious reserve hardly seems perplexing to a present-day reader. After all the Nuer, in good measure correctly, identified him with the colonial regime, which at the time was conducting a campaign of military repression against them.

Evans-Pritchard's simultaneous account of, and lack of accountability to, the political context of his fieldwork appears particularly disconcerting in the one instance where he and a Nuer man named Cuol enter a textualized dialogue. The fieldworker attempts a British introduction by asking Cuol his name and the name of his lineage. Cuol in response uses a series of maneuvers to resist giving both names and in the process asks: "Why do you want to know the name of my lineage?" and "What will you do with it if I tell you? Will you take it to your country?" The narrator interprets the conversation in the following terms: "I defy the most patient ethnologist to make headway against this kind of opposition. One is just driven crazy by it. Indeed, after a few weeks of associating solely with Nuer one displays, if the pun be allowed, the most evident symptoms of 'Nuerosis'" (13). The narrator depicts Cuol's "opposition" complexly. It is at once bullheaded, admirable, and perverse. His opposition is enjoyed as an assertion of Nuer values of freedom and autonomy, and it appears perverse because it subverts "innocent" ethnographic inquiry. Furthermore, it is measured against a norm (which probably is alien to the Nuer) of courteous conduct that requires strangers, on first meeting, to introduce themselves by giving their names. The narrator finds that the fault in this unhappy encounter lies with Nuer character, rather than with historically specific circumstances.[7] Yet the reader should consider that, just two pages before, Evans-Pritchard has described how a government force raided a Nuer camp, "took hostages, and threatened to take many more" (11). Cuol had, not a character disorder, but good reasons for resisting inquiry and asking who wanted to know his name and the name of his lineage.

The narrator's complaints about how the fieldworker was treated have to do with fundamental difficulties the Nuer form of life posed for anyone bent on gathering ethnographic information, as described in the following:

7. This discursive tactic of eternalizing and universalizing (as "timeless" and "homogeneous" Nuer culture) much more specifically motivated human conduct has, of course, been studied in its political context by Edward Said (1978).

As soon as I began to discuss a custom with one man another would interrupt the conversation in pursuance of some affair of his own or by an exchange of pleasantries and jokes. The men came at milking-time and some of them remained till mid-day. Then the girls, who had just finished dairy-work, arrived and insisted on attention. . . . These endless visits entailed constant badinage and interruption and, although they offered opportunity for improving my knowledge of the Nuer language, imposed a severe strain. (14)

In depicting the play of power relations between investigator and informants, the fieldworker combines a perception that the Nuer subverted his efforts to interview them with a strangely ethnocentric yearning to have had private conversations with them. Although the fieldworker's hardships appear convincing, his complaints (which in retrospect seem a euphemistic foreshadowing of Malinowski's already written, but not yet published, diary) also serve to lend his account an air of forthright realism. The narrator has assumed the persona of an honest man.

In the end, far from undermining his account, the narrator's often contradictory confessions enhance his credibility by creating a sense of his reliability as a fieldworker. Consider, for example, the following passage: "As I could not use the easier and shorter method of working though regular informants I had to fall back on direct observation of, and participation in, the everyday life of the people. From the door of my tent I could see what was happening in camp or village and every moment was spent in Nuer company" (15). The Nuer, in other words, forced him to become a participant-observer. The fieldworker, turning adversity to his advantage, could always, by looking from the door of his tent, survey the Nuer as they went about their daily lives.[8]

In retrospect, the fieldworker's mode of surveillance uncomfortably resembles Michel Foucault's Panopticon, the site from which the (disciplining) disciplines enjoy gazing upon (and subjecting) their subjects. Yet Evans-Pritchard, as suited his historical circumstances, separated power and surveillance from the gathering of ethnographic information. The greatest imperial advantage granted the fieldworker, of course, was a certain guarantee of his physical safety as he went about the business of collecting data. His "information" was gathered, as he put it, in "particles" from "each Nuer I met being used as a

8. Stocking (1983) has discussed the tent as a topos of anthropology. For Malinowski, however, the tent was an ambivalent site from which the ethnographer looked in two directions: outward, gazing on the village, and inward, escaping to read novels and simply to be alone. Stocking characterizes Malinowski's turning inward in these terms: "Pulling its flaps behind him, he could to some extent shut out the native world and retire to his novels when the strain of the very intensive study of a very limited area became too great" (1983 : 97).

source of knowledge," rather than having been collected (as it was among the Azande) "in chunks supplied by selected and trained informants" (15). Beneath the self-irony, Evans-Pritchard boldly asserts that his methodology is more powerful than working with paid informants.

By this point, as the introduction draws to a close, the narrator Evans-Pritchard says the following:

I do not make far-reaching claims. I believe that I have understood the chief values of the Nuer and am able to present a true outline of their social structure, but I regard, and have designed, this volume as a contribution to the ethnology of a particular area rather than as a detailed sociological study, and I shall be content if it is accepted as such. (15)

In his introductory persona the narrator asks his readers to set aside the context of colonial domination and view his study as a "true outline," an incomplete, yet objective, scientific account.

The introductory section of *The Nuer* parallels that of *Montaillou* in doing the rhetorical work of separating the context of colonial domination from the production of ethnographic knowledge. Indeed, just as Fournier disappears from the text after the introduction, the fieldworker who engages his informants in dialogue plays no role in the analysis of Nuer modes of livelihood and political institutions. If Le Roy Ladurie converts interrogation into overhearing and cataloguing, Evans-Pritchard transforms lively dialogue into listening and envisioning. The tale of the fieldworker as lone heroic victim establishes his innocence from colonial domination and validates his credentials as a disinterested scientist. Other than his interest in discovering the truth, Evans-Pritchard appears in the persona of a man without an axe to grind: the detached ironic observer.

The Rhetoric of Objectivity Reviewed

Evans-Pritchard's object of scientific knowledge is social structure rather than historical contingencies and political action. His lucid modes of discourse (which Clifford Geertz [1983a] has called African transparencies) render the social order singularly visible. This expository elegance derives from the well-defined project of developing a "body of scientific theory" about "primitive peoples" (261). Evans-Pritchard defines this project's master concept, social structure, as follows:

By social structure we mean relations between groups which have a high degree of consistency and constancy. The groups remain the same irrespective

of their specific content of individuals at any particular moment, so that generation after generation of people pass through them. Men are born into
them, or enter them later in life and move out of them at death; the structure
endures. (262)

By this definition, social structure resembles a house with many rooms
that people pass through over the course of their lifetimes: the people
come and go, but the house remains the same. Both Evans-Pritchard
and Le Roy Ladurie equate the structures that last the longest with
those that matter the most. Yet the long timespan directly links the historian and his subjects, whereas social structure creates differences
that separate the ethnographer from the Nuer.

Notions of Nuer character often emerge through the analysis of
social structure. Thus the people appear portrayed as "primitive" in
their social conformity and their lack of individuality. The narrator,
following a disciplinary norm, verbally represents the people with the
group noun (the Nuer) or the masculine pronoun (he) rather than
with more individuating personal names. One frequently, for example, encounters statements in the distanced normalizing mode of
discourse, such as the following: "When a man feels that he has suffered an injury there is no authority to whom he can make a com-
plaint and from whom he can obtain redress, so he at once challenges
the man who has wronged him to a duel and the challenge must be
accepted" (151). Evans-Pritchard fails to discuss, for example, what
happens when, or how it happens that, a man does not take up the
challenge. Surely a Nuer man has a certain leeway in deciding whether
or not he has been wronged. Only someone pathologically oversocialized could follow such programmed normative commands without
exception or contextual qualification.

When Evans-Pritchard characterizes Nuer society, he often resembles Le Roy Ladurie in speaking of absences rather than pres-
ences. Consider, for example, the following passages:

The Nuer cannot be said to be stratified into classes. (7)

Indeed, the Nuer have no government, and their state might be described as
an ordered anarchy. Likewise they lack law, if we understand by the term
judgments delivered by an independent and impartial authority which has,
also, power to enforce its decisions. (6)

The lack of governmental organs among the Nuer, the absence of legal institutions, of developed leadership, and, generally, of organized political life is
remarkable. (181)

The Nuer, in other words, lack the obvious (to a Western eye) institutions of political order. They have no social classes, no state, no law, no
leadership.

Evans-Pritchard goes on to describe the Nuer as close to nature because of their simple material culture, as seen in the following:

It will be seen that the Nuer political system is consistent with their oecology. (4)

A people whose material culture is as simple as that of the Nuer are highly dependent on their environment. (16)

Evans-Pritchard overextends his assertions and verbally locates the Nuer in a mythic (past?) age of implements made neither of iron nor of stone, but of flora and fauna: "Taken with the earlier list of uses of cattle we can say that the Nuer do not live in an iron age or even a stone age, but in an age, whatever it may be called, in which plants and beasts furnish technological necessities" (87). The Nuer remain putatively more enmeshed in their primitive pre–Stone Age niche than we in ours. Despite the formal elegance of their social structure, they also appear closer to nature than we are.

In a manner comparable to Le Roy Ladurie's assertions about the shepherd Pierre Maury, the narrator claims that Nuer character is consistent with their environment, their mode of subsistence, and their political system, as in the following passages:

Such a life nurtures the qualities of the shepherd—courage, love of fighting, and contempt of hunger and hardship—rather than shapes the industrious character of the peasant. (26)

Some outstanding traits in Nuer character may be said to be consistent with their low technology and scanty food-supply. . . . The qualities which have been mentioned, courage, generosity, patience, pride, loyalty, stubborness, and independence, are the virtues the Nuer themselves extol, and these values can be shown to be very appropriate to their simple mode of life and to the simple set of social relations it engenders. (90)

The ordered anarchy in which they live accords well with their character, for it is impossible to live among Nuer and conceive of rulers ruling over them. The Nuer is a product of hard and egalitarian upbringing, is deeply democratic, and is easily roused to violence. His turbulent spirit finds any restraint irksome and no man recognizes a superior. (181)

Nuer character corresponds all too elegantly with their pastoral way of life.[9] Their pastoral character is also defined by contrast with their putative opposites: sedentary peasants. Peasants, it should be noted, do not otherwise appear in Evans-Pritchard's text. Yet their presence in this context, as foils for characterizing "the qualities of the shepherd," curiously echoes one of their rhetorical uses in *Montaillou*.

9. Elsewhere I have called generalizing through series of such questionable correspondences the rhetoric of control (Rosaldo 1978). It surprised me to find the device, common among colonial officials, used by Evans-Pritchard.

Pastoral Modes of Domination

Curiously enough, the ethnographer and the historian come together in asserting that transhumant pastoralism engenders democratic values, rugged individualism, fierce pride, and a warrior spirit. Not unlike cowboys and other self-sufficient male heroes, the Nuer appear to embody idealized characteristics of a certain masculine imagination. Although militarily "pacified" by colonial troops, the Nuer remain, as initially suggested by their resistance to ethnographic inquiry, indomitable in character. Symbolically, they represent an ideal of human liberty, even in the midst of colonial domination.

The distinctive subjectivity attributed to pastoralists perhaps resembles that of fieldworkers who travel, yet stay in one place. Speaking from a position of culturally rooted mobility, ethnographers often invoke "my people" or "my village," meaning, of course, the people among whom, or the place where, they did their field research. In asserting their authority to represent the lives of their subjects, ethnographers take great pains to distinguish themselves, on the one hand, from tourists and, on the other, from stationary missionaries and colonial officials. Ethnographers' career itineraries can halfseriously, half-playfully be likened to the patterned movements of transhumant pastoralists, rather than of nomads (tourists) or peasants (missionaries and colonial officials). It seems fitting that a discourse that denies the domination that makes its knowledge possible idealizes, as alter egos, shepherds rather than peasants. Pastoralists, like individual tourists (not to be confused with the tourist industry), exercise domination less readily than peasants, missionaries, or colonial officials.

Yet a question remains. Why use the literary pastoral to represent, presumably in a documentary rather than fictional mode, the lives of actual shepherds? The pastoral mode, after all, derives from the court, and its shepherds usually turn out to have been royalty dressed in rustic garb. As a literary mode, it stands far removed from either late medieval French shepherds or contemporary Nilotic cattle herders. Instead it embodies a distinctive sense of courtesy that Kenneth Burke has aptly characterized as "the rhetoric of courtship between contrasted social classes" (1969:123). In earlier literary epochs this courtship occurred between nobles and commoners, lords and vassals, and masters and servants. The displaced modern pastoral analogously emerges in interactions between town and country, middle class and working class, and colonizer and colonized.[10]

10. Northorp Frye has asserted that the displaced modern pastoral "preserves the theme of escape from society to the extent of idealizing a simplified life in the country

The pastoral makes possible a peculiar civility in relationships that cross social boundaries. It permits a polite tenderness that more direct ways of acknowledging inequality could inhibit. Its courtesy becomes respect, even admiration. Evans-Pritchard and Le Roy Ladurie clearly esteemed "their shepherds." Yet the pastoral also licences patronizing attitudes of condescension, such as reverence for a simplicity "we" have lost (compare Clifford's paper in this volume). For Evans-Pritchard and Le Roy Ladurie the pastoral mode becomes self-serving because the shepherd symbolizes that point beyond domination where neutral ethnographic truth can collect itself.

The use of the pastoral at once justifies and betrays the introductory efforts to suppress the interplay of power and knowledge. Thus the narrators can enjoy relations suffused with a tender courtesy that appears to transcend inequality and domination. Yet the pastoral mode obliquely reveals inequalities in the relations that produced ethnographic knowledge. Repressed in introductory narratives, contexts of domination return in courtly disguise. The quality of human relations embodied in the figures of the inquisitor and the fieldworker still haunt the authors. Through a literary metamorphosis, the figures of domination reappear, neither as inquisitor nor as fieldworker, but now as "natives" in shepherds' clothing.

---

or on the frontier" (1971:43). This version of the pastoral often informs ethnographic writing. In reading *The Nuer* and *Montaillou* I have been concerned with the content of idealization, and its purposes.

This paper has benefited from comments by Talal Asad, Amy Burce, James Clifford, Vincent Crapanzano, Michael Fischer, George Marcus, Kirin Narayan, Mary Pratt, Paul Rabinow, Robert Thornton, Stephen Tyler, and Sylvia Yanagisako.

JAMES CLIFFORD

On Ethnographic Allegory

1. a story in which people, things and happenings have another meaning, as in a fable or parable: allegories are used for teaching or explaining.

2. the presentation of ideas by means of such stories. . . .[1]

In a recent essay on narrative Victor Turner argues that social performances enact powerful stories—mythic and commonsensical—that provide the social process "with a rhetoric, a mode of emplotment, and a meaning" (1980:153). In what follows I treat ethnography itself as a performance emplotted by powerful stories. Embodied in written reports, these stories simultaneously describe real cultural events and make additional, moral, ideological, and even cosmological statements. Ethnographic writing is allegorical at the level both of its content (what it says about cultures and their histories) and of its form (what is implied by its mode of textualization).

An apparently simple example will introduce my approach. Marjorie Shostak begins her book *Nisa: The Life and Words of a !Kung Woman* with a story of childbirth the !Kung way—outside the village, alone. Here are some excerpts:

I lay there and felt the pains as they came, over and over again. Then I felt something wet, the beginning of the childbirth. I thought, "Eh hey, maybe it is

1. *Webster's New Twentieth Century Dictionary*, 2nd ed. In literary studies definitions of allegory have ranged from Angus Fletcher's (1964:2) loose characterization ("In the simplest terms, allegory says one thing and means another") to Todorov's reassertion (1973:63) of a stricter sense: "First of all, allegory implies the existence of at least two meanings for the same words; according to some critics, the first meaning must disappear, while others require that the two be present together. Secondly, this double meaning is indicated in the work in an *explicit* fashion: it does not proceed from the reader's interpretation (whether arbitrary or not)." According to Quintilian, any continuous or extended metaphor develops into allegory; and as Northrop Frye (1971:91) observes, "Within the boundaries of literature we find a kind of sliding scale, ranging from the most explicitly allegorical, consistent with being literature at all, at one extreme, to the most elusive, anti-explicit and anti-allegorical at the other." The various "second meanings" of ethnographic allegory I shall be tracing here are all textually explicit. But ethnographies slide along Frye's scale, exhibiting strong allegorical features, usually without marking themselves *as* allegories.

the child." I got up, took a blanket and covered Tashay with it; he was still sleeping. Then I took another blanket and my smaller duiker skin covering and I left. Was I not the only one? The only other woman was Tashay's grand-mother, and she was asleep in her hut. So, just as I was, I left. I walked a short distance from the village and sat down beside a tree. . . . After she was born, I sat there; I didn't know what to do. I had no sense. She lay there, moving her arms about, trying to suck her fingers. She started to cry. I just sat there, look-ing at her. I thought, "Is this my child? Who gave birth to this child?" Then I thought, "A big thing like that? How could it possibly have come out from my genitals?" I sat there and looked at her, looked and looked and looked. (1981 : 1–3)

The story has great immediacy. Nisa's voice is unmistakable, the experience sharply evoked: "She lay there, moving her arms about, trying to suck her fingers." But as readers we do more than register a unique event. The story's unfolding requires us, first, to imagine a dif-ferent *cultural* norm (!Kung birth, alone in the bush) and then to rec-ognize a common *human* experience (the quiet heroism of childbirth, feelings of postpartum wonder and doubt). The story of an occur-rence somewhere in the Kalahari Desert cannot remain just that. It implies both local cultural meanings and a general story of birth. A difference is posited and transcended. Moreover, Nisa's story tells us (how could it not?) something basic about woman's experience. Shostak's life of a !Kung individual inevitably becomes an allegory of (female) humanity.

I argue below that these kinds of transcendent meanings are not abstractions or interpretations "added" to the original "simple" ac-count. Rather, they are the conditions of its meaningfulness. Ethno-graphic texts are inescapably allegorical, and a serious acceptance of this fact changes the ways they can be written and read. Using Shostak's experiment as a case study I examine a recent tendency to distinguish allegorical levels as specific "voices" within the text. I argue, finally, that the very activity of ethnographic *writing*—seen as inscription or textualization—enacts a redemptive Western allegory. This pervasive structure needs to be perceived and weighed against other possible emplotments for the performance of ethnography.

∿∿

Literary description always opens onto another scene set, so to speak, "behind" the this-worldly things it purports to depict.
MICHEL BEAUJOUR, "Some Paradoxes of Description"

Allegory (Gr. *allos*, "other," and *agoreuein*, "to speak") usually denotes a practice in which a narrative fiction continuously refers to another pattern of ideas or events. It is a representation that "inter-prets" itself. I am using the term allegory in the expanded sense re-

claimed for it by recent critical discussions, notably those of Angus
Fletcher (1964) and Paul De Man (1979). Any story has a propensity
to generate another story in the mind of its reader (or hearer), to repeat and displace some prior story. To focus on ethnographic allegory
in preference, say, to ethnographic "ideology"—although the political
dimensions are always present (Jameson 1981)—draws attention to
aspects of cultural description that have until recently been mini-
mized. A recognition of allegory emphasizes the fact that realistic portraits, to the extent that they are "convincing" or "rich," are extended
metaphors, patterns of associations that point to coherent (theoretical, esthetic, moral) additional meanings. Allegory (more strongly
than "interpretation") calls to mind the poetic, traditional, cosmological nature of such writing processes.

Allegory draws special attention to the *narrative* character of cultural representations, to the stories built into the representational
process itself. It also breaks down the seamless quality of cultural description by adding a temporal aspect to the process of reading. One
level of meaning in a text will always generate other levels. Thus the
rhetoric of presence that has prevailed in much post-romantic literature (and in much "symbolic anthropology") is interrupted. De Man's
critique of the valorization of symbols over allegory in romantic esthetics also questions the project of realism (De Man 1969). The claim
that nonallegorical description was possible—a position underlying
both positivist literalism and realist synecdoche (the organic, functional, or "typical" relationship of parts to wholes)—was closely allied
to the romantic search for unmediated meaning in the event. Positivism, realism, and romanticism—nineteenth-century ingredients of
twentieth-century anthropology—all rejected the "false" artifice of
rhetoric along with allegory's supposed abstractness. Allegory violated
the canons both of empirical science and of artistic spontaneity (Ong
1971:6–9). It was too deductive, too much an open imposition of
meaning on sensible evidence. The recent "revival" of rhetoric by
a diverse group of literary and cultural theorists (Roland Barthes,
Kenneth Burke, Gerard Genette, Michel de Certeau, Hayden White,
Paul De Man, and Michel Beaujour among others) has thrown serious
doubt on the positivist-romantic-realist consensus. In ethnography
the current turn to rhetoric coincides with a period of political and
epistemological reevaluation in which the constructed, imposed nature of representational authority has become unusually visible and
contested. Allegory prompts us to say of any cultural description not
"this represents, or symbolizes, that" but rather, "this is a (morally
charged) *story* about that."[2]

2. An "allegorical anthropology" is suggested fairly explicitly in recent works by
Boon (1977, 1982), Crapanzano (1980), Taussig (1984), and Tyler (1984a).

The specific accounts contained in ethnographies can never be limited to a project of scientific description so long as the guiding task of the work is to make the (often strange) behavior of a different way of life humanly comprehensible. To say that exotic behavior and symbols make sense either in "human" or "cultural" terms is to supply the same sorts of allegorical added meanings that appear in older narratives that saw actions as "spiritually" significant. Culturalist and humanist allegories stand behind the controlled fictions of difference and similitude that we call ethnographic accounts. What is maintained in these texts is a double attention to the descriptive surface and to more abstract, comparative, and explanatory levels of meaning. This twofold structure is set out by Coleridge in a classic definition.

We may then safely define allegorical writing as the employment of one set of agents and images with actions and accompaniments correspondent, so as to convey, while in disguise, either moral qualities or conceptions of the mind that are not in themselves objects of the senses, or other images, agents, fortunes, and circumstances so that the difference is everywhere presented to the eye or imagination, while the likeness is suggested to the mind; and this connectedly, so that the parts combine to form a consistent whole. (1936:30)

What one *sees* in a coherent ethnographic account, the imaged construct of the other, is connected in a continuous double structure with what one *understands*. At times, the structure is too blatant: "During the ceramic manufacturing process, women converse gently, quietly, always without conflict, about ecosystem dynamics . . ." (Whitten 1978:847). Usually it is less obvious and thus more realistic. Adapting Coleridge's formula, what appears descriptively to the senses (and primarily, as he suggests, to the observing eye) seems to be "other," while what is suggested by the coherent series of perceptions is an underlying similitude. Strange behavior is portrayed as meaningful within a common network of symbols—a common ground of understandable activity valid for both observer and observed, and by implication for all human groups. Thus ethnography's narrative of specific differences presupposes, and always refers to, an abstract plane of similarity.

It is worth noting, though I cannot pursue the theme here, that before the emergence of secular anthropology as a science of *human* and *cultural* phenomena, ethnographic accounts were connected to different allegorical referents. Father Lafitau's famous comparison (1724) of Native American customs with those of the ancient Hebrews and Egyptians exemplifies an earlier tendency to map descriptions of the other onto conceptions of the "*premiers temps*." More or less explicit biblical or classical allegories abound in the early descriptions of the New World. For as Johannes Fabian (1983) argues, there has been a pervasive tendency to prefigure others in a temporally distinct, but locatable, space (earlier) within an assumed progress of Western history. Cultural anthropology in the twentieth century has tended to replace (though never completely) these historical allegories with humanist allegories. It has eschewed a search for origins in favor of seeking human similarities and cultural differences. But the representational process itself has not essentially changed. Most descriptions of others continue to assume and refer to elemental or transcendent levels of truth.

This conclusion emerges clearly from the recent Mead-Freeman controversy.[3] Two competing portrayals of Samoan life are cast as scientific projects; but both configure the other as a morally charged alter ego. Mead claimed to be conducting a controlled "experiment" in the field, "testing" the universality of stressful adolescence by examining a counter instance empirically. But despite Boasian rhetoric about the "laboratory" of fieldwork, Mead's experiment produced a message of broad ethical and political significance. Like Ruth Benedict in *Patterns of Culture* (1934), she held a liberal, pluralist vision, responding to the dilemmas of a "complex" American society. The ethnographic stories Mead and Benedict told were manifestly linked to the situation of a culture struggling with diverse values, with an apparent breakdown of established traditions, with utopian visions of human malleability and fears of disaggregation. Their ethnographies were "fables of identity," to adapt Northrop Frye's title (1963). Their openly allegorical purpose was not a kind of moral or expository frame for empirical descriptions, something added on in prefaces and conclusions. The entire project of inventing and representing "cultures" was, for Mead and Benedict, a pedagogical, ethical undertaking.

Mead's "experiment" in controlled cultural variation now looks less like science than allegory—a too sharply focused story of Samoa suggesting a possible America. Derek Freeman's critique ignores any properly literary dimensions in ethnographic work, however, and instead applies its own brand of scientism, inspired by recent developments in sociobiology. As Freeman sees it, Mead was simply wrong about Samoans. They are not the casual, permissive people she made famous, but are beset by all the usual human tensions. They are violent. They get ulcers. The main body of his critique is a massing of counterexamples drawn from the historical record and from his own fieldwork. In 170 pages of empirical overkill, he successfully shows what was already explicit for an alert reader of *Coming of Age in Samoa*: that Mead constructed a foreshortened picture, designed to propose

3. Mead (1923), Freeman (1983). I have drawn on my review of Freeman in the *Times Literary Supplement*, May 13, 1983, 475–76, which explores the literary dimensions of the controversy. For another treatment in this vein, see Porter 1984.

moral, practical lessons for American society. But as Freeman heaps up instances of Samoan anxiety and violence, the allegorical frame for his own undertaking begins to emerge. Clearly something more is getting expressed than simply the "darker side," as Freeman puts it, of Samoan life. In a revealing final page he admits as much, countering Mead's "Apollonian" sense of cultural balance with biology's "Dionysian" human nature (essential, emotional, etc.). But what is the scientific status of a "refutation" that can be subsumed so neatly by a Western mythic opposition? One is left with a stark contrast: Mead's attractive, sexually liberated, calm Pacific world, and now Freeman's Samoa of seething tensions, strict controls, and violent outbursts. Indeed Mead and Freeman form a kind of diptych, whose opposing panels signify a recurrent Western ambivalence about the "primitive." One is reminded of Melville's *Typee*, a sensuous paradise woven through with dread, the threat of violence.

ᴧᴧ

Le transfert de l'Empire de la Chine à l'Empire de soi-même est constant.
VICTOR SEGALEN

A scientific ethnography normally establishes a privileged allegorical register it identifies as "theory," "interpretation," or "explanation." But once *all* meaningful levels in a text, including theories and interpretations, are recognized as allegorical, it becomes difficult to view one of them as privileged, accounting for the rest. Once this anchor is dislodged, the staging and valuing of multiple allegorical registers, or "voices," becomes an important area of concern for ethnographic writers. Recently this has sometimes meant giving indigenous discourse a semi-independent status in the textual whole, interrupting the privileged monotone of "scientific" representation.[4] Much ethnography, taking its distance from totalizing anthropology, seeks to evoke multiple (but not limitless) allegories.

Marjorie Shostak's *Nisa* exemplifies, and wrestles with, the problem of presenting and mediating multiple stories.[5] I shall dwell on it at some length. Shostak explicitly stages three allegorical registers: (1) the representation of a coherent cultural subject as source of scientific knowledge (Nisa is a "!Kung woman"); (2) the construction of a gendered subject (Shostak asks: what is it to be a woman?); (3) the story of a mode of ethnographic production and relationship (an intimate dia-

4. On the origins of this "monotone," see De Certeau 1983 : 128.
5. The rest of this section is an expanded version of my review of *Nisa* in the *Times Literary Supplement*, September 17, 1982, 994–95.

logue). Nisa is the pseudonym of a fifty-year-old woman who has lived most of her life in semi-nomadic conditions. Marjorie Shostak belongs to a Harvard-based research group that has studied the !Kung San hunter-gatherers since the 1950s. The complex truths that emerge from this "life and words" are not limited to an individual or to her surrounding cultural world.

The book's three registers are in crucial respects discrepant. First, the autobiography, cross-checked against other !Kung women's lives, is inserted within an ongoing cultural interpretation (to which it adds "depth"). Second, this shaped experience soon becomes a story of "women's" existence, a story that rhymes closely with many of the experiences and issues highlighted in recent feminist thought. Third, *Nisa* narrates an intercultural encounter in which two individuals collaborate to produce a specific domain of truth. The ethnographic encounter itself becomes, here, the subject of the book, a fable of communication, rapport, and, finally, a kind of fictional, but potent, kinship. *Nisa* is thus manifestly an allegory of scientific comprehension, operating at the levels both of cultural description and of a search for human origins. (Along with other students of gatherer-hunters, the Harvard project—Shostak included—tend to see in this longest stage of human cultural development a baseline for human nature.) *Nisa* is a Western feminist allegory, part of the reinvention of the general category "woman" in the 1970s and 80s. *Nisa* is an allegory of ethnography, of contact and comprehension.

A braided narrative, the book moves constantly, at times awkwardly, between its three meaningful registers. *Nisa* is like many works that portray common human experiences, conflicts, joys, work, and so on. But the text Shostak has made is original in the way it refuses to blend its three registers into a seamless, "full" representation. They remain separate, in dramatic tension. This polyvocality is appropriate to the book's predicament, that of many self-conscious ethnographic writers who find it difficult to speak of well-defined "others" from a stable, distanced position. Difference invades the text; it can no longer be represented; it must be enacted.

Nisa's first register, that of cultural science, holds its subject in firm relation to a social world. It explains Nisa's personality in terms of !Kung ways, and it uses her experience to nuance and correct generalizations about her group. If *Nisa* reveals intersubjective mechanisms in unusual depth, its polyvocal construction shows, too, that the transition to scientific knowledge is not smooth. The personal does not yield to the general without loss. Shostak's research was based on systematic interviews with more than a score of !Kung women. From these conversations she amassed a body of data large enough to reveal typical attitudes, activities, and experiences. But Shostak was dissatisfied by the lack of depth in her interviews, and this led her to seek out an informant able to provide a detailed personal narrative. Nisa was quite unusual in her ability to recall and explain her life; moreover there developed a strong resonance between her stories and Shostak's personal concerns. This posed a problem for the expectations of a generalizing social science.

At the end of her first sojourn in the field, Shostak was troubled by a suspicion that her interlocutor might be too idiosyncratic. Nisa had known severe pain; her life as she recalled it was often violent. Most previous accounts of the !Kung, like Elizabeth Marshall Thomas's *The Harmless People* (1959), had shown them to be peace-loving. "Did I really want to be the one to balance the picture?" (350). On a return trip to the Kalahari, Shostak found reassurance. Though Nisa still exerted a special fascination, she now appeared less unusual. And the ethnographer became "more sure than ever that our work together could and should move forward. The interviews I was conducting with other women were proving to me that Nisa was fundamentally similar to those around her. She was unusually articulate, and she had suffered greater than average loss, but in most other important respects she was a typical !Kung woman" (358).

Roland Barthes (1981) has written poignantly of an impossible science of the individual. An insistent tug toward the general is felt throughout *Nisa*, and it is not without pain that we find Nisa generalized, tied to "an interpretation of !Kung life" (350). The book's scientific discourse, tirelessly contextual, typifying, is braided through the other two voices, introducing each of the fifteen thematic sections of the life with a few pages of background. ("Once a marriage has survived a few years beyond the young wife's first menstruation, the relationship between the spouses becomes more equal" [169]. And so forth.) Indeed, one sometimes feels that the scientific discourse functions in the text as a kind of brake on the book's other voices, whose meanings are excessively personal and intersubjective. There is a real discrepancy. For at the same time that Nisa's story contributes to better generalizations about the !Kung, its very specificity, and the particular circumstances of its making, create meanings that are resistant to the demands of a typifying science.

The book's second and third registers are sharply distinct from the first. Their structure is dialogical, and at times each seems to exist primarily in response to the other. Nisa's life has its own textual autonomy, as a distinct narrative spoken in characteristic, believable tones. But it is manifestly the product of a collaboration. This is particularly true of its overall shape, a full lifespan—fifteen chapters including

"Earliest Memories," "Family Life," "Discovering Sex," "Trial Mar-riages," "Marriage," "Motherhood and Loss," "Women and Men," "Taking Lovers," "A Healing Ritual," "Growing Older." Although at the start of the interviews Nisa had mapped out her life, sketching the main areas to be covered, the thematic roster appears to be Shostak's. Indeed, by casting Nisa's discourse in the shape of a "life," Shostak ad-dresses two rather different audiences. On one side, this intensely personal collection of memories is made suitable for scientific typifica-tion as a "life-history" or "life-cycle." On the other, Nisa's life brings into play a potent and pervasive mechanism for the production of meaning in the West—the exemplary, coherent self (or rather, the self pulling itself together in autobiography). There is nothing universal or natural about the fictional processes of biography and autobiogra-phy (Gusdorf 1956; Olney 1972; Lejeune 1975). Living does not easily organize itself into a continuous narrative. When Nisa says, as she often does, "We lived in that place, eating things. Then we left and went somewhere else," or simply, "we lived and lived" (69), the hum of unmarked, impersonal existence can be heard. From this blurred background, a narrative shape emerges in the occasion of speaking, simultaneously to oneself and another. Nisa tells her life, a process textually dramatized in Shostak's book.

As alter ego, provoker, and editor of the discourse, Shostak makes a number of significant interventions. A good deal of cutting and re-arranging transforms overlapping stories into "a life" that does not repeat itself unduly and that develops by recognizable steps and pas-sages. Nisa's distinct voice emerges. But Shostak has systematically re-moved her own interventions (though they can often be sensed in Nisa's response). She has also taken out a variety of narrative markers: her friend's habitual comment at the end of a story, "the wind has taken that away," or at the start, "I will break open the story and tell you what's there"; or in the middle, "What am I trying to do? Here I am sitting, talking about one story, and another runs right into my head and into my thoughts!" (40). Shostak has clearly thought care-fully about the framing of her transcripts, and one cannot have every-thing—the performance with all its divagations, and also an easily un-derstandable story. If Nisa's words were to be widely read, concessions had to be made to the requirements of biographical allegory, to a readership practiced in the ethical interpretation of selves. By these formal means the book's second discourse, Nisa's spoken life, is brought close to its readers, becoming a narration that makes eloquent "hu-man" sense.

The book's third distinct register is Shostak's personal account of fieldwork. "Teach me what it is to be a !Kung woman" was the question she asked of her informants (349). If Nisa responded with peculiar aptness, her words also seemed to answer another question, "What is it to be a woman?" Shostak told her informants "that I wanted to learn what it meant to be a woman in their culture so I could better understand what it meant in my own." With Nisa, the relationship became, in !Kung terms, that of an aunt talking to a young niece, to "a girl-woman, recently married, struggling with the issues of love, marriage, sexuality, work and identity" (4). The younger woman ("niece," sometimes "daughter") is instructed by an experienced elder in the arts and pains of womanhood. The transforming relationship ends with an equality in affection and respect, and with a final word, potent in feminist meaning: "sister" (371). Nisa speaks, throughout, not as a neutral witness but as a person giving specific kinds of advice to someone of a particular age with manifest questions and desires. She is not an "informant" speaking *cultural* truths, as if to everyone and no one, providing information rather than circumstantial responses.

In her account, Shostak describes a search for personal knowledge, for something going beyond the usual ethnographic rapport. She hopes that intimacy with a !Kung woman will, somehow, enlarge or deepen her sense of being a modern Western woman. Without drawing explicit lessons from Nisa's experience, she dramatizes through her own quest the way a narrated life makes sense, allegorically, *for another*. Nisa's story is revealed as a joint production, the outcome of an encounter that cannot be rewritten as a subject-object dichotomy. Something more than explaining or representing the life and words of another is going on—something more open-ended. The book is part of a new interest in revaluing subjective (more accurately, intersubjective) aspects of research. It emerges from a crucial moment of feminist politics and epistemology: consciousness raising and the sharing of experiences by women. A commonality is produced that, by bringing separate lives together, empowers personal action, recognizes a common estate. This moment of recent feminist consciousness is allegorized in *Nisa*'s fable of its own relationality. (In other ethnographies, traditionally masculine stories of initiation and penetration differently stage the productive encounter of self and other.)[6] Shostak's explicit feminist allegory thus reflects a specific moment in which the construction of "woman's" experience is given center stage. It is a moment of continuing importance; but it has been challenged by recent countercurrents within feminist theory. The assertion of common female qualities (and oppressions) across racial, ethnic, and class lines is newly problematic. And in some quarters "woman" is

6. On ethnography as an allegory of conquest and initiation, see Clifford 1983b.

seen, not as a locus of experience, but as a shifting subjective position not reducible to any essence.[7]

Shostak's allegory seems to register these countercurrents in its occasionally complex accounts of the processes of play and transference, which produce the final inscription of commonality. For the book's intimate relationships are based on subtle, reciprocal movements of doubling, imagination, and desire, movements allegorized in one of the stories Shostak tells in counterpoint to Nisa's narrative—an incident turning on the value of a girl-woman's body.

One day I noticed a twelve-year-old girl, whose breasts had just started to develop, looking into the small mirror beside the driver's window of our Land Rover. She looked intently at her face, then, on tiptoe, examined her breasts and as much of her body as she could see, then went to her face again. She stepped back to see more, moved in again for a closer look. She was a lovely girl, although not outstanding in any way except being in the full health and beauty of youth. She saw me watching. I teased in the !Kung manner I had by then thoroughly learned, "So ugly! How is such a young girl already so ugly?" She laughed. I asked, "You don't agree?" She beamed, "No, not at all. I'm beautiful!" She continued to look at herself. I said, "Beautiful? Perhaps my eyes have become broken with age that I can't see where it is?" She said, "Everywhere— my face, my body. There is no ugliness at all." These remarks were said easily, with a broad smile, but without arrogance. The pleasure she felt in her changing body was as evident as the absence of conflict about it. (270)

A great deal of the book is here: an old voice, a young voice, a mirror . . . talk of self-possession. Narcissism, a term of deviance applied to women of the West, is transfigured. We notice, too, that it is the ethnographer, assuming a voice of age, who has brought a mirror, just as Nisa provides an allegorical mirror when Shostak takes the role of youth. Ethnography gains subjective "depth" through the sorts of roles, reflections, and reversals dramatized here. The writer, and her readers, can be both young (learning) and old (knowing). They can simultaneously listen, and "give voice to," the other.[8] Nisa's readers follow—and prolong—the play of a desire. They imagine, in the mir-

7. On racial and class divisions within feminism, see the rethinking of Rich (1979), and the work of Hull, Scott, and Smith (1982), Hooks (1981), and Moraga (1983). Strong feminist critiques of essentialism may be found in Wittig (1981) and Haraway (1985).

8. Ethnographies often present themselves as fictions of learning, the acquisition of knowledge, and finally of authority to understand and represent another culture. The researcher begins in a child's relationship to adult culture, and ends by speaking with the wisdom of experience. It is interesting to observe how, in the text, an author's enunciative modes may shift back and forth between learning from and speaking for the other. This fictional freedom is crucial to ethnography's allegorical appeal: the simultaneous reconstruction of a culture and a knowing self, a double "coming of age in Samoa."

ror of the other, a guileless self-possession, an uncomplicated feeling of "attractiveness" that Shostak translates as "I have work," "I am productive," "I have worth" (270).

Anthropological fieldwork has been represented as both a scientific "laboratory" and a personal "rite of passage." The two metaphors capture nicely the discipline's impossible attempt to fuse objective and subjective practices. Until recently, this impossibility was masked by marginalizing the intersubjective foundations of fieldwork, by excluding them from serious ethnographic texts, relegating them to prefaces, memoirs, anecdotes, confessions, and so forth. Lately this set of disciplinary rules is giving way. The new tendency to name and quote informants more fully and to introduce personal elements into the text is altering ethnography's discursive strategy and mode of authority. Much of our knowledge about other cultures must now be seen as contingent, the problematic outcome of intersubjective dialogue, translation, and projection. This poses fundamental problems for any science that moves predominantly from the particular to the general, that can make use of personal truths only as examples of typical phenomena or as exceptions to collective patterns.

Once the ethnographic process is accorded its full complexity of historicized dialogical relations, what formerly seemed to be empirical/interpretive accounts of generalized cultural facts (statements and attributions concerning "the !Kung," "the Samoans," etc.) now appear as just one level of allegory. Such accounts may be complex and truthful; and they are, in principle, susceptible to refutation, assuming access to the same pool of cultural facts. But as written versions based on fieldwork, these accounts are clearly no longer *the* story, but a story among other stories. *Nisa*'s discordant allegorical registers—the book's three, never quite manageable, "voices"—reflect a troubled, inventive moment in the history of cross-cultural representation.

ᨇ

> Welcome of Tears *is a beautiful book, combining the stories of a vanishing people and the growth of an anthropologist.*
>
> MARGARET MEAD, blurb for the paperback edition
> of Charles Wagley's *Welcome of Tears*

Ethnographic texts are not only, or predominantly, allegories. Indeed, as we have seen, they struggle to limit the play of their "extra" meanings, subordinating them to mimetic, referential functions. This struggle (which often involves disputes over what will count as "scientific" theory and what as "literary" invention or "ideological" projection) maintains disciplinary and generic conventions. If ethnography as a tool for positive science is to be preserved, such conventions must

mask, or direct, multiple allegorical processes. For may not every extended description, stylistic turn, story, or metaphor be read to mean
something else? (Need we accept the three explicit levels of allegory in
a book like *Nisa*? What about its photographs, which tell their own
story?) Are not readings themselves undecidable? Critics like De Man
(1979) rigorously adopt such a position, arguing that the choice of a
dominant rhetoric, figure, or narrative mode in a text is always an imperfect attempt to impose a reading or range of readings on an interpretive process that is open-ended, a series of displaced "meanings"
with no full stop. But whereas the free play of readings may in theory
be infinite, there are, at any historical moment, a limited range of canonical and emergent allegories available to the competent reader
(the reader whose interpretation will be deemed plausible by a specific
community). These structures of meaning are historically bounded
and coercive. There is, in practice, no "free play."

Within this historical predicament, the critique of stories and patterns that persistently inform cross-cultural accounts remains an important political as well as scientific task. In the remainder of this essay
I explore a broad, orienting allegory (or more accurately, a pattern of
possible allegories) that has recently emerged as a contested area—a
structure of retrospection that may be called "ethnographic pastoral."
Shostak's book and the Harvard hunter-gatherer studies, to the extent
that they engage in a search for fundamental, desirable human traits,
are enmeshed in this structure.

In a trenchant article, "The Use and Abuse of Anthropology: Reflections on Feminism and Cross-Cultural Understanding," Michelle
Rosaldo has questioned a persistent tendency to appropriate ethnographic data in the form of a search for origins. Analyses of social
"givens" such as gender and sexuality show an almost reflexive
need for anthropological just-so-stories. Beginning with Simone de
Beauvoir's founding question, "What is woman?" scholarly discussions
"move . . . to a diagnosis of contemporary subordination and from
then on to the queries 'Were things always as they are today?' and then
'When did "it" start?'" (1980:391). Enter examples drawn from ethnography. In a practice not essentially different from that of Herbert
Spencer, Henry Maine, Durkheim, Engels, or Freud, it is assumed
that evidence from "simple" societies will illuminate the origins
and structure of contemporary cultural patterns. Rosaldo notes that
most scientific anthropologists have, since the early twentieth century,
abandoned the evolutionary search for origins, but her essay suggests
that the reflex is pervasive and enduring. Moreover, even scientific
ethnographers cannot fully control the meanings—readings—provoked by their accounts. This is especially true of representations that

have not historicized their objects, portraying exotic societies in an "ethnographic present" (which is always, in fact, a past). This synchronic suspension effectively textualizes the other, and gives the sense of a reality not in temporal flux, not in the same ambiguous, moving *historical* present that includes and situates the other, the ethnographer, and the reader. "Allochronic" representations, to use Johannes Fabian's term, have been pervasive in twentieth-century scientific ethnography. They invite allegorical appropriations in the mythologizing mode Rosaldo repudiates.

Even the most coolly analytic accounts may be built on this retrospective appropriation. E. E. Evans-Pritchard's *The Nuer* (1940) is a case in point, for it portrays an appealingly harmonious anarchy, a society uncorrupted by a Fall. Henrika Kuklick (1984) has analyzed *The Nuer* (in the context of a broad trend in British political anthropology concerned with acephalous "tribal" societies) as a political allegory reinscribing a recurrent "folk model" of Anglo-Saxon democracy. When Evans-Pritchard writes, "There is no master and no servant in their society, but only equals who regard themselves as God's noblest creation," it is not difficult to hear echoes of a long political tradition of nostalgia for "an egalitarian, contractual union" of free individuals. Edenic overtones are occasionally underscored, as always with Evans-Pritchard, drily.

Though I have spoken of time and units of time the Nuer have no expression equivalent to "time" in our language, and they cannot, therefore, as we can, speak of time as though it were something actual, which passes, can be wasted, can be saved, and so forth. I do not think that they ever experience the same feeling of fighting against time or of having to coordinate activities with an abstract passage of time, because their points of reference are mainly the activities themselves, which are generally of a leisurely character. Events follow a logical order, but they are not controlled by an abstract system, there being no autonomous points of reference to which activities have to conform with precision. Nuer are fortunate. (103)

For a readership caught up in the post-Darwinian bourgeois experience of time—a linear, relentless progress leading nowhere certain and permitting no pause or cyclic return, the cultural islands out of time (or "without history") described by many ethnographers have a persistent prelapsarian appeal. We note, however, the ironic structure (which need not imply an ironic tone) of such allegories. For they are presented through the detour of an ethnographic subjectivity whose attitude toward the other is one of participant-observation, or better perhaps, belief-skepticism (See Webster 1982:93). Nuer are fortunate. (We are unfortunate.) The appeal is fictional, the temporal ease and attractive anarchy of Nuer society are distant, irretrievable. They are lost qualities, textually recovered.

This ironic appeal belongs to a broad ideological pattern that has oriented much, perhaps most, twentieth century cross-cultural representation. "For us, primitive societies [*Naturvölker*] are ephemeral. . . . At the very instant they become known to us they are doomed." Thus, Adolph Bastian in 1881 (quoted in Fabian 1983:122). In 1921, Bronislaw Malinowski: "Ethnology is in the sadly ludicrous, not to say tragic position, that at the very moment when it begins to put its workshop in order, to forge its proper tools, to start ready for work on its appointed task, the material of its study melts away with hopeless rapidity" (1961:xv). Authentic Trobriand society, he implied, was not long for this world. Writing in the 1950s, Claude Lévi-Strauss saw a global process of entropy. *Tristes Tropiques* sadly portrays differentiated social structures disintegrating into global homogeneity under the shock of contact with a potent monoculture. A Rousseauian quest for "elementary" forms of human collectivity leads Lévi-Strauss to the Nambikwara. But their world is falling apart. "I had been looking for a society reduced to its simplest expression. That of the Nambikwara was so truly simple that all I could find in it was individual human beings" (1975:317).

The theme of the vanishing primitive, of the end of traditional society (the very act of naming it "traditional" implies a rupture), is pervasive in ethnographic writing. It is, in Raymond Williams's phrase, a "structure of feeling" (1973:12). Undeniably, ways of life can, in a meaningful sense, "die"; populations are regularly violently disrupted, sometimes exterminated. Traditions are constantly being lost. But the persistent and repetitious "disappearance" of social forms at the moment of their ethnographic representation demands analysis as a narrative structure. A few years ago the *American Ethnologist* printed an article based on recent fieldwork among the Nambikwara—who are still something more than "individual human beings." And living Trobriand culture has been the object of recent field study (Weiner 1976). The now-familiar film *Trobriand Cricket* shows a very distinct way of life, reinventing itself under the conditions of colonialism and early nationhood.

Ethnography's disappearing object is, then, in significant degree, a rhetorical construct legitimating a representational practice: "salvage" ethnography in its widest sense. The other is lost, in disintegrating time and space, but saved in the text. The rationale for focusing one's attention on vanishing lore, for rescuing in writing the knowledge of old people, may be strong (though it depends on local circumstances and cannot any longer be generalized). I do not wish to deny specific cases of disappearing customs and languages, or to challenge the value of recording such phenomena. I do, however, question the assumption that with rapid change something essential ("culture"), a coherent differential identity, vanishes. And I question, too, the mode of scientific and moral authority associated with salvage, or redemptive, ethnography. It is assumed that the other society is weak and "needs" to be represented by an outsider (and that what matters in its life is its past, not present or future). The recorder and interpreter of fragile custom is custodian of an essence, unimpeachable witness to an authenticity. (Moreover, since the "true" culture has always vanished, the salvaged version cannot be easily refuted.)

Such attitudes, though they persist, are diminishing. Few anthropologists today would embrace the logic of ethnography in the terms in which it was enunciated in Franz Boas's time, as a last-chance rescue operation. But the allegory of salvage is deeply ingrained. Indeed, I shall argue in a moment that it is built into the conception and practice of ethnography as a process of writing, specifically of textualization. Every description or interpretation that conceives itself as "bringing a culture into writing," moving from oral-discursive experience (the "native's," the fieldworker's) to a written version of that experience (the ethnographic text) is enacting the structure of "salvage." To the extent that the ethnographic process is seen as inscription (rather than, for example, as transcription, or dialogue) the representation will continue to enact a potent, and questionable, allegorical structure.

This structure is appropriately located within a long Western tradition of pastoral (a topic also developed by Renato Rosaldo in this volume). Raymond Williams's *The Country and the City* (1973), while drawing on an established tradition of scholarship on pastoral (Empson 1950, Kermode 1952, Frye 1971, Poggioli 1975, among others) strains toward a global scope wide enough to accommodate ethnographic writing. He shows how a fundamental contrast between city and country aligns itself with other pervasive oppositions: civilized and primitive, West and "non-West," future and past. He analyzes a complex, inventive, strongly patterned set of responses to social dislocation and change, stretching from classical antiquity to the present. Williams traces the constant reemergence of a conventionalized pattern of retrospection that laments the loss of a "good" country, a place where authentic social and natural contacts were once possible. He soon, however, notes an unsettling regression. For each time one finds a writer looking back to a happier place, to a lost, "organic" moment, one finds another writer of that earlier period lamenting a similar, previous disappearance. The ultimate referent is, of course, Eden (9–12).

Williams does not dismiss this structure as simply nostalgic, which it manifestly is; but rather follows out a very complex set of temporal, spatial, and moral positions. He notes that pastoral frequently involves a *critical nostalgia*, a way (as Diamond [1974] argues for a concept of the primitive) to break with the hegemonic, corrupt present by asserting the reality of a radical alternative. Edward Sapir's "Culture, Genuine and Spurious" (1966) recapitulates these critical pastoral values. And indeed every imagined authenticity presupposes, and is produced by, a present circumstance of felt inauthenticity. But Williams's treatment suggests that such projections need not be consistently located in the past; or, what amounts to the same thing, that the "genuine" elements of cultural life need not be repetitiously encoded as fragile, threatened, and transient. This sense of pervasive social fragmentation, of a constant disruption of "natural" relations, is characteristic of a subjectivity Williams loosely connects with city life and with romanticism. The self, cut loose from viable collective ties, is an identity in search of wholeness, having internalized loss and embarked on an endless search for authenticity. Wholeness by definition becomes a thing of the past (rural, primitive, childlike) accessible only as a fiction, grasped from a stance of incomplete involvement. George Eliot's novels epitomize this situation of participant-observation in a "common condition . . . a knowable community, belong[ing] ideally in the past." *Middlemarch*, for example, is projected a generation back from the time of its writing to 1830. And this is approximately the temporal distance that many conventional ethnographies assume when they describe a passing reality, "traditional" life, in the present tense. The fiction of a knowable community "can be recreated there for a widely ranging moral action. But the real step that has been taken is withdrawal from any full response to an existing society. Value is in the past, as a general retrospective condition, and is in the present only as a particular and private sensibility, the individual moral action" (180).

In George Eliot we can see the development of a style of sociological writing that will describe whole cultures (knowable worlds) from a specific temporal distance and with a presumption of their transience. This will be accomplished from a loving, detailed, but ultimately disengaged, standpoint. Historical worlds will be salvaged as textual fabrications disconnected from ongoing lived milieux and suitable for moral, allegorical appropriation by individual readers. In properly *ethnographic* pastoral this textualizing structure is generalized beyond the dissociations of nineteenth-century England to a wider capitalist topography of Western/non-Western, city/country oppositions. "Primitive," nonliterate, underdeveloped, tribal societies are constantly yielding to progress, "losing" their traditions. "In the name of science, we anthropologists compose requiems," writes Robert Murphy (1984). But the most problematic, and politically charged, aspect of this "pastoral" encodation is its relentless placement of others in a present-becoming-past. What would it require, for example, consistently to associate the inventive, resilient, enormously varied societies of Melanesia with the cultural *future* of the planet? How might ethnographies be differently conceived if this standpoint could be seriously adopted? Pastoral allegories of cultural loss and textual rescue would, in any event, have to be transformed.[9]

Pervasive assumptions about ethnography as writing would also have to be altered. For allegories of salvage are implied by the very practice of textualization that is generally assumed to be at the core of cultural description. Whatever else an ethnography does, it translates experience into text. There are various ways of effecting this translation, ways that have significant ethical and political consequences. One can "write up" the results of an individual experience of research. This may generate a realistic account of the unwritten experience of another group or person. One can present this textualization as the outcome of observation, of interpretation, of dialogue. One can construct an ethnography composed of dialogues. One can feature multiple voices, or a single voice. One can portray the other as a stable, essential whole, or one can show it to be the product of a narrative of discovery, in specific historical circumstances. I have discussed some of these choices elsewhere (1983a). What is irreducible, in all of them, is the assumption that ethnography brings experience and discourse into writing.

Though this is manifestly the case, and indeed reflects a kind of common sense, it is not an innocent common sense. Since antiquity the story of a passage from the oral/aural into writing has been a complex and charged one. Every ethnography enacts such a movement, and this is one source of the peculiar authority that finds both rescue and irretrievable loss—a kind of death in life—in the making of texts from events and dialogues. Words and deeds are transient (and au-

9. In my reading, the most powerful attempt to unthink this temporal setup, by means of an ethnographic invention of Melanesia, is the work of Roy Wagner (1979, 1980). He opposes, perhaps too sharply, Western "anticipations of the past" with Melanesian "anticipations of the future." The former are associated with the idea of culture as a structuring tradition (1979:162). Hugh Brody's *Maps and Dreams* (1982) offers a subtle and precise attempt to portray the hunting life of Beaver Indians in northwest Canada as they confront world-system forces, an oil pipeline, hunting for sport, etc. He presents his work as a political collaboration. And he is careful to keep the future open, uncertain, walking a fine line between narratives of "survival," "acculturation," and "impact."

thentic), writing endures (as supplementarity and artifice). The text embalms the event as it extends its "meaning." Since Socrates' refusal to write, itself powerfully written by Plato, a profound ambivalence toward the passage from oral to literate has characterized Western thinking. And much of the power and pathos of ethnography derives from the fact that it has situated its practice within this crucial transition. The fieldworker presides over, and controls in some degree, the making of a text out of life. His or her descriptions and interpretations become part of the "consultable record of what man has said" (Geertz 1973:30). The text is a record of something enunciated, in a *past*. The structure, if not the thematic content, of pastoral is repeated.

A small parable may give a sense of why this allegory of ethnographic rescue and loss has recently become less self-evident. It is a true parable.[10] A student of African ethno-history is conducting field research in Gabon. He is concerned with the Mpongwé, a coastal group who, in the nineteenth century, were active in contacts with European traders and colonists. The "tribe" still exists, in the region of Libreville, and the ethno-historian has arranged to interview the current Mpongwé chief about traditional life, religious ritual, and so on. In preparation for his interview the researcher consults a compendium of local custom compiled in the early twentieth century by a Gabonese Christian and pioneering ethnographer, the Abbé Raponda-Walker. Before meeting with the Mpongwé chief the ethnographer copies out a list of religious terms, institutions and concepts, recorded and defined by Raponda-Walker. The interview will follow this list, checking whether the customs persist, and if so, with what innovations. At first things go smoothly, with the Mpongwé authority·providing descriptions and interpretations of the terms suggested, or else noting that a practice has been abandoned. After a time, however, when the researcher asks about a particular word, the chief seems uncertain, knits his brows. "Just a moment," he says cheerfully, and disappears into his house to return with a copy of Raponda-Walker's compendium. For the rest of the interview the book lies open on his lap.

Versions of this story, in increasing numbers, are to be heard in the folklore of ethnography. Suddenly cultural data cease to move smoothly from oral performance into descriptive writing. Now data also move from text to text, inscription becomes transcription. Both informant and researcher are readers and re-*writers* of a cultural invention. This is not to say, as some might, that the interview has ended

10. My thanks to Henry Bucher for this true story. I have told it as a parable, both because it is one, and because I suspect he would tell it somewhat differently, having been there.

in a sterile short circuit. Nor need one, like Socrates in the *Phaedrus*, lament the erosion of memory by literacy. The interview has not, suddenly, become "inauthentic," the data merely imposed. Rather, what one must reckon with are new conditions of ethnographic production. First, it is no longer possible to act as if the outside researcher is the sole, or primary, bringer of the culture into writing. This has, in fact, seldom been the case. However, there has been a consistent tendency among fieldworkers to hide, discredit, or marginalize prior written accounts (by missionaries, travelers, administrators, local authorities, even other ethnographers). The fieldworker, typically, starts from scratch, from a research *experience*, rather than from reading or transcribing. The field is not conceived of as already filled with texts. Yet this intertextual predicament is more and more the case (Larcom 1983). Second, "informants" increasingly read and write. They interpret prior versions of their culture, as well as those being written by ethnographic scholars. Work with texts—the process of inscription, rewriting, and so forth—is no longer (if it ever was) the exclusive domain of outside authorities. "Nonliterate" cultures are already textualized; there are few, if any, "virgin" lifeways to be violated and preserved by writing. Third, a very widespread, empowering distinction has been eroded: the division of the globe into literate and nonliterate peoples. This distinction is no longer widely accurate, as non-Western, "tribal" peoples become increasingly literate. But furthermore, once one begins to doubt the ethnographer's monopoly on the power to inscribe, one begins to see the "writing" activities that have always been pursued by native collaborators—from an Ambrym islander's sketch (in a famous gesture) of an intricate kinship system in the sand for A. B. Deacon to the Sioux George Sword's book-length cultural description found in the papers of James Walker. (See the Introduction of this volume, p. 15.)

But the most subversive challenge to the allegory of textualization I have been discussing here is found in the work of Derrida (1974). Perhaps the most enduring effect of his revival of "grammatology" has been to expand what was conventionally thought of as writing. *Alphabetic* writing, he argues, is a restrictive definition that ties the broad range of marks, spatial articulations, gestures, and other inscriptions at work in human cultures too closely to the representation of speech, the oral/aural word. In opposing logocentric representation to *écriture*, he radically extends the definition of the "written," in effect smudging its clear distinction from the "spoken." There is no need here to pursue in detail a disorienting project that is by now well known. What matters for ethnography is the claim that *all* human groups write—if they articulate, classify, possess an "oral-literature," or inscribe their world in ritual acts. They repeatedly "textualize" meanings. Thus, in Derrida's epistemology, the writing of ethnography cannot be seen as a drastically new form of cultural inscription, as an exterior imposition on a "pure," unwritten oral/aural universe. The logos is not primary and the *gramme* its mere secondary representation.

Seen in this light, the processes of ethnographic writing appear more complex. If, as Derrida would say, the cultures studied by anthropologists are always already writing themselves, the special status of the fieldworker-scholar who "brings the culture into writing" is undercut. Who, in fact, writes a myth that is recited into a tape recorder, or copied down to become part of field notes? Who writes (in a sense going beyond transcription) an interpretation of custom produced through intense conversations with knowledgeable native collaborators? I have argued that such questions can, and should, generate a rethinking of ethnographic authority (Clifford 1983a). In the present context I want merely to underline the pervasive challenge, both historical and theoretical in origin, that presently confronts the allegory of ethnographic practice as textualization.

It is important to keep the allegorical dimensions in mind. For in the West the passage from oral to literate is a potent recurring *story*— of power, corruption, and loss. It replicates (and to an extent produces) the structure of pastoral that has been pervasive in twentieth-century ethnography. Logocentric writing is conventionally conceived to be a *representation* of authentic speech. Pre-literate (the phrase contains a story) societies are oral societies; writing comes to them from "outside," an intrusion from a wider world. Whether brought by missionary, trader, or ethnographer, writing is both empowering (a necessary, effective way of storing and manipulating knowledge) and corrupting (a loss of immediacy, of the face-to-face communication Socrates cherished, of the presence and intimacy of speech). A complex and fertile recent debate has circled around the valorization, historical significance, and epistemological status of writing.[11] Whatever may or may not have been settled in the debate, there is no doubt of what has become unsettled: the sharp distinction of the world's cultures into literate and pre-literate; the notion that ethnographic textualization is a process that enacts a fundamental transition from oral experience to written representation; the assumption that something essential is lost when a culture becomes "ethnographic"; the strangely ambivalent authority of a practice that salvages as text a cultural life becoming past.

These components of what I have called ethnographic pastoral no

---

11. The "debate" centers on the confrontation of Ong (1967, 1977, 1982) and Derrida (1973, 1974). Tyler (1978, 1984b) tries to work past the opposition. Goody (1977) and Eisenstein (1979) have made important recent contributions.

longer appear as common sense. Reading and writing are generalized. If the ethnographer reads culture over the native's shoulder, the native also reads over the ethnographer's shoulder as he or she writes each cultural description. Fieldworkers are increasingly constrained in what they publish by the reactions of those previously classified as nonliterate. Novels by a Samoan (Alfred Wendt) can challenge the portrait of his people by a distinguished anthropologist. The notion that writing is a corruption, that something irretrievably pure is lost when a cultural world is textualized is, after Derrida, seen to be a pervasive, contestable, Western allegory. Walter Ong and others have shown that something is, indeed, lost with the generalization of writing. But authentic culture is not that something—to be gathered up in its fragile, final truth by an ethnographer or by anyone else.

Modern allegory, Walter Benjamin (1977) tells us, is based on a sense of the world as transient and fragmentary. "History" is grasped as a process, not of inventive life, but of "irresistible decay." The material analogue of allegory is thus the "ruin" (178), an always-disappearing structure that invites imaginative reconstruction. Benjamin observes that "appreciation of the transience of things, and the concern to redeem them for eternity, is one of the strongest impulses in allegory" (quoted by Wolin 1982:71). My account of ethnographic pastoral suggests that this "impulse" is to be resisted, not by abandoning allegory—an impossible aim—but by opening ourselves to different histories.

∿∿

Allegories are secured . . . by teaching people to read in certain ways.
TALAL ASAD (comment on this essay at the Santa Fe seminar)

I have explored some important allegorical forms that express "cosmological" patterns of order and disorder, fables of personal (gendered) identity, and politicized models of temporality. The future of these forms is uncertain; they are being rewritten and criticized in current practice. A few conclusions, or at least assertions, may be drawn from this exploration.

• There is no way definitely, surgically, to separate the factual from the allegorical in cultural accounts. The data of ethnography make sense only within patterned arrangements and narratives, and these are conventional, political, and meaningful in a more than referential sense. Cultural facts are not true and cultural allegories false. In the human sciences the relation of fact to allegory is a domain of struggle and institutional discipline.

The meanings of an ethnographic account are uncontrollable. Neither an author's intention, nor disciplinary training, nor the rules of genre can limit the readings of a text that will emerge with new historical, scientific, or political projects. But if ethnographies are susceptible to multiple interpretations, these are not at any given moment infinite, or merely "subjective" (in the pejorative sense). Reading is indeterminate only to the extent that history itself is open-ended. If there is a common resistance to the recognition of allegory, a fear that it leads to a nihilism of reading, this is not a realistic fear. It confuses contests for meaning with disorder. And often it reflects a wish to preserve an "objective" rhetoric, refusing to locate its own mode of production within inventive culture and historical change.

A recognition of allegory inescapably poses the political and ethical dimensions of ethnographic writing. It suggests that these be manifested, not hidden. In this light, the open allegorizing of a Mead or a Benedict enacts a certain probity—properly exposing itself to the accusation of having *used* tribal societies for pedagogical purposes. (Let those free of such purposes cast the first stone!) One need not, of course, purvey heavy-handed "messages," or twist cultural facts (as presently known) to a political purpose. I would suggest as a model of allegorical tact Marcel Mauss's *The Gift*. No one would deny its scientific importance or scholarly commitment. Yet from the outset, and especially in its concluding chapter, the work's aim is patent: "to draw conclusions of a moral nature about some of the problems confronting us in our present economic crisis" (1967:2). The book was written in response to the breakdown of European reciprocity in World War I. The troubling proximity it shows between exchange and warfare, the image of the round table evoked at the end, these and other urgent resonances mark the work as a socialist-humanist allegory addressed to the political world of the twenties. This is not the work's only "content." The many rereadings *The Gift* has generated testify to its productivity as a text. It can even be read—in certain graduate seminars—as a classic comparative study of exchange, with admonitions to skim over the final chapter. This is a sad mistake. For it misses the opportunity to learn from an admirable example of science deploying itself *in* history.

A recognition of allegory complicates the writing and reading of ethnographies in potentially fruitful ways. A tendency emerges to specify and separate different allegorical registers within the text. The marking off of extended indigenous discourses shows the ethnography to be a hierarchical structure of powerful stories that translate, encounter, and recontextualize other powerful stories. It is a palimpsest (Owens 1980). Moreover, an awareness of allegory heightens awareness of the narratives, and other temporal setups, implicitly or explicitly at work. Is the redemptive structure of salvage-textualization being replaced? By what new allegories? Of conflict? Of emergence? Of syncretism? [12]

Finally, a recognition of allegory requires that as readers and writers of ethnographies, we struggle to confront and take responsibility for our systematic constructions of others and of ourselves through others. This recognition need not ultimately lead to an ironic position—though it must contend with profound ironies. If we are condemned to tell stories we cannot control, may we not, at least, tell stories we believe to be true.

12. For recent changes in these underlying stories, see note 9, above, and Bruner 1985. See also James Boon's 1983 exploration of anthropology's satiric dimensions. A partial way out can perhaps be envisioned in the pre-modern current that Harry Berger has called "strong" or "metapastoral"—a tradition he finds in the writing of Sidney, Spenser, Shakespeare, Cervantes, Milton, Marvell, and Pope. "Such pastoral constructs within itself an image of its generic traditions in order to criticize them and, in the process, performs a critique on the limits of its own enterprise even as it ironically displays its delight in the activity it criticizes" (1984:2). Modern ethnographic examples are rare, although much of Lévi-Strauss's *Tristes Tropiques* certainly qualifies.

For helpful criticisms of this paper I would like to thank Richard Handler, Susan Gevirtz, David Schneider, Harry Berger, and the Santa Fe seminar participants, especially Michael Fischer.

STEPHEN A. TYLER

Post-Modern Ethnography: From Document of the Occult to Occult Document

First Voice: Context

The paper that follows this introduction is part of a group of essays written at various times and in response to various influences. Nonetheless, each essay anticipates, alludes to, builds on, or presupposes the others. Each deals in one way or another with discourse and rhetoric, and each characterizes the tension between the possible worlds of common sense and the impossible worlds of science and politics. Together they tell how the rhetorical modes of ethics (*ethos*), science (*eidos*), and politics (*pathos*) are sensorial allegories whose root metaphors "saying/hearing," "seeing/showing," "doing/acting" respectively create the discourses of value, representation, and work. All of the essays speak of the ethnographic contextualization of the rhetorics of science and politics and tell how the rhetoric of ethnography is neither scientific nor political, but is, as the prefix *ethno-* implies, ethical. They also speak of the suffix *-graphy* in reminder of the fact that ethnography itself is contextualized by a technology of written communication.

Neither part of the search for universal knowledge, nor an instrument for the suppression/emancipation of peoples, nor just another mode of discourse on a par with those of science and politics, ethnography is instead a superordinate discourse to which all other discourses are relativized and in which they find their meaning and justification. Ethnography's superordination is the consequence of its "imperfection." Neither self-perfecting in the manner of scientific discourse nor totalizing in the manner of political discourse, it is defined neither by a reflexive attention to its own rules nor by the performative instrumentality of those rules. Defined neither by form nor by relation to an external object, it produces no idealizations of form and performance, no fictionalized realities or realities fictionalized. Its transcendence is not that of a meta-language—of a language superior by means of its greater perfection of form—nor that of a unity created by synthesis and sublation, nor of *praxis* and practical application. Transcendent then, neither by theory nor by practice, nor by their synthesis, it *describes* no knowledge and *produces* no action. It transcends instead by *evoking* what cannot be known discursively or performed perfectly, though all know it as if discursively and perform it as if perfectly.

Evocation is neither presentation nor representation. It presents no objects and represents none, yet it makes available through absence what can be conceived but not presented. It is thus beyond truth and immune to the judgment of performance. It overcomes the separation of the sensible and the conceivable, of form and content, of self and other, of language and the world.

Evocation—that is to say, "ethnography"—is the discourse of the post-modern world, for the world that made science, and that science made, has disappeared, and scientific thought is now an archaic mode of consciousness surviving for a while yet in degraded form without the ethnographic context that created and sustained it. Scientific thought succumbed because it violated the first law of culture, which says that "the more man controls anything, the more uncontrollable both become." In the totalizing rhetoric of its mythology, science purported to be its own justification and sought to control and autonomize its discourse. Yet its only justification was proof, for which there could be no justification within its own discourse, and the more it controlled its discourse by subjecting it to the criterion of proof, the more uncontrollable its discourse became. Its own activity constantly fragmented the unity of knowledge it sought to project. The more it knew, the more there was to know.

All its textual strategies—its method—depended on a prior and critical disjunction of language and the world. It made visual perception unmediated by concepts the origin of knowledge about the world, and it made language the means by which that knowledge appeared in descriptions. Science depended, in other words, on the descriptive adequacy of language as a representation of the world, but in order to move from individual percept to agreed-upon perception, it also needed a language of communicative adequacy that could enable consensus in the community of scientists. In the end, science failed because it could not reconcile the competing demands of representation and communication. Every move to enhance representation threatened communication and every agreement in communication was the sign of a new failure in representation.

Science adopted a model of language as a self-perfecting form of closed communication that achieved closure by making language itself the object of description. But closure was bought at the cost of descriptive adequacy. The more language became its own object, the less it had to say about anything else. So, the language of science became the object of science, and what had begun as perception unmediated by concepts became conception unmediated by percepts. The unity of communication brought about by language displaced the unity of perception that language had formerly wrought. Language as communication displaced language as representation, and as science communicated better and better about itself, it had less and less to say about the world. In an excess of democracy, agreement among scientists became more important than the nature of nature.

Still, this would not have been fatal had it not been for the stubborn refusal of language to perfect itself. As science increasingly defined itself as the mode of discourse that had its own discourse as its object, every move to perfect that discourse and fill every gap of proof revealed ever-new imperfections. Every self-perfecting, self-corrective move created local orders that spawned new imperfections requiring new corrections. Instead of a coherent system of knowledge, science created a welter of local orders unrelated to one another and beyond the control of anyone. Scientific knowledge was systematized only by the unity of a rational method that produced greater and greater irrationality. The utopian unity of science disappeared from sight along with all the other unreal objects of scientific fantasy.

Caught up in the fascination of this glass bead game with its ever-changing rules of play and promise of the always new and different, scientists fulfilled in their discourse that dream of capitalist production in which new self-destructing products automatically remove themselves from competition with still newer self-destructing products created to fill an insatiable demand for the consumption of the latest scientific breakthrough, the latest change in the rules of the game. In this world of ever-changing fashions, the provincial was the player who continued to play a game that had already been abandoned by those in the "forefront" or on the "cutting edge" of research.

As science came to be thought of more and more as a game, it became distanced from *praxis* and disrupted the taken-for-granted relation between theory and practice. What consistent practice could flow from an inconstant theory that understood its significance as a play in a game? The less theory was guided and stimulated by a reflexive relation to practical application, the less it could justify itself as the source of practice. And since the infinite game led only to provisional knowledge, ever subject to revision as a consequence of changes in the rules, it produced no universal knowledge and could not justify itself by holding out the promise that it would. Its involution closed off both the return to the concrete world of practice and the transit to the wholly transcendental world of universal knowledge. Consequently, it had to look outside its own discourse for justification, to seek legitimation in a discourse that was other than its own and not subject to its rules. It needed a discourse that could not be part of the self-perfecting discourse of science or foundational in any scientifically acceptable way.

Science chose an uneasy compromise, subjugating itself both to the discourse of work (politics and industry) and the discourse of value (ethics and aesthetics), but since politics and industry controlled the means of play and could always threaten to withhold the funds on which the game depended, science succumbed more and more to limitations on play imposed in the interests of its masters.

Enlisted first as the propaganda arm of science, asserting the lie of theory and basic research as the source of practice and technological innovation, the discourse of value eventually became the ideological means for the justification of work, and all talk of value was linked inseparably to objects and to performance relative to objects—the reality fictions of work. What had originally presented itself as the context of practical reality within which the aesthetics of the play of science would find its meaning and justification became the condition of a bureaucratic unreality establishing the limits of reality through the exercise of power disguised as reason. All discourse was reduced to the rhetoric of work. But, at this moment of its triumph of total control, do we sense the first tremors of the eruption of the uncontrollable?

This is the tale of the origin of the post-modern world as told by Habermas (1975, 1984) and Lyotard (1979)—allowing for certain intentional interpretive liberties. It is the framing story for a post-modern ethnography.

Free Voice: Post-Modern Ethnography

A post-modern ethnography is a cooperatively evolved text consisting of fragments of discourse intended to evoke in the minds of both reader and writer an emergent fantasy of a possible world of commonsense reality, and thus to provoke an aesthetic integration that will have a therapeutic effect. It is, in a word, poetry—not in its textual form, but in its return to the original context and function of poetry, which, by means of its performative break with everyday

speech, evoked memories of the *ethos* of the community and thereby
provoked hearers to act ethically (cf. Jaeger 1945:3–76). Post-
modern ethnography attempts to recreate textually this spiral of poetic and ritual performance. Like them, it defamiliarizes commonsense reality in a bracketed context of performance, evokes a fantasy
whole abducted from fragments, and then returns participants to the
world of common sense—transformed, renewed, and sacralized. It
has the allegorical import, though not the narrative form, of a vision
quest or religious parable. The break with everyday reality is a journey apart into strange lands with occult practices—into the heart of
darkness—where fragments of the fantastic whirl about in the vortex
of the quester's disoriented consciousness, until, arrived at the mael-
strom's center, he loses consciousness at the very moment of the mi-
raculous, restorative vision, and then, unconscious, is cast up onto the
familiar, but forever transformed, shores of the commonplace world.
Post-modern ethnography is not a new departure, not another rupture in the form of discourse of the sort we have come to expect as the
norm of modernist esthetics' scientist emphasis on experimental
novelty, but a self-conscious return to an earlier and more powerful
notion of the ethical character of all discourse, as captured in the ancient significance of the family of terms "ethos," "ethnos," "ethics."

Because post-modern ethnography privileges "discourse" over
"text," it foregrounds dialogue as opposed to monologue, and emphasizes the cooperative and collaborative nature of the ethnographic
situation in contrast to the ideology of the transcendental observer. In
fact, it rejects the ideology of "observer-observed," there being nothing observed and no one who is observer. There is instead the mutual,
dialogical production of a discourse, of a story of sorts. We better
understand the ethnographic context as one of cooperative story
making that, in one of its ideal forms, would result in a polyphonic
text, none of whose participants would have the final word in the form
of a framing story or encompassing synthesis—a discourse on the discourse. It might be just the dialogue itself, or possibly a series of juxtaposed paratactic tellings of a shared circumstance, as in the Synoptic
Gospels, or perhaps only a sequence of separate tellings in search of
a common theme, or even a contrapuntal interweaving of tellings, or
of a theme and variations (cf. Marcus and Cushman 1982, Clifford
1983a). Unlike the traditional teller of tales or his folklorist counterpart, the ethnographer would not focus on monophonic performance
and narrativity, though neither would he necessarily exclude them if
they were appropriate in context.

I do not wish to suggest that such a text would resemble an edited
collection of authored papers, one of those authorless books pro-

duced by committee, or an accidental collage like an issue of the *American Anthropologist*. These three used together, though, do characterize a ubiquitous ethnographic form called the "newspaper." In fact, had there been a modernist movement in ethnography, it would have taken the newspaper as its literary model. The collection and the collage preserve differences of perspective, but differ on the dimension of accident vs. purpose, though we can all think of edited collections that are in fact collages, so little do their selections relate to common themes or topics that their presence in the same volume seems accidental, and we are all familiar with thematized collages like the newspaper, whose items are minimally linked by the common theme, "here are today's relevances for nobody in particular as put together by nobody in particular."

Polyphony is a means of perspectival relativity and is not just an evasion of authorial responsibility or a guilty excess of democracy, though, as Vico might say, it articulates best with that social form, and it does correspond with the realities of fieldwork in places sensitive to the issue of power as symbolized in the subject-object relationship between he who represents and she who is represented. And it is not that ethnographers have never before used the idea of authorless texts, for myths and folktales, even when related by someone, are pure examples of the form, though we must think in that case of a committee extended in time whose participants never convene to compose the work.

The point is that questions of form are not prior, the form itself should emerge out of the joint work of the ethnographer and his native partners. The emphasis is on the emergent character of textualization, textualization being just the initial interpretive move that provides a negotiated text for the reader to interpret. The hermeneutic process is not restricted to the reader's relationship to the text, but includes as well the interpretive practices of the parties to the originating dialogue. In this respect, the model of post-modern ethnography is not the newspaper but that original ethnography—the Bible (cf. Kelber 1983).

The emergent and cooperative nature of textualization also indexes a different ideological attitude toward the ethnographic other and the uses of ethnography. The history of ethnographic writing chronicles a cumulative sequence of different attitudes toward the other that implicate different uses of ethnography. In the eighteenth century, the dominant mode was "ethnography as allegory," centering around the key concept of utopianism in which the "noble savage" played his ennobling role as a therapeutic image. In the nineteenth century, the "savage" was no longer noble; she was either "fallen," in the continuing biblical allegory, or a figure of therapeutic irony—a minatory Satanic finger, or an instance of the primordial "primitive," a "living fossil" signifying past imperfection healed by time in the emerging evolutionary allegory. In the twentieth century, the "savage" was no longer even "primitive." She was only "data" and "evidence," the critical disproving instance in the positivist rhetoric of political liberalism. Later, in the structuralist and semioticist revival of seventeenth-century rationalism, he again became pure "difference," a formal pattern of collocated signs totally robbed of therapeutic significance. Now, in addition to these, each of which, or some combination of them, still feeds the imagination of some ethnographer somewhere, she has become the instrument of the ethnographer's "experience," the ethnographer having become the focus of "difference" in a perverse version of the romanticism that has always been in ethnography, no matter how desperately repressed and marginalized by the objective impulses of seekers for pure data. As in the utopianism of the eighteenth century, the other is the means of the author's alienation from his own sick culture, but the savage of the twentieth century is sick too; neutered, like the rest of us, by the dark forces of the "world system," IT has lost the healing art.

Having perceived the limiting meaning of the second member of the compound term "ethnography" ("-graphy" fr. *graphein* "to write"), some ethnographers have tamed the savage, not with the pen, but with the tape recorder, reducing him to a "straight man," as in the script of some obscure comic routine, for even as they think to have returned to "oral performance" or "dialogue," in order that the native have a place in the text, they exercise total control over her discourse and steal the only thing she has left—her voice. Others, in full and guiltless knowledge of their crime, celebrate it in "ethnopoetry," while the rest, like Sartre, their faces half-turned from the offending pen, write on in atonement—little finger of the left hand on the "erase" button, index finger on the "play" button—in the sign of the cuckold-counterfeiting voice in text.

Like Derrida, they have missed the true import of "discourse," which is "the other as us," for the point of discourse is not how to make a better representation, but how to avoid representation. In their textualization of pseudo-discourse they have accomplished a terrorist alienation more complete than that of the positivists. It may be that all textualization is alienation, but it is certainly true that non-participatory textualization is alienation—"not us"—and there is no therapy in alienation.

As the utopians knew, ethnography can perform a therapeutic purpose in evoking a participatory reality, but they were wrong in thinking that reality could be explicitly projected in text. It is this echo, then, of participatory reality that post-modern ethnography seeks to evoke by means of a participatory text in which no one has the exclusive right of synoptic transcendence. Because it is participatory and emergent, post-modern ethnography cannot have a predetermined form, for it could happen that participants might decide that textualization itself is inappropriate—as have many informants in the past, though their objections were seldom taken to be significant in themselves, being treated instead as impediments to the ethnographer's monophonic text. Whatever form the text takes—if any—it will stress sonorant relativity, not only between the text and the community of discourse of which it is a part—the usual sense of "cultural relativity"— but within the text itself as a constitutive feature of the text.

Though post-modern ethnography privileges discourse, it does not locate itself exclusively within the problematics of a single tradition of discourse, and seeks, in particular, to avoid grounding itself in the theoretical and commonsense categories of the hegemonic Western tradition. It thus relativizes discourse not just to form—that familiar perversion of the modernist; nor to authorial intention—that conceit of the romantics; nor to a foundational world beyond discourse—that desperate grasping for a separate reality of the mystic and scientist alike; nor even to history and ideology—those refuges of the hermeneuticist; nor even less to language—that hypostasized abstraction of the linguist; nor, ultimately, even to discourse—that Nietzschean playground of world-lost signifiers of the structuralist and grammatologist, but to all or none of these, for it is anarchic, though not for the sake of anarchy but because it refuses to become a fetishized object among objects—to be dismantled, compared, classified, and neutered in that parody of scientiific scrutiny known as criticism. The ethnographic text is not only not *an* object, it is not *the* object; it is instead a means, the meditative vehicle for a transcendence of time and place that is not just transcendental but a transcendental return to time and place.

Because its meaning is not in it but in an understanding, of which it is only a consumed fragment, it is no longer cursed with the task of representation. The key word in understanding this difference is "evoke," for if a discourse can be said to "evoke," then it need not represent what it evokes, though it may be a means to a representation. Since evocation is nonrepresentational, it is not to be understood as a sign function, for it is not a "symbol of," nor does it "symbolize" what it evokes. The post-modern text has moved beyond the representational function of signs and has cast off the encumbrances of the substitution of appearances, those "absences" and "differences" of the grammatologist. It is not a presence that calls into being something that was absent; it is a coming to be of what was neither there present nor absent, for we are not to understand "evocation" as linking two differences in time and place, as something that evokes and something else evoked. Evocation is a unity, a single event or process, and we must resist the temptation of grammar that would make us think that the propositional form "x evokes y" must mean that x and y are different entities linked by a third rather peculiar "process-entity" called "evoke," and that, moreover, x must precede y in time, and consequently x must be a condition of y or y a result of x. These are all illusions of grammar, which make us dismember unities into discrete entities and punctuate events. We might think to correct this situation by writing English nonlineally, as if it were Chinese, in imitation of Ernest Fenellosa and Ezra Pound: evo$\overset{x}{\underset{y}{k}}$es, but since we could still read lineally "x evokes y," and the elements x, "evokes," and y are as discrete as ever, this is no solution. Perhaps the best we can do, short of inventing some new logograph, is a Heideggerian "evoking," or better yet, be wary of the snares of grammar.

The whole point of "evoking" rather than "representing" is that it frees ethnography from *mimesis* and the inappropriate mode of scientific rhetoric that entails "objects," "facts," "descriptions," "inductions," "generalizations," "verification," "experiment," "truth," and like concepts that, except as empty invocations, have no parallels either in the experience of ethnographic fieldwork or in the writing of ethnographies. The urge to conform to the canons of scientific rhetoric has made the easy realism of natural history the dominant mode of ethnographic prose, but it has been an illusory realism, promoting, on the one hand, the absurdity of "describing" nonentities such as "culture" or "society" as if they were fully observable, though somewhat ungainly, bugs, and, on the other, the equally ridiculous behaviorist pretense of "describing" repetitive patterns of action in isolation from the discourse that actors use in constituting and situating their action, and all in simpleminded surety that the observers' grounding discourse is itself an objective form sufficient to the task of describing acts. The problem with the realism of natural history is not, as is often claimed, the complexity of the so-called object of observation, nor failure to apply sufficiently rigorous and replicable methods, nor even less the seeming intractability of the language of description. It is instead a failure of the whole visualist ideology of referential discourse, with its rhetoric of "describing," "comparing," "classifying," and "generalizing," and its presumption of representational signification. In ethnography there are no "things" there to be the objects of a description, the original appearances that the language of description "represents" as indexical objects for comparison, classification, and generalization; there is rather a discourse, and that too, no thing, despite the misguided claims of such translational models of ethnography as structuralism, ethno-science, and dialogue, which attempt to represent either native discourse or its unconscious patterns, and thus recommit the crime of natural history in the mind.

Ethnographic discourse is itself neither an object to be represented nor a representation of an object. Consequently the visualist rhetoric of representation, depending from the concreteness of the written word—of *de-scribere*—subverts the ethical purport of ethnography and can only give us as replacement a sense of incompleteness and failure, since its goals and means are always out of reach.

Ethnographic discourse is not part of a project whose aim is the creation of universal knowledge. It disowns the Mephistophelian urge to power through knowledge, for that, too, is a consequence of representation. To represent means to have a kind of magical power over appearances, to be able to bring into presence what is absent, and that is why writing, the most powerful means of representation, was called "*grammarye*," a magical act. The true historical significance of writing is that it has increased our capacity to create totalistic illusions with which to have power over things or over others as if they were things. The whole ideology of representational signification is an ideology of power. To break its spell we would have to attack writing, totalistic representational signification, and authorial authority, but all this has already been accomplished for us. Ong (1977) has made us aware of the effects of writing by reminding us of the world of oral expression that contrasts with it. Benjamin (1978) and Adorno (1977) have counterposed the ideology of the "fragment" to that of the whole, and Derrida (1974) has made the author the creature of writing rather than its creator. Post-modern ethnography builds its program not so much from their principles as from the rubble of their deconstruction.

A post-modern ethnography is fragmentary because it cannot be otherwise. Life in the field is itself fragmentary, not at all organized around familiar ethnological categories such as kinship, economy, and religion, and except for unusual informants like the Dogon sage Ogotemmêli, the natives seem to lack communicable visions of a shared, integrated whole; nor do particular experiences present themselves, even to the most hardened sociologist, as conveniently labeled synecdoches, microcosms, or allegories of wholes, cultural or theoretical. At best, we make do with a collection of indexical anecdotes or telling particulars with which to portend that larger unity beyond explicit textualization. It is not just that we cannot see the forest for the trees, but that we have come to feel that there are no forests where the trees are too far apart, just as patches make quilts only if the spaces between them are small enough.

We confirm in our ethnographies our consciousness of the fragmentary nature of the post-modern world, for nothing so well defines our world as the absence of a synthesizing allegory, or perhaps it is only a paralysis of choice brought on by our knowledge of the inexhaustible supply of such allegories that makes us refuse the moment of aesthetic totalization, the story of stories, the hypostatized whole.

But there are other reasons, too. We know that these textual transcendentals, these invocations of holism, of functionally integrated systems are literary tropes, the vehicles that carry imagination from the part to the whole, the concrete to the abstract, and knowing them for what they are, whether mechanismic or organismic, makes us suspect the rational order they promise.

More important than these, though, is the idea that the transcendental transit, the holistic moment is neither textually determined nor the exclusive right of the author, being instead the functional interaction of text-author-reader. It is not some secret hidden in the text, or between texts; nor in the mind of the author and only poorly expressed/repressed by him; nor in the reader's interpretation, no matter what his critical persuasion—if any. It is not the negative dialectics of Theodor Adorno, for its paratactic oppositions are participatory functions rather than textual forms. They derive from dialogue rather than the monophonic internal dialectic of the author with his text. Even though Adorno argues that the essay, by means of negative dialectics, aims at the liquidation of all viewpoints, it cannot achieve this goal so long as it is monophonic, projected from the viewpoint of a single author. It expresses only the cognitive utopia of the author (Kauffmann 1981 : 343–53). Unlike negative dialectics, the oppositions of dialogue need not be held in unresolved suspension without the possibility of transcendence, but like negative dialectics, post-modern ethnography does not practice synthesis within the text. The synoptic transit is a nonsynthetic transcendence that is evoked by, not immanent in, the text. The text has the paradoxical capacity to evoke transcendence without synthesis, without creating within itself formal devices and conceptual strategies of transcendental order. In common with Adorno's program, it avoids any supposition of a harmony between the logical-conceptual order of the text and the order of things, and it attempts to eliminate the subject-object nexus by refusing the possibility of their separation or of the dominance of one over the other in the form of the text-as-mirror-of-thought. It accomplishes a cognitive utopia not of the author's subjectivity or of the reader's, but of the author-text-reader, an emergent mind that has no individual locus, being instead an infinity of possible loci.

Here, then, is a new kind of holism, one that is emergent rather than given, and one that emerges through the reflexivity of text-author-reader and privileges no member of this trinity as the exclusive locus or means of the whole. Moreover, this emergent whole is neither a theoretical object nor an object of theoretical knowledge, and is consequently neither evoked by explicit methods nor the derivational source of practices. It does not motivate or enable practice in the expected manner of the usual theory-practice correlation. It is not, in other words, a dialectical synthesis of the manifold of impressions that neutralizes their differences in a higher-order pattern of their same type. It is neither an abstract "thing" nor an abstraction from "things," and is thus not the product of an inference whose line of development could be traced step-by-step from the concrete particulars of its origins, through transformations, to its abstract and universal terminus.

It goes against the grain of induction, deduction, synthesis, and the whole movement to "symbol," for its mode of inference is abductive, and the elements it conjoins, though used up in the fantasy, do not deliver up their separateness in the resolution of some organic totality. In Sir William Hamilton's way of speaking, they are similar to correlatives such as part-whole and cause-effect, the one unthinkable without the other, a conjunction of terms that mutually explicate but do not determine each other or induce a synthetic reduction. They express the "Law of the Conditioned": "All positive thought lies between two extremes, neither of which we can conceive as possible, and yet as mutual contradictories, the one or the other we must recognize as necessary" (1863:211).

Just as the metaphor of the upward spiral into the Platonic "other of unity," the "light of reason," the "higher, rational" realm of conscious thought and faceless abstraction—into the future, mind excarnate—is inappropriate, so, too, is the opposite metaphor of descent "beneath the surface" into the Plutonic "other of separation," the "lower" gyre of the unconscious, where dwell in mutual antagonism the dark forces of the irrational animal and the demonic rational powers of "underlying structures"—into the past, in memory, the mind carnal and incarnate.

The ancient metaphor of thought as movement, a species of motion, bequeathed to us by Aristotle, is in question here, for it is the simultaneous juxtaposition of these contrary motions and their mutually neutralizing conflict that enables the whole I seek to evoke, that stillness at the center where there is neither higher nor lower, forward

nor back, past nor future, when space and time cancel each other out
in that familiar fantasy we all know as the everyday, commonplace
world, that breach in time, that ever present, never present simultaneity of reality and fantasy that is the return to the commonsense
world, floating, like the Lord Brahmā, motionless in the surfaceless
void, all potentiality suspended within us in perfect realization, a return that is not a climax, terminus, stable image, or homeostatic equi-
librium, but a reduction of tension as the moment of transcendence
simultaneously approaches, draws near, and departs without having
arrived. And that is why the post-modern ethnography is an occult
document; it is an enigmatic, paradoxical, and esoteric conjunction of
reality and fantasy that evokes the constructed simultaneity we know
as naive realism. It conjoins reality and fantasy, for it speaks of the
occult in the language of naive realism and of the everyday in occult
language, and makes the reason of the one the reasonableness of the
other. It is a fantasy reality of a reality fantasy whose aim is to evoke in
reader and writer alike some intimation of a possible world already
given to us in fantasy and commonsense, those foundations of our
knowledge that cannot themselves be the objects of our knowledge,
"for as by them we know all else, by nought else can they be known.
We know them indeed, but only in the fact that with them and through
them we know" (Hamilton 1863:255).

Post-modern ethnography is a return to the idea of aesthetic
integration as therapy once captured in the sense of Proto-Indo-
European *ar- ("way of being," "orderly and harmonious arrangement of the parts of a whole"), from which have come English "art,"
"rite," and "ritual," that family of concepts so closely connected with
the idea of restorative harmony, of "therapy" in its original sense of
"ritual substitute" (cf. Hittite tarpan-alli), and with the poet as therá-
pon, "attendant of the Muse." Post-modern ethnography is an object
of meditation that provokes a rupture with the commonsense world
and evokes an aesthetic integration whose therapeutic effect is worked
out in the restoration of the commonsense world. Unlike science, it is
not an instrument of immortality, for it does not hold out the false
hope of a permanent, utopian transcendence, which can only be
achieved by devaluing and falsifying the commonsense world and
thereby creating in us a sense of permanent alienation from everyday
life as we live in constant expectation of the messianic deliverance
from it that can never come, or comes only with death, and science
thus encourages us to die too soon. Instead, it departs from the commonsense world only in order to reconfirm it and to return us to it
renewed and mindful of our renewal.

Because the post-modern world is a post-scientific world without the illusion of a transcendental, neither transcendental science nor transcendental religion can be at home in it, for that which is inhospitable to the transcendence by abstraction of the one must also be unfriendly to the similar character of the other. Neither the scientific illusion of reality nor the religious reality of illusion is congruent with the reality of fantasy in the fantasy reality of the post-modern world. Post-modern ethnography captures this mood of the post-modern world, for it, too, does not move toward abstraction, away from life, but back to experience. It aims not to foster the growth of knowledge but to restructure experience; not to understand objective reality, for that is already established by common sense, nor to explain how we understand, for that is impossible, but to reassimilate, to reintegrate the self in society and to restructure the conduct of everyday life.

Save in the commonsense world, discourse cannot autonomously determine its rhetorical effects. Neither its form nor its authorial intention determine how it will be understood, for it is impossible in text or speech to eliminate ambiguity and to structure totally for all time the auditor's purposes and interests. Her reading and listening are as much expressions of her intentions and will as is the author's writing and speaking. Not even the conjunction and consequence of their joint interests and purposes in a shared interpretation deny ambiguity and affirm determinative meaning; it only expresses a temporary sufficiency for present purposes and conditions that will be insufficient for other purposes and different conditions. Even less can the text, by means of its form, dictate its interpretation, for it cannot control the powers of its readers. They respond to a text out of various states of ignorance, irreceptivity, disbelief, and hypersensitivity to form. They are immune in the first extreme to any nuance of form, reading through it, not by means of it, unconscious of it except perhaps in confusion or annoyance. In the second extreme a paranoid conviction of authorial deceit feeds a search for hidden meanings— and the finding of them; or, in one with heightened sensibility to the necessary structures of thought and language, the search is less for things hidden by the author than for things hidden from the author by the structure of language and thought. Of these latter two, the one thinks the author a charlatan, the other a dupe, but to both the text is a coded secret hiding a necessary inner meaning irresponsive to those obscuring or concealing appearances of outer contingencies that implicate a community of belief. Because the text can eliminate neither ambiguity nor the subjectivity of its authors and readers, it is bound to be misread, so much so that we might conclude, in a parody of Bloom, that the meaning of the text is the sum of its misreadings.

Such may indeed be the fate of the text, but the meaning of this inherent failure to control ambiguity and subjectivity is that it provides good reason for rejecting the model of scientific rhetoric, that Cartesian pretense that ideas are effable in clear, unambiguous, objective, and logical expression, for the inner form of a text is not logical, except in parody, but paradoxical and enigmatic, not so much ineffable, as over-effable, illimitably effable, possessing a surplus of effability that must always exceed the means of its effability, so that the infinite possibility of its effability becomes the condition of its ineffability, and the interpretation of a text must struggle against this surplus of meaning, not with its obscurity or poverty.

For post-modern ethnography the implication is, if not clear, at least apparent that its text will be projected neither in the form of this inner paradox nor in the form of a deceptive outer logic, but as the tension between them, neither denying ambiguity nor endorsing it, neither subverting subjectivity nor denying objectivity, expressing instead their interaction in the subjective creation of ambiguous objectivities that enable unambiguous subjectivity. The ethnographic text will thus achieve its purposes not by revealing them, but by making purposes possible. It will be a text of the physical, the spoken, and the performed, an evocation of quotidian experience, a palpable reality that uses everyday speech to suggest what is ineffable, not through abstraction, but by means of the concrete. It will be a text to read not with the eyes alone, but with the ears in order to hear "the voices of the pages" (St. Bernard, quoted in Stock 1983:408).

Other Voices: Supplement

Yes, but what you really mean is don't you think that how is it possible that what you're trying to say is . . .

1. Consensus in form and content belong to the other kind of discourse, and whose ethics is not the question. If one is deaf to the tune one need not dance to it, and besides there is no presentation of an ethic, only the possibility of its influence.

2. No, there is no instance of a post-modern ethnography, even though all ethnography is post-modern in effect, nor is one likely, though some recent writing has the right spirit, for example Crapanzano (1980), Tedlock (1983) and Majnep and Bulmer (1977). The point anyway is not how to create a post-modern ethnography or what form it ought to take. The point is that it might take any form but never be completely realized. Every attempt will always be incomplete, insufficient, lacking in some way, but this is not a defect since it is the means that enables transcendence. Transcendence comes from imperfection not from perfection.

3. No, it is not a question of form, of a manner of writing as such, and even though I speak of polyphony and perspectival relativity, fragmentation, and so on, these are not necessary components of form. There is here no aesthetic of form. Lyotard (1979:80) notes two possibilities. Let us call one "writing at the limit," where we seek to push against limits imposed by conventions of syntax, meaning, and genre, and let us call the other "writing within the limit," writing so clear and commonsensical that its very reasonableness evokes what is beyond reason. In both cases the writing is anti-genre, anti-form.

4. Perspective is the wrong metaphor. It conjures images appropriate to descriptive writing, writing in thought pictures or hieroglyphs. It is not a business of "seeing" at all, for that is the metaphor of science, nor is it a "doing"; that is the metaphor of politics. There is no attempt to go beyond language by means of vision and action. Polyphony is a better metaphor because it evokes sound and hearing and simultaneity and harmony, not pictures and seeing and sequence and line. Prose accomplishes at most only a kind of sequential polyphony until the reader adds his voice to it.

5. Yes, it is a form of realism; it describes no objects and makes no break between describing and what is being described. It does not describe, for there is nothing it could describe. So much for the idea of ethnography as a "description of reality." Descriptions of reality are only imitations of reality. Their mode is *mimetic*, but their *mimesis* creates only illusions of reality, as in the fictional realities of science. That is the price that must be paid for making language do the work of the eyes.

6. Perception has nothing to do with it. An ethnography is no account of a rationalized movement from percept to concept. It begins and ends in concepts. There is no origin in perception, no priority to vision, and no data of observation.

7. No, it is not surrealism. It is the realism of the commonsense world, which is only surreal in the fictions of science and in the science of fiction. Whose commonsense? Why, anybody's, which is not to say everybody's, as Thomas Reid (1895:692−701) did.

8. Translation? Not if we think of it as fording a stream that separates one text from another and changing languages in midstream. This is *mimesis* of language, one language copying another, which never makes a copy anyway, but a more or less contorted original. Though this form of *mimesis* offends less than that of vision, it is still a silly idea to suppose that one might render the meanings of another folk in terms already known to us just as if

the others had never been there at all. For it is not for us to know the meaning for them unless it is already known to us both, and thus needs no translation, but only a kind of reminding. So, there is no originating text to play the part of the missing object. No object of any kind precedes and constrains the ethnography. It creates its own objects in its unfolding and the reader supplies the rest.

9. But what of the experience of the ethnographer? Surely that amounts to something prior since the ethnography is at the very least a record of that experience. No, it is not a record of experience at all; it is the means of experience. That experience became experience only in the writing of the ethnography. Before that it was only a disconnected array of chance happenings. No experience preceded the ethnography. The experience was the ethnography. Experience is no more an object independent of the ethnography than all the others—behavior, meanings, texts, and so on.

10. No origin outside the text—just literature then, or an odd kind of lit. crit.? Yes, literature, but not in the sense of total self-reflexivity, of literature about itself and nothing else. An ethnography does not invite movement from text to text alone. It is not just a collection of clever allusions to other texts, though it can obviously do that as well as any other text. It evokes what can never be put into a text by any writer, and that is the common-sense understanding of the reader. An ethnography is not the author's cognitive utopia since no author can fully control the reader's response. Her text depends on the reader's supplementation. The incompleteness of the text implicates the work of the reader, and his work derives as much, if not more, from the oral world of everyday expression and commonsense understanding as it does from the world of text.

11. Post-modern ethnography denies the illusion of a self-perfecting discourse. No corrective movements from text to object and back again in the manner of empiricism, and no supplemental, self-reflexive movements from flawed sublation to scatheless transcendent mark its course. Each text retains a separate sense within the discourse without being subordinated to a grand evolutionary myth of ultimate perfectibility. Each text is akin to a Leibnizian monad, perfect in its imperfectibility.

Post-modern ethnography foregoes the tale of the past as error and denies the myth of the future as utopia. No one believes anymore in the unconditioned future. The past at least has the advantage of having been. Modernism, like Christianity, taught us to value postponement, to look ahead to a scientific utopia, to devalue the past, and negate the present. In contrast, the post-modern world is in a sense timeless; past, present, and future co-exist in all discourse, and so we may say with equal sense that all repetitions are fictive and all differences are illusions. We may say that conservation is not of objects but of time. Objects change, but time does not, which makes it reasonable for us to say that when we see the same object twice it is not the same. No thing is the same, just time, which is no thing and not perceivable. To speak in the language of identities, to say "I saw the same thing," or "it has changed," or "it has moved" requires a changed time and change-less objects and subjects, but a discourse can make all three—time, subject, and object—what it will. It is not enslaved by the hege-mony of the noun, by the perception of changeless objects by changeless subjects.

Dispersed authorship mirrors this dispersed self, this incon-stant subject, just as the incompleteness of the text mirrors the dissolution of the object, but post-modern ethnography is not thereby anonymous in the manner of bureaucratic discourse or of a television serial. It is neither the *DSM III* (*Diagnostic and Statis-tical Manual*), that terrorist bludgeon of the psychiatrist, the face-less ponderosity of "the manic-depressive personality is character-ized by," nor the exploitative pseudo-narrative of "Dallas," with its insidious hiss in the ears of the poor of: "See, the rich are rich but miserable."

An ethnography is a fantasy, but it is not, like these, a fiction, for the idea of fiction entails a locus of judgment outside the fic-tion, whereas an ethnography weaves a locus of judgment within itself, and that locus, that evocation of reality, is also a fantasy. It is not a reality fantasy like "Dallas," nor a fantasy reality like the *DSM III*; it is a reality fantasy of a fantasy reality. That is to say, it is realism, the evocation of a possible world of reality already known to us in fantasy.

12. The critical function of ethnography derives from the fact that it makes its own contextual grounding part of the ques-tion and not from hawking pictures of alternative ways of life as instruments of utopian reform.

13. A conflicted form? Yes, full of unresolved conflict, but not agonistic, not violent like science nor an instrument of violence like politics. It has none of the rape of the scientist's "looking at," or of the macho braggadocio of "let's see," or of the deployment of armies of argument, or of the subjugation of the weak in the poli-tician's "doing to." Seeking neither the reason that makes power nor the power that makes reason, it founds in the receptivity of

"listening to" and in the mutuality of "talking with." It takes its metaphor from another part of the sensorium and replaces the monologue of the bullhorn with dialogue.

14. I call ethnography a meditative vehicle because we come to it neither as to a map of knowledge nor as a guide to action, nor even for entertainment. We come to it as the start of a different kind of journey.

The paper given at the Santa Fe seminar on the Making of Ethnographic Texts has been revised and "sandwiched" between the "Context" and "Supplement" appearing here. Both "Context" and "Supplement" were written after the seminar and are as much dialogical responses to seminar papers and discussion as they are the working out of themes and conflicts in these parerga to *The Said and the Unsaid* (Tyler 1978).

TALAL ASAD

The Concept of Cultural Translation in British Social Anthropology

Introduction

All anthropologists are familiar with E. B. Tylor's famous definition of culture: "Culture or Civilization, taken in its wide ethnographic sense, is that complex whole which includes knowledge, belief, art, morals, law, custom, and any other capabilities and habits acquired by man as a member of society." It would be interesting to trace how and when this notion of culture, with its enumeration of "capabilities and habits" and its emphasis on what Linton called *social heredity* (focusing on the process of learning), was transformed into the notion of a *text*—that is, into something resembling an inscribed discourse. One obvious clue to this change is to be found in the way that a notion of *language* as the precondition of historical continuity and social learning ("cultivation") came to dominate the perspective of social anthropologists. In a general way, of course, such an interest in language predates Tylor, but in the nineteenth and early twentieth centuries it tended to be central to varieties of nationalist literary theory and education (cf. Eagleton 1983:ch. 2) rather than to the other human sciences. When and in what ways did it become crucial for British social anthropology? I do not intend to attempt such a history here, but merely to remind ourselves that the phrase "the translation of cultures," which increasingly since the 1950s has become an almost banal description of the distinctive task of social anthropology, was not always so much in evidence. I want to stress that this apparent shift is not identical with the old pre-Functionalism/Functionalism periodization. Nor is it simply a matter of a direct interest in language and meaning that was previously lacking (Crick 1976). Bronislaw Malinowski, one of the founders of the so-called Functionalist school, wrote much on "primitive language" and collected enormous quantities of linguistic material (proverbs, kinship terminology, magical spells, and so on) for anthropological analysis. But he never thought of his work in terms of the translation of cultures.

Godfrey Lienhardt's paper "Modes of Thought" (1954) is possibly one of the earliest—certainly one of the most subtle—examples of the use of this notion of translation explicitly to describe a central task of social anthropology. "The problem of describing to others how members of a remote tribe think then begins to appear largely as one of translation, of making the coherence primitive thought has in the languages it really lives in, as clear as possible in our own" (97). This statement is quoted and criticized in the article by Ernest Gellner that I analyze in the next section, and I shall return to it in the context of Gellner's argument. Here I draw attention briefly to Lienhardt's use of the word "translation" to refer not to linguistic matter per se, but to "modes of thought" that are embodied in such matter. It may not be without significance, incidentally, that Lienhardt has a background in English literature, that he was a pupil of F. R. Leavis's at Cambridge before he became a pupil and collaborator of E. E. Evans-Pritchard's at Oxford.

Oxford is, of course, famous as the anthropological center in Britain most self-conscious about its concern with "the translation of cultures." The best-known introductory textbook to emerge from that center, John Beattie's *Other Cultures* (1964), emphasized the centrality of the "problem of translation" for social anthropology and distinguished (but did not separate) "culture" from "language" in a way that was becoming familiar to anthropologists—though not necessarily therefore entirely clear (see pp. 89–90).

It is interesting to find Edmund Leach, who has never been associated with Oxford, employing the same notion in his conclusion to a historical sketch of social anthropology a decade later:

Let me recapitulate. We started by emphasizing how different are "the others"—and made them not only different but remote and inferior. Sentimentally we then took the opposite track and argued that all human beings are alike; we can understand Trobrianders or the Barotse because their motivations are just the same as our own; but that didn't work either, "the others" remained obstinately other. But now we have come to see that the essential problem is one of translation. The linguists have shown us that all translation is difficult, and that perfect translation is usually impossible. And yet we know that for practical purposes a tolerably satisfactory translation is always possible even when the original "text" is highly abstruse. Languages are different but not so different as all that. Looked at in this way social anthropologists are engaged in establishing a methodology for the translation of cultural language. (Leach 1973:772)

Even Max Gluckman (1973:905), responding shortly afterward to Leach, accepts the centrality of "cultural translation," while proposing a very different genealogy for that anthropological practice.

Yet despite the general agreement with which this notion has been accepted as part of the self-definition of British social anthropology, it has received little systematic examination from within the profession. One partial exception is Rodney Needham's *Belief, Language, and Experience* (1972). This is a complex, scholarly work that deserves extended treatment. Here, however, I wish to concentrate on a shorter text, Ernest Gellner's "Concepts and Society," which appears to be fairly widely used in undergraduate courses at British universities and is still available in several popular collections. I propose, therefore, to devote the next section to a detailed examination of that essay and then to take up some points that emerge from my discussion in the sections that follow.

A Theoretical Text

Gellner's "Concepts and Society" is concerned with the way in which Functionalist anthropologists deal with problems of interpreting and translating the discourse of alien societies. His basic argument is that (a) contemporary anthropologists insist on interpreting exotic concepts and beliefs within a social context, but that (b) in doing so they ensure that apparently absurd or incoherent assertions are always given an acceptable meaning, and that (c) while the contextual method of interpretation is in principle valid, the "excessive charity" that usually goes with it is not. The paper contains several diagrams intended to fix and clarify the relevant cultural processes visually.

Gellner introduces the problem of interpretation by reference to Kurt Samuelsson's *Religion and Economic Action* (1961), which is an economic historian's attack on the Weberian Protestant-ethic thesis. Samuelsson takes issue with the fact that Weber and his supporters have reinterpreted religious texts in a way that enables them to extract meanings that confirm the thesis. Gellner presents this example merely to bring out more sharply the contrasting position of the Functionalist anthropologist:

I am not concerned, nor competent, to argue whether Samuelsson's employment, in this particular case, of his tacit principle that one must not reinterpret the assertions one actually finds, is valid. What is relevant here is that if such a principle is made explicit and generalized, it would make nonsense of most sociological studies of the relationship of belief and conduct. We shall find anthropologists driven to employ the very opposite principle, the insistence rather than refusal of contextual re-interpretation. (20)

But this modest disclaimer of competence allows too many interesting questions to drift by. To begin with, it calls for no great competence to note that Samuelsson does not hold to the principle that one must *never* reinterpret. Nor does he insist that there is *never* a significant connection between a religious text and its social context, but only that the conclusion the Weber thesis seeks to make cannot be established. (See, e.g., Samuelsson 1961:69.) There is, furthermore, a real contrast that Gellner might have picked up between the Samuelsson example and the typical anthropologist's predicament. For economic historians and sociologists involved in the Weber debate, historical texts are a primary datum in relation to which the social contexts must be reconstructed. The anthropological fieldworker begins with a social situation within which something is said, and it is the cultural significance of these enunciations that must be reconstructed. This is not to say, of course, that the historian can ever approach his archival material without some conception of its historical context, or that the fieldworker can define the social situation independently of what was said within it. The contrast, such as it is, is one of orientation, which follows from the fact that the historian is *given a text* and the ethnographer has *to construct one*.

Instead of investigating this important contrast, Gellner rushes along to define and commend what he calls "moderate Functionalism" as a method, which

consists of the insistence on the fact that concepts and beliefs do not exist in isolation, in texts or in individual minds, but in the life of men and societies. The activities and institutions, in the context of which a word or phrase or set of phrases is used, must be known before that word or those phrases can be understood, before we can really speak of a *concept* or a *belief*. (22)

This is well put, and, even if it has been said before, it is worth restating. At this point the reader might expect a discussion of the different ways in which language is encountered by the ethnographer in the field, how utterances are produced, verbal meanings organized, rhetorical effects attained, and culturally appropriate responses elicited. After all, Wittgenstein had already sensitized British philosophers to the complexity of language-in-use, and J. L. Austin had set up distinctions between the different levels of speech production and reception in a way that foreshadowed what anthropologists would later call the ethnography of speaking. But Gellner had previously rejected the suggestion that this philosophical movement had anything of value to teach (see his polemic in *Words and Things* 1959), and like other critics, he always insisted that its concern with understanding everyday language was merely a disguise for defending established ways of speaking about the world, for denying that it was possible for such speech-ways to be illogical or absurd. Gellner has always been determined to maintain the distinction between defending and explaining "concepts and beliefs" and to warn against the kind of anthropological translation that rules out a priori the critical distance necessary for explaining how concepts actually function, for "to understand the *working* of the concepts of a society," he writes, "is to understand its institutions" (p. 18; see also note 1 on the same page).

This is why Gellner's brief statement about moderate Functionalism quoted above leads him immediately to a discussion of Durkheim's *Elementary Forms of the Religious Life,* which, besides being "one of the fountainheads of Functionalism in general" (22), is concerned to explain rather than to defend concepts—to explain, more precisely, "the compulsive nature of our categorial concepts" (22) in terms of certain collective processes. Thus:

Our contemporary invocations of the functional, social-context approach to the study and interpretation of concepts is in various ways very different from Durkheim's. Durkheim was not so much concerned to defend the concepts of primitive societies: in their setting, they did not need a defence, and in the setting of modern and changing societies he was not anxious to defend what was archaic, nor loath to suggest that some intellectual luggage might well be archaic. He was really concerned to explain the compulsiveness of what in practice did not seem to need any defence (and in so doing, he claimed he was solving the problem of knowledge whose solution had in his view evaded Kant and others, and to be solving it without falling into either empiricism or apriorism). Whether he was successful I do not propose to discuss: for a variety of reasons it seems to me that he was not. (23)

It is clear that Gellner has recognized the basic project of *Elementary Forms*—namely, its attempt to explain the compulsive nature of socially defined concepts—but he moves too hastily from a consideration of what might be involved in such a problem to a dismissal of Durkheim's attempt at explanation. The possibility that a priori *denunciation* may not further the purposes of explanation any better than *defense* does not seem to be envisaged in "Concepts and Society." Instead, the reader is reminded, by way of quotation from Lienhardt, that the contemporary anthropologist typically "appears to make it a condition of a good translation that it conveys the coherence which he assumes is there to be found in primitive thought" (26). So we have here what I think is a misleading contrast—Durkheim's attempt to explain versus the contemporary anthropologist's attempt to defend. I shall return to this point later, but here I want to insist that to argue for a form of coherence by which a discourse is held together is not ipso facto to justify or defend that discourse; it is merely to take an essential step in the problem of explaining its *compulsiveness*. Anyone familiar with psychoanalysis would take this point quite easily. We might put it another way: the criterion of abstract "coherence" or "logicality" (Gellner tends to use these and other terms interchangeably) is not always, and in every case, decisive for accepting or rejecting discourse. This is because, as Gellner himself correctly observes, "Language functions in a variety of ways other than 'referring to objects'" (25). Not every utterance is an *assertion*. There are many things that language-in-use does, *and is intended to do*, which explains why we may respond positively to discourse that may seem inadequate from a narrow "logical" point of view. The functions of a particular language, the intentions of a particular discourse, are of course part of what every competent ethnographer tries to grasp before he can attempt an adequate translation into his own language.

Gellner does seem half-aware of this point, but quickly brushes it aside in his eagerness to display to Functionalist anthropologists their "excessive charity" in cultural translation.

The situation, facing a social anthropologist who wishes to interpret a concept, assertion or doctrine in an alien culture, is basically simple. He is, say, faced with an assertion S in the local language. He has at his disposal the large or infinite set of possible sentences in his own language. . . .

He may not be wholly happy about this situation, but he cannot avoid it. There is no third language which could mediate between the native language and his own, in which equivalences could be stated and which would avoid the pitfalls arising from the fact that his own language has its own way of handling the world, which may not be those of the native language studied, and which consequently are liable to distort that which is being translated.

Naively, people sometimes think that *reality* itself could be this kind of mediator and "third language." . . . For a variety of powerful reasons, this is of course no good. (24–25)

Again, this sensible statement might seem to some readers to support the demand that the ethnographer must try to reconstruct the various ways in which the "native language" handles the world, conveys information, and constitutes experience, before translating an alien discourse into the language of his ethnographic text. But Gellner's account proceeds in a different, and very dubious, direction.

Having located an equivalent English sentence, he continues, the anthropologist notices that it inevitably carries a value connotation—that it is, in other words, either Good or Bad. "I do not say 'true' or 'false', for this only arises with regard to some types of assertion. With regard to others, other dichotomies, such as 'meaningful' and 'absurd' or 'sensible' or 'silly' might apply. I deliberately use the 'Good' and 'Bad' so as to cover all such possible polar alternatives, whichever might best apply to the equivalent of S" (27).

Have we not got here some very curious assumptions, which no practiced translator would ever make? The first is that evaluative discrimination is always a matter of choosing between polar alternatives, and second, that evaluative distinctions are finally reducible to "Good" and "Bad." Clearly neither of these assumptions is acceptable when stated as a general rule. And then there is the suggestion that the translator's task necessarily involves matching sentence for sentence. But if the skilled translator looks first for any principle of coherence in the discourse to be translated, and then tries to reproduce that coherence as nearly as he can in his own language, there cannot be a general rule as to what units the translator will employ—sentences, paragraphs, or even larger units of discourse. To turn my point around: the appropriateness of the unit employed itself depends on the principle of coherence.

But Gellner's parable of the anthropologist-translator requires the assumption that it is sentences that the latter matches, because that makes it easier to display how the sin of excessive charity occurs. Having made an initial equivalence between a sentence in the local language and one in his own, the anthropologist notices that the English sentence carries a "Bad" impression. This worries the anthropologist because, so runs Gellner's parable, an ethnographic account giving such an impression might be thought to be disparaging the natives he has studied, and to disparage other cultures is a sign of ethnocentrism, and ethnocentrism in turn is a symptom of poor anthropology according to the doctrines of Functionalist anthropology. Functionalist method requires that sentences always be evaluated in terms of their own social context. So the worried anthropologist reinterprets the original sentence, with a more flexible and careful use of the contextual method, in order to produce a "Good" translation.

The sin of excessive charity, and the contextual method itself, are together linked, Gellner writes, to the relativistic-functionalist view of thought that goes back to the Enlightenment:

The (unresolved) dilemma, which the thought of the Enlightenment faced, was between a relativistic-functionalist view of thought, and the absolutist claims of enlightened Reason. Viewing man as part of nature, as enlightened Reason requires, it wished to see his cognitive and evaluative activities as parts of nature too, and hence as varying, legitimately, from organism to organism and context to context. (This is the relativistic-functionalist view.) But at the same time in recommending life according to Reason and Nature, it wished at the very least to exempt this view itself (and, in practice, some others) from such a relativism. (31)

Typically, Gellner's philosophical formulation presents this "unresolved dilemma" as an abstract opposition between two concepts—"a relativistic-functionalist view of thought" and "the absolutist claims of enlightened Reason." But how do these two "concepts" work as "correlates of . . . the institutions of [Western] society"? (cf. Gellner, p. 18). It would not be difficult to argue that the claims of "enlightened Reason" are *materially* more successful in Third World countries than many relativistic views, that they have exerted greater *authority* than the latter in the development of industrial economies and the formation of nation states. We shall have occasion to discuss this further when examining translation as a process of power. The point is that "the absolutist claims of enlightened Reason" are in effect *an institutionalized force*, and that as such it is by definition committed to *advancing* into and appropriating alien territory, and that its opponents (whether explicitly relativistic or not) are by definition *defensive*. Thus when Gellner continues on the same page to characterize this abstract dilemma in the attitudes of anthropologists, he fails to consider what "cultural translation" might involve when it is considered as institutionalized *practice* given the wider relationship of unequal societies. For it is not the abstract logic of what individual Western anthropologists *say* in their ethnographies, but the concrete logic of what their countries (and perhaps they themselves) *do* in their relations with the Third World that should form the starting point for this particular discussion. The dilemmas of "relativism" appear differently depending on whether we think of abstracted understanding or of historically situated practices.

However, Gellner says he is not in principle against anthropological relativism. "My main point about tolerance-engendering contextual interpretation," he writes, "is that it calls for caution" (32). But why such caution is reserved for "tolerance-engendering" as opposed to *in*tolerance-engendering contextual interpretations is not explained. After all, Gellner insisted earlier that all translated sentences are bound to be received either as "Good" or as "Bad." Why should we be suspicious only of those that appear "Good"? If "it is the *prior* determination that S, the indigenous affirmation, be interpreted favourably, which determines just how much context will be taken into consideration" (33), can we perhaps escape this vicious circularity by adopting an *unsympathetic* attitude? Gellner does not address himself directly to this possibility here, but one must assume that it cannot be a solution, especially in view of the claim that "there is nothing [*sic*] in the nature of things or societies to dictate visibly just how much context is relevant to any given utterance, or how the context should be described" (33).

Yet can this last remark be meant seriously? *Nothing*?! How, then, is communication even between individuals in the same society ever

possible? Why does one ever say to foreigners that they have misunderstood something they heard or saw? Does social learning produce no skills in the discrimination of relevant contexts? The answers
to these questions should be obvious, and they are connected with the
fact that the anthropologist's translation is not merely a matter of
matching sentences in the abstract, but of *learning to live another form of
life* and to speak another kind of language. Which contexts are relevant in different discursive events is something one learns in the
course of living, and even though it is often very difficult to verbalize
that knowledge, it is still knowledge about something "in the nature of
society," about some aspect of living, that indicates (although it does
not "dictate") just how much context is relevant to any given utterance. The point, of course, is not that the ethnographer cannot know
what context is appropriate for giving sense to typical statements, or
that he is induced to be more charitable than he should be in translating them, but that his attempts at translation may meet with problems
rooted in the linguistic materials he works with *and* the social conditions he works in—both in the field and in his own society. More on
this later.

The latter half of Gellner's essay is devoted to examples from ethnographic studies in order to display, first, excessive charity in translation, and then, the explanatory advantages of taking a *critical* look at
the logic of alien religious discourse.

The first set of examples comes from Evans-Pritchard's *Nuer Religion* (1956), in which odd-sounding initial translations of Nuer religious discourse, such as the notorious statement that "a twin is a bird,"
are reinterpreted. "This kind of statement," Gellner observes,
"appears to be in conflict with the principle of identity or non-
contradiction, or with common sense, or with manifest observable
fact: human twins are *not* birds, and vice versa" (34). According to
Gellner, Evans-Pritchard's reinterpretation absolves Nuer thought
from the charge of "pre-logical mentality" by an arbitrary use of the
contextual method. The apparent absurdity is reinterpreted to deny
that Nuer beliefs conflict with manifest fact by relating the meaning of
the "absurd" statement to "logical" behavior. Gellner indicates how
this is done by quoting (with the deliberate omission of one significant
sentence) from Evans-Pritchard:

no contradiction is involved in the statement which, on the contrary, appears
quite sensible and even true, to one who presents the idea to himself in the
Nuer language and within their system of religious thought. [He does not
then take their statements about twins any more literally than they make and
understand them themselves.] *They are not saying that a twin has a beak, feathers,
and so forth. Nor in their everyday relations as twins do Nuers speak of them as birds or*

act towards them as though they were birds. (35. Sentence in brackets omitted by
Gellner; emphasis supplied by Gellner.)

At this point Gellner breaks off the quotation and interjects in
mock despair: "But what, then, *would* count as pre-logical thought?
Only, presumably, the behaviour of a totally demented person, suffering from permanent hallucinations, who *would* treat something which
is perceptibly a human being as though it had all the attributes of a
bird" (35). So eager is Gellner to nail utterances that must count as
expressions of "pre-logical thought" (why *is* he so eager?) that he does
not pause to consider carefully what Evans-Pritchard is trying to
do. In fact, Evans-Pritchard devotes several pages to explaining this
strange sentence. It is plain that he is concerned to *explain* (in terms of
Nuer social life), not to *justify* (in terms of Western commonsense, or
Western values). The aim of this kind of exegesis is certainly not to
persuade Western readers to adopt Nuer religious practices. Nor does
it rule out the possibility that individual speakers make mistakes or
utter absurdities in their religious discourse when employing their
traditional ways of thinking. It is not clear, therefore, why Gellner
should point to this example from *Nuer Religion* to substantiate his
charge of excessive charity on the part of Functionalist anthropologists. Evans-Pritchard is trying to explain the coherence that gives
Nuer religious discourse its sense, not to defend that sense as having a
universal status—after all, Evans-Pritchard himself was a Catholic
both before and after his monograph on Nuer religion was written.

Now whether Evans-Pritchard succeeds in explaining the basic coherence of Nuer religious discourse is, of course, another question.
Several British anthropologists—for example, Raymond Firth (1966)
—(though not, to my knowledge, any Nuer themselves) have disputed
aspects of Evans-Pritchard's interpretation. But such disagreements
are still about different ways of making sense of Nuer religious discourse, not about too much or too little "charity" in translation. In fact
contrary to Gellner's allegations, Evans-Pritchard's exegesis *does* make
quite explicit apparent "contradictions," or at least ambiguities, in
Nuer concepts—for example, between the notion of "a supreme and
omnipresent being" and that of "lesser spirits," both of which are cate-
gorized as *kwoth*. And it is precisely because Evans-Pritchard insists on
keeping the different senses of *kwoth* together as parts of "one concept" and does not treat them as homonyms (as Malinowski might
have done by relating the word to different contexts of use) that
the Nuer concept of spirit might be said to be "contradictory." But
whether the identification of ambiguities and "contradictions" in the
basic conceptual repertoire of a language provides obvious evidence
of "pre-logical thought" is, of course, a different issue—I would sug-

gest that only someone with a very naive understanding of what was involved in translation could think that it does.

Yet Gellner's discourse typically evades the issues it seems to be raising, in a style that seeks to hurry the reader along over a series of archly phrased disclaimers:

> I do not wish to be misunderstood: I am *not* arguing that Evans-Pritchard's account of Nuer concepts is a bad one. (Nor am I anxious to revive a doctrine of pre-logical mentality *a la* Lévy-Bruhl.) On the contrary, I have the greatest admiration for it. What I am anxious to argue is that contextual interpretation, which offers an account of what assertions "really mean" in opposition to what they seem to mean in isolation, does not by itself clinch matters. (38)

Now who would have claimed it did? Certainly Evans-Pritchard does not. In any case the opposition between a "contextual interpretation" and one that is not contextual is entirely spurious. Nothing has meaning "in isolation." The problem is always, what kind of context?

But that is something Gellner never discusses, except by suggesting that the answer must involve a vicious circularity—or by uttering repeated warnings against "excessive" charity (when is charity not "excessive"?). He appears unaware that for the translator the problem of determining the relevant kind of context in each case is solved by *skill* in the use of the languages concerned, not by an a priori "attitude" of intolerance or tolerance. And skill is something that is *learned*—that is, something that is necessarily circular, but not viciously so. We are dealing not with an abstract matching of two sets of sentences, but with a social practice rooted in modes of life. A translator may make mistakes, or he may knowingly misrepresent something—much as people make mistakes or lie in everyday life. But we cannot produce a general principle for identifying such things, particularly not through warnings to be careful of "the contextual method of interpretation."

And so to another of Gellner's charming disclaimers: "To say all this is not to argue for a scepticism or agnosticism concerning what members of alien languages mean, still less to argue for an abstention from the contextual method of interpretation. (On the contrary, I shall argue for a fuller use of it, fuller in the sense of allowing for the possibility that what people mean is sometimes absurd.)" (39). The charm of this statement consists in Gellner's cheeky appropriation of his opponent's method to strengthen his own distinctive position.

But before that is done, we are given further examples of the tolerance-engendering contextual method at work in Leach's *Political Systems of Highland Burma*. Thus according to Leach, Kachin statements about the supernatural world are "in the last analysis, nothing more than ways of describing the formal relationships that exist between real persons and real groups in ordinary Kachin society" (quoted on p. 40). At this point Gellner intervenes: "It is possible to discern what has happened. Leach's exegetic procedures have also saved the Kachins from being credited with what they *appear* to be saying" and thus made it possible "to attribute meaning to assertions which might otherwise be found to lack it" (41). Gellner goes on to insist that he is not concerned to dispute Leach's interpretations, but merely "to show how the range of context, and the manner in which the context is seen, necessarily affect the interpretation" (41). This is a significant remark, because it is indeed not Leach's reductionism to which Gellner objects (we shall find him insisting on it himself later in connection with Berber religious ideology) but to the fact that this example of reductionism—which Gellner misleadingly calls "contextualism"—seems to defend, rather than to attack, the cultural discourse concerned.

Gellner's demonstration of how "the *uncharitable* may be 'contextualist' in the second, deeper and better sense" (42) begins by presenting a fictitious word in a fictitious society—the word "boble," used in a way remarkably like the English word "noble." Thus we are told that it can be applied to people who actually display certain habitual forms of conduct, as well as to people who occupy a particular social status irrespective of their behavior. "But the point is: the society in question does not distinguish *two concepts*, boble (a) and boble (b). It only uses the word boble tout court" (42). The logic of bobility is then analyzed further to show how

bobility is a conceptual device by which the privileged class of the society in question acquires some of the prestige of certain virtues respected in that society, without the inconvenience of needing to practice it, thanks to the fact that the same word is applied either to practitioners of those virtues or to occupiers of favoured positions. It is, at the same time, a manner of reinforcing the appeal of those virtues, by associating them, through the use of the same appellation, with prestige and power. But all this needs to be said, and to say it is to bring out the internal logical incoherence of the concept—an incoherence which, indeed, is socially functional. (42)

In fact the concept of "bobility" is not shown to be *incoherent*—even if it be accepted that the ambiguity of the *word* allows it to be used in political discourse to consolidate the legitimacy of a ruling class (and therefore, in principle, also to undermine that legitimacy). Gellner's satisfied conclusion to his fictional example is surely far too hasty: "What this shows, however, is that the over-charitable interpreter, determined to defend the concepts he is investigating from the charge of logical incoherence, is bound to misdescribe the social situation. *To make sense of the concept is to make nonsense of the society*" (42, emphasis added). Clearly the word "bobility" makes sense to its users in particular statements (or they would not use it), and it makes sense also, although of a different kind, to Gellner, who states that by deceiving its users it somehow upholds a social structure. Sense or nonsense, like truth or falsehood, applies to *statements* and not to abstract concepts. There seems to me no evidence here of a "nonsensical" concept, because there is no analysis of socially situated statements.

But there is also a more important failure evident in this example: the lack of any attempt to explore its *coherence*—that which makes its social effect such a powerful possibility. Of course, political discourse employs lies, half-truths, logical trickery, and so on. Yet that is not what gives it its *compulsive* character, any more than the use of true or clear statements does, and compulsiveness is precisely what is involved in Gellner's example. It is not the abstract logical status of concepts that is relevant here, but the way in which specific political discourses seem to mobilize or direct the behavior of people within given cultural situations. The compulsiveness of "bobility" as a political concept is a feature not of gullible minds but of coherent discourses and practices. That is why it is essential for a translator of powerful political ideologies to attempt to convey something of this coherence. To make *non-sense* of the concept is to make nonsense of the society.

Gellner's final example comes from his own fieldwork among the central Moroccan Berbers, and is intended to clinch the argument that an uncharitable contextualist makes better sense of the society he describes by emphasizing the incoherence of its concepts: "Two concepts are relevant," he writes, "*baraka* and *agurram* (pl. *igurramen*). *Baraka* is a word which can mean simply 'enough', but it also means plenitude, and above all blessedness manifested amongst other things in prosperity and the power to cause prosperity in others by supernatural means. An *agurram* is a possessor of *baraka*" (43).

Igurramen—translated as "saints" in Gellner's later writings (e.g., 1969)—are a fairly privileged and influential minority in the tribal society of central Moroccan Berbers who act as foci of religious values and also as mediators and arbitrators amongst the tribal population with whom they live. "The local belief is that they are selected by God. Moreover, God makes his choice manifest by endowing those whom he has selected with certain characteristics, including magical powers, and great generosity, prosperity, a consider-the-lilies attitude, pacifism, and so forth" (43).

This is Gellner's "translation." But his too-fluent use of a religious vocabulary with strong, and perhaps irrelevant, Christian overtones must prompt doubts and questions at this point. What precisely are the behavior and discourses translated here as "a consider-the-lilies attitude," "makes his choice manifest," and "endowing," for instance? Do the Berbers believe that God *endows* their "saints" with dispositional characteristics such as "great generosity and pacifism," or do they take it rather that these characteristics are *conditions* of saintliness, of the closeness of *igurramen* to God? Do the Berbers really behave as though religious and moral *virtues* were "manifestations" of divine choice? What do they say and how do they behave when people fail to display the virtues they *ought* to have? By whom is an *agurram's* behavior conceptualized as a "consider-the-lilies attitude," given that he has both family and property, and that this fact is taken by the Berbers to be perfectly in order? Gellner does not give the reader the relevant evidence for answering these important questions, whose significance for his translation will emerge in a moment.

> The reality of the situation is, however, that the *igurramen* are in fact selected by the surrounding ordinary tribesmen who use their services, by being called to perform those services and being preferred to the rival candidates for their performance. What appears to be *vox Dei* is in reality *vox populi*. Moreover, the matter of the blessed characteristics, the stigmata [sic] of *agurram*-hood is more complicated. It is essential that successful candidates to *agurram* status be *credited* with these characteristics, but it is equally essential, at any rate with regard to some of them, that they should not really possess them. For instance, an *agurram* who was extremely generous in a consider-the-lilies spirit would soon be impoverished and, as such, fail by another crucial test, that of prosperity.
>
> There is here a crucial divergence between concept and reality, a divergence which moreover is quite essential for the working of the social system. (43–44)

It is not at all clear from the account given by Gellner what is meant by the statement, "The local belief is that they are selected by God"—"selected" for what exactly? For being arbitrators? But arbitration must be initiated by one or other member of the tribal society, and that fact can hardly be unknown to the tribesmen. For being pacific? But pacifism is a virtue, not a reward. For worldly success and prosperity? But that cannot be a local *definition* of saintliness, or the French colonial rulers would have been regarded as more saintly than any *agurram*.

It is really no great explanatory achievement for a European anthropologist to inform his agnostic and/or modern European readers that the Berbers believe in a particular kind of direct intervention of the deity in their affairs, that they are of course mistaken in this belief, and that this mistaken belief can have social consequences. In this kind of exercise we do not learn *what* they believe, but only *that* what they believe is quite wrong: thus, the Berbers believe that God "selects" *igurramen*; we know God does not exist (or if some of us still "believe" he does, we "know" he does not intervene directly in secular history); ergo the "selector" must be another agent whom the tribesmen

do not know as the agent—in fact, the surrounding tribesmen themselves. The *igurramen* are "selected" (for a particular social role? for a
moral virtue? for a religious destiny?) by the people. The "selection"
appears to be *vox Dei* and is in reality *vox populi*. Or is it?

In reality the social process described by the anthropologist as "selection" is the locus of a *vox* only if it is pretended that that process
constitutes a cultural text. For a text must have an author—the one
who makes his voice heard through it. And if that voice cannot be
God's, it must be someone else's—the people's. Thus Gellner the athe-
ist insists on answering a theological question: who speaks through
history, through society? In this particular case, the answer depends
on the text containing at once the "real," unconscious meaning and its
appropriate translation. This fusion of signifier and signified is especially evident in the way in which the Islamic concept of *baraka* is made
to sound remarkably like the Christian concept of grace as portrayed
by an eighteenth-century skeptic, so that the conditions defining the
agurram's baraka are referred to with a knowing Gibbonian smile as
"stigmata"—and by that deft sign, a portion of the Berber cultural
text is at once constructed (made up) and designated (shown up)
within Gellner's text, as exquisite a union of word and thing as any to
be found in all his writings.

But society is not a text that communicates itself to the skilled
reader. It is people who speak. And the ultimate meaning of what
they say does not reside in society—society is the cultural condition in
which speakers act and are acted upon. The privileged position that
Gellner accords himself for decoding the *real* meaning of what the
Berbers say (regardless of what they think they say) can be maintained
only by someone who supposes that translating other cultures is essentially a matter of matching written sentences in two languages,
such that the second set of sentences becomes the "real meaning" of
the first—an operation the anthropologist alone controls, from field
notebook to printed ethnography. In other words, it is the privileged
position of someone who does not, and can afford not to, engage in a
genuine dialogue with those he or she once lived with and now *writes*
about (cf. Asad, ed. 1973:17).

In the middle of his article, when discussing anthropological relativism, Gellner complains that "anthropologists were relativistic, tolerant, contextually-comprehending vis-à-vis the savages who are after
all some distance away, but absolutistic, intolerant vis-à-vis their immediate neighbours or predecessors, the members of our own society
who do not share their comprehending outlook and are themselves
'ethnocentric' . . ." (31).

Why have I tried to insist in this paper that anyone concerned
with translating from other cultures must look for coherence in dis-

courses, and yet devoted so many pages to showing that Gellner's text is largely incoherent? The reason is quite simple: Gellner and I speak the same language, belong to the same academic profession, live in the same society. In taking up a critical stance toward his text I am *contesting* what he says, not *translating* it, and the radical difference between these two activities is precisely what I insist on. Still, the purpose of my argument is not to express an attitude of "intolerance" toward an "immediate neighbour," but to try and identify incoherences in his text that call for remedy, because the anthropological task of translation deserves to be made more coherent. The purpose of this criticism, therefore, is to further a collective endeavor. Criticizing "savages who are after all some distance away," in an ethnographic monograph they cannot read, does not seem to me to have the same kind of purpose. In order for criticism to be responsible, it must always be addressed to someone who can contest it.

The Inequality of Languages

A careful reading of Gellner's paper shows that although he raises a number of important questions, he not only fails to answer them, but misses some of the most crucial aspects of the problem with which the ethnographer is engaged. The most interesting of these, it seems to me, is the problem of what one might call "unequal languages"—and it is this I want now to discuss in some detail.

All good translation seeks to reproduce the structure of an alien discourse within the translator's own language. How that structure (or "coherence") is reproduced will, of course, depend on the genre concerned ("poetry," "scientific analysis," "narrative," etc.), on the resources of the translator's language, as well as on the interests of the translator and/or his readership. All successful translation is premised on the fact that it is addressed within a specific language, and therefore also to a specific set of practices, a specific form of life. The further that form of life is from the original, the less mechanical is the reproduction. As Walter Benjamin wrote: "The language of a translation can—in fact must—let itself go, so that it gives voice to the *intentio* of the original not as reproduction but as harmony, as a supplement to the language in which it expresses itself, as its own kind of *intentio*" (1969:79). It is, incidentally, for the reader to evaluate that *intentio*, not for the translator to preempt the evaluation. A good translation should always precede a critique. And we can turn this around by saying that a good critique is always an "internal" critique—that is, one based on some shared understanding, on a joint life, which it aims to enlarge and make more coherent. Such a critique—no less than the object of criticism—is a point of view, a (contra) *version*, having only provisional and limited authority.

What happens when the languages concerned are so remote that it is very difficult to rewrite a harmonious *intentio*? Rudolf Pannwitz, quoted in the Benjamin essay on which I have just drawn, makes the following observation:

Our translations, even the best ones, proceed from a wrong premise. They want to turn Hindi, Greek, English into German instead of turning German into Hindi, Greek, English. Our translators have a far greater reverence for the usage of their own language than for the spirit of the foreign works. . . . The basic error of the translator is that he preserves the state in which his own language happens to be instead of allowing his language to be powerfully affected by the foreign tongue. Particularly when translating from a language very remote from his own he must go back to the primal elements of language itself and penetrate to the point where work, image, and tone converge. He must expand and deepen his language by means of the foreign language. (1969:80–81)

This call to transform a language in order to translate the coherence of the original, poses an interesting challenge to the person satisfied with an absurd-sounding translation on the assumption that the original must have been equally absurd: the good translator does not immediately assume that unusual difficulty in conveying the sense of an alien discourse denotes a fault in the latter, but instead critically examines the normal state of his or her *own* language. The relevant question therefore is not how tolerant an *attitude* the translator ought to display toward the original author (an abstract ethical dilemma), but how she can test the tolerance of her own language for assuming unaccustomed forms.

But this pushing beyond the limits of one's habitual usages, this breaking down and reshaping of one's own language through the process of translation, is never an easy business, in part because (if I may be allowed a hypostatization) it depends on the willingness of the translator's *language* to subject itself to this transforming power. I attribute, somewhat fictitiously, volition to the language because I want to emphasize that the matter is largely something the translator cannot determine by individual activity (any more than the individual speaker can affect the evolution of his or her language)—that it is governed by institutionally defined power relations between the languages/modes of life concerned. To put it crudely: because the languages of Third World societies—including, of course, the societies that social anthropologists have traditionally studied—are "weaker" in relation to Western languages (and today, especially to English), they are more likely to submit to forcible transformation in the translation process than the other way around. The reason for this is, first, that in their political-economic relations with Third World countries, Western nations have the greater ability to manipulate the latter. And, second, Western languages produce and deploy *desired* knowledge more readily than Third World languages do. (The knowledge that Third World languages deploy more easily is not sought by Western societies in quite the same way, or for the same reason.)

Take modern Arabic as an example. Since the early nineteenth century there has been a growing volume of material translated from European languages—especially French and English—into Arabic. This includes scientific texts as well as "social science," "history," "philosophy," and "literature." And from the nineteenth century, Arabic as a language has begun as a result to undergo a transformation (lexical, grammatical, semantic) that is far more radical than anything to be identified in European languages—a transformation that has pushed it to approximate to the latter more closely than in the past. Such transformations signal inequalities in the power (i.e., in the *capacities*) of the respective languages in relation to the *dominant* forms of discourse that have been and are still being translated. There are varieties of knowledge to be learnt, but also a host of models to be imitated and reproduced. In some cases knowledge of these models is a precondition for the production of more knowledge; in other cases it is an end in itself, a mimetic gesture of power, an expression of desire for transformation. A recognition of this well-known fact reminds us that industrial capitalism transforms not only modes of production but also kinds of knowledge and styles of life in the Third World. And with them, forms of language. The result of half-transformed styles of life will make for ambiguities, which an unskillful Western translator may simplify in the direction of his own "strong" language.

What does this argument imply for the anthropological concept of cultural translation? That perhaps there is a greater stiffness in ethnographic linguistic conventions, a greater intrinsic resistance than can be overcome by individual experiments in modes of ethnographic representation.

In his perceptive essay "Modes of Thought," which Gellner criticizes for making over-charitable assumptions about the coherence of "primitive thought," Lienhardt has this to say:

When we live with savages and speak their languages, learning to represent their experience to ourselves in their way, we come as near to thinking like them as we can without ceasing to be ourselves. Eventually, we try to represent their conceptions systematically in the logical constructs we have been brought up to use; and we hope, at best, thus to reconcile what can be expressed in their languages, with what can be expressed in ours. We mediate between their habits of thought, which we have acquired with them, and those of our own society; in doing so, it is not finally some mysterious "primitive philoso-phy" that we are exploring, but the further potentialities of our thought and language. (1954:96–97)

In the field, as Lienhardt rightly suggests, the process of translation takes place at the very moment the ethnographer engages with a spe-cific mode of life—just as a child does in learning to grow up within a specific culture. He learns to find his way in a new environment, and a new language. And like a child he needs to verbalize *explicitly* what the proper way of doing things is, because that is how learning pro-ceeds. (Cf. A. R. Luria on "synpraxic speech" in Luria and Yudovich 1971:50.) When the child/anthropologist becomes adept at adult ways, what he has learnt becomes *implicit*—as assumptions informing a shared mode of life, with all its resonances and areas of unclarity.

But learning to live a new mode of life is not the same as learning about another mode of life. When anthropologists return to their countries, they must write up "their people," and they must do so in the conventions of representation already circumscribed (already "written around," "bounded") by their discipline, institutional life, and wider society. "Cultural translation" must accommodate itself to a different language not only in the sense of English as opposed to Dinka, or English as opposed to Kabbashi Arabic, but also in the sense of a British, middle class, academic game as opposed to the modes of life of the "tribal" Sudan. The stiffness of a powerful established structure of life, with its own discursive games, its own "strong" lan-guages, is what among other things finally determines the effective-ness of the translation. The translation is addressed to a very specific audience, which is waiting to read *about* another mode of life and to manipulate the text it reads according to established rules, not to learn *to live* a new mode of life.

If Benjamin was right in proposing that translation may require not a mechanical reproduction of the original but a harmonization with its *intentio*, it follows that there is no reason why this should be done only in the same mode. Indeed, it could be argued that "trans-lating" an alien form of life, another culture, is not always done best through the representational discourse of ethnography, that under certain conditions a dramatic performance, the execution of a dance, or the playing of a piece of music might be more apt. These would all be *productions* of the original and not mere interpretations: trans-formed instances of the original, not authoritative textual representa-tions of it (cf. Hollander 1959). But would they be thought of by most social anthropologists as valid exercises in the "translation of culture"? I think not, because they all raise an entirely different dimension of the relationship between the anthropological "work" and its audience, the question of different *uses* (practices), as opposed merely to different *writings and readings* (meanings) of that work. And as social anthropologists we are trained to translate other cultural languages as texts, not to introduce or enlarge cultural capacities, learnt from other ways of living, into our own. It seems to me very likely that the notion of culture as *text* has reinforced this view of our task, because it facilitates the assumption that translation is *essentially* a matter of verbal representation.

Reading Other Cultures

This inequality in the power of languages, together with the fact that the anthropologist typically writes about an illiterate (or at any rate non-English-speaking) population for a largely academic, English-speaking audience, encourages a tendency I would now like to discuss: the tendency to read the *implicit* in alien cultures.

According to many social anthropologists, the object of ethnographic translation is not the historically situated speech (that is the task of the folklorist or the linguist), but "culture," and to translate culture the anthropologist must first read and then reinscribe the implicit meanings that lie beneath/within/beyond situated speech. Mary Douglas puts this nicely:

The anthropologist who draws out the whole scheme of the cosmos which is implied in [the observed] practices does the primitive culture great violence if he seems to present the cosmology as a systematic philosophy subscribed to consciously by individuals. . . . So the primitive world view which I have defined above is rarely itself an object of contemplation and speculation in the primitive culture. It has evolved as the appanage of other social institutions. To this extent it is produced indirectly, and to this extent the primitive culture must be taken to be unaware of itself, unconscious of its own conditions. (1966:91)

One difference between the anthropologist and the linguist in the matter of translation is perhaps this: that whereas the latter is immediately faced with a specific piece of discourse produced within the society studied, a discourse that is *then* textualized, the former must construct the discourse *as* a cultural text in terms of meanings *implicit* in a range of practices. The construction of cultural discourse and its translation thus seem to be facets of a single act. This point is brought out in Douglas's comments on her own translations of the meanings of the pangolin cult among the Lele:

There are no Lele books of theology or philosophy to state the meaning of the cult. The metaphysical implications have not been expressed to me in so many words by Lele, nor did I even eavesdrop a conversation between diviners covering this ground. . . .

What kind of evidence for the meaning of this cult, or of any cult, can be sensibly demanded? It can have many different levels and kinds of meaning. But the one on which I ground my argument is the meaning which emerges out of a pattern in which the parts can incontestably be shown to be regularly related. No one member of the society is necessarily aware of the whole pattern, any more than speakers are able to be explicit about the linguistic patterns they employ. (1966:173–74)

I've suggested elsewhere (Asad 1983a) that the attribution of implicit meanings to an alien practice *regardless of whether they are acknowledged by its agents* is a characteristic form of theological exercise, with an ancient history. Here I want to note that reference to the linguistic patterns produced by speakers does not make a good analogy because linguistic *patterns* are not meanings to be translated, they are rules to be systematically described and analysed. A native speaker is aware of how such patterns should be produced even when he cannot verbalize that knowledge explicitly in the form of rules. The apparent lack of ability to verbalize such social knowledge does not necessarily constitute evidence of unconscious meanings (cf. Dummett 1981). The concept of "unconscious meaning" belongs to a theory of the repressive unconscious, such as Freud's, in which a person may be said to "know" something unconsciously.

The business of identifying unconscious meanings in the task of "cultural translation" is therefore perhaps better compared to the activity of the psychoanalyst than to that of the linguist. Indeed British anthropologists have sometimes presented their work in precisely these terms. Thus David Pocock, a pupil of Evans-Pritchard's, writes:

In short, the work of the social anthropologist may be regarded as a highly complex act of translation in which author and translator collaborate. A more precise analogy is that of the relation between the psychoanalyst and his subject. The analyst enters the private world of his subject in order to learn the grammar of his private language. If the analysis goes no further it is no different in kind from the understanding which may exist between any two people who know each other well.[!] It becomes scientific to the extent that the private language of intimate understanding is translated into a public language, however specialized from the layman's point of view, which in this case is the language of psychologists. But the particular act of translation does not distort the private experience of the subject and ideally it is, at least potentially, acceptable to him as a scientific representation of it. Similarly, the model of Nuer political life which emerges in Professor Evans-Pritchard's work is a scientific model meaningful to his fellow-sociologists as sociologists, and it is effective because it is *potentially acceptable to the Nuer in some ideal situation in which they could be supposed to be interested in themselves as men living in society.* The collaboration of natural scientists may from this point of view be seen as devel-

oping language enabling certain people to communicate with increasing subtlety about a distinct area of natural phenomena which is defined by the name
of the particular science. Their science is, in the literal meaning of the term,
their commonsense, their common meaning. To move from this common
sense to the "common sense" of the wider public involves again an act of
translation. The situation of social anthropology, or sociology in general, is
not at this level so very different. The difference lies in the fact that sociological phenomena are objectively studied only to the extent that their subjective meaning is taken into account and that the people studied are potentially capable of sharing the sociological consciousness that the sociologist has
of them. (1961 : 88–89; emphasis added)

I have quoted this remarkable passage in full because it states very lucidly a position that is, I think, broadly acceptable to many anthropologists who would otherwise consider themselves to be engaged in very
different kinds of enterprise. I have quoted it also because the nature
of the collaboration between "author and translator" is neatly brought
out in the subsequent reference to the psychoanalyst as scientist: if the
anthropological translator, like the analyst, has final authority in determining the subject's meanings—it is then the former who becomes
the real author of the latter. In this view, "cultural translation" is a
matter of determining implicit meanings—not the meanings the native speaker actually acknowledges in his speech, not even the meanings the native listener necessarily accepts, but those he is "potentially
capable of sharing" with scientific authority "in some ideal situation":
it is when he can say, for example, with Gellner, that *vox Dei* is in reality *vox populi*, that he utters the true meaning of his traditional discourse, an essential meaning of his culture. The fact that in that "ideal
situation" he would no longer be a Muslim Berber tribesman, but
something coming to resemble Professor Gellner, does not appear to
worry such cultural translators.

This power to create meanings for a subject through the notion of
the "implicit" or the "unconscious," *to authorize them*, has of course
been discussed for the analyst-analysand relationship (e.g., recently in
Malcolm 1982). It has not, to my knowledge, been considered with regard to what the cultural translator does. There are, of course, important differences in the case of the anthropologist. It may be pointed
out that the latter does not *impose* his translation on the members of
the society whose cultural discourse he unravels, that his ethnography
is therefore not authoritative in the way the analyst's case study is. The
analysand comes to the analyst, or is referred to the latter by those
with authority over him, as a patient in need of help. The anthropologist, by contrast, comes to the society he wants to read, he sees himself
as a learner, not as a guide, and he withdraws from the society when
he has adequate information to inscribe its culture. He does not con-

sider the society, and neither do its members consider themselves to be, sick: the society is never subject to the anthropologist's authority.

But this argument is not quite as conclusive as it may seem at first sight. It remains the case that the ethnographer's translation/representation of a particular culture is inevitably a textual construct, that as representation it cannot normally be contested by the people to whom it is attributed, and that as a "scientific text" it eventually becomes a privileged element in the potential store of historical memory for the nonliterate society concerned. In modern and modernizing societies, inscribed records have a greater power to shape, to reform, selves and institutions than folk memories do. They even construct folk memories. The anthropologist's monograph may return, retranslated, into a "weaker" Third World language. In the long run, therefore, it is not the personal authority of the ethnographer, but the social authority of his ethnography that matters. And that authority is inscribed in the institutionalized forces of industrial capitalist society (see page 158 above), which are constantly *tending* to push the meanings of various Third World societies in a single direction. This is not to say that there are no resistances to this tendency. But "resistance" in itself indicates the presence of a dominant force.

I must stress I am not arguing that ethnography plays any great role in the reformation of other cultures. In this respect the effects of ethnography cannot be compared with some other forms of representing societies—for example, television films produced in the West that are sold to Third World countries. (That anthropologists recognize the power of television is reflected, incidentally, in the increasing number of anthropological films being made for the medium in Britain.) Still less can the effects of ethnography compare with the political, economic, and military constraints of the world system. My point is only that the process of "cultural translation" is inevitably enmeshed in conditions of power—professional, national, international. And among these conditions is the authority of ethnographers to uncover the implicit meanings of subordinate societies. Given that that is so, the interesting question for enquiry is not whether, and if so to what extent, anthropologists should be relativists or rationalists, critical or charitable, toward other cultures, but how power enters into the process of "cultural translation," seen both as a discursive and as a nondiscursive practice.

Conclusion

For some years I have been exercised by this puzzle. How is it that the approach exemplified by Gellner's paper remains attractive to so many academics in spite of its being demonstrably faulty? Is it perhaps because they are intimidated by a *style*? We know, of course, that anthropologists, like other academics, learn not merely to use a scholarly language, but to fear it, to admire it, to be captivated by it. Yet this does not quite answer the question because it does not tell us *why* such a scholarly style should capture so many intelligent people. I now put forward this tentative solution. What we have here is a style easy to teach, to learn, and to reproduce (in examination answers, assessment essays, and dissertations). It is a style that facilitates the textualization of other cultures, that encourages the construction of diagrammatic answers to complex cultural questions, and that is well suited to arranging foreign cultural concepts in clearly marked heaps of "sense" or "nonsense." Apart from being easy to teach and to imitate, this style promises visible results that can readily be graded. Such a style must surely be at a premium in an established university discipline that aspires to *standards* of scientific objectivity. Is the popularity of this style, then, not a reflection of the kind of pedagogic institution we inhabit?

Although it is now many years since Gellner's paper was first published, it represents a doctrinal position that is still popular today. I have in mind the sociologism according to which religious ideologies are said to get their real meaning from the political or economic structure, and the self-confirming methodology according to which this reductive semantic principle is evident to the (authoritative) anthropologist and not to the people being written about. This position therefore assumes that it is not only possible but necessary for the anthropologist to act as translator and critic at one and the same time. I regard this position as untenable, and think that it is relations and practices of power that give it a measure of viability. (For a critical discussion of this position as it relates to Islamic history, see Asad 1980.)

The positive point I have tried to make in the course of my interrogation of Gellner's text has to do with what I have called the inequality of languages. I have proposed that the anthropological enterprise of cultural translation may be vitiated by the fact that there are asymmetrical tendencies and pressures in the languages of dominated and dominant societies. And I have suggested that anthropologists need to explore these processes in order to determine how far they go in defining the possibilities and the limits of effective translation.

In addition to the members of the Santa Fe seminar who discussed an early draft of this article—and especially Paul Rabinow, who commented on it at length—I wish to thank Tanya Baker, John Dixon, Rodney Needham, and Keith Nield for their helpful criticism.

GEORGE E. MARCUS

Contemporary Problems
of Ethnography in
the Modern World System

Ethnographies have always been written in the context of
historic change: the formation of state systems and the evolution
of a world political economy. But aside from the use of a few well-
established techniques for taking into account change, history, and political economy,[1] ethnographers of an interpretive bent—more inter-

1. The two most common modes for self-consciously fixing ethnography in historic time are what I shall call the salvage mode and the redemptive mode. In the salvage mode, the ethnographer portrays himself as "before the deluge," so to speak.
Signs of fundamental change are apparent, but the ethnographer is able to salvage a
cultural state on the verge of transformation. This rhetoric is most transparent when a
succession of ethnographers writing on the same cultural subject position themselves
historically in the same momentous way; each ethnographer is "before the deluge," but
nonetheless each finds a culture he or she can relate to previous representations without
much sensitivity to historical change between periods of fieldwork. In the redemptive
mode, the ethnographer demonstrates the survival of distinctive and authentic cultural
systems despite undeniable changes. The redemption of cultural authenticity is often
undertaken and measured against some imputed pre-modern or pre-capitalist state—
the "golden age" motif—or else a spatial, rather than temporal, preserve is found for
cultural authenticity amidst transformation—the anthropologist's odyssey up-river or
to the back country to situate fieldwork where "they still do it." Rabinow's Moroccan
fieldwork (1977) as epic journey employs this narrative posture, but in the end, he ex-
plodes the illusion that the pure ethnographic subject can be found even in the back
country. In his recent sophisticated Samoan ethnography, Shore (1982) elides the historic context by this move of finding spatially a place for ethnography free of the un-
wanted complications of a compellingly present world-historical political economy.
There are many similar examples of magisterial ethnographies that make their contributions at the cost of such maneuvers. What is finally shaking ethnography free of these
ahistorical modes of taking account of the historical contexts of its production are experiments either oriented explicitly to locating their subjects within the framework of
historicist world-system perspectives or probing the nature of historical consciousness
in their subjects' lives. The latter kind of experiment, involving the simultaneous representation of multiple temporal perspectives, opens up ethnography to issues of history
and historical narrative in unprecedented ways, which go far beyond merely embedding ethnographic subjects more effectively in Western historical narratives. Renato
Rosaldo's recent account (1980) of the Ilongot histories is a key experiment in this vein.
He, too, ends with a "before the deluge" motif, but the sense of being on the verge of

ested in problems of cultural meaning than in social action—have not generally represented the ways in which closely observed cultural worlds are embedded in larger, more impersonal systems. Nor have they portrayed the role of these worlds in the sort of events and processes that make history, so to speak, perhaps because ethnography as description has never been particularly ambitious in this way. Change and the larger frameworks of local politics have usually been treated in separate theoretical or conceptual discourse with some ethnographic detail added for illustration. The descriptive space of ethnographies itself has not seemed an appropriate context for working through conceptual problems of this larger order. The world of larger systems and events has thus often been seen as externally impinging on and bounding little worlds, but not as integral to them.

In anthropology and all other human sciences at the moment, "high" theoretical discourse—the body of ideas that authoritatively unify a field—is in disarray. The most interesting and provocative theoretical works now are precisely those that point to practice (see Ortner 1984), that is, to a bottom-up reformulation of classic questions, which hinges on how the previously taken-for-granted facts of high theory are to be represented.[2] These works constitute renewed assaults on positivist perspectives, rearmed by the postwar hermeneutic, phenomenological, and semiotic fashions in Continental philosophy that are finally having an impact on Anglo-American social thought. The concepts of structure on which such perspectives depended are really processes that must be understood from the point of view of the actor, a realization that raises problems of interpretation and presents opportunities for innovation in writing accounts of social reality.

This shift of theoretical concern toward problems of microsocial description and contextuality can hardly be attributed to intellectual

---

fundamental transformation is far more convincing in his text because it grows out of an account in which the forms of Ilongot historic consciousness intersecting with our privileging of global world history have been the unrelieved focus.

2. During the mid-1970s, this practice-focused attack on positivist high theory was itself conducted within the genre of abstract theoretical discussion, separate from, and pointing to, genres of practice. By the 1980s, this critique has moved to a suspension of paradigmatic authority and a questioning of the utility of system building in favor of free play and experimentation in the specific rendering of accounts of social life. A perfect example of the shift in emphasis toward the more substantively ethnographic and experimental among the "high" theory treatments of the challenge to positivism is the evolving work of Richard J. Bernstein. In his *The Restructuring of Social and Political Theory*, published in 1976, Bernstein, like Anthony Giddens (1979), monitors the challenge to predominant Anglo-American social theory and endorses the apparent evolution of a new kind of theory. In his *Beyond Objectivism and Relativism: Science, Hermeneutics, and Practice*, published in 1983, Bernstein focuses strongly on practice. Significantly, he ends with a plea for the production of open-ended dialogic works, which is precisely where the most radically experimental ethnographies have been heading.

fashions alone. Even continuing efforts to build macro perspectives are infused with concerns about matters of micro description and interpretation. In the field of political economy, which can be seen as a continuing commentary upon world conditions in terms most relevant to Western officialdom and statecraft, the major recent innovation in efforts at macro system building has been the world-system perspective introduced by Immanuel Wallerstein during the early 1970s. The adequacy of Wallerstein's center-periphery formulation and his overview interpretations of history are the subject of lively debate, dependent significantly on discussions of local situations. The important influence and appeal of his work has been the introduction of a framework for the intimate reassociation of history and social theory. This has as its practical research imperative the doing of local-level studies of processes and their social construction—in other words, of ethnography sensitive to its context of historical political economy.[3]

What the appropriate facts of social theory are and how to represent them combining both interpretation and explanation is thus a current topic of widespread interest that can be posed rhetorically and repetitively in theoretical discourse, but can only be pursued in the doing of fieldwork and the writing of ethnography. This is why ethnography—hitherto widely viewed outside anthropology as marginal in both its practice (mere description) and its subject matter (the primitive, the exotic, alien other)—has been appropriated by a number of fields that sometimes recognize anthropology's labor in this vineyard, and sometimes do not.[4]

---

3. This move toward the ethnographic in American academic political economy, I would argue, is related to a widely perceived decline of the post–World War II international order in which America has held a hegemonic position and to an undermining of the American form of the welfare state itself. A sense of profound transition in the foundations of domestic and international reality, as seen from the American perspective, has in turn been reflected intellectually in a widespread retreat from theoretically centralized and organized fields of knowledge. Goals of organizing scholarly practice in such diverse fields as history, the social sciences, literature, art, and architecture have given way to fragmentation and a spirit of experimentation that aims to explore ways to evoke and represent diversity in social life—to convey the richness of experience, to probe the meaning of details of everyday life, to remember symbols and associations long forgotten. Among the vehicles of experimentation, precocious in relation to this trend, is ethnography in anthropology.

4. At the present moment, anthropology both attracts and repels those caught by the spirit of experimentation in a diversity of fields. It is ethnography that primarily attracts. We find philosophers, literary critics, historians, and political economists reading ethnographies of the Balinese and Azande, not out of intrinsic interest in the subject matter, but for their distinctive textual devices and modes of exploring theoretical issues in the process of ethnographic representation itself. It is the traditional subject matter of anthropology—the primitive or alien other—that primarily repels, or, rather, undercuts the full potential of anthropology's relevance in a widespread intellectual

   This paper explores how the conventions of ethnographic writing and the enthographic posture of authority merge in single texts with the kind of analytic tasks of macrosocial theory mentioned above. Indeed, ethnography has shown the effects of major events and large systems on the everyday life of those usually portrayed as victims (the subjects of ethnography have usually been victims, or, because of modern enthography's commitment to social criticism, they have at least been portrayed as such), but it has rarely been directed to answering macrosociological questions about the causes of events or the constitution of major systems and processes, usually represented more formally and abstractly in other conceptual languages.[5] I shall address

---

trend, which it has long anticipated. The figure of the primitive or the alien other is no longer as compelling as it was in similar experimental periods (e.g., the late nineteenth century and the 1920s and 1930s). Global homogenization is more credible than ever before, and though the challenge to discover and represent cultural diversity is strong, doing so in terms of spatio-temporal cultural preserves of otherness seems outmoded. Rather, the strongest forms of difference are now defined within our own capitalist cultural realm, gender and lifestyle constructs being two prominent fields of representation for exploring difference. The Samoan or Trobriand islander, juxtaposed to us, is no longer as convincing or believable a figure for an alternative way of being as he once was in a less saliently perceived world order of interpenetrating common concerns. What is more, linked to this perception of the declining significance of the primitive is the notion that anthropology is losing its raison d'etre. It is unfortunate, and certainly an artifact of current intellectual moods, both that strong evidence running counter to perceptions of homogenization is ignored for lack of interest, and that anthropology has been received in such a limited way, associated more with its exotic subject matter than with its distinctive mode of understanding reality.

   5. A sense of experimentation pervades contemporary ethnographic writing even among those who continue to write well within the tradition of realist conventions. What motivates experiments is the recognition of a much more complex world, which challenges the traditional modes of representing cultural difference in ethnographic writing. I view the experimental responses to this challenge as moving in two divergent directions. One trend of experimentation is intensely concerned with getting at the representation of authentic other-cultural experience, with going beyond existing interpretive or symbolic perspectives on cultural meaning toward the most deep-seated and radical level at which difference can be evoked. Some of these experiments, those that fix on differing cultural constructions of the person, remain true to realist conventions. Others shift more radically to modernist concerns with textual form; other cultural experience can only be evoked or represented by a fundamental change in the way we think about the construction of ethnographic texts. Dialogic interchanges between ethnographer and other, the sharing of textual authority with subjects themselves, autobiographical recounting as the only appropriate form for merging other cultural experience with the ethnographer's own—these are all attempts to change radically the way the conventional subject matter of ethnography has been constituted in order to convey authentically other cultural experience.

   The other trend of experimentation, and the one to which I limit myself in this paper, is relatively well satisfied with the means interpretive anthropology has developed to represent cultural difference, but instead explores new and more effective ways in which ethnographic texts can take account of the manner in which world-historical political economy constitutes their subjects. These experiments remain well within realist conventions, but they are no less innovative in the kinds of texts they generate.

in detail one major variety of such contemporary experimentation with the ethnographic genre—namely, its contribution to the understanding of the operation of capitalist political economy. The general points made in the next section about the textual strategies of such experiments will then be developed by an extended commentary on Paul Willis's *Learning to Labour* (1981).

Ethnography and the Invisible Hand

Since the mid-1970s there has been no shortage of works addressing what Anthony Giddens (1979) has called the central problems of social theory: the integration of action perspectives, standing for the positivist paradigm predominant in postwar Anglo-American social thought, with meaning perspectives, standing for the interpretive paradigm, which has effectively challenged it. But few such works have been posed as theories of practice, eliding for the moment the penchant in Western social thought for abstract, all-encompassing paradigmatic structures to theory (Bourdieu's *Outline of a Theory of Practice* [1977] is perhaps the key, and most influential, exception). Even rarer are works fully recognizing that the challenge of interpretive approaches does not really pose a problem of grand theoretical synthesis so much as problems of textual representation.[6]

Perhaps the most sophisticated statement of the intimate linkage between knowledge of modern society and its representation in realist genres of writing is in the works of British literary and cultural critic Raymond Williams. It is worth quoting him at length from a book-length series of interviews that survey his writings:

It is very striking that the classic technique devised in response to the impossibility of understanding contemporary society from experience, the statistical

6. One recent volume that does seem to locate the problem of integrating systems and meaning perspectives in that of textual representation is *Advances in Social Theory and Methodology*, edited by K. Knorr-Cetina and A. V. Cicourel (1981). As Knorr-Cetina frames the problem, advances in the study of microprocesses during the past decade or so have overwhelmed those in the study of macrosystems. The question then is not how micro and macro perspectives can be equally integrated, but how macro perspectives can be brought back into accounts of microsituations and processes. Knorr-Cetina reviews three techniques for integrating micro and macro levels textually. First, the macrosystem may be portrayed as the mere summation of microsituations or processes. Second, the macro may be represented as a result of the totality of unintended consequences emanating from the multitude of microsituations. Third, macrosystems may be represented as they are subtly imagined or registered within the ongoing life processes of an intensely studied and interpreted microsituation. Knorr-Cetina dismisses the first technique, as do I. Of the remaining two, she finds the third most attractive and least problematic.

mode of analysis, had its precise origins within the period of which you are speaking. For without the combination of statistical theory . . . and arrangements for collection of statistical data . . . the society that was emerging out of the industrial revolution was literally unknowable. I tried to develop this contrast in *The Country and the City* between the knowable community, a term used with irony because what is known is shown to be incomplete, and the new sense of the darkly unknowable. . . . New forms had to be devised to penetrate what was rightly perceived to be to a large extent obscure. . . . From the industrial revolution onwards, qualitatively altering a permanent problem, there has developed a type of society which is less interpretable from experience—meaning by experience a lived contact with the available articulations, including their comparison. The result is that we have become increasingly conscious of the positive power of techniques of analysis, which at their maximum are capable of interpreting, let us say, the movements of an integrated world economy, and of the negative qualities of a naive observation which can never gain knowledge of realities like these. . . . Experience becomes a forbidden word, whereas what we ought to say about it is that it is a limited word, for there are many kinds of knowledge it will never give us, in any of its ordinary senses.

The general problem which has exercised many producers—perhaps more often in plays than in novels—is whether to break with the realist tradition altogether or to try to extend it. I think there is a case for seeing how far certain areas which the bourgeois form typically excluded could now be integrated in the novel. . . . That has produced extreme complications for the traditional form because it did depend, in my view, on the idea of a knowable community, and now we are faced with the fact that this cannot be called a community and is not knowable in former ways. The result is an extreme crisis of form. . . . But I think that a much more extensive theoretical discussion of the possibilities in *all* the available forms is necessary. . . . Alongside this theoretical debate we need a lot of examples of practice, so that people can see how far a particular form can be taken. We must be very experimental about it. (Williams 1981: 164–65, 272–73)

For this experimental and ethnographic moment in the history of Western social theory, Williams has precisely defined text construction as the crucible for integrating the macro into the micro, combining accounts of impersonal systems into representations of local life as cultural forms both autonomous and constituted by the larger order. It is not important that Williams is talking about the novel, whereas we are dealing with ethnography and interpretive analysis. With the latter in fashion, practical problems of description and exposition have become much like the problems of the socialist realist novel in the twentieth century, Williams's primary concern.

Williams shares the English Marxist tradition, and particularly its emphasis on culture, with those who seem to be producing the most sophisticated realist ethnography, sensitive to problems of cultural meaning, yet insistent on embedding analyses of everyday life in Marxist perspectives on capitalist political economy. He has obviously been a major influence on Marxist scholars of culture, especially those, such as Paul Willis, who have found a textual medium in ethnography. Williams defines the problem for those ethnographers concerned as writers equally with forms of life and world systems.

Given the past commitment of anthropology to holistic representation and allusion in ethnography, how might an adequate account be constructed in the terms we have so far discussed? What is holism once the line between the local worlds of subjects and the global world of systems becomes radically blurred? How, then, is the representational space of the realist ethnography to be textually bounded and contained in the compelling recognition of the larger systems contexts of any ethnographic subjects? Two modes of text construction suggest themselves.

First, by sequential narrative and the effect of simultaneity, the ethnographer might try in a single text to represent multiple, blindly interdependent locales, each explored ethnographically and mutually linked by the intended and unintended consequences of activities within them. If the intent were merely to demonstrate random interdependencies by which everyone is unexpectedly connected to everyone else in the modern world, if only you looked hard enough, this would be an absurd and pointless project—to show, say, the connection between mental health in America and the price of tea in China. Rather, the point of this kind of project would be to start with some prior view of a system and to provide an ethnographic account of it, by showing the forms of local life that the system encompasses, and then leading to novel or revised views of the nature of the system itself, translating its abstract qualities into more fully human terms.

Markets (Adam Smith's invisible hand) and capitalist modes of production, distribution, and consumption (Marx's version of the invisible hand—commodity fetishism) are perhaps the most obvious views of systems as objects for experimentation with multi-locale ethnographies. These would explore two or more locales and show their interconnections over time and simultaneously. While there are texts like this in fiction (for example, Aleksander Solzhenitsyn's *The First Circle*), I know of none in the literature of ethnography. However, such multi-locale ethnography is often evoked these days, especially among certain political economists, as a sort of ideal for experimentation in realist ethnography.

The difficulties of writing such a work are well illustrated by existing journalistic accounts that do approximate the ethnographic, such as Stephen Fay's *Beyond Greed* (1982), an inquiry into the recent attempt by the Hunt brothers of Dallas and their Saudi allies to corner the world silver market. The narrative complexity is considerable in an account like this, which in fact is dealing with the human dimensions of the operation of the invisible hand, markets, in capitalist societies. To tell his story, Fay has to juggle over a dozen locales and actors' perspectives, simultaneously and blindly influencing one another, and in addition he must sustain a narrative sequence of events. He explains how commodity markets work; he speculates about what the Hunts of Dallas are thinking, as well as portraying their social background; he does the same for the Saudis; he explains the operations of federal regulatory agencies and other bureaucracies, as well as their response to events; he explains the perspectives and actions of other major commodity traders; and he describes man-on-the-street and industry reactions to the crisis in the silver market. Now this is the kind of subject that ethnography ought to be able to take on, especially if it intends to say something about the culture of capitalist societies. Fay's book is a demonstration and successful handling (for a journalist, if perhaps not for an ethnographer) of the practical difficulties in constructing a multi-locale account of a system or a major social drama encompassed by it.

In the second, much more manageable, mode, the ethnographer constructs the text around a strategically selected locale, treating the system as background, albeit without losing sight of the fact that it is integrally constitutive of cultural life within the bounded subject matter. The rhetorical and self-conscious emphasis on the strategic and purposeful situating of ethnography is an important move in such works, linking it to broader issues of political economy. The fact is that the situating of most anthropological ethnography—why this group rather than another, why this locale rather than another—has not been acknowledged as a major problem, or at least as an issue that relates to any broader aim of research. Instead, it has often been dictated by opportunity. Not so with an ethnography sensitive to political economy, which must answer the question, "Why precisely are you in this locale rather than another?" This rhetorical self-consciousness about the selection and bounding of the ethnographic subject should be seen as a practical foreshortening of the ideal, but less manageable, multi-locale systems ethnography. Other options or alternatives for situating the ethnography are always present. One is obliged to be self-consciously justifying (or strategic) in the placement of ethnography precisely because of sensitivity to the broader system representation that is at stake, foreshortened by the practical advantage of ethnography fixed in a single locale.

These two modes are thus not mutually exclusive conceptually—the second is a compromised version of the first—but textually they are. In his study of working class youth in a school setting, Willis writes in the second mode of strategically situated ethnography, discussed in the next section. Here it is interesting to note that Willis and other ethnographers who write explicitly within the Marxist theoretical tradition (e.g., Michael Taussig in *The Devil and Commodity Fetishism in South America*) have the powerful advantage of placing the larger order in the background while focusing intensely upon a closely observed locale as ethnographic subject. Because familiarity, or at least acquaintance, with the Marxist framework can be assumed on the part of the reader, much of the work of inventing a representation of the larger order is accomplished merely by orienting or referring the situated ethnography to issues of Marxist theory. The Marxist system is *there*, so to speak, to be invoked. A commitment to it by the ethnographer makes it available as an image of system worked into the ethnography. (I am not, of couse, suggesting that this is why the commitment is made by a writer, and in the current fragmentation of paradigms, some version of a Marxist framework is available through more eclectic forms of it, such as world-system theory, to scholars with no previous commitment to Marxism.) It is the most sophisticated and coherent framework for conceptualizing modern societies to survive the nineteenth century. Exploring the cultural meanings of the production of labor or commodity fetishism provides textual means for bringing the larger order into the space of ethnography.

Thus, it might be expected that with this advantage, the most sophisticated experiments in ethnography sensitive to political economy might initially arise within the Marxist tradition, or at least a Marxist framework, and this seems to be the case. Of course, eventually the ready-made Marxist construct may not be an advantage. It is a short cut that can leave many of the ambiguities in Marxist macro-system concepts unpacked, even though ethnographers are working creatively within it. Furthermore, it can stand in the way of the possible invention of new system perspectives working up from ethnography. Conversely, ethnographic projects potentially provide powerful internal critiques and adaptations of the Marxist theory of capitalism to changing global conditions. In any case, the Marxist system imagery remains the most convenient and comprehensive framework for embedding single-locale ethnography in political economy.

Paul Willis's *Learning to Labour*

Willis's subject is, broadly speaking, how best to understand labor in capitalist society—how it is constituted as cultural experience. As Karl Polanyi emphasized in *The Great Transformation* (1944), the reduction of any human resource to a commodity by market discipline must necessarily be incomplete and a fiction. There is a need to demystify commodity fetishism of various sorts and to understand labor as a fully human process. The cultural and social study of working classes has been the major rationale for bottom-up, ethnographic studies in the Marxist tradition, and particularly in the British Marxist tradition.

There is a very long tradition in England of focusing attention on the problem of the poor, extending from the inception of market capitalism and the parallel development of a science of economics to the present. The initiation of an ethnographic tradition within Marxism through Engels's firsthand accounts of the working class and factory conditions in Manchester was just a continuation of this line of inquiry in British intellectual life, but now encompassed within the most systematic and powerful theoretical framework for understanding modern Western political economy. The interest in the everyday life and conditions of the working classes has continued among social scientists and literary critics who identify themselves as Marxists and socialists. Willis's study of working class boys at school is firmly and self-consciously within this tradition, and his ethnography is meant to improve upon the quality of understanding class formation processes that have long been the focal concern of Marxist scholars in England.

Specifically, Willis strategically locates his subject matter as the oppositional culture that white working class males create in school. His ethnography is replete with references to other locales in which his subjects live, such as the home, street, and dance hall, but he chooses the school environment because this is where class conflict has a day-to-day manifestation, and it is where the critical development of class consciousness occurs among nonconformist youths, a consciousness and set of orientations they take to the shop floor after leaving school. Willis's key argument resides in the irony that a cultural form created from resistance to dominant class indoctrination in the school becomes the adaptive means of accommodation to factory life.

Willis's ethnographic focus is a group of twelve boys in a working class school, linked by friendship and a mutual recognition of the conspiracy in their nonconformism. Willis notes that control studies were done among conformist boys of middle-class background, labelled "ear'oles" by the nonconformists, and also among conformist working class lads. But these other references are only brought occasionally into the text. Centrally he is concerned with a representation of the oppositional culture among his twelve lads, and with some shifting to shop floor and home environments (discussions with parents) to show how the focally represented oppositional culture created from school experience resonates in these other critical locales (the home locale and parental perspective show that the culture is generationally reproduced, but also that the school, not the home, is its site of formation; the shop floor locale shows the continuity of oppositional culture in the work context and its very different consequences). So there is a very specific and strategic circumscribing of the system portrayed in the text for the purposes of Willis's argument. He pays some attention to middle class culture, as manifested in staff and other students, and he recognizes distinct perspectives for girls, West Indians, and Asians, but mainly he keeps to a school-situated ethnography of his twelve nonconformist boys.

This ethnography, arranged by topical headings, is presented as verbatim discussions among the lads, with the author present as interlocutor. Straightforward commentary elaborating on the discourse alternates with cuttings of dialogue from group discussions with Willis. There are occasional descriptions of the atmosphere of the school as a place, but the reporting of dialogue is the main form of ethnographic evidence employed by Willis. The distinctiveness of the ethnography thus lies not so much in its sustained narrative technique, but in its constructive moves: how it defines topics, shifts from one locale to another, juxtaposes other perspectives and thus brings the larger world, in which the youths are embedded, occasionally into focus.

The most salient organizational move in the text is its bifurcation into a first part labelled "Ethnography" and a second part labelled "Analysis." Clearly Willis sees ethnography primarily as a method, and in text organization it must be set off and represented as such. This first part is presumably the data, but it is as much analysis as description. The second part, "Analysis," is really a theoretical reflection on the first part, as well as a manifesto for the value of ethnography in research on political economy. It relies on jargon and abstractions, but is rhetorically constructed upon references back to the naturalist representation of the boys' culture of the first part. Clearly Willis sees the need to abstract the theoretical contribution of ethnography from the actual writing of ethnographic description. This is not the simple description/theory dichotomy that seems to be presented. There are two different levels of analytic discourse, the second relying for its effect on the fact of the first preceding it. The first part provides a certain authority for the validity and authenticity of the theoretical elaborations of the second part. By separating ethnography from analysis, Willis gains a freedom of exposition, in which his own elaborations of the lads' embedded critique of capitalism seem a natural extension of this critique by taking off from an ethnographic platform. Only in the appendix does he self-critically demonstrate his authorial artifice. There he presents verbatim dialogue depicting the boys' reaction to their reading of his book. They can relate to their own words, but not to Willis's interpretive elaborations of their world view. Appropriately, he argues that this failure of recognition is itself a validation of their rejection of "mental" labor, which scholarly products embody, in favor of "manual" labor and immediate experience, an opposition at the heart of working class culture. Thus, whether in fact, on close inspection, the theoretical discussions of part 2 can be derived from the ethnographic discussions of part 1 is an open question; the point is that rhetorically they are effectively so derived.

Before proceeding to a discussion of Willis's specific claims for ethnography, it is worth stating briefly why this particular work merits so much attention. Despite several flaws,[7] which Willis confronts in a revealing afterword added to the American edition, *Learning to Labour*, in its ambition and grasp of the problems of achieving a text that probes the experience of its subjects while adequately representing the larger order in which they are implicated, stands as the state of the art for ethnographies that remain within realist (or, as Willis categorizes them, naturalist) conventions of writing.[8] There is a self-

---

7. Perhaps the most devastating flaw, from the perspective of a methodologically minded social science, is the self-fulfilling and circular manner in which Willis selected his sample and makes broader claims from it. Though he did control studies among conformist working class youth, he by fiat draws his boundary of concern around the manifestly cultural form of nonconformist boys without examining the process by which some become conformist and others do not. Rather he is interested in the *given* of nonconformism and sees it as the heart of working class consciousness and culture. The problem and process of variation do not bother him much. This is perhaps the ideological bias of the work. While it is an immensely attractive project to locate and evoke vividly a cultural form in origin and then to show its continuities in other locales, Willis's work is flawed. This stacking of the deck in sampling would not be so noticeable if Willis did not explicitly employ the rhetoric of formalist sociology's concern with method in his writing. Generalization from ethnography is a classic problem, and is even more saliently so in ethnography sensitive to political economy, but to adopt the methodologist's rhetoric to weaken the suggestive power of ethnography, which is traditionally where its will to generalize has lain.

8. Other recent works that experiment with the representation of the experience of ethnographic subjects and the systems of political economy that interpenetrate their lives are Michael Taussig's *The Devil and Commodity Fetishism in South America* (1980) and the paper by Daniel Bertaux and Isabelle Bertaux-Wiame (1981) on the survival of artisanal bakeries in France. The latter very much resembles Willis's effort, except that its subject is the petite bourgeoisie rather than the working class. Taussig's book is presented less self-consciously as ethnography and more as an argument about the folk critical perspective on capitalism creatively developed by those being proletarianized (in this, his book shares an important claim with Willis's ethnography, from which is derived much of the attraction and promise of interpretive ethnography that is sensitive to political economy: that it can discuss and articulate for the literate middle classes novel and insightful critiques of society embedded in the talk and life worlds of those most patently victimized by capitalism). Nonetheless, Taussig depends on his authority as an ethnographer, even though the ethnography remains in the wings and is only

critical subtext of hedges that runs through Willis's book and wrestles with all the previously discussed problems associated with the writing of ethnographies sensitive to political economy. It strains between the two textual modes we have discussed: it takes the form of strategically situated ethnography, but constantly has the ideal of multi-locale ethnography in view. As we shall see, it develops both of the alternatives for merging the macro and micro perspectives that Karin Knorr-Cetina (1981) reviews (see footnote 6). It embraces the conventions of realism, yet understands their limitations. By the inclusion of the above mentioned appendix, in which the reactions of the subjects to the ethnographer's account of them are sampled, it signals awareness of a possible hermeneutic critique of its claims, and of the persisting problem of translating the oral into the literary. Finally, it provides the strongest possible statement of the importance of ethnography for the reconstruction of high theory by complexifying the determination of events and actions at any point in an abstractly conceived social order. Willis demonstrates what statistical approaches cannot do and how they in fact oversimplify. The book is written with a strong commitment to Marxist theory, but it recognizes the value of similar kinds of ethnographic studies beyond the critical focus upon the working class. It is thus the most comprehensive meditation on a trend of experimentation that seeks to adapt the writing of ethnography to take into account larger issues of political economy and broader vistas of representation.

Willis's Main Conceptual Moves

The idea of cultural forms forged by resistance and accommodation to capitalist institutions. In opening his study, Willis says, "I view the cultural, not simply as a set of transferred internal structures (as in the usual notions of socialisation) nor as the passive result of the action of dominant ideology downwards (as in certain kinds of Marxism), but at least in part as the product of collective human praxis" (4). Appropriate to a Marxist for whom *the* problematic given is the capitalist overlay upon human diversity, culture is not what preexists this historic overlay, but is how humans whose lives are structurally defined by institutionally enacted capitalist principles respond to them in their

---

selectively brought on stage, so to speak, to provide a legitimating rhetoric for his mixed-mode, self-consciously moralistic and broadly transcendent purpose. Neither Taussig nor Bertaux and Bertaux-Wiame have written the kind of probing, meditative subtext about the nature of such ethnography that Willis has. Nor have they touched as comprehensively on so many major issues of writing such ethnography.

everyday life and experience. A cultural form thus arises from a group's class position in an institutional order, and its representation and analysis are the purpose of ethnographic research and writing. For Willis, the radical nature of ethnography is that it ends by redefining capitalist structure itself in human terms—to elucidate cultural forms demonstrates what the human meanings of structure are.

In this, Willis is very close to current notions of culture informing the writing of ethnography in American anthropology. But where Willis radically diverges from anthropological constructions of culture for the purposes of writing about it is in his view of its integrally interstitial and constitutive character bound up with a given order of political economy. Culture is not sui generis, but is class culture or subculture, entailing its formation in historic process—it originates in processes of resistance and accommodation to historically momentous trends of institution building. A cultural form is thus forged in class conflict.

Now this view of culture suits Willis very well, because working classes as distinctive cultural forms—meat for the ethnographer—are pure inventions of a particular world historical system of political economy. In the industrial West, class culture *is* the only culture that defines the form of life of many people. Anthropologists, specialists in the study of those on the margins of world historical trends emanating from the West, are accustomed to staging culture as an integral spatio-temporal isolate, not without its own internal contradictions, but at least with its own integrity against the world, so to speak. This is much different from the Marxist emphasis, which views culture as a product of struggle; there is no self-contained integrity entailed in the concept; it is a function of critique and acceptance in thought and action among those variously situated in a system of political economy, which is not finally monolithic, once viewed from the perspective of an ethnography of cultural forms, but rather a diversity of responses to the enacted principles of capitalist political economy.

The problem for contemporary ethnographic experiments in anthropology is how to synthesize these two emphases in the textual representation of culture, since around the world anthropologists often deal these days with subjects for whom both emphases apply. The anthropological bias is to emphasize or give priority reality to the precapitalist dimensions of the lives of ethnographic subjects. Willis's view of culture is an important corrective to this. Conversely, as we shall see, Willis's predicament of having to invest richness of meaning in "thin" cultural forms purely generated by responses to capitalism is not faced by most anthropologists. (Compare Taussig 1980 with Willis: The former has a rich body of lore with which to represent a resistance-and-accommodation view of proletarian culture, even though he does overplay the off-stage image of pre-capitalist cultural purity among his subjects; the latter strains to invest positive meaning and richness in a cultural form that seems entirely oppositional.)

Finally, Willis makes a strong argument for the irreducibility and autonomy of the cultural level of analysis, very similar to the foundational postulate of such American cultural theorists as David Schneider and Clifford Geertz. There is a reifying bias built into this postulate. In Willis's book it becomes more apparent as he moves from ethnographic representation to the more abstractly analytic section, and especially when he makes a strong plea in the afterword for the value of the ethnographic as an approach within Marxism. For Willis, this radical insistence on the irreducibility and the autonomy of the cultural, at whatever cost in reification, is a safeguard against the penchant in Western (or bourgeois) social thought to devalue or marginalize what the cultural emphasizes: the concreteness and commonsensicality of everyday life, intractable to formulations of structural determination as a privileged mode of discourse in bourgeois society (which also infects much Marxist writing). As Willis states:

> The main point here, though, is not to attempt an exact taxonomy of "cultural forms" or a rigorous theoretical conceptualization of "the cultural." What I want to emphasize in the general approach of this book is the way that the field of symbolic and material, lived relations should be represented in their own concreteness, at their own level, without continually reducing them, mechanistically, to basic determining structures. Social reproduction and contradiction must be shown not as abstract entities, but as embedded dynamically within the real lives of real people in a way that is not simple "correspondence" or "reflection" of unchanged, somehow "deeper" structures. . . . Agents' intentions do not proceed from themselves, but are bound up in the complex way in which structures are inhabited through "cultural forms". . . .
>
> The role of ethnography is to show the cultural viewpoint of the oppressed, their "hidden" knowledges and resistances as well as the basis on which entrapping "decisions" are taken in some sense of liberty, but which nevertheless help to produce "structure." This is, in part, the project of showing the capacities of the working class to generate, albeit ambiguous, complex, and often ironic, collective and cultural forms of knowledge not reducible to the bourgeois forms—and the importance of this is as one of the bases for political change. (1981:201–3)

Thus, like the anthropological ethnographer, Willis defines an autonomous culture concept that facilitates the authentic depiction of human diversity and difference against the bias to elide it, but his agenda, unlike the anthropologist's, has a self-consciously political definition. Furthermore, in Willis's agenda, the staging of the cultural for the purpose of ethnographic representation is primarily a means to the end of elucidation of an embedded critique of capitalist society in working class life, a conceptual move to which we now turn.

The ethnographer's articulation of the critical theory embedded in working class experience. One of the great current attractions of ethnography to traditions of cultural criticism in the West, and especially the Marxist tradition, is the move that Willis makes (as does Taussig) in letting ethnography demonstrate that the most powerful and novel criticisms of capitalist society lie embedded in the everyday conditions and talk of ethnographic subjects, more powerful and novel even than the contributions of intellectuals whose self-conscious task cultural criticism has been. The ethnographer is the midwife, as it were, who delivers and articulates what is vernacularly expressed in working class lives, and for that matter, middle class lives.

Having the critique come from the subject rather than the author as critic can be seen as a move to shift the responsibility of criticism to those who are represented as social actors, and in so doing, to find a new and powerful authenticity for works of cultural criticism. The traditional quest of ethnography, in anthropology at least, for the "native's point of view" becomes in its guise of cultural criticism a search for an authentic critical theory, embodied in the lives of the victims of macrosocial systems, who are most often the subject of ethnography. Incidentally, this move also fulfills Knorr-Cetina's favored mode of integrating the macro with the micro in that the extracted and articulated critical theory of the subject is also a representation encapsulated in the micro-focused enthography, of his folk understanding of the macrosocial system. As Willis states:

This is why the ethnography of visible forms is limited. The external, more obviously creative, varied and sometimes random features must be read back to their heart. The logic of living must be traced to the heart of its conceptual relationships if we are to understand the social creativity of a culture. This always concerns, at some level, a recognition of, and action upon, the particularity of its place within a determinate social structure.

One of the most profound reasons why this social creativity cannot be expressed rationally at the surface of the culture is that it is truly only half the story. It really *does not* proceed with a pure expressive purpose from the center of the culture. We must posit the penetration [Willis's jargon for perceptive understandings of capitalist reality in the lads' own idiom] as a clean and coherent insight in order to say what it is, but the concrete forms of cultures, as ethnography insistently reminds us, do not allow single pure dynamics. In their very formation these "insights" are distorted, turned and deposited into other forms—such as subjective affirmation of manual labour—which make it hard to believe there has ever been, or could ever be, even a notion of a rational kernel, never mind that it should be easily expressed. This means, amongst other things, that we must distinguish between the level of the cultural and the level of practical consciousness in our specification of creativity and rationality. (1981 : 121–22)

Thus, Willis defines the appropriate function of the ethnographer as midwife. The lads embody the critical insights, but in an engaged, stunted way, which the ethnographer can register. Thus, it is for the ethnographer to bring out and clarify the insights as well as to explain why they may lead to unintended consequences or inaction. As Willis says, "It is the apparent cultural ascension of the working class which brings the hell of its own real present" (122).

It is worth remarking on why this posture of the ethnographer as midwife to indigenous critical theory is such an appealing move in Marxist cultural analysis, especially in its persisting focus on the working class (historically well defined in England). This class is the "chosen people" who most experience the contradictions of capitalism, and the state of whose consciousness is a matter of perennial debate among Marxist intellectuals. And so Willis says, "It [the working class potential for insight] is embedded in the only class in the capitalist social formation which does not have a structurally based vested interest in mystifying itself. . . . The working class does not *have* to believe the dominant ideology. It does not need the mask of democracy to cover its face of oppression. The very existence and consciousness of the middle class is deeply integrated into that structure which gives it dominance" (123).

By his ethnographic midwifery among the proletariat, Willis reveals that they, and not the intellectuals, embody the most powerful critique of capitalism, and this is as it should be, given their strategic position in Marxist theory. Willis's ethnography thus proposes to resolve the longstanding embarrassment in Marxism of the need for radical middle class intellectuals (or intellectuals of working class origin) to be the articulate consciousness of working class masses. Willis presumes to show that they can speak equally and effectively for themselves (but without his being self-critical enough about the hermeneutic problems of realizing this claim textually, discussed below).

In summary form, Willis sees the heart of his subjects' criticism of capitalism in the distinction they make between mental and manual labor, their elaborate rejection of the former and their embracing of the latter as the central male-oriented ethos of their cultural form. The lads see behind the ideology of schooling in preparing students for work to the real nature of work—to the nature of labor power, as a commodity like no other, in Willis's terms. Most importantly, the youths reject qualifications as the means to social mobility. For them, all jobs are the same and equally meaningless; they take refuge and satisfaction in a youth subculture that emphasizes adventure and virile experience. Manual labor is an emblem of this emphasis—it stands for masculinity and opposition to authority. The oppositional culture at school develops the means of taking informal control of the production process. Most proximately, the "ear'oles," or conformist students, stand as foils for the lads and the embodiment of the world of qualifications leading to middle class mystifications of work, which they reject.

So, the lads turn out to confirm basic Marxist notions of the central role of the reduction of labor to a commodity in capitalist production. Ethnography in Willis's hands thus powerfully validates Marxist theory by authenticating its claims among the most important ethnographic subjects of all, the working class. Much of Willis's claim hinges on his ability to persuade the reader by textual artifice of the meaningfulness of the boys' nonconformist behavior against the middle class tendency to dismiss it as mindless deviance, alienation, or delinquency. We shall consider below whether the investiture of the boys' oppositional culture with the respectability of meaning—the foundation from which grows a critical theory embodied in everyday experience—is effectively achieved.

The system beyond the ethnographic locale enacted in the irony of unintended consequences. The postulate of unintended consequences is a means by which an ethnographer can push analysis beyond the locale of primary fieldwork to representations of the macro-system (conventionally conceived as abstract structures) in cultural, structurally contingent terms. Willis makes full use of this move, which Knorr-Cetina discusses (see footnote 6) as one of the modes of bringing macro perspectives back into the current reign of productivity in micro perspectives. In fact, the central argument of the book is the one about the unintended consequences of the lads' oppositional culture formed at school: how they systematically disqualify themselves from middle class jobs as the ironic effect of class conflict in the schools; how, without coercion, youths funnel themselves onto the shop floor. As Willis concludes the ethnography section of his book:

There is also a sense in which, despite the ravages—fairly well contained at this point anyway—manual work stands for something and is a way of contributing to and substantiating a certain view of life which criticises, scorns and devalues others as well as putting the self, as they feel it, in some elusive way ahead of the game. These feelings arise precisely from a sense of their own labour power which has been learnt and truly appropriated as insight and self-advance within the depths of the counter-school culture as it develops specific class forms in the institutional context. It is difficult to think how attitudes of such strength and informal and personal validity could have been formed in any other way. It is they, not formal schooling, which carry "the lads" over into a certain application to the productive process. In a sense, therefore, there is an element of self-domination in the acceptance of subordinate roles in western capitalism. However, this damnation is experienced, paradoxically, as a form of true learning, appropriation and as a kind of resistance. How are we to understand this? (1981:113)

This is the framing question Willis uses to organize his elaborations of the second, analysis part of the book. Though it is the need for cash that finally pushes the lads into the productive process, it is masculine chauvinism, forged in opposition to school, that adapts them to the shop floor and provides the line of continuity between the two locales.

The unintended-consequences move may be a nice solution to the problem of macro-system representation in ethnography whose spirit is interpretive, but it is also the most notably hedged dimension of Willis's account. He is constantly hedging against the circularity of making an argument of such general implication from so small a sample and from his recognition, but systematic eliding, of other variant responses to school both among middle class and conformist working class lads (see footnote 7); he also hedges against the danger of an "oversocialized" view of his own nonconformist subjects, as thorough products of the cultural form that is, finally, Willis's abstracted focus of analysis. Furthermore, the unintended-consequences move seems very close to old-fashioned functionalist teleology, albeit an ironic form of it—agents do what they do in their various contexts, and hey presto! there is neat order in the system. A certain recognition of the messiness of real life is simply added to conventional notions of functionalist order. This is indeed an improvement on past moves of representing the social system, but it is hardly a bold break with easy notions of order.

A Commentary on Textual Moves Used to Achieve the Above Conceptual Arguments

Willis's Hermeneutic Sensitivity

I would just like to mark a recognition here that, no matter how modified, participant observation and the methods under its aegis, display a tendency towards naturalism and therefore to conservatism. The ethnographic account is a supremely ex post facto product of the actual uncertainty of life. There develops, unwilled, a false unity which asks, "What follows next?" "How did it end?" "What makes sense of it?". The subjects stand too square in their self-

referenced world. The method is also patronising and condescending—is it
possible to imagine the ethnographic account upwards in a class society? . . .
The ethnographic account, for all its biases insists upon a level of human
agency which is persistently overlooked or denied but which increases in importance all the time for other levels of the social whole. Although the world
is never directly "knowable," and cannot empirically present itself in the way
that the ethnographic account seems sometimes to suggest, it must nevertheless be specifically registered somewhere in theory if theory pretends to any
relevance at all. (Willis 1981 : 194)

At issue here is the hermeneutic critique of Willis's claim to have
extracted a working class critical theory from the words and actions of
his subjects, a theory that happens powerfully to confirm Marxist theory. We should recall, in this regard, the central constructive move of
Willis's text—the distinct separation of ethnography from analysis.
This move may be a function of Willis's retention of a rhetoric of
positivist sociologism that represents ethnography as merely a method
and the reporting of data. Nevertheless, this constructive division
most importantly frames a legitimated, autonomous analytic voice
through which Willis can develop a theoretical discourse in a language
to which he is accustomed, while relying on reference back to the ethnography section as a suggestion that it is not really his voice, but a
mediation of what is embodied in the ethnography of the lads, conceived, significantly, as verbatim interview transcripts. So, we might
say that the representation of working class experience is not at all
Willis's primary goal; rather, Willis develops ethnographic representations of working class experience to refer to it in a way that serves his
theoretical exposition. Ethnography gives body to Willis's book, but it
is not in itself the main point.

There is at least a hint of a sleight-of-hand here, and what a hermeneutic sensitivity incorporated in the narrative of ethnography
does is to impose standards of puritanical honesty upon claims, such
as those at the heart of Willis's text, about who speaks for whom, and
what is actually being authentically represented. Does Willis's articulated critical theory of capitalism really come from the lads? Does the
ethnographer discover such insights, as is argued, or does he evoke
them in his subjects in his engagement with them, or, most crudely,
does he merely assert by fiat that what he is saying in his own words is
an accurate gloss of what the subjects have said and meant? These are
very old epistemological problems central to the practice of ethnography, which are currently being probed in the impact that hermeneutic
philosophy is having on anthropological thought. Perhaps, most centrally, the issue is one of translating the orality of the subjects into the
literacy of the ethnographer—in this case, the talk of the lads into the

jargon-laden, dense prose of Willis in his commentaries and theoretical elaborations.

Given the disarray of paradigms I have mentioned, it is a seductive idea at the moment to liberal and radical cultural critics in search of some direction that the necessary insights are *there* in the lives of subjects, to be unearthed by careful interpretation within a genre such as ethnography. As a result, the special appeal of the kind of claim Willis makes does tend to blunt the skepticism of hermeneutic self-criticism, and it gets off rather easily. To make the claim passionately and evocatively is sufficient to win over middle class readers to a move that transfers the burden of criticism to the subject and modifies the function of the analyst with very attractive implications for the contemporary predicaments of theory.

How much hermeneutic sensitivity is there, then, in Willis's book? Willis is very shrewd indeed about the limitations of ethnography and the possible objections to his claim that he has in fact authentically spoken for the lads, but the important point here is that this awareness is not an integral part of his text, nor for him a foundation of writing ethnography. As in so many realist accounts, hermeneutic shrewdness, when it is present, is marginalized (as in the *very* shrewd appendix previously discussed and in Willis's afterword admissions about the limitations of naturalism in ethnographic accounts—see the quotation above). So while hermeneutically aware on the margins, Willis keeps his distance from his subjects; the sort of engagement out of which hermeneutic reflection arises is only a leitmotif in his text and not an integral component of either its ethnographic representations or the analysis that follows.

The Dominant Bourgeois World Evoked Rather Than Juxtaposed Ethnographically

Since my main focus was on the culture of the "lads," the "ear'oles" necessarily became something of a dramatic foil for their activity and creativity. . . . Nevertheless, the general case I am arguing is that, in different ways, all social agents have a hand collectively in constructing their own destiny, doing so in a way which is not simply determined from outside and which often enjoys the labyrinthine complexity of a "cultural form." But this cannot be said all at once! And if the ethnographic act of "giving life" to one particular "cultural form" seems to take life from others, to make others look anemic, then this should not be taken to mean that "social theory" is true only for the former. This book should not encourage the dismissal or marginalization of the more conformist in school, but should encourage concrete research in them from similar perspectives to uncover the complexity and promise of their social existence. (Willis 1981:207)

Willis entertains the possibility that the same conceptual moves he has made in regard to the working class could be made, with as productive results, in regard to various segments of the dominant bourgeoisie. What belies this possibility is the fact that Willis himself does not choose to represent in these ethnographic ways the larger class world beyond that of his working class subjects, even though he did do "control" fieldwork among the "ear'oles" and the text is sprinkled with insights about the cultural form of the dominant class in contrast to that of the lads. Rather, instead of cross-class parallel juxtapositions of ethnography, he chooses to evoke the capitalist world in a vague, personified way. Rather than depend on the kind of ethnography he does for his focal working class subjects, he relies on the ethnographically unexamined images of class-structured society built into the tradition of Marxist theory. This is, as I have noted, both an advantage of writing ethnography within the Marxist tradition (it provides a ready-made, classic, and familiar means of evoking the macrosocial order) and a disadvantage (the use of ready-made macro images tends to caricature the darkly unknowable world in contrast with the ethnographically elucidated world of working class subjects).

Rather than juxtaposing ethnographic representations of different classes, Willis presents an ethnography of the working class, and just *assumes* an ethnographic perspective on the middle class by contrast (incidentally, Willis is aware of this problem, as indicated in the above quotation: "But this cannot be said all at once!"). Thus, he makes the lads real, but he chooses to reify the larger system in which they live. This is inconsistent with the spirit of the ethnographic approach he eloquently promotes. What is "the system" for the lads is the other's (the middle class) cultural form. The textual problem here is carefully representing one form of life while caricaturing those of the others beyond it as "the system."

At stake here is the validity of the "unintended-consequences" construction of the system, linking ethnographic locales. While Willis limits himself in demonstrating the workings of the system as unintended consequences to the youths' cultural evolution in the school and on the shop floor, for consistency he must also argue that relations *between* classes, whose cultural forms are often situated in different ethnographic locales (*except* for the school), are also characterized by linkages of unintended consequences emanating from activity ethnographically recounted. If all participants in the capitalist social order develop creative cultural forms of accommodation and resistance like the lads, then how on the cultural level, can capitalism and its dominant classes be made to appear more directed, ideologically bound, and intentional than the lads as victims? If the system thoroughly operates by unwitting interdependencies and unintended, but coordinated, consequences, then it would be difficult to sustain the conventional way of representing the dominant class or classes in Marxist theory. As long as Willis personifies and caricatures the system beyond the ethnographic representation of the working class, he need not come to terms with this difficulty. If he had instead constructed his text on cross-class ethnographic juxtapositions, he would have had to face the full implications of his unintended consequences more squarely.

Investing Meaning in the Lads' Lives

Finally, all of Willis's conceptual moves depend on his ability to persuade the reader that the youths' culture is in fact positively mean-ing*ful* and creative, that they are on to something, rather than just being the alienated class both in conditions of work and spirit. The critical move is to dissociate the world of work, which the lads do clearly see as meaningless, from the world of experience, which they celebrate and creatively elaborate as a form of rebellion. Because Willis refers only obliquely to the richest context for the persuasive representation of working class creativity—youth popular culture— he is left with rather thin materials through which to evoke the style and creativity of the boys' experience. There is thus a straining and special pleading in his repeated praise of the meaningful content of their oppositional culture, which, though passionately asserted (as if there were much more to it than he can tell us within the confines of ethnography), still rings hollow. For example, as Willis states:

Thus the whole nature of "really doing things", of being physically active in the world, of giving labour power in a certain way, is seen by "the lads" not simply as a defensive measure, or as a negative response, but as an affirmation and expression of what it seems has been genuinely and creatively learned. It speaks of a distinct maturity, a practice of ability and perspective, that others are felt not to have. Despite its intrinsic meaninglessness manual labour, at least at this period in their lives, comes to mean for "the lads" in Hammer-town an assertion of their freedom and a specific kind of power in the world. (1981:104)

Obviously, Willis has great admiration for the meaning that his subjects are able to derive from the meaninglessness of their place in society. But in expressing such admiration, he cannot escape suggesting the inauthenticity of it and the self-deception involved, without a much more direct treatment of working class popular culture. Willis finally retreats from his enthusiasm for the lads' oppositional cultures when he responds sympathetically to the complaints of feminists in the afterword, written for the American edition of *Learning to Labour*: what meaning the lads' lives have for them is built on the oppression of women. In the text itself, Willis does acknowledge in passing the racism and sexism that frame his subjects' oppositional culture, centered on virile masculinity, but he does not confront them seriously until the reflective afterword. So, in a sense, the textual move of investing meaning in what might be viewed as meaningless, anarchic lives, is done in a "he doth protest too much" manner, and finally with considerable ambivalence. Yet, as the rhetoric necessary both for convincing ethnographic representations and claims drawn from them, the successful handling of this textual move would seem fundamental.

Conclusion

The book is not an attempt to give a full *anthropological* account of the full range of the whole life process of twelve individuals—which indeed would have had to take in much else, including their physical and emotional development, sexuality, experience in the family, and their detailed existence in a whole neighbourhood and sweep of local life. I was concentrating on *certain* cultural and symbolic processes within a relatively discrete "cultural form," focused mainly in the school, and on the transition to work which touched upon many of these things, certainly, but not as a neutral taxonomical charting of them. Perhaps we should call this a "cultural ethnography" to distinguish it from anthropological approaches. (Willis 1981 : 217–18)

Anthropologists may be disconcerted and irritated by the way in which Willis as ethnographer distances himself from the same project in anthropology by trivializing the purpose of the latter as nondirected, inflexible holism; taxonomic description for its own sake, without a redeeming point or argument. Nonetheless, Willis does pose the challenge for the anthropological tradition of ethnography, underlain perhaps by an unattainable ideal of holism not to be taken literally, to apply ethnography to projects of broader purpose and theoretical significance, like his own. This entails the writing of mixed-genre texts, similar to those envisioned by Raymond Williams for social realism, in which ethnographic representation and authority would be a variably salient component. Contrary to Willis's outmoded perception of the state of ethnography within anthropology, such mixed-genre texts, sensitive to both the inner lives of subjects and the nature of world historical political economy, are a major concern of the trend of experimentation in contemporary anthropology that we have been discussing.

Appendix: Short Takes on Other Experimental Uses of Ethnography in Addressing Problems of Political Economy and Social Theory

I shall very briefly deal with two other kinds of mixed-genre texts in the move toward ethnographies that ambitiously take on problems of social theory, political economy, and history. In one kind of text, it is the conventions of ethnographic representation that are left in the background, marginalized, or subordinated to a purpose that contributes to the explanation of momentous historic events; in the other kind of text, ethnographic representation is the focus, if not obsession, while the world of historic political economy, although brought into the text, gets subtly shifted to the background by a strategy of evocation rather than by substantive representation. In both cases, the texts are written from the experience of fieldwork and the authority derived from it, but there is no simple correlation between fieldwork done and symmetrical text as reportage written from that experience. Rather, in both cases, and most saliently in the first, ethnographic detail shares textual space with other varieties of writing, including historical narrative, literary exegesis, and autobiographical confession.

Ethnography and Revolutionary Upheaval

The particular concern here is how the writing of ethnography can be adapted to address classic historic questions of causation, those that require explanations of major events. The question of social and political revolutions is an excellent, perennial case in point. For the ethnographer, much depends on serendipity and opportunity—where and when the ethnographer was situated in relation to the event. Ethnography that has concerned itself with great revolutions has usually been situated to recount the effects of revolution on everyday life in the form of village studies. For me, the most vivid village-level ethnography registering post-revolutionary conditions is William Hinton's *Fanshen* (1966), with its striking account of how a revolutionary social theory is applied in the reclassification and reshaping of local village society.

But ethnography could do much more if ethnographers in opportune circumstances wrote accounts of greater ambition. With the careful textual use of ethnographic representation, they could enter into the central debates about the origin and course of revolutionary processes themselves. Michael Fischer's *Iran: From Religious Dispute to Revolution* (1980) is a prime, if not unique, example of a mixed-genre account in which the rhetorical fixing of the ethnographer's authority and the careful introduction of ethnographic detail shape an argument dealing with the causation and origins of revolution rather than its effects. The critical ethnographic representations are those of Shi'ite religious education, which Fischer studied in Qum before the revolution. The book itself opens with the fixing of ethnographic authority, with Fischer engaged in discussion with an ayatollah. Indeed, this establishes that "he was there," but it does much more than this, since it is a presentation of the reality and medium of Shi'ite ideology and world view itself, inseparable from the styles of discourse in which it is expressed. From this beginning onward, the ethnography of Shi'ite culture is threaded through a text that alternates between historical narrative, moment-to-moment reporting of revolutionary events, sociological class analysis, textual exegesis, and the ethnographic representation of life in Qum itself. Though it is much harder to pin down as ethnography than Willis's explicitly labelled study, Fischer's book nonetheless depends, as does Willis's book, on strategically situated ethnography, and self-consciously so. Thus, when the ethnographer takes on debates about momentous events (and the macro systems of political economy they implicate), ethnography itself moves from center place to play a peripatetic role in text construction.

Ethnography and the Modern Essay: Undermining Realist Representation in an Uncertain World

And what of those who view the representation of larger, impersonal systems within the narrative space of ethnography as untenable, yet are sensitive to trends in political economy and still see the need to evoke them in some way? This is the predicament of the more radical, modernist experiments in ethnography—those turning away from realist conventions toward elaborate experimentation with form and attention to reciprocity of perspectives, the dialogic context of fieldwork, and even to the incorporation of multiple authorial voices in the conventional single-author-controlled text. Much more strongly than Raymond Williams, who holds to realism, such experimental writers feel that radically interpretive ethnographies can never gain knowledge of the realities that statistics can—they perhaps do not even recognize the priority or privileged validity of such abstractly represented realities. They seek rather a means of evoking the world without representing it.

The modernist form of the essay perhaps meets this need. It opposes conventional systematic analysis, absolves the writer from having to develop the broader implications of his thought (while nonetheless indicating that there are such implications) or of having to tie loose ends together. The essayist can mystify the world, leave his subjects' actions open-ended as to their global implications, from a rhetorical posture of profound half-understanding, half-bewilderment with the world in which the ethnographic subject and the ethnographer live. This is thus a form well suited to a time such as the present, when paradigms are in disarray, problems intractable, and phenomena only partly understood. It is finally a hedge on the holistic commitments of anthropological ethnography. The open-ended mystery of phenomena partly explained ("there are always alternative interpretations") is an essential feature of the rhetoric of the experimental posture. Unlike realist ethnography, which can be backgrounded when the text squarely addresses great events, the modernist ethnographic essay grapples with the textual problem of how the world is to serve as backdrop once conventional techniques of realistic representation are ruled out.

Perhaps the most intensive and explicit reflection on the essay as a form of writing appropriate to modernity is that of Theodor Adorno (see Kauffmann 1981), and especially his refusal to impose order through writing on a world whose essence is its fragmentary character. Rather than attempting to represent the system or major events by an orderly account of them, to which realism is partial, the modern essay permits, or rather sanctions, the ultimate hedge—it legitimates fragmentation, rough edges, and the self-conscious aim of achieving an effect that disturbs the reader. The essay in this modernist sense is thus a particularly appropriate self-conscious posture for the most radically experimental ethnographies. They want to change the conventional focus in ethnography and thus the perception of readers. As noted, they shift focus to the dialogic and the reciprocity of perspectives involved in any ethnographic project. They want to say something about the modern world as much, if not more, by self-conscious attention to the form of the ethnographic text as by direct attention to the bounded world of the ethnographic subject.

The subtlety of this use of the essay is that whether or not the subject is explicitly viewed as living in a fragmented world system, at the level of her experience and that of the ethnographer the broader world is evoked indirectly through the attempt in ethnographic writing to convey alien experience. This is the radical approach to the representation of cultural difference in a world where the salience of difference has diminished, at least among Western middle class

readerships. Such ethnography seeks to convey the quality of its subjects' experience, free of the mediation of customs and institutions,
concepts that carry an embedded bias toward seeing order, where on
the level of experience such order is not felt or imagined to the same
degree. The ethnography as modern essay profoundly disrupts the
commitment to holism that is at the heart of most realist ethnography
and that is increasingly problematic (as the hedges in Willis's text indicate). It does not promise that its subjects are part of a larger order.
Instead, by the open-endedness of the form, it evokes a broader world
of uncertain order—this is the pose the modernist essay cultivates supremely. In a sense, with the appropriate rhetoric of the essay, modernist ethnography declines the problematic of the modes of ethnography sensitive to political economy that we have discussed, while
being similarly motivated by the predicament of writing ethnography
in recognition of a world for which the twentieth-century ethnographic paradigm now seems inadequate. The rhetoric of the modern
essay as a guide to constructing ethnography is merely very strong
medicine, compared to Willis's or Fischer's moves to merge the perspectives of ethnography and political economy.

Actual examples of ethnography set in the rhetoric of the modern
essay are few, although it is the kind of text writers either aspire to or
entertain the possibility of and then shy away from in experimental
times. Vincent Crapanzano's *Tuhami: Portrait of a Moroccan* (1980) and,
more recently, his *Waiting* (1985) are perhaps the most prominent existing experimental ethnographies that can be viewed as employing
the rhetoric of the modern essay. The latter work in particular, which
uses the dialogic capturing of multiple voices to expose the condition
of entrapment among the whites of contemporary South Africa, reveals the inherent concern of such modernist techniques with political
economy. Far from being insular and parochial, the discourse of the
whites in the pleasant South African countryside is full of "knowing"
irony about their own position and that of their society globally. Likewise, in *Tuhami*, the form of the text as well as its subject—a spirit-
possessed proletarian tilemaker—serves as a statement about colonial
and post-colonial Algerian society.

A sustained tolerance of incompleteness and indeterminateness
about the order in the world that lies beyond the experience of ethnographic subjects, intensely focused upon, seems to be a key rhetorical
marker in modernist ethnography. For example, one common idea of
text construction is to string together a set of separate essays dealing
with different themes or interpretations of the same subject (if its actual style were not that of the cocksure English essayist, combined
with a heavy dose of scientistic certainty, Gregory Bateson's *Naven*

[1936] might be seen in its actual narrative structure and spirit as an early example of the ethnography as modern essay; indeed it was written during a time of profound global uncertainty like the contemporary period; the oddness of *Naven* is its mingling of behaviorist and hermeneutic concerns). Furthermore, the ethnography as essay often defines itself as such by a prominent metacommentary on the difficulties of doing ethnography in the modern world, while doing it. In general, then, it is the revealed modernist consciousness of the ethnographic writer, troubled by the interpretive task at hand, that embeds in the text references to the broader world she and her subjects share. I view modernist experiments as the current outer limit to the ways ethnography as a matter of textual strategy handles the micro-macro integration problem with which this paper began.

MICHAEL M. J. FISCHER

Ethnicity and the Post-Modern Arts of Memory

I

Conclusions and Re-Visions

History as celebrated by Mnemosoune is a deciphering of the invisible, a geography of the supernatural. . . . It throws a bridge between the world of the living and that beyond to which everything that leaves the light of day must return. It brings about an "evocation" of the past. . . . Memory appears as a source of immortality. . . . JEAN-PIERRE VERNANT

Our period is not defined by the triumph of technology for technology's sake, as it is not defined by art for art's sake, as it is not defined by nihilism. It is action for a world to come, transcendence of its period—transcendence of self which calls for epiphany of the Other. EMANUEL LEVINAS

This paper brings together two indirectly related ethnographic phenomena of the 1970s and 1980s—the florescence of ethnic autobiography and the academic fascination with textual theories of deferred, hidden, or occulted meaning[1]—in order to ask whether

NOTE: My use of "post-modern" in this essay follows that of Jean-François Lyotard (1979): it is that moment of modernism that defines itself against an immediate past ("post") and that is skeptically inquisitive about all grounds of authority, assumption, or convention ("modernism"). Lyotard's definition allows for cycles of modernism that decay and renew, as well as drawing attention to the various techniques for questioning and deorienting/reorienting—techniques ranging from surrealism in the arts to developments in the natural sciences (fractals, catastrophe theory, pragmatic paradoxes, undecidables). Alternative definitions of post-modernism as either an unlabeled aftermath of early twentieth-century modernisms—or, as Fredric Jameson would have it, a retreat from politically charged modernism back into bourgeois complacency—empty the term of any substantive meaning and (in Jameson's case) assert unsubstantiated negative political evaluations. An allied usage of post-modern to that employed here, and to which I am also indebted, is that of Stephen Tyler (see this volume).

1. For reasons of space, this second phenomenon will have to remain an undersong, only alluded to periodically. "Occulted" is a key term from Stephen Tyler's essay in this volume, an essay with which the present paper is intended to resonate. "Deferred" invokes Jacques Derrida's efforts to show how metaphors depend on and create new displacements from meanings in other texts, how no text exists in and of itself. "Hidden" refers to Walter Benjamin's attempts at "revelation" or recovery of meanings sedi-

they can revitalize our ways of thinking about how culture operates and refashion our practice of ethnography as a mode of cultural criticism. Just as the travel account and the ethnography served as forms for explorations of the "primitive" world (see Pratt in this volume) and the realist novel served as the form for explorations of bourgeois manners and the self in early industrial society, so ethnic autobiography and autobiographical fiction can perhaps serve as key forms for explorations of pluralist, post-industrial, late twentieth-century society.

The recent proliferation of autobiographical works that take ethnicity as a focal puzzle seems to be poorly accommodated within the traditional sociological literature on ethnicity. Works such as Maxine Hong Kingston's *The Woman Warrior* (1976), Michael Arlen's *Passage to Ararat* (1975), and Marita Golden's *Migrations of the Heart* (1983) are inadequately comprehended through discussions of group solidarity, traditional values, family mobility, political mobilization, or similar sociological categories. Immigrant novels of rebellion against the family, intermarriage, and acculturation are more relevant to these sociological conceptions.

What the newer works bring home forcefully is, *first*, the paradoxical sense that ethnicity is something reinvented and reinterpreted in each generation by each individual and that it is often something quite puzzling to the individual, something over which he or she lacks control. Ethnicity is not something that is simply passed on from generation to generation, taught and learned; it is something dynamic, often unsuccessfully repressed or avoided. It can be potent even when not consciously taught; it is something that institutionalized teaching easily makes chauvinist, sterile, and superficial, something that emerges in full—often liberating—flower only through struggle. Insofar as ethnicity is a deeply rooted emotional component of identity, it is often transmitted less through cognitive language or learning (to which sociology has almost entirely restricted itself) than through

---

mented in layers of language. Others who have become theoreticians of interest for the present mood include Harold Bloom (like Derrida, concerned with intertextuality—in his terms, "the anxiety of influence"); Sigmund Freud and Jacques Lacan (as semioticians interested in the dynamics of what Freud called "the soul," locating what is repressed, implicit, mediated, or what Tyler calls the "unsaid"); Wilhelm Dilthey, Clifford Geertz, and Victor Turner (as exploring constructivist understandings of symbolic meaning, in Geertz's phrase "models of and models for"); Hans-Georg Gadamer (for his articulation of meaning elicited through the juxtaposition of historical horizons and cultural traditions); Friedrich Nietzsche and Michel Foucault (for their inquiries into the hegemonic power of language); Max and Uriel Weinreich and Michel Serres (for their concerns with inter-reference and interlinguistics). It is no coincidence that the interest in these authors—renewed interest in the case of Freud, Nietzsche, and Benjamin—(a reaction against the New Criticism of the 1960s in literature, and against Parsonianism in anthropology) appears contemporaneously with the florescence of ethnic autobiography. There is a commonality of inquiry characteristic of the present moment.

processes analogous to the dreaming and transference of psychoanalytic encounters.

Second, what is discovered and reinvented in the new works about
ethnicity is, perhaps increasingly, something new: to be Chinese-
American is not the same thing as being Chinese in America. In this
sense there is no role model for becoming Chinese-American. It is a
matter of finding a voice or style that does not violate one's several
components of identity. In part, such a process of assuming an ethnic
identity is an insistence on a pluralist, multidimensional, or multifaceted concept of self: one can be many different things, and this
personal sense can be a crucible for a wider social ethos of pluralism.

Third, the search or struggle for a sense of ethnic identity is a
(re-)invention and discovery of a vision, both ethical and future-
oriented. Whereas the search for coherence is grounded in a connection to the past, the meaning abstracted from that past, an important
criterion of coherence, is an ethic workable for the future. Such visions can take a number of forms: they can be both culturally specific
(e.g., the biblical strains of black victories over oppression) and dialectically formed as critiques of hegemonic ideologies (e.g., as alternatives to the melting pot rhetoric of assimilation to the bland, neutral
style of the conformist 1950s).

Two preliminary examples are both retrospective accounts expressing surprise at the power of politically charged crystallizations.
In *American Immigrants in Israel* (1981), Kevin Avruch quotes an American who wryly recalls exploding at SDSers who attacked Israel in
1967, giving them Israel's case in great detail: "At the time, I didn't
know where that attitude and all that information came from." Similarly, Marita Golden remembers being in high school when Martin
Luther King was assassinated:

The days after King's death saw an invisible barricade of tensions rise between
the white and black students at Western High School. The black students did
not know then that in a few months many of us would repudiate our white
friends, no longer finding them "relevant." Finding instead their mere presence inconsistent with a "commitment to the struggle," which is what our lives
became overnight. (p. 15)

These passages illustrate a lack of explicit knowledge, a sense of the
buried coming to the surface, and the compulsion of an "id-like"
force. The *id*, as Freud originally used the term, was merely *das Es*,
the it-ness of experience, made particularly potent for the German-
speaking child, who is referred to in the neuter—*das Kind*—and who
only gradually develops an acknowledged, engendered, individuated
self. The recognition of something about one's essential being thus
seems to stem from outside one's immediate consciousness and con-

trol, and yet requires an effort of self-definition.[2] Ethnicity in its contemporary form is thus neither, as the sociological literature would have it, simply a matter of group process (support systems), nor a matter of transition (assimilation), nor a matter of straightforward transmission from generation to generation (socialization).

In some ways, the contemporary reinvention of ethnic identity through remembering is nothing new. The Pythagorean notion of memory (which fascinated Plato) also conceived of the world as one of oblivion, of superficial appearances behind which lay the hidden realities. Only the soul that engaged in memory exercises, in recollections, in preserving the knowledge of this world when proceeding to the next and avoiding the waters of Lethe (or Ameles) when returning to this world from the celestial realms would be able to escape the cycles of rebirth, the flux of meaningless repetitions, and the entropy toward reductions of human beings into mechanical or bestial ciphers. Only through memory, honed by constant exercise and effort, could one purge the sins of past lives, purify the soul, ascend and escape from oblivious repetitions.[3]

So, too, contemporary ethnic re-creations are given impetus by the fear not merely of being levelled into identical industrial hominids, but of losing an ethical (celestial) vision that might serve to renew the self and ethnic group as well as contribute to a richer, powerfully dynamic pluralist society. In exploring why white America produces biographies, while black America produces autobiographies, Arnold Rampersad (1983) points out that autobiography (at least in its most potent forms) is predicated on a moral vision, on a vibrant relation between a sense of self and a community, on a retrospective or prophetic appeal to a community of spirit, be it religious or social, or on what Hans-Georg Gadamer might call a feel for a moral tradition.

Ethnic anxiety, that feeling welling up out of mysterious depths, is not the only interesting aspect of contemporary expressions of ethnicity. Rather, they seem to be a reflex of more general cultural processes. To a Westerner, late twentieth-century society globally seems to be characterized by surface homogenization, by the erosion of public enactments of tradition, by the loss of ritual and historical rootedness. Cultural elements seem to be increasingly fragmented, volitional, arbitrary matters of personal style. Celebrations and rituals in the United States, for instance, often seem to be ironic, reflecting good-natured nonbelief, skeptical, hedonistic, and commercial in overtone.[4] And yet, clearly, these are reactions to the superficialities of such sit-

2. On Freud's usage, see Bruno Bettleheim (1983).
3. On Pythagorean and Platonic notions of memory, see Jean-Pierre Vernant (1965/1983).
4. Wilcomb E. Washburn, in Victor Turner, ed. 1982, 299.

uations: as Benjamin and Freud in differing ways pointed out, language itself contains sedimented layers of emotionally resonant metaphors, knowledge, and associations, which when paid attention to can be experienced as discoveries and revelations. Indeed, much of the contemporary philosophical mood (in literary criticism and anthropology, as well as in philosophy) is to inquire into what is hidden in language, what is deferred by signs, what is pointed to, what is repressed, implicit, or mediated.

What thus seem initially to be individualistic autobiographical searchings turn out to be revelations of traditions, re-collections of disseminated identities and of the divine sparks from the breaking of the vessels. These are a modern version of the Pythagorean arts of memory: retrospection to gain a vision for the future. In so becoming, the searches also turn out to be powerful critiques of several contemporary rhetorics of domination.

In a period when the writing and reception of ethnography are subjects of much interest and debate among anthropologists (see Marcus and Fischer 1986), the perspectives on ethnicity embodied in autobiographical literature suggest new ways of reading and writing ethnographies.

II

Disseminations and Pro-Vocations

The word's power does not consist in its explicit content—if, generally speaking, there is such a thing—but in the diversion that is involved in it.
                                                    CHAIM NACHMAN BIALIK

The strategy of this paper is threefold: ethnographic listening, attention to cultural criticism, and attention to experimental writing. First of all, the strategy is to listen to the voices of several ethnic groups through autobiographies. Autobiography was chosen because, like ethnography, it has a commitment to the actual. Autobiographical fiction was also included because the modalities of veracity in our age can no longer (if they ever could) be limited to the conventions of realism. Indeed, as Murray Baumgarten rightly points out, ever since the massive linguistic disturbances of Nazi Deutsch, Stalinist Russian, and other forms of twentieth-century double-think, including the deadening language of American officialese, "realism as trust in language is no longer readily available"; it is as if "surrealist montage, cubist collage, and existentialist parable are the only appropriate possibilities" (1982:117). Moreover, the conventions of realism, especially as practiced in traditional ethnography, themselves contain and are made coherent through allegorical metaphors (see Clifford in this volume).

Indirection (vide Bialik above) is inherent in language use and should be exploited consciously rather than ignored, denied, and allowed to mislead. During the past two decades ethnic autobiographers have produced brilliant explorations aimed at rediscovering the sources of language, and thereby also the nature of modern reality.

In thinking about how to read, analyze, and interpret these contemporary autobiographical texts, it occurred to me that the ethnic search is a mirror of the bifocality that has always been part of the anthropological rationale: seeing others against a background of ourselves, and ourselves against a background of others. The juxtaposing of exotic customs to familiar ones, or the relativizing of taken-for-granted assumptions, has always been the kind of cultural criticism promised by anthropology. This bifocality, or reciprocity of perspectives, has become increasingly important in a world of growing interdependence between societies: members of cultures described are increasingly critical readers of ethnography. No longer can rhetorical figures of the "primitive" or the "exotic" be used with impunity: audiences have become multiple. "Bifocality" moreover must increasingly be a shorthand for "two or more" cultures in juxtaposition and comparison. Successful cross-cultural comparison requires at least a third case to avoid simplistic better-worse judgments, to foster multiple axes of comparison,[5] and to evoke a sense of the larger universes in which cultures are situated (see also Marcus in this volume). Cultures and ethnicities as sets are more like families of resemblances than simple typological trees.

The ethnic, the ethnographer, and the cross-cultural scholar in general often begin with a personal empathetic "dual tracking," seeking in the other clarification for processes in the self. One thinks perhaps of the great Islamic scholar and Catholic mystic Louis Massignon, who used Sufism as a proxy for his own dilemmas in a post-Christian, anti-mystical world. Examples could be multiplied. Among the most sensitive and best anthropological works are those that bring personal engagements of this sort into play, albeit usually only as a subtext, rarely highlighted or explicitly acknowledged. One thinks of the association between the late Victor Turner's engagement with Ndembu ritual and symbols and his turn to Catholicism; of Stanley Tambiah's work on Buddhism in Thailand, which, unlike so much written about Buddhism by Westerners, treats it with respect as a potent political force, in an oblique attempt to understand its dynamics in his own troubled homeland of Sri Lanka; and perhaps even of Lévi-Strauss,

5. This was the subject of a conference organized by M. C. Bateson at Coolfont, West Virginia, in June 1984, under the auspices of the Intercultural Foundation, with support from the Wenner-Gren Foundation, the Smithsonian Institution, and the Georgetown University Center for Intercultural Studies.

whose work on American Indian mythologies might be understood as an act of atonement for a world destroyed, parallel to the creation of the Talmud—that is, a preservation together with a critical apparatus permitting regenerative use by future generations.[6] Such engagement need not be ethnic or religious in content: Steven Feld's accounting of Kaluli aesthetics, utilizing his performer's knowledge and skills as well as his academic ones, is one of the finest recent examples. He is able to provide not merely a convincing description but, more important, a critical apparatus[7] that gives the reader a set of conceptual tools with sensory and cognitive bases radically different from our own.

It should be clear that I am not advocating a reductive reading of ethnographies in terms of the biographies of their authors. It is true that professionals may adjust their readings of ethnographies according to their knowledge of the writers. This makes reading richer and more informed. It allows the reader to bring to the text many of the nuances, tacit understandings, and implicit perspectives that informed the writer—to bring, as Plato might say, a dead text to fuller life.[8] But in the case of casual or unsophisticated readers, reading in terms of the biography of the writer can be invidious and destructive, explaining away the text rather than enriching it. What I am suggesting instead is a reading of ethnographies as the juxtaposition of two or more cultural traditions and paying attention both in reading and in constructing ethnographies to the ways in which the juxtaposition of cultural traditions works on both the conscious and unconscious levels. For many the search in another tradition, such as perhaps Golden's in Nigeria or my own in Iran, can serve as a way of exploring one's own past, now disappeared forever. One needs authentic anchorages

6. The Talmud discusses the minutiae of temple worship, a form of worship long gone by the time the Talmud was written. It thereby transformed what once were rules of ritual into a tool for developing argumentation and dialectical skills (Neusner 1981). So, too, Lévi-Strauss has tried to collect myths, many of which no longer function in their original contexts, and, by collating them and suggesting procedures for interpreting them, has made them live again as the subjects of intellectual discussion and intellectual growth (see Handleman 1982). No one, for instance, will ever again be able to analyze a single incident, symbolic figure, or single myth variant apart from other variants and other relevant myths, or be able to ignore the notion of myth as a kind of language with rules of syntax and meanings generated systematically through contrastive differences of usage of incidents, characters, or symbols.

7. Feld's account moves from a textual analysis of a poem built around the call of an abandoned child, to an analysis of the Kaluli typologies of birds based on sounds, to a musical analysis of songs such as those used in the Gisaro ritual, to the Kaluli rhetorical analysis of the ways words are made poetic, and to an analysis of the Kaluli vocabulary and theory of music, in which sonic structure is coded in metaphors of the movement of water. Kaluli music, poetry, aesthetics, and epistemology in general are built around sound, in striking contrast to Western epistemology, which privileges vision (see also Tyler 1984c).

8. See Plato's *Phaedrus* and the commentary on it by Jacques Derrida in his *Disseminations*.

that can allow a kind of dual or multiple tracking (between self and other), that generate a rich, sympathetic curiosity for detail and cultural logic, that can be subjected to mutual criticism or mutual revelation from both traditions. At the same time, one needs a check against assimilating the other to the self, seeing only what is similar or different. One must avoid comparison by strict dualistic contrast. A third, fourth, or fifth comparison inevitably involves multidimensionality, and a sense of larger universes of significance. In ethnic autobiographies, the trying on of alternative identities is one technique for achieving this multidimensionality.

The strategy for writing this paper, then, has been to juxtapose five sets of autobiographical writings, those of Armenian-Americans, Chinese-Americans, Afro-Americans, Mexican-Americans, and Native Americans. The idea is to allow multiple sets of voices to speak for themselves, with my own author's voice muted and marginalized as commentary. While it remains true that I stage these voices, the reader is directed to the originals; the text is not hermetically sealed, but points beyond itself. Parallel writings from my own ethnic tradition are evoked in the introductions and conclusions as points of further contact, in order, as Tzevtan Todorov puts it (1982/1984:250–51), to avoid "the temptation to reproduce the voices of these figures 'as they really are': to try to do away with my own presence 'for the other's sake' . . . [or] to subjugate the other to myself, to make him into a marionette."

What emerges as a conclusion is not simply that parallel processes operate across American ethnic identities, but a sense that these ethnicities constitute only a family of resemblances, that ethnicity cannot be reduced to identical sociological functions, that ethnicity is a process of inter-reference between two or more cultural traditions, and that these dynamics of intercultural knowledge provide reservoirs for renewing humane values. Ethnic memory is thus, or ought to be, future, not past, oriented.

If multiple voices are engaged in this experiment, so, too, it is hoped, will multiple readerships. By invoking the discourses of a number of different groups, access is provided to them for rejoinder. The discourse of the text is not sealed by a professional rhetoric or authority that denies standing to nonprofessional interlocutors. At the same time, it draws members of these different ethnic discourses into the comparative project of anthropology. It does not allow ethnics to protest merely on the terms of their intuitive understandings of their own rhetorics, but attempts to conceive of such intuition as but one valid source of knowledge.

Finally, the ability of texts such as those reviewed in this paper to deliver cultural criticism without the stereotypic distortions that traditional cross-cultural categorizations have often produced is an important model for ethnography. No greater indictments of racism in America exist than Charlie Mingus's *Beneath the Underdog*, Raul Salinas's "A Trip Through the Mind Jail," the angry writings of Frank Chin, the portraits of trauma by James Welch or Gerald Vizenor. None of these, however, merely indicts, and certainly none blames only oppressors outside the self and ethnic group; all fictively demonstrate the creation of new identities and worlds. Rather than naive efforts at direct representation, they suggest or evoke cultural emergence (see Tyler in this volume). One of the reasons for the relative sense that these portraits are less stereotyped is their attention to the ineffectiveness of textual techniques—that is, the self-conscious employment of such devices as transference, dream-translation, talk-story, multiple voices and perspectives, the highlighting of humorous inversions and dialectical juxtaposition of identities/traditions/cultures, and the critique of hegemonic discourses. In the fashionable jargon of the day, they illustrate intertextuality, inter-reference, and the interlinguistic modalities of post-modernist knowledge. On the practical level, such self-conscious and virtuoso technique could contribute to a reinvigorated ethnographic literature, one that can again fulfill the anthropological promise of cultural criticism: of making our taken-for-granted ways recognizable as sociocultural constructions for which we can exercise responsibility.

In the working draft of this paper, the five sources (ethnicities) of ethnic autobiography each provided a separate section. I attempted to suggest something about the range or historical trajectory of autobiographical writing within each ethnicity, as well as to highlight in each section a different sense of, and technique for capturing, ethnicity. That organization, although close to the ethnographic discovery strategy, proved unwieldy for readers. In the present draft, I have reversed the hierarchical stress: each section focuses on a writing tactic, yet I retain the division by ethnicity because there does seem to be some connection between particular experiences of ethnic groups and the techniques used to capture, reveal, or exorcise those experiences. This does not mean that any tactic or technique is used exclusively by writers of a given ethnicity. (Quite the contrary: all these techniques are available to, and are used by, writers of all ethnicities.) However, what a simple organization by technique alone would endanger is the sense of historical trajectory of writing in each ethnic tradition.[9]

9. For instance, Amerindian writing draws on a long tradition of philosophical, mythic, and simply humorous engagement with trickster figures. Black autobiographical writing is also a long-established tradition. One can trace it back to the slave narratives of Muslim West Africans (and others) brought to America, and, more immediately in the modern period, black autobiographies contributed to the core development of the post–World War II civil rights movement. That movement is hard to conceive of with-

A simple organization by technique alone also leads to the danger of reducing the polyphony and texture of multiple styles of any ethnic writing tradition into a mere example for a univocal argument.

Among the elements of texture (apart from style, multiple techniques, and dialogue with predecessors) are explorations of psychoanalytic and feminist perspectives. It is striking the degree to which contemporary autobiographers are fond of deploying psychoanalytic language and/or logic to describe or model ethnic processes. Somewhat less innovative are the ways ethnicity is engendered. Cultural heritage is often figured in paternal or maternal imagery. Children pattern themselves, after all, on both same and opposite sex parents (or other adults) in complex, often reactive, ways. One ethnographic way to ask if and how contemporary debates about gender roles are reflected here is to pay attention to both male and female authors, male and female imagery.

We proceed from the pain of silence to the wisdom of laughter.

Transference

My ancestors talk
to me in dangling
myths.

Each word a riddle
each dream
heirless.

On sunny days
I bury
words.

They put out roots
and coil around
forgotten syntax.

Next spring a full
blown anecdote
will sprout. DIANA DER HOVANESSIAN, "Learning an Ancestral Tongue"[10]

---

out thinking of Ralph Ellison's *Invisible Man* (1952), Claude Brown's *Manchild in the Promised Land* (1965), Maya Angelou's *I Know Why the Caged Bird Sings* (1969), *The Autobiography of Malcolm X* (with Alex Haley, 1973), Eldridge Cleaver's *Soul on Ice* (1968). Chinese-American (like Mexican-American) writing has generated class-linked differential reactions. Some Chinese-Americans whose families did not experience the railroads, sweatshops, and Chinatowns resent Kingston's books as giving further credence to stereotypes. Male writers, such as Frank Chin and Jeffrey Paul Chan, have also criticized Kingston for pandering to stereotypic exoticism, rather than creating alternative visions (Kim 1982).

10. Compare William Saroyan carrying fragments of his father's writings on scraps of paper, like seeds that inspire his imagination (*Here Comes There Goes You Know Who*, p. 36).

Michael Arlen's *Passage to Ararat* (1975) is an archetypical text for displaying the "transference" mechanisms of ethnicity, and for coming to terms with an id-like force, experienced as defining one's self, yet coming from without. Crucial here is the conquest of an anxiety that manifests itself through repetition of behavioral patterns, and that cannot be articulated in rational language but can only be acted out. The analogy here is with the third of the three modes of communication routinely distinguished in psychoanalytic therapy: cognitive, rational, conscious investigation; translation from dreams into linear, textlike verbalizations (thereby introducing the distortions of the mediating language); and transference, in which no text is produced, but rather a repetition toward the analyst of behavior patterns previously established toward some prior significant other.

Michael Arlen's ethnic anxiety begins with the silence of his father about the Armenian past. By attempting to spare children knowledge of painful past experiences, parents often create an obsessive void in the child that must be explored and filled in. Arlen claims he has no obvious childhood experiences except the warmth and family happiness of eating in the Golden Horde Restaurant (a favorite, as well, of William Saroyan's). Yet the silence of his father is a dramatically enacted ambivalence full of import for the son: the father attempts and spectacularly fails to become English, changes his name, (although a writer) does not write or talk about Armenians, marries another exile (a Greek-American), dresses "with the meticulous care of the idle or insecure," attempts to hold court at the St. Regis Hotel, comes home to meals "devoid of taste or personality," paces in "a little room euphemistically called the library," sends his children to boarding school, and eventually moves to America when anti-foreign speeches are made in Parliament. In America, he feels himself an ineffectual Armenian, abetted by his uncertainty about how to treat his children; yet he lands his first American job with what his son remembers as a virtuoso triumph of Armenian wile: movie producer Louis Mayer asks him what he is going to do; he responds that he has been talking to Sam Goldwyn (who had told him to try racehorses). Mayer: How much did he offer you? Arlen, Sr.: Not enough. Mayer: How about $1,500 for thirty weeks? Arlen: I'll take it.

Michael Arlen's statement about the Golden Horde Restaurant being his only real Armenian childhood experience is followed by a statement of ambivalence about his father. Indeed his text is structured —beginning, middle, and end—with paternal imagery. Beginning:

I was only slightly curious about my Armenian background—or so I thought, although if I had understood how to acknowledge such matters, I might have known that I was haunted by it. Mostly I was afraid of it. . . . What was I afraid of? . . . Probably of being exposed in some way, or pulled down by the connection: that association of difference . . . with something deeply pejorative . . . And in the end I came to hate my father for my fear. . . . I loved him too . . . He was my father. But also I was afraid of him. Something always lay between us—something unspoken and (it seemed) unreachable. We were strangers. (1975:7)

Arlen describes the ambivalences (paralleling his father's) generated in himself: the childhood fears that his Anglo-American camouflage would come undone (terror for himself when he sees a Jewish boy being beaten; a Scottish boy asserting that Arlen could not possibly be English); the fear of getting too emotionally close to Armenians; and above all, being unable to read about the massacres of the Armenians by the Ottomans (becoming angry, but irrationally not at the Ottomans).[11]

To exorcise this anxiety, Arlen visits Soviet Armenia. Initially the ambivalence recurs: inability to feel anything at the monuments; anger at the tourists' slurs and stereotypes about Armenians confided to him as apparently simply an American tourist. Eventually, however, there is engagement, a movement outside of himself, a recognition of connections between his personal dilemmas and those of other Armenians. Arlen ignites the anger of his Armenian guide by asking about Armenian submissiveness to the Ottomans, their collusion in their own second-class status. The guide accuses him of wanting to tear down his father ("Fatherland, father. It is the same thing" [1975:98].): "'All that Anglo-Saxon coolness and detachment. . . . Not like a proper son!' . . . And then Sarkis suddenly took my hands in his, and I looked into his face and saw that he was crying" (ibid: 99).

Following this cathartic breakthrough, a picture of an eighteenth-century merchant from Erzurum brings an associative flash. The face reminds Arlen of his father: "burning eyes in a composed, impassive face": "I realized at that moment that to be an Armenian, to have lived as an Armenian, was to have become something crazy . . . crazed, that deep thing—deep where the deep-sea souls of human beings twist and turn" (ibid: 103).[12] His father had attempted to free him of the pain of the past, but suddenly Michael Arlen remembers his father telling him "with suprising severity and intensity" (p. 139) when he was eight to learn to box. Arlen speculates on the effects of centuries

---

11. Compare Saroyan's distorted anger at his father (ibid., p. 36).

12. Compare Saroyan's comic version, as Bedrosian (1982:287) aptly characterizes it: "Homeless except for each other, forced to create an entire heritage through a chance meeting, demonstrating through their boyant, child-like spirits that life is comic after all, [and adding further historical-epic depth] these Armenians remind us of the irrepressible and wacky daredevils of Sassoon."

of provocation from the surrounding majority population, Armenian protest, mob response (the classic dynamic, Margaret Bedrosian comments, of a bully committing a misdeed on the sly, then feigning being wronged when the victim cries out; and she cites the Ottoman interior minister Talaat Bey: "We've been reproached for making no distinction between the innocent Armenians and the guilty, but that was utterly impossible in view of the fact that those who were innocent today might be guilty tomorrow" [Bedrosian 1982: 234]). Such an environment leads to a turning inward: "The eyes [of the portrait] seemed almost to burn out at me. Burning eyes in a frozen face . . . did he set his expression, freeze part of himself, his face—all save the eyes, which no man can control—and tap his finger on the coffee cup, and curl and uncurl his hand inside his well-cut pocket . . . and *manage?*" (102–3). Such an environment Arlen speculates leads to arts of miniaturization, in this case not a creative expression through smallness, but an obsessive gesture, an effort to become invisible.

Anxiety confronted, diagnosis explored, the book ends again with the father, with dreams as an index of the liberation achieved. Michael Arlen recalls his father's anxiety dreams about *his* father: not being able to understand his Armenian. Michael Arlen reflects that he, Michael, no longer dreams so frequently of his father (his passage to Ararat has been liberating). As he puts it, the need to set the father free has been met (p. 292).

Arlen's text is straightforward and self-conscious,[13] describing ethnic anxiety as an approach-avoidance to a past that is larger than oneself, that is recognized by others as defining of one's identity, and yet that does not seem to come from one's own experience. It makes one feel not in control of one's own being. It is a historical reality principle: individual experience cannot be accounted for by itself. It expresses itself in repetitions.[14] Yet he concludes weakly on a false note. He claims his is a tale of conquest, of finding peace and security: "How strange to finally meet one's past: to simply meet it, the way one might finally acknowledge a person who had been in one's company a long while, 'So it's you'" (253). Anxiety, he seems to say, is relieved by establishing continuity with the past where previously there was breach, silence, anxiety. There seems to be almost a failure here to create for the future, something perhaps figured in the text by the absence of his American-Greek mother.

13. "What [is] one to make of such a story? I use the word 'make' in the sense of 'to fashion'; or . . . 'to re-create'" (p. 177).
14. Michael Arlen the writer, his father the writer; the father as the immigrant to America, the guide in Soviet Armenia, the eighteenth-century Erzurum merchant; the Armenian heritage in general.

Michael Arlen is but one of a gradually growing number of Armenian literary voices, several of whom have been reviewed in a recent dissertation by Margaret Bedrosian. The theme of puzzlement, of obscure fathers, is a strong recurrent one, but maternal imagery can be equally strong.[15] In another medium, the painter Arshile Gorky uses images of his mother and transferencelike techniques of indirection, repetition, and reworking. Gorky (born Vosdanig Adoian in 1904 of a line of thirty-eight generations of priests) was a survivor of the massacres, child of a mother who died of starvation at thirty-nine, not eating so that her children might live. He chose the names "the bitter one" (Gorky) and Achilles (Arshile) whose wrath kept him from battle until a new wrath impelled him to act. Abstraction and expressionism were for him techniques, not of spontaneity and the autonomous unconscious, but of masking vulnerable truths. During World War II, he issued an invitation for a course in camouflage: "An epidemic of destruction sweeps through the world today. The mind of civilized man is set to stop it. What the enemy would destroy, however, he must first see. To confuse and paralyze his vision is the role of camouflage" (quoted in Bedrosian 1982: 355). His paintings are carefully reworked images: of his mother, of his natal village near Lake Van, of the family garden in that village, of the Tree of the Cross used by villagers to attach supplications to God. His slogans were clear: "From our Armenian experience will I create new forms to ignite minds and massage hearts!"; "Having a tradition enables you to tackle new problems with authority, with solid footing."

Transference, the return of the repressed in new forms, and repetitions with their distortions are all mechanisms through which ethnicity is generated. They also suggest possible writing tactics. Three uses of transference and repetition can be distinguished in recent ethnographic writing. First, there is the discovery or eliciting of psychological patterns of transference proper among ethnographic subjects, as in the work of Gananath Obeyesekere (1981), where, moreover, such systematic patterns generate new social forms. Second, there is the analysis of change through intended repetitions that in fact work through misappropriation or distortion. The classic such highlighting of the indirection of cultural dynamics is Marx's observations on the French Revolution using borrowed language and costumes from the Roman Republic and on history never working out

15. See for instance the two lovely poems by David Kherdian about an old man ("Dedeh Dedeh") and an old woman ("Sparrow"), each representing the Armenian past, reproduced in Bedrosian (1982).

the same way the second time.[16] Marshall Sahlins's recent book on Captain Cook and the structural changes Hawaiian society underwent in the period following his death similarly exploits the delineation of intended repetition or reproduction of cultural forms leading to unintended distortion, inversion, and change. Third, and perhaps most intriguing, there is the suggestion of Vincent Crapanzano in *Tuhami* (1980) that in part the dynamic of the interviews between himself and Tuhami was one of mutual transference, with Tuhami placing the ethnographer in the uncomfortable role of curer. Crapanzano suggests that many ethnographic situations partake of this ambiguity: informants present and tailor information as if the anthropologist were a government official, a physician, or other agent of aid or danger; the anthropologist is placed in positions that constrain his actions, and he, too, creates roles for the informant. In other words the emergence of ethnographic knowledge is not unlike the creation of ethnic identity. Crapanzano hints at this also in an article reporting a possession case, where he interviews the husband, Muhammad, and his wife interviews the wife, Dawia.[17] Not only do the possessed couple present different versions of the same event, but these versions depend upon the interlocutors, there being perhaps even a mild rivalry between the two ethnographers. By recognizing such dynamics of gaining information and insight, anthropologists' informants-collaborators gain a more dynamic role, and we begin to see our own bases of knowledge as more subtly constructed through the action of others. Our knowledge is shown to be less objective, more negotiated by human interests, and the subject for greater responsibility in the interactions and ethical honesty of fieldwork (in Tyler's sense in this volume).

Dream-Work

Maxine Hong Kingston's *The Woman Warrior* (1975) is an archetypical text for displaying ethnicity processes analogous to translations of dreams. Just as a dream needs to be translated into a text or linear verbal discourse so that it can be analyzed by someone who has not experienced the visual imagery, so Kingston's text is developed as a series of fragments of traditional stories, myths, and customs imposed by parents, but not adequately explained, at critical points of her childhood, which thus are embedded in consciousness to be worked out through, and integrated with, ongoing experience. This

16. See the opening passages of *The Eighteenth Brumaire of Louis Bonaparte*.
17. "Muhammad and Dawia" in V. Crapanzano and V. Garrison, eds. (1977).

process of integration is analogous to that experienced by the analysand in psychoanalytic therapy, who must translate from the imagery of dreams into verbal discourse so that both he and the analyst can reason through it. The process of articulating what it means to be Chinese-American, for Kingston, is the process of creating a text that can be interrogated and made coherent.

The first fragment, "No Name Woman," is the tale of a father's sister who has an illegitimate child, is forced by the enraged villagers to have the child in a pigsty, and who then commits suicide. The story, says Kingston, was told to warn young girls ("now that you have started to menstruate" [5]), but also to test the American-born children's ability to establish realities: to distinguish what is peculiar to one's family, to poverty, to Chineseness. The obscure story gains force as Kingston considers the alternative possible interpretations it might contain: was this aunt coerced (a figure of female obedience) or was she an active temptress: indeed why, since she was married to a husband off in America, was she still in her natal home rather than in her husband's parents' house—previous transgressions? The aunt became an allegory of internal struggles for the adolescent Kingston: all young women wish to be attractive to the opposite sex, but selectively: how to make a Chinese fall in love with me, but not Caucasians, Negroes, or Japanese? Ambiguities explode: women are, of course, devalued in Chinese society, yet this aunt's father had had only sons before the aunt was born and had attempted to trade a boy-infant for a girl-infant: presumably, he loved his only daughter and perhaps encouraged her rebelliousness.

The ambiguities of the woman's role are elaborated in "White Tiger." Kingston was taught she would grow up to be wife and slave, yet she was also taught the song of the warrior woman—a variant of the great Nishan Shaman legend [18]—who avenged her family like a man. The story of Fa Mu Lan, the warrior woman, is of going up the mountain into the clouds, where she learns spiritual and physical strength, biding her time until at twenty-two she returns to become a warrior. The parallel for Kingston is the unreal devaluation of girls in her Chinese communal setting, from which she finds an escape into American society, where she can become a strong person in her own right. Like Fa Mu Lan, she feels she must stay away until strong enough to return and reform the stifling Chinese immigrant community.

18. On the Nishan Shaman, see Stephen Durant (1979). In the Manchu story, the resolution between the statuses of (a) the powerful female shaman who teases and taunts the wealthy and powerful and (b) the widowed daughter-in-law (urun, "work woman") is to take the shaman's implements away, making her again merely an urun. This, as Kingston's version shows, is hardly a necessary resolution.

"Shaman" is about the ghost stories Kingston's mother told as work stories to chill the heat in the family laundry; tales of heroes who would eat anything in great quantities ("The emperors used to eat the peaked hump of purple dromedaries . . . Eat! Eat! my mother would shout . . . the blood pudding awobble in the middle of the table."); stories of wartime horrors. Her mother was a woman of accomplishment and strength: she had a diploma from a school of midwifery, and knew how to recite genealogies to talk back her children's frightened spirits after nightmares and horror films. Such familial powers can also be repressive ("Chinese do not smile for photographs. Their faces command relatives in foreign lands—'send money'—and posterity forever—'put food in front of this picture'") and regressive (whenever she would return home, Kingston would regress into fear of ghosts, nightmares of wartime airplanes, and lethargic illness).

These and other "talk stories" in the volume (and the companion volume *Chinamen*) show how stories can become powerful sources of strength, how they work differently for each generation, how they are but fragmentary bits that have to be translated, integrated, and reworked. ("Unless I see her life branching into mine, she gives me no ancestral help.") Part of the fragmentary context of the stories, of the unexplained customs, of the paranoia about non-Chinese, and of the general secrecy about origins is grounded in survival tactics that the immigrants developed against the discriminatory immigration policies of the United States against Asians. People changed names, lied about their ages and ports of entry, and generally covered their tracks so that their lives became unintelligible to their children (who being half-American were not entirely trustworthy either). Non-Chinese are called ghosts, but for the American-Chinese children, ghosts are the bizarre fragments of past, tradition, and familial self-overprotectiveness that must be externalized and tamed.

"Dream-work" can be prospective, as well as retrospective: daydreams as well as working through past experiences. Frank Chin, Jeffrey Paul Chan, and Shawn Hsu Wong, as well as Kingston, utilize the dilemmas of Chinese-American males to explore further the novelties of Chinese-Americanness suggested in "White Tiger." Kingston there describes the need to get away from Chinatown to gain the strength to redeem (recover, change, and create) her identity. The further task is to construct or find images that are neither Chinese nor European. There are no clear role models for being Chinese-American. Being Chinese-American exists only as an exploratory project, a matter of finding a voice and style. Among the exploratory tactics are efforts to claim America, to assert aggressive sexual identity, to imaginatively try on other minority experiences, and to question both hegemonic white ideological categories and those of Chinatown.

This project is doubly important for writers: for personal self-definition, and also to overcome those publishers and critics who consistently reject any writings contradicting popular racist views of Asian-Americans as either totally exotic, as no different from anyone else (denial of culture), or, finally, as model minorities (humble, well-mannered, law-abiding, family-oriented, hard-working, education-seeking).

In response, as Elaine Kim describes (1982), Frank Chin calls himself a Chinatown cowboy, insisting on his roots in the American West and his manly ruggedness. This pose is particularly useful against the exotic stereotype of Chinese as "pigtailed heathens in silk gowns and slippers, whispering Confucian aphorisms about filial piety." The pose is also useful against the model minority stereotype used: (a) to depreciate blacks; (b) to deny the history of Chinese-Americans (Chinese do not turn to the government for aid because for so long the government was hostile to their legal status and they thus had to hide from the government, with the consequence that poverty, suicide, and tuberculosis flourished in Chinatown unnoticed by white society); (c) and to emasculate Asian-American males. Chin recalls the classic situation in school where blacks and Chicanos are asked why they cannot be like the Chinese: stay out of trouble, mind your folks, study hard, and obey the laws: "And there we chinamen were, in Lincoln Elementary School, Oakland, California, in a world where manliness counts for everything, surrounded by bad blacks and bad Mexican kids . . . suddenly stripped and shaved bare by this cop with no manly style of my own, unless it was sissiness" (quoted by Kim, p. 178).

If these racist, ideological stereotypes need be countered, so, too, Chinatown needs to be exposed. Chin images Chinatown as decaying beneath an exotic façade, as a senile living corpse, populated by inhabitants imaged as bugs, spiders, and frogs, engaged in activities imaged as funerals (preservation of decaying pasts under ivory masks). Heroes—cowboys—must escape to survive. Like Kingston, Chin moved out, preferring to build strength in Seattle, returning only on temporary forays to the battleground of change in San Francisco. In his writing, Chin attempts to create a tough, aggressive, back-talking young male hero, an adolescent sexuality and aggression that are perhaps signs of a new voice and identity not yet found.

Jeffrey Paul Chan, Kim notes, writes not dissimilarly: both use the image of Chinatown as a chicken coop. In his search for a new style for the Chinese-American, Chan also plays with the roles of other minorities, especially that of the American Indian. The Indian is attractive because he has (to outsiders) unquestionable roots in America. This is a theme that both Kingston and Shawn Hsu Wong also develop: the need particularly of Chinese-American males to mark and appropriate the land. Wong's narrator is haunted by the ghosts of grandfathers who built the railroads, imagining their struggles, their letters home to China, and even fantasizes himself as an old night train filled with Chinamen, running along the tracks, heart burning like a red hot engine. These grandfathers laid roots in the land, like "roots of giant trees," like "sharp talons in the earth of my country." Rainsford, the narrator of *Homebase* (1979), has a white girlfriend, who patronizes him, telling him that he is the product of the richest and oldest culture in the world, a civilization that invented many of the components of modern life, making him feel even sharper anxiety about having nothing of his own in America. He rejects this "love," and she, classically, tells him to go back where he came from: go home. But home is here. It is an American Indian who shows him how to find his American roots: he should retrace where his people have been, all over America, see the town he is named after. He does this, determined that America "must give me legends with spirit," and dreaming of a reconciliation with a Chinese-American girl in Wisconsin whose grandfather from China had fled the West Coast. In *Chinamen*, Kingston, too, emphasizes the theme of men claiming America, writing of railroad workers—heroic and masculine at times such as the strike of 1869: bare-chested, muscular young gods—victimized, kept womanless, dying in the wilderness. But, says one of them, "We're marking the land now."

Dream-work—simultaneously the integration of dissonant past fragments and the daydreaming "trying-on" of alternative possible identities—is both descriptive of one way (or one set of ways) ethnicity works and suggests a writing tactic of fragments. Here, too, Crapanzano's *Tuhami*, referred to above, might serve as an example of a recent ethnographic text that exploits this tactic. The reader is presented with a puzzle: to help the author analyze bits of interviews in which the informant draws equally on reality and fantasy for metaphors with which to describe the impossibilities of his existence. Tuhami is a member of Morocco's subproletariat; the style of his discourse perhaps illustrates what Pierre Bourdieu provocatively calls the truncated consciousness of many members of such subproletariats.[19] If so, Crapanzano's recording of Tuhami might provide an access to the discourse of an emergent new social class, analogous to the emergent discourse of Chinese-American writers' concern with chicken coops and railroads, cowboys and Indians. Other similar writ-

19. "The Disenchantment of the World," in *Algeria 1960* (New York: Cambridge University Press, 1979).

ing tactics are easily imaginable, such as the use of the juxtaposed viewpoints of different informants and/or authors,[20] and Rashomon-like descriptions from different perspectives.[21]

Alternative Selves and Bifocality

Two recent black autobiographies by Charles Mingus and Marita Golden develop the notion of multiple selves and examine the reality constraints on enacting alternative selves. They also explore the use of alternative selves to challenge dominant hegemonic ideologies, the one by applying an ethnic aesthetic (thus being ethnographic in style as well as content), the other by pioneering the bifocality that anthropology has always promised. Alice Walker, another black writer, notes: "When I look at people in Iran and Cuba, they look like kin folk" (Bradley 1984: 35–36). This is echoed by Maxine Hong Kingston and American Indian writer Leslie Marmon Silko, who portray young men in American uniform in southeast Asia severely disturbed by the inability to distinguish the enemy from kinfolk. As a humanist cultural criticism of nationalist, class, and other hegemonic political discourses, these observations signal the potential for a powerful counter rhetoric, similar to those developed by the small nations of Europe, those on the wrong side of history, whose "disabused view of history" is the "source of their culture, of their wisdom, of the 'non-serious spirit' that mocks grandeur and glory" (Kundera 1984).

Mingus's *Beneath the Underdog* (1971) utilizes a tripartite self as narrator; a telling to a psychiatrist as the overall narrative frame; and an obsessive focus on a father figure. The tripartite self is introduced on the first page, and reflected upon again near the last (p. 255): an inborn, ever-loving gentle soul who always gets taken; a frightened animal that, from experience, learns to attack for fear of being attacked; and a distanced third who stands apart watching the other two. The three selves appear throughout the text as alternating, inter-braided voices—like the call-and-response of a jazz session—keeping the reader alert to perspective and circumstance.

Equally striking is Mingus's textual strategy of posing the autobiography as a telling, a talk-story, to a Jewish psychiatrist ("remem-

20. Recent examples of such "polyphony" are *Birds of My Kalam Country* by Ian Majnep and Ralph Bulmer (1977), and *Piman Shamanism* by Donald M. Bahr, Juan Gregorio, David I. Lopez, and Albert Alvarez (1974).

21. See the discussion of N. Scott Momaday below, or in anthropology see Richard Price's *First-Time* (1983) in which oral accounts are juxtaposed to archival ones; or Renato Rosaldo's *Ilongot Headhunting* (1980) which pursues a similar goal more discursively.

ber saying you came to me not only because I'm a psychiatrist but also because I'm a Jew? And therefore could relate to your problems?" p. 7). This allows the author to play with four subdevices, like improvisatory jazz themes that reappear periodically. First, there are the psychological devices of fabrication (involving the reader in sorting out the puzzles of identity, control by the self versus control by outside forces), and changing the subject or crying (signals of blockages, avoidances, pain, and irrational compulsions). Second, the theme of pimping is used as a multi-register metaphor. It describes the narrator's use of women as a childish way to prove his manhood (breaking out of subordination and dependency—the pimp as master—by imposing subordination on others). It is a metaphor of economic survival, of the dilemmas of black musicians who cannot make it on music alone, but must prostitute themselves and others, meaning among other things a regressive dependence on women ("He wanted to make it alone without any help from women or anyone else," p. 132). That is, narrator as both pimp and prostitute. And it is a bitter description of the racist economic system controlled by whites ("Jazz is big business to the white man and you can't move without him. We just work-ants," p. 137). The third device is recurrent dreams about Fats Navarro, a Florida-born Cuban musician who died at twenty-six of tuberculosis and narcotic addiction, who serves throughout the book as an alter ego to whom the project of writing a book is confided. The book is to achieve liberation, both economic (fantasies of fat royalties) and spiritual. The dreams include meditations on a death wish, centering on the idea that one can die (only?) when one works out one's karma, precisely what was denied Fats.

Finally, the use of the father figuration is, of course, also part of the narration to the psychiatrist—the fourth subdevice—but it also introduces an element of choice and retracing of genealogical connection ("Some day I may choose another father to teach me," p. 96). Mingus's father appears first in his childhood traumas (being dropped on his head, having his dog shot by a neighbor, kindergarten accusations of being a sexual pervert, and above all paternal beatings and threats of castration for bedwetting, later discovered to be due to damaged kidneys). The father gave him his first musical instrument, but being emotionally unresponsive also set up a longing for a real father. (The father's own anxiety structure is analyzed as stemming from being a frustrated architect condemned to life in the Post Office, and as manifesting itself by teaching his children a false, racist sense of superiority on the grounds that they were light-skinned.) Midbook, Mingus returns to find out about his father, and hears yet again that he is not fully black, that he is a descendant of Abraham Lincoln's cousin, and that

"a lot of talking about freedom . . . [is] a waste of time 'cause even a
slave could have inner freedom if he wanted it."
"That's brainwashing by the white man."
"Careful, boy—you ain't totally black." (95)

White connections are not the only troubling ones. Class prejudices
within the black community also threaten young Mingus. The father
advises: "So tell them your grandfather was an African chieftain
named Mingus" (96). There is also a certain amount of play with alternative ethnic masks. Mingus grows up in Watts and is light-skinned; in
the mirror he thinks he can see strains of Indian, African, Mexican,
Asian, and white, and he worries that he is "a little of everything,
wholly nothing" (50).

Mexican is a major alternative identity ("Mexican Moods").[22] His
first girlfriend when aged five was Mexican; so was a girl who almost
snagged him into marriage at seventeen. Later, in San Francisco, a
Jewish musician had tried to give him a break in a white union: he was
accepted as Mexican until a black musician turned him in. Jewishness
is another ethnicity played with, particularly through his Jewish psychiatrist and the psychiatrists at Bellevue, who initially seem like Nazis
threatening lobotomy, but who eventually midwife a feeling of respect
and love:

The truth is doctor, I'm insecure and I'm black and I'm scared to death of
poverty and especially poverty alone. I'm helpless without a woman, afraid of
tomorrow. . . . It was easy to be proud and feel contempt and say to these
beautiful women, "I don't want your dirty money!" so that was one good thing
that happened in Bellevue, having a feeling of love and respect for them
again. . . . My music is evidence of my soul's will to live beyond my sperm's
grave. (245–46)

The wild humor, excessive sexuality, and anguish of Mingus's style
help pose the contradictions and puzzles of his ethnic search: the differences among the women upon whom he depends—two mistresses,
a middle class black wife, and a blond nurse; the tentative trying on of
other minorities' identities; the hint of exploring African connections;
and the sense of mixed blood or heritage. Mingus's critique of racism
is poignant, macabrely humorous, a verbal jazz-blues, sophisticated in
style and technique, wielding an ethnic aesthetic to bring the reader to
a perspective and understanding.

Marita Golden's *Migrations of the Heart* (1983) explores the African
connections more directly, and illustrates a different form of critique,
perhaps less innovative in style, but pioneering an old promise of anthropology to be a "bifocal" mode of cultural criticism. Golden mar-

22. The name of the album that in 1962 he said was his best.

ries a Nigerian and goes to Nigeria to reexperience her American-
ness. The marriage fails. The story is a painful, yet eventually
strengthening, recognition that identity is not to be constructed with
the free will of romantic fantasy. There are reality principles that constrain: traditions, growth patterns, and dynamics beyond the ego. Several schemata structure Golden's text: repetitions of the father figure,
countervailing but secondary mother figures (mother, mother-in-
law), rebellions and gradual tempering into mature womanhood, and
a skillful portrait of the devastating dynamics of an intercultural marriage that does not work.

The patriarchal figures (father and husband) with which she
struggles seem to be the primary vehicles for ethnicity-work.

[My father] was as assured as a panther . . . he bequeathed to me—gold
nuggets of fact, myth, legend. . . . By his own definition he was "a black man
and proud of it." . . . Africa: "It wasn't dark until the white man got there."
Cleopatra: "I don't care WHAT they teach you in school, she was a black
woman." . . . the exploits of Toussaint L'Ouverture. (3–4)

Yet also:

He was a hard, nearly impossible man to love when love meant exclusive
rights to his soul . . . he relied [on his many women] . . . to enhance the im-
provisational nature of his life. (3–4)

Her African lover, then husband, is almost a double to her father. His
assurance first attracts her:

enveloped in the aura of supreme confidence that blossomed around all the
Africans I had ever met . . . I'd read about my past and now it sat across from
me in a steak house, placid, and even a bit smug. . . . I rubbed my fingers
across his hand. "What're you doing?" he asked. "I want some of your confidence to rub off on me," I said. (50–51)

Both men have areas of reticence she cannot penetrate. With her father the mutual lack of understanding is manifested in his demand
that she get rid of her "natural" hair-do, in his (and her) inability to
share grief when her mother dies, and in his taking up with another
woman, whom she resents. With her husband, the mutual lack of
understanding lies in his familial and patriarchal traditions, for instance, his sharing of economic resources with his fraternal group at
the expense of his conjugal family. Initially she finds the patriarchal,
masculine Nigerian culture attractive:

Lagos is an aggressively masculine city, and its men exude a dogmatic confidence. . . . it was this masculinity that made the men so undeniably attractive.
Nigeria was their country to destroy or save. That knowledge made them

stride and preen in self-appreciation. This assurance became for an Afro-American woman a gaily wrapped gift to be opened anew every day. (84)

Ultimately, she feels the assumptions of this culture to be devastatingly denying of her sense of self. Women, she is told by another wife, are forgiven almost everything as long as they fulfill the duty to set the stage on which their men live. Life is complicated in Nigeria, particularly when her fiancé resists marriage until he feels financially independent, when she finds a job and he cannot, later when he demands a child before she is ready, and when he gives money to raise his brother's children at the expense of her comfort.

The primary frames of Golden's book are the portraits of a marriage gone awry, partly for reasons of culturally conflicting assumptions, and of a woman gradually freeing herself from dependencies and unexamined notions of identity. But what is important here are the reflections on what it is to be a black American—again, an identity to be created, and a sociological reality to be struggled for. Just as Africa is initially an over-romanticized image of "my past," an image of self-confidence, one that inevitably is shaken by a closer look— Nigeria has its own problems, an American does not slip so easily into an African set of roles—so, too, America is not to be accepted in its realities of racism or individual fantasies (such as those of her father). Golden returns from her ordeal in Africa to Boston (Boston because it is not Washington or New York, where she grew up and where there are too many regressive pulls). There she finds the racial atmosphere almost unbearable. One has the feeling, however, that she will now help to change the situation simply by being a stronger, richer person.

This use of Africa is what anthropological cultural criticism ought to be about: a dialectical or two-directional journey examining the realities of both sides of cultural differences so that they may mutually question each other, and thereby generate a realistic image of human possibilities and a self-confidence for the explorer grounded in comparative understanding rather than ethnocentrism. It is perhaps what Margaret Mead promised in *Coming of Age in Samoa* and *Sex and Temperament in Three Primitive Societies*, and failed fully to deliver. These influential books helped Americans see that American adolescent patterns of rebelliousness and American sex roles were not "natural," but culturally molded, and so might be altered through different child-rearing methods. Such cultural criticism of America worked by juxtaposing alternative patterns elsewhere in the world: that is, real world examples, not utopian fantasies. In today's more sophisticated world, we know that the Samoan and New Guinea societies are more complicated than Margaret Mead described, as also is America. Marita

Golden's narrative points to some of the complexities on both sides of any cultural divide that need to be addressed in contemporary anthropological efforts at cultural criticism (see further Marcus and Fischer 1986).

Inter-reference

And Louie would come through—
melodramatic music, like in the
mono—tan tan taran!—Cruz
Diablo, El Charro Negro! Bogard
smile (his smile is deadly as
his viasas!). He dug roles, man,
and names—like blackie, little
Louie . . .

JOSE MONTOYA, "El Louie"

Within the dark morada average
chains rattle and clacking prayer
    wheels jolt
the hissing spine to uncoil wailing
    tongues
of Nahuatl converts who slowly
    wreath
rosary whips to flay one another

BERNICE ZAMORA, "Restless
Serpents"

Perhaps the most striking feature of Mexican-American writing, present in other ethnic writing too, but brought to its most explicit and dramatic level here, is interlinguistic play: interference, alternation, inter-reference. This was the subject of the first Armenian poem cited above. It is clear in the texture of black English. Some Mexican-American writers use Spanish, others English, some have alternating/mirroring pages or chapters of Spanish and English (reciprocal translations). Chicano literary journals (*El Grito, Entrelinas, Revista Chicano-Riquena*) are resolutely bilingual. Spanish phrases occur within the flow of English, and Spanish words and grammatical structure take on changes influenced by English. Indeed, for some *pochismo* or *calo*, the Chicano slang, takes on a privileged role. Says Bernice Zamora:

I like to think of Calo as the language of Chicano literature . . . It is evolving as a literary mode, and the writers I enjoy most for their consistency of Calo are Cecilio Camavillo, Jose Montoya, and Raul Salinas. I am fond of Calo because of the usage of English phonemes with Spanish gerund or verb endings . . . eskipiando [skipping] . . . Indios pasando we watchando. . . . I teach Calo with the premise that it is a conflict of languages resolved. (Quoted in Bruce-Nova 1980a: 209)

Ricardo Sanchez provides an example of bilingual insistence:

Soy un manito por herencia y un pachuco por experiencia [I am a native New Mexican by heritage and a pachuco by experience] . . . I was born number 13, the first one in the family to be born outside of New Mexico and Colorado since somewhere en el siglo 16 [in the sixteenth century] . . . soy mestizo [I'm a mestizo], scion to the beautiful and turbulent reality of indo-hispanic concatenation, ay, mi abuela materna [my maternal grandmother] was born in

the tewa pueblo of san juan, there between taos and española . . . un mundo
ni español ni indígena: ay, mundo de policolores [a world neither spanish nor
indian: ay, world of polycolors] when mindsouls se ponen a reconfigurar
[start to restructure] new horizons. (Bruce-Nova 1980a: 221)

But of far more interest than simply linguistic interference or code
switching, and the education debate generated over bilingualism, is the
fact, as Michel Serres puts it, "Il faut lire l'interférence comme inter-
référence" (it is necessary to read interference as inter-reference).[23]
What keeps the interlinguistic situation vital is not merely the continuing waves of Mexicans entering the United States and the flow back
and forth across the border, so that gradual disappearance in an English environment is less likely, but the cultural vitality of references to
Mexican history, Spanish civilization, and pre-Columbian civilization,
as well as to particular Chicano styles (such as the pachuco "zoot suit"
subculture of El Paso and Los Angeles celebrated in Montoya's "El
Louie," a figure paralleling the black Staggerlee)[24] or cultural environments (such as the Penitentes cult of New Mexico described in
the opening poem of Zamora's "Restless Serpents").

Poetic autobiography—and the outright novelistic fiction of
Rudolfo Anaya, Ron Arias, and Rolando Hinojosa—has perhaps
been more boldly experimental here than prose autobiography. But,
if one considers Jose Antonio Villarreal's *Pocho* (1959) as a veiled autobiography (it is often counted as the first major Chicano novel, although Villarreal does not like the label "Chicano"), then together
with Ernesto Galarza's *Barrio Boy* (1971), Richard Rodriguez's *Hunger
of Memory* (1981), and Sandra Cisneros's ("semi-autobiographical")
The House on Mango Street (1983), prose autobiography has set out
many of the thematic preoccupations of Chicano writing.

Villarreal establishes the themes of immigration, dealing with
Mexican religious and sexual inhibitions, and familial relations in
Pocho. In *The Fifth Horseman* (1974) he reworks the Mexican genre of
novels about the 1910 revolution so as to create a positive ancestral
figure for the contemporary Chicano: a protagonist who after the
"success" of the revolution refuses to join the victorious army in plun-
dering the people, and, staying true to the revolution, flees to the
United States. Villarreal's father, indeed, fought for Pancho Villa,
coming in 1921 first to Texas and then to California. (Both father and
son returned eventually to Mexico; the son recently once again returned to the States.) Galarza's *Barrio Boy* styles itself as originating in
oral vignettes, and thereby explores the preoccupation of Chicano

23. *L'Interférence* (1972:157), cited by Baumgarten (1982:154), who develops
the notion himself with reference to Jewish-American writing, especially Yiddish-
influenced writing, but not limited to that set of inter-references.
24. See Greil Marcus's chapter on Sly Stone in his *Mystery Train* (1975).

writers with preserving what has been largely an oral culture, albeit attached to the worlds of Hispanic literacy. Rodriguez's *Hunger of Memory* is an argument for English as the medium of instruction in schools, retaining Spanish only as a language of intimacy; its descriptions of the two very different worlds are intended to deny that success in North America can be accompanied by retaining the communal richness of the barrio. Rodriguez has roused a storm of controversy, exposing deep class divisions among Mexican-Americans, but also pointing to the ambiguity of middle class Mexican-American writers using the figure of the poor as a vehicle of expression rather than writing about their own experiences. Many Chicano commentators acknowledge the didactic nature of Chicano writing in the 1960s as a key component of the rise of a political movement. Cisneros is one of a number of writers who have begun to write more directly of themselves; she uses a fragmentary, richly evocative, vignette style, in English.

The antagonism/anxiety directed towards Rodriguez's autobiographic argument, as well as the commentary on the political didacticism of earlier Chicano writing, pose the key issues for the creation of authentically inter-referential ethnic voices, as well as alerting us to the diversity within the Chicano (not to mention the larger Hispanic-American) community: diversity of class, of region (in Mexico; Texas vs. California vs. Chicago), of genealogy (pride in Spain vs. pride in pre-Columbian ancestry).

The most famous poems of the Chicano movement, for example, Rudolpho's "Corky," Gonzales's "I am Joaquin," Alurista (Alberto Urista)'s *Floricanto en Aztlan*, and Abelardo Delgado's "Stupid America," are open searches for enabling histories of Chicano identity. "I am Joaquin" builds on Mexican history, picturing the United States as a neurotic evil giant (invader of Mexico; demander of assimilation into a whirlpool or melting pot that would deny Mexican-Americans their ancestry) and the Chicano nation as a counter giant in the process of creation through blood sacrifices (of the past and perhaps future: the example of Israel is posed). Alurista, influenced by Carlos Casteneda, constructs a somewhat different heroic past, centered less on Hispanic-Mexican history, and more on a pre-Columbian mythos (*flori-canto*, "flower-song," is a Spanish translation of the Nahuatl for "poetry"); Aztlan, the region of northern Mexico including what is now the southwestern United States, is a realm of ancient wisdom, far older than the Anglo settlements and more in tune with the harmonies of nature and the universe. Delgado's short poem exposes the inability of Anglo America to recognize in Chicanos their rich antiquity, creative modernity, and synthetic fertility. Chicano knives can be put

to use in creative sculpture, as in the past *santeros* carved religious figures; Hispanic modernity in painting (Picasso) outpaced Anglo, and
barrio graffiti could be much more, given the chance; literature,
too, can be powerfully synthesized out of a bicultural situation: witness this poem:

> stupid america, see that chicano
> with the big knife
> in his steady hand
> he doesn't want to knife you
> he wants to sit on a bench
> and carve christfigures
> but you won't let him.
>
> . . . .
>
> he is the picasso
> of your western states
> but he will die
> with one thousand masterpieces
> hanging only from his mind.

Inter-reference here encompasses both folk tradition (*santeros*) and
high modernism in the Hispanic world (Picasso), bringing them to
consciousness in Anglo America (the English medium), while criticizing the oppression and cultural deprivation imposed by America.

The search for enabling histories and myths in much early Chicano writing took the form of seeking out *cuentos* (stories), and much
of the literary ideology was one of capturing and preserving an oral
culture. Galarza's *Barrio Boy* presents itself as a written version of oral
vignettes told to the family. Tomas Rivera's *y no se lo tragó la tierra* (*and
the earth did not part*) alternates a short anecdote with a longer vignette
vividly recreating archetypical crises and dilemmas of the exploited
poor Chicanos of Texas; the effect is of a collective voice of the people,
powerful and searing, with that eternal, but not ahistorical, quality of
folktales, the quality that Walter Benjamin identified as coming from
shared experience. Curers and grandparents, often female (*curan-
deras, abuelitas*), figure as important sources of tradition, of mysterious
knowledge, and of cultural strength: the *curandera* Ultima in Rudolfo
Anaya's *Bless Me Ultima* (1972) is one of the richest of these figures;
Fausto in Ron Arias's *The Road to Tamazunchale* (1975) is a comic male
abuelito counterpart. Both Anaya and Arias move beyond retelling of
oral folk culture, using "magical realism" to create a richly inventive
universe pregnant with Chicano associations. Ultima is still a healing
figure, using traditional lore on the side of good. A former encyclope-
dia salesman, Fausto is already a very modernist old man, who instead

of passively yielding to failing health, brilliantly creates an active end game, hanging out with a young teenager, inventing relations with a Peruvian llama herder, transporting himself to ancient Cuzco, acting as a coyote to bring wetbacks into the United States, and teaching them how to earn a living without working by playing corpse. Thanks perhaps to knowledge gained from his encyclopedias, Fausto's end game is full of allusions and parodies. Rolando Hinojosa's *Rites and Witnesses* (1982) works the oral mode in a wildly comic, but less magical, direction, being largely constructed of dialogues set in major institutions that manipulate his characters' lives in mythical Klail City, Belken County, south Texas (a bank that knows everyone's genealogies and business, in all senses, the better to stay one step ahead of them in manipulating real estate, politics, careers, ranching, and banking; the Army, which brings together a Chicano from Klail City and a Cajun from Louisiana to fight in Asia under Sgt. Hatalski). Satire here functions like a hall of mirrors to reality, rather than attempting to create a counter world. It is a series of mirrors that reflect deeply, with a scalpel's precision, revealing ever deeper layers like a *cuento de nunca acabar* (story without end).

Two autobiographical poems that like "Stupid America" depend less on creating new myths of Mexican or Aztlan pasts illustrate the richness of inter-reference: Raul Salinas's "A Trip Through the Mind Jail" (1969) written in jail and dedicated to Eldridge Cleaver, reflecting on the destruction of his childhood barrio in Austin, Texas; and Bernice Zamora's "Restless Serpents." Salinas elegantly reviews the trajectory of childhood and youth, thereby making a powerful indictment of the oppression in these barrios. The first half of the poem describes childhood scenes of playing in chuck-holed streets, learning game playing that turns aggressivity inward, bribing girls with Juicy Fruit gum (an apt euphemism, using a prepackaged, sterile consumer good from outside for seducing tabooed objectives), ethnic rejection at school, and being scared by La Llorona (the weeping woman who inhabits streams and kidnaps naughty children). The second half parallels the first in the transformations of youth: hanging out at Spanish Town Cafe, the "first grown-up (13) hangout" (13 = marijuana), sniffing gas, drinking muscatel, chased by the llorona of police sirens, painting graffiti (pachuco "could-be artists"). The barrio is gone, but "You live on, captive in the lonely cell blocks of my mind." The poem, dedicated to Cleaver, names Chicano barrios across the States. The poem's description is a powerful indictment, but the poem's result is strength: "you keep me away from INSANITY's hungry jaws," providing "identity . . . a sense of belonging," which is "so essential to adult days of imprisonment."

We turn finally to Bernice Zamora's *Restless Serpents*. The beauty here, in part, lies in the way she injects a female (she rejects "feminist")[25] point of view, counterposing it as a healing potential against the self-destructiveness of the male worlds depicted by Salinas, Montoya ("El Louie"), and the Penitentes cult she describes. The cult of flagellation during Easter week is fascinating and attracts her to its pilgrimage center; but as a woman she is not allowed into the center. She offers an alternative imagery, of locomotion to the center (swimming instead of riding up dry arroyos), of natural cycles of life-giving blood (instead of the exclusively male death-dealing blood sacrifices of flagellation and mock crucifixion). The serpents perhaps are the self-renewing (periodically skin-shedding) images of ancient Mexico (the descending plumed serpent gods). As Bruce-Nova (1982) puts it, at the beginning of Zamora's 58-poem book, the mythic beasts are restless, wanting their due; the cosmic order is out of phase, the rituals are wrong, inwardly turned, self-destructive aggression; at the end an alternative ritual, nuanced in the imagery of communion and the sex act, male ingested by female, soothes the serpents. Other women writers too use this subtle technique of undermining an initial point of view and showing it in a different light through women's eyes. Evangelina Vigil's "Dumb Broad" describes a woman in fast 8 A.M. bumper-to-bumper traffic with both hands off the wheel, the rear view mirror turned perpendicular, as she teases her hair, fixes her lipstick, puts on eyeshadow, and so on; the poem ends triumphantly with her "sporting a splendid hair-do," tuning the radio, lighting a cigarette, and being handed coffee, the refrain "dumb broad" now, as it ends the poem, being subverted, almost a commuter's "El Louie."

It could be said that inter-reference is what ethnicity is essentially all about, but rarely is the contribution of interlinguistic context so clear and so obviously rich as a vehicle for future creativity: between English and Hispanic worlds; among subcultural styles, mass culture, and "high" culture; between male and female worlds. The subversiveness of alternative perspectives (feminist, minority) for the taken-for-granted assumptions of dominant ideologies, and the polyphony of multiple voices (English, Spanish), are models for more textured, nuanced, and realistic ethnography.[26]

25. Feminism, Zamora says, ignores race. The Chicana's relation to Chicano men she says is different from that of feminists with their men, owing among other reasons to the loss of Chicano men to white women. She sees a parallel problem for black women. (See interview in Bruce-Nova 1980:214.)

26. See again here note 21 above.

Ironic Humor

. . . the yet unseen translation where Indians have been backed up into and on long liquor nights, working in their minds, the anger and madness will come forth in tongues and fury

SIMON ORTIZ, "Irish Poets on Saturday Night and an Indian"

Tricksters must learn better how to balance the forces of good and evil through humor in the urban world

GERALD VIZENOR, *Wordarrows*

Perhaps nothing defines the present conditions of knowledge so well as irony. Ever more aware, in ever more precise ways, of the complexity of social life, writers have had to find ways to incorporate, acknowledge, and exploit our increasingly empirical understandings of the context, perspective, instability, conflict, contradiction, competition, and multilayered communications that characterize reality. Irony is a self-conscious mode of understanding and of writing, which reflects and models the recognition that all conceptualizations are limited, that what is socially maintained as truth is often politically motivated. Stylistically, irony employs rhetorical devices that signal real or feigned disbelief on the part of the author towards her or his own statements; it often centers on the recognition of the problematic nature of language; and so it revels—or wallows—in satirical techniques.[27]

Recent Amerindian autobiographies and autobiographical fiction and poetry are among the most sophisticated exemplars of the use of ironic humor as a survival skill, a tool for acknowledging complexity, a means of exposing or subverting oppressive hegemonic ideologies, and an art for affirming life in the face of objective troubles. The techniques of transference, talk-stories, multiple voices or perspectives, and alternative selves are all given depth or expanding resonances through ironic twists. Thus, talk-stories or narrative connections to the past, to the animated cosmos, and to the present are presented as the healing medicine not only for Indians but for Americans and modern folk at large. Searing portraits of Indian pain are wielded to expose white poets' appropriations of Indian holism with nature as romanticizing, trivializing, and hegemonic whitewashing. Openness to construction of new identities is promoted by the fact

27. Hayden White, from whom this characterization is adapted, has described the efforts of nineteenth-century historiography and social theory to overcome the irony of the Enlightenment—by rhetorical strategies of romance, tragedy, and comedy—only to end in an even more sophisticated and thorough irony (White 1973). For the present century, see Marcus and Fischer (1986), Lyotard (1979), and the recent essays of Tyler, including the one in this volume.

that almost all writers acknowledge a creative sense of being of mixed heritage.

N. Scott Momaday, perhaps the high priest of the healing power of the word ("The possibilities of storytelling are precisely those of understanding the human experience"),[28] is a skillful experimenter with multiple voices and perspectives. His first memoir, *The Way to Rainy Mountain* (1969), traces the migration route of the Kiowas from Montana to Oklahoma, each chapter told in three voices: that of eternal legendary stories; that of historical anecdote or ethnographic observation, often a single sentence or two in impersonal, flat, descriptive or scientific prose; and that of a personal reminiscence, often lyrical and evocative of a mood. Personal experience, cultural norm or generalization, and visionary tale are thus interbraided so as to capture, and re-present in mutual reinforcement, the separate levels of meaningfulness, while at the same time exposing and heightening the rhetorical vehicles that shape these levels. A lean, sparse, yet sharp and multidimensional, poetic effect is achieved.

In a second memoir, *The Names* (1976), Momaday plays with childhood fantasies, seeing himself sometimes as a white confronting hostile, dumb, unappealing Indians, and at other times seeing himself as the Indian. Such options come both from his experience and his genealogy. Momaday is Kiowa on his father's side, and his mother styled herself as an Indian, although only one of her great grandmothers was Cherokee. She was not accepted by the Kiowa, and the family moved to New Mexico, where Momaday had experiences with the Navajo, Tanoan Pueblo, and being a member of a gang of white toughs. Momaday's life history, his physical features, and his ideas about the potencies of story telling are incorporated into the character of John Big Bluff Tosameh (along with the introduction to *The Way to Rainy Mountain*) in his Pulitzer–prize winning novel *House Made of Dawn* (1968). The focal character of this novel, Abel, is a victim of illegitimacy (not knowing his father or his father's heritage, Navajo perhaps) and exclusion by other Indians. Abel is a transformation of the figure of Ira Hayes (the Pima Indian who helped raise the flag at Iwo Jima and after the war fell mortal victim to the role, provided by white society, of outcast alcoholic Indian). Abel, too, is a veteran, but his problems are primarily caused by Indians and non-Anglos. He is an embarrassment to Tosameh by fulfilling the white stereotypes of the violent, superstitious, inarticulate Indian. He is redeemed by returning to his dying grandfather and entering a ceremonial race the grandfather had once won. Through the ritual he is able (Abel?) to

28. From the introduction to Vizenor's *Wordarrows*.

recall the Navajo prayer song, "House Made of Dawn," which earlier he had unsuccessfully sought.

Leslie Marmon Silko (a mixed blood Laguna)'s *Ceremony* (1977) deals with the same issues in very similar ways. She, too, uses the device of an Indian traumatized by war (in his memories the killing of Japanese merges with the death of his uncle Josiah; his prayers to stop the Philippine rains cause him guilt for the drought and loss of animals suffered by his family and people: "Tayo didn't know how to explain . . . that he had not killed . . . but that he had done things far worse"). She, too, uses character types to explore the proper integration with the present world. Tayo, the protagonist, is half-Mexican, half-Laguna, and thus looked down on by his long-suffering Christian Laguna aunt. The latter's son, Rocky, adopts white outlooks and education, and is thought to be the family's great hope to escape Indian poverty. He, however, is killed in the Philippines (wrong solution), causing Tayo to add survivor's guilt to his confusions. Emo, Harley, and Leroy are the stereotypic Indian veterans who try to recapture their sense of belonging to America by drinking and telling stories of their more potent days. Emo carries around a little bag of teeth of Japanese soldiers he has killed, and eventually turns his frustration on his fellow victims, killing his two buddies. It is Tayo in the end who represents the path out of the mixtures and confusions of the Indian—and of modern America.

His redemption comes through two old medicine men, particularly Old Betonie who lives on skid row in Gallup. Old Betonie not only insists that one must confront the sickness-witchery in oneself and not take the easy way out, writing off all whites ("It was Indian witchery that made white people" [139]), for witchery works largely through fear, but he also insists that the healing ceremonies themselves must change ("things which don't shift and grow are dead" [133]). Indeed, his ritual implements consist of cardboard boxes, old clothing and rags, dry roots, twigs, sage, mountain tobacco, wool, newspapers, telephone books (to keep track of names), calendars, coke bottles, pouches and bags, and deer-hoof clackers: "In the old days it was simple. A medicine person could get by without all these things. All these things have stories alive in them" (123). Ceremonies and stories are not just entertainment: "They are all we have to fight off illness and death" (2). Tayo must confront the witchery in himself, in his fellow veterans, and in America. The climax occurs along the chain-link fence of a uranium mine near an atomic test site. The problem of the Indian is analogous to that of the whites:

> Then they grew away from the earth . . .
> sun . . . plants and animals . . .

> when they look
> they see only objects
> The world is a dead thing for them . . .
> They fear the world.
> They destroy what they fear.
> They fear themselves.

Humor is a critical component of the healing talk-stories that re-establish connections to the past, to the cosmos, and to the present. Humor is a survival skill against witchery and evil. Gerald Vizenor, a half-Chippewa (Anishinabe) Indian activist, is a major practitioner of the fine art of the trickster. *Wordarrows* (1978b) is a series of portraits drawn from his experience as director of the American Indian Employment and Guidance Center in Minneapolis, which also informs his comic novel *Darkness in St. Louis Bearheart* (1978a). He says he refused to work with the Communist Party, which attempted to support his organizing activities, "because in addition to political reasons—there was too little humor in communist speech, making it impossible to know the hearts of the speakers" (1978b: 17). The portraits in *Wordarrows* are full of sadness, but also small absurdist victories. There is Baptiste Saint Simon IV or "Bat Four," told by his father that he is stupid and a backward and a fool, who tries to become a trickster, balancing energies of good and evil, but "hard as he tried, and in good humor, he failed as a trickster and settled for the role of a fool. Evil was too much for him to balance. As a fool . . . he was a brilliant success," talking hilarious nonsense to get his case dismissed in court, to weasel money out of his social worker, and so on (1978b: 54). There is the "conference savage," or "nomadic committee bear," who never washes or changes his clothes, goes to all the conferences, and sleeps with white women as a kind of "foul bear racism test." And there is the story of the cripple who sells his wooden leg for a drink (the leg has a label on it to be mailed back), for which the white moral is "stop drinking," but the tribal moral is to find free booze with a wooden leg. No wonder there is thus also "Custer on the Slipstream," a Bureau of Indian Affairs employee and reincarnation of Custer, who suffers his own nightmares of humiliation at the hands of the Indians, and so spends all his time in his padded chair. *Darkness in St. Louis Bearheart*, which gets a preview in *Wordarrows*, is an absurdist comedy set after the collapse of American civilization, after oil runs out and the government takes back the trees on the reservations for fuel, forcing a pilgrimage of the Indians from their sacred forest lands, led by Proude Cedarfair (clowns and tricksters). Along the way they meet and overcome a series of enemies, such as Sir Cecil Staples, the monarch of unleaded gasoline, who wagers five gallons worth of gas against the bettor's life; the fast-food fascists, who hang witches from the rafters to season before cutting them up for take-out orders; and the government regional word hospitals, modelled on the BIA, set up on the theory of Congress that social problems and crime are caused by language, words, grammar, and conversations. (Sir Cecil Staples's mother had been sterilized by the government for having illegitimate children while on welfare; so she became a truck driver and took to kidnapping children from shopping malls, raising them in her truck, and when they were grown, setting them out at rest-stops.)

James Welch (of Blackfeet and Gros Ventre parentage) uses a grimmer sort of ironic comedy. His novel *Winter in the Blood* is about a Blackfeet man whose emotions become frozen (shadowy inversions of Michael Arlen's eighteenth-century Armenian merchant) in an inverted Western: the cowboy here is the Indian whose horse is out of control and who watches helplessly as a death occurs (the tableau happens twice, framing the text). Welch also writes poetry. With sensitive irony, in "Arizona Highways" Welch writes of love for a Navajo girl: he feels cut off from his ethnic (general Indian) roots by his education and craft as a poet; he feels white ("a little pale"), flabby ("belly soft as hers"), and overdressed ("my shoes too clean"). Instead of being an inappropriate lover, he tries to be a spiritual guide, but feels himself instead a malevolent ghost. Such irony can be searing, as in "Harlem Montana: Just off the Reservation":

> We need no runners here. Booze is law . . .
> When you die, if you die, you will remember
> the three young bucks who shot the grocery up,
> locked themselves in and cried for days, we're rich
> help us, oh God, we're rich.

Several meanings coalesce here, as Michael Castro points out (1983: 165): the image of desperation in poverty, the despair of having locked themselves in from both white and Indian worlds, unable to use the riches of either. The imagery of the inability to discover and express one's identity, of being adrift and lost between worlds, recurs:

> In stunted light, Bear Child tells a story
> to the mirror. He acts his name out,
> creeks muscling gorges fill his glass
> with gumbo. The bear crawls on all fours
> and barks like a dog. Slithering snake-wise
> he balances a nickel on his nose. The effect
> a snake in heat.   ("D-Y BAR")

Castro again: Bear Child cannot find himself, let alone the traditional wisdom and power of his bear namesake and totem; his attempts at recovery through acting out his name are but a pathetic charade, and Welch leaves him at the bar, "head down, the dormant bear."

These images of pain are cautions against the trivializing, superficial romanticism with which many whites attempt to appropriate Indian consciousness. "Many Indian writers perceived [Gary] Snyder's
acclaimed book [*Turtle Island*] as part of a new cavalry charge into
their territory by wild-eyed neo-romantics seeking to possess not
merely their land, as had the invaders of the previous century, but
their very spirit" (Castro 1983 : 159). Thus Silko:

Ironically, as white poets attempt to cast off their Anglo-American values,
their Anglo-American origins, they violate a fundamental belief held by the
tribal people they desire to emulate: they deny their history, their very origins. The writing of imitation "Indian" poems then, is pathetic evidence that
in more than two hundred years, Anglo-Americans have failed to create a satisfactory identity for themselves. (Quoted in Castro 1983 : 213)

Again, commenting on Maurice Kenny (a Mohawk)'s refusal to play
"savior and warrior, priest and poet . . . savage and prophet, angel of
death and apostle of truth," Castro says (169):

Kenny comically reminds us of how the eagerness of spiritually starved whites
to romanticize the Native American denies the Indian's contemporary reality
and humanity, at the same time obfuscating the fact that what America has
become is now our common problem:

> Again I spoke of hunger:
> A "Big Mac" would do, instant coffee
> plastic pizza, anything but holy water.

Irony and humor are tactics that ethnographers have only slowly
come to appreciate, albeit recently with increasing interest. A number
of analyses now exist of previously unnoticed or misunderstood ironies (either intended or unintentionally revealing) in past ethnographic writing—see Crapanzano in this volume, James Boon (1972)
on Lévi-Strauss, Don Handelman (1979) on Bateson. Increasingly attention is being paid to the uses of laughter among ethnographic subjects (Bakhtin 1965, Karp 1985, Fischer 1984). Ethnographers are
pointing out the rhetorical devices they employ (Marcus and Fischer
1986). Considerable potential still exists, however, to construct texts
utilizing humor and other devices that draw attention to their own
limitations and degree of accuracy, and that do so with aesthetic elegance, and are pleasurable to read, rather than with pedantic laboredness. The stylist closest to such an ambition in anthropology is, perhaps, Lévi-Strauss (and in literary criticism, Jacques Derrida). This, I
recognize, is a personal judgment, and neither Lévi-Strauss nor Derrida are unproblematic. They are less models to emulate than examples on which to build in more accessible, replicable ways. For the
time being, pedantic laboredness is also difficult to avoid, because edi-

tors and readers still need to be educated to understand such texts. Subtlety is a quality that seems often (but not necessarily) to run counter to the canons of explicitness and univocal meaning expected in scientific writing. But, as Stephen Tyler has eloquently pointed out, the demand for univocal meaning is often self-defeating (Tyler 1978).

III

Re-Collections and Introductions

Postmodern knowledge . . . refines our sensitivity to differences and reinforces our ability to tolerate the incommensurable.
JEAN-FRANÇOIS LYOTARD, *The Postmodern Condition*

Ethnicity is merely one domain, or one exemplar, of a more general pattern of cultural dynamics in the late twentieth century. Ethnic autobiographical writing parallels, mirrors, and exemplifies contemporary theories of textuality, of knowledge, and of culture. Both forms of writing suggest powerful modes of cultural criticism. They are post-modern in their deployment of a series of techniques: bifocality or reciprocity of perspectives, juxtapositioning of multiple realities, intertextuality and inter-referentiality, and comparison through families of resemblance. Insofar as the present age is one of increasing potentialities for dialogue, as well as conflict, among cultures, lessons for writing ethnography may be taken from writers both on ethnicity and on textuality, knowledge, and culture.

Ethnicity. Substantively what have we learned? First, that the different ethnicities constitute a family of resemblances: similar, not identical; each enriching because of its inter-references, not reducible to mechanical functions of solidarity, mutual aid, political mobilization, or socialization. It is the inter-references, the interweaving of cultural threads from different arenas, that give ethnicity its phoenix-like capacities for reinvigoration and reinspiration. To kill this play between cultures, between realities, is to kill a reservoir that sustains and renews humane attitudes.

In the modern, technological, secular world, ethnicity has become a puzzling quest to those afflicted by it. But rather than establishing a sense of exclusivity or separation, resolutions of contemporary ethnicity tend toward a pluralistic universalism, a textured sense of being American. (We are all ethnics, in one sense, perhaps; but only some feel ethnicity as a compelling force,[29] only some have an ear for

29. See George Lipsitz's "The Meaning of Memory: Class, Family, and Ethnicity in Early Network Television" (forthcoming) for an analysis of mechanisms operating im-

the music of its revelations.) Not only is the individualism of ethnic searches—posing the struggles of self-definition as idiosyncratic—humanistically tempered by the recognition that parallel processes affect individuals across the cultural spectrum, but the tolerance and pluralism of American society should be reinforced by this recognition. The recreation of ethnicity in each generation, accomplished through dream- and transferencelike processes, as much as through cognitive language, leads to efforts to recover, fill in, act out, unravel, and reveal. Though the compulsions, repressions, and searches are individual, the resolution (finding peace, strength, purpose, vision) is a revelation of cultural artifice. Not only does this revelation help delegitimize and place in perspective the hegemonic power of repressive political or majority discourses, it sensitizes us to important wider cultural dynamics in the post-religious, post-immigrant, technological and secular societies of the late twentieth century. In these societies processes of immigration and cultural interaction have not slowed; quite the contrary. There is increasingly a diversity of cultural tapestry that is not—as many have assumed—being homogenized into blandness. The great challenge is whether this richness can be turned into a resource for intellectual and cultural reinvigoration.

The possibility always exists that the exploration of elements of tradition will remain superficial, merely transitional to disappearance. In the first generation of immigration, problems are communal and family-related; in later ones vestiges remain at the personal level, and they, too, will disappear. This is the traditional sociological stance: the Yiddish theater is replaced by assimilated Jewish writers like Bernard Malamud, Philip Roth, and Saul Bellow, and they, too, will pass. There is, however, another, more exciting possibility—that there are cultural resources in traditions that can be recovered and reworked into enriching tools for the present, as Arshile Gorky deploys his mother through his painting. It is, suggests Robert Alter (1982), not Roth, Malamud, and Bellow who define a Jewish renaissance in America—indeed, they are totally encapsulated in immigrant adjustments—but rather, the establishment of a new serious, post-orthodox, Jewish scholarship by such writers as linguists Uriel and Max Weinreich, historians Jacob Neusner and Gershom Scholem, philosophers Hannah Arendt and Emanuel Levinas, and literary critics Harold Bloom and Robert Alter himself, all resolutely modern, yet able to involve the past in a dialogue generating new perspectives for the present and future.[30] Or more generously, as Murray Baumgarten suggests (1982),

---

perfectly and ultimately unsuccessfully to homogenize, coopt, and suppress interest in ethnicity.

30. Eric Gould makes a similar point in contrasting the work of Edmond Jabès with the Jewish ethnic novels of mid-century America (Gould, ed. 1985:xvi).

what is enduring about Malamud, Roth, Bellow, Singer, and Henry Roth is the *interference* between Yiddish and English that the texture and idiom of their English preserves, reworks, and gifts back with new richness to English; and the *inter-references* to dual or multiple cultural traditions. Jewish ethnicity and other ethnicities have always grown in an interlinguistic context. The future of Jewish writing may depend upon the creation of a renewed inter-referential style: Cynthia Ozick (1983) would do it through the recreation in English of a liturgical and midrashic voice; Shmuel Agnon and Jorge Luis Borges do it through a mirroring play in which ancient narratives are placed in modern settings with resolutions echoing ancient texts. One of the most important of contemporary Jewish projects in ethnicity is Jewish feminism, particularly by those who feel themselves orthodox (e.g., Greenberg 1981; Heschel 1983; Prell-Foldes 1978). For here is a context, par excellence, demanding *hiddush* (creative interpretation), informed knowledge of the texts and traditions of the past so rich that new possibilities may be discovered.

Writing Tactics.   Contemporary ethnic autobiographies partake of the mood of meta-discourse, of drawing attention to their own linguistic and fictive nature, of using the narrator as an inscribed figure within the text whose manipulation calls attention to authority structures, of encouraging the reader to self-consciously participate in the production of meaning. This is quite different from previous autobiographical conventions. There were once times and cultural formations when there was little self-reflection, little expression of interiority, and autobiography served as a moral didactic form in which the subject/narrator was little more than a sum of conventions, useful today primarily for exploring the logic and grounding of those moralities (Fischer 1982b, 1983). Romantic poetics made the author/narrator and his or her interiority central: knowledge itself was thought inseparable from the cultivation of individual minds. Realism again deemphasized the individual, elevating social and historical references, making the individual the locus of social process: this is the moment of the classic immigrant-assimilation story of struggle between marginal individual and on the one side family/community and on the other side noncommunal society. The characteristic of contemporary writing of encouraging participation of the reader in the production of meaning—often drawing on parodic imitation of rationalistic convention (Kingston, Mingus, Vizenor), or using fragments or incompleteness to force the reader to make the connections (Kingston, Cisneros, Momaday)—is not merely descriptive of how ethnicity is experienced, but more importantly is an ethical device attempting to activate in the reader a desire for *communitas* with others, while preserving rather than effacing differences.

Ethnography as Cultural Critique.   Rather than repeat the ethnographic codas to each of the five writing tactics discussed in part II of this paper, which conceptually belong here,[31] it is best to end with a challenge, a call for a renewed beginning. Not much ethnography yet exists that fulfills the anthropological promise of a fully bifocal cultural criticism. Or rather, what exists was drafted with less sophisticated audiences in mind than exist today on all the continents of our common earth.

Cultural criticism that operates dialectically among possible cultural and ethnic identifications is one important direction in which the current ferment about ethnography seems to lead. If this is true, then finding a context for ethnographic projects in the provocative literature on modern ethnicity can only enhance their critical potential.

31. The idea of the paper was that the sections of part II should be staged "to speak for themselves." Because the first draft did not achieve this goal in a way readers found illuminating, the second draft (printed here) has reverted to a more traditional authorial guiding voice. A third, future version, when both author and readers have become more expert, would again remove the intrusive interpretations to this place of re-collection and reconsideration—by reader and author—as to how to do it better.

The ideas for this paper were first developed in a course at Rice University on American Culture, and I am indebted to the student participants. For stimulating discussions I would like to thank members of the Rice Circle for Anthropology (in 1982–84 comprised of George Marcus, Stephen Tyler, Tulio Maranhao, Julie Taylor, Ivan Karp, Lane Kaufmann, Gene Holland, myself, and occasional others), as well as the participants in the seminar "The Making of Ethnographic Texts," particularly Renato Rosaldo, who led the discussion of the first draft of this paper, and James Clifford, who made helpful suggestions at a later stage.

This paper is dedicated to the memory of my father, Eric Fischer, who read from it at his last seder table (while it was being delivered in Santa Fe) and who died as it was being polished a year later just before Shavuot. His own first and last English-language books—*The Passing of the European Age* (Cambridge, Mass., 1943) and *Minorities and Minority Problems* (Takoma Park, Md., 1980)—are very much concerned with similar issues.

PAUL RABINOW

Representations Are Social Facts: Modernity and Post-Modernity in Anthropology

Beyond Epistemology

In his influential book *Philosophy and the Mirror of Nature* (1979), Richard Rorty argues that epistemology as the study of mental representations arose in a particular historical epoch, the seventeenth century; developed in a specific society, that of Europe; and eventually triumphed in philosophy by being closely linked to the professional claims of one group, nineteenth-century German professors of philosophy. For Rorty, this turn was not a fortuitous one: "The desire for a theory of knowledge is a desire for constraint—a desire to find 'foundations' to which one might cling, frameworks beyond which one must not stray, objects which impose themselves, representations which cannot be gainsaid" (315). Radicalizing Thomas Kuhn, Rorty portrays our obsession with epistemology as an accidental, but eventually sterile, turning in Western culture.

Pragmatic and American, Rorty's book has a moral: modern professional philosophy represents the "triumph of the quest for certainty over the quest for reason" (61). The chief culprit in this melodrama is Western philosophy's concern with epistemology, the equation of knowledge with internal representations and the correct evaluation of those representations. Let me briefly outline Rorty's argument, add some important specifications by Ian Hacking, then claim that Michel Foucault has developed a position that enables us to supplement Rorty in important ways. In the rest of the paper I explore some ways in which these lines of thought are relevant to discourses about the other. Specifically, in the second section I discuss recent debates about the making of ethnographic texts; in the third section, some differences between feminist anthropology and anthropological feminism; and, finally, in the fourth section, I put forward one line of research, my own.

Philosophers, Rorty argues, have crowned their discipline the queen of the sciences. This coronation rests on their claim to be the specialists on universal problems and their ability to provide us with a sure foundation for all knowledge. Philosophy's realm is the mind; its privileged insights establish its claim to be the discipline that judges all other disciplines. This conception of philosophy is, however, a recent historical development. For the Greeks there was no sharp division between external reality and internal representations. Unlike Aristotle, Descartes's conception of knowing rests on having correct representations in an internal space, the mind. Rorty makes the point by saying: "The novelty was the notion of a single inner space in which bodily and perceptual sensations (confused ideas of sense and imagination in Descartes's phrase), mathematical truths, moral rules, the idea of God, moods of depression, and all the rest of what we now call 'mental' were objects of quasi-observation" (50). Although not all of these elements were new ones, Descartes successfully combined them into a new problematic, setting aside Aristotle's concept of reason as a grasp of universals: beginning in the seventeenth century, knowledge became internal, representational, and judgmental. Modern philosophy was born when a knowing subject endowed with consciousness and its representational contents became the central problem for thought, the paradigm of all knowing.

The modern notion of epistemology, then, turns on the clarification and judgment of the subject's representations. "To know is to represent accurately what is outside the mind; so to understand the possibility and nature of knowledge is to understand the way in which the mind is able to construct such representations. Philosophy's eternal concern is to be a general theory of representations, a theory which will divide culture up into the areas which represent reality well, those which represent it less well, and those which do not represent it at all (despite their pretense of doing so)" (3). The knowledge arrived at through the examination of representations about "reality" and "the knowing subject" would be universal. This universal knowledge is, of course, science.

It was only at the end of the Enlightenment that the fully elaborated conception of philosophy as the judge of all possible knowledge appeared and was canonized in the work of Immanuel Kant. "The eventual demarcation of philosophy from science was made possible by the notion that philosophy's core was a 'theory of knowledge', a theory distinct from the sciences because it was their foundation," Rorty argues (132). Kant established as a priori the Cartesian claim that we have certainty only about ideas. Kant, "by taking everything we say to be about something we have constituted, made it possible for epistemology to be thought of as a foundational science. . . . He thus en-

abled philosophy professors to see themselves as presiding over a tribunal of pure reason, able to determine whether other disciplines
were staying within the legal limits set by the 'structure' of their subject matters" (139).

As a discipline whose proper activity is grounding claims to knowledge, philosophy was developed by nineteenth-century neo-Kantians
and institutionalized in nineteenth-century German universities. Carv-
ing out a space between ideology and empirical psychology, German
philosophy wrote its own history, producing our modern canon of the
"greats." This task was completed by the end of the nineteenth century. The narrative of the history of philosophy as a series of great
thinkers continues today in introductory philosophy courses. Philosophy's claim to intellectual preeminence lasted only for a short time,
however, and by the 1920s, only philosophers and undergraduates
believed that philosophy was uniquely qualified to ground and judge
cultural production. Neither Einstein nor Picasso was overly concerned with what Husserl might have thought of them.

Although philosophy departments continue to teach epistemology, there is a counter tradition in modern thought that followed another path. "Wittgenstein, Heidegger and Dewey are in agreement that
the notion of knowledge as accurate representation, made possible by
special mental processes, and intelligible through a general theory of
representation, needs to be abandoned," Rorty observes (6). These
thinkers did not seek to construct alternate and better theories of the
mind or knowledge. Their aim was not to improve epistemology but
to play a different game. Rorty calls this game hermeneutics. By this,
he simply means knowledge without foundations; a knowledge that
essentially amounts to edifying conversation. Rorty has so far told us
very little about the content of this conversation, perhaps because
there is very little to tell. As with Wittgenstein, Heidegger, and, in a
different way, Dewey, Rorty is faced with the fact, troubling or amusing, that once the historical or logical deconstruction of Western philosophy has been accomplished, there is really nothing special left for
philosophers to do. Once it is seen that philosophy does not found or
legitimate the claims to knowledge of other disciplines, its task becomes one of commenting on their works and engaging them in
conversation.

Truth versus Truth or Falsity

Even if one accepts Rorty's deconstruction of epistemology,
the consequences of such a move remain very open. Before exploring
some of them, it seems important to underline the point that rejecting
epistemology does not mean rejecting truth, reason, or standards of

judgment. This point is made very succinctly by Ian Hacking in "Language, Truth, and Reason" (1982). Parallel to Rorty's distinction of certainty versus reason, Hacking draws a distinction between those philosophies involved in the quest for truth and those—which he calls styles of thinking, so as not to limit them to modern philosophy—that open up new possibilities by proceeding in terms of "truth or falsehood."

Hacking puts forward what is basically a simple point: what is currently taken as "truth" is dependent on a prior historical event—the emergence of a style of thinking about truth and falsity that established the conditions for entertaining a proposition as being capable of being taken as true or false in the first place. Hacking puts it this way: "By reasoning I don't mean logic. I mean the very opposite, for logic is the preservation of truth, while a style of reasoning is what brings in the possibility of truth or falsehood. . . . styles of reasoning create the possibility of truth and falsehood. Deduction and induction merely preserve it" (56–57). Hacking is not "against" logic, only against its claims to found and ground all truth. Logic is fine in its own domain, but that domain is a limited one.

By drawing this distinction one avoids the problem of totally relativizing reason or of turning different historical conceptions of truth and falsity into a question of subjectivism. These conceptions are historical and social facts. This point is well put by Hacking when he says: "Hence although whichever propositions are true may depend on the data, the fact that they are candidates for being true is a consequence of an historical event" (56). That the analytical tools we use when we investigate a set of problems—geometry for the Greeks, experimental method in the seventeenth century, or statistics in modern social science—have shifted is explainable without recourse to some truth denying relativism. Furthermore, science understood in this way remains quite objective "simply because the styles of reasoning that we employ determine what counts as objectivity. . . . Propositions of the sort that necessarily require reasoning to be substantiated have a positivity, a being true or false, only in consequence of the styles of reasoning in which they occur" (49, 65). What Foucault has called the regime, or game, of truth and falsity is both a component and a product of historical practices. Other procedures and other objects could have filled the bill just as well and have been just as true.

Hacking distinguishes between everyday, commonsensical reasoning that does not need to apply any elaborate set of reasons and those more specialized domains that do. There is both a cultural and a historical plurality of these specialized domains and of historically and culturally diverse styles associated with them. From the acceptance of a diversity of historical styles of reasoning, of methods, and objects,

Hacking draws the conclusion that thinkers frequently got things right, solved problems, and established truths. But, he argues, this does not imply that we should search for a unified Popperian realm of the true; rather, a la Paul Feyerabend, we should keep our options in inquiry as open as possible. The Greeks, Hacking reminds us, had no concept, or use, of statistics, a fact that invalidates neither Greek science nor statistics as such. This position is not relativism, but it is not imperialism either. Rorty calls his version of all this hermeneutics. Hacking calls his anarcho-rationalism. "Anarcho-rationalism is tolerance for other people combined with the discipline of one's own standards of truth and reason" (65). Let us call it good science.

Michel Foucault has also considered many of these issues in parallel, but not identical, fashion. His *Archaeology of Knowledge* (1976) and *Discourse on Language* (1976) are perhaps the most developed attempts to present, if not a theory of what Hacking refers to as "truth or falsity" and "styles of thought," then at least an analytic of them. Although the details of Foucault's systematization of how discursive objects, enunciative modalities, concepts, and discursive strategies are formed and transformed is beyond the scope of this paper,[1] several points are relevant here. Let us merely take one example as illustrative. In the *Discourse on Language* Foucault discusses some of the constraints on, and conditions for, the production of truth, understood as statements capable of being taken seriously as true or false. Among others, Foucault examines the existence of scientific disciplines. He says:

For a discipline to exist, there must be the possibility of formulating—and of doing so ad infinitum—fresh propositions. . . . These propositions must conform to specific conditions of objects, subject, methods etc. . . . Within its own limits, every discipline recognises as true and false propositions, but it repulses a whole teratology of learning. . . . In short, a proposition must fulfill some onerous and complex conditions before it can be admitted within a discipline; before it can be pronounced true or false it must be, as Monsieur Canguilhem might say, "within the true." (1976:223–24)

Foucault gives the example of Mendel: "Mendel spoke of objects, employed methods and placed himself within a theoretical perspective totally alien to the biology of his time. . . . Mendel spoke the truth, but he was not *dans le vrai* of contemporary biological discourse" (224). The demonstration of the richness of this style of thinking has been the great strength of Foucault, Georges Canguilhem, and other French practitioners of the history and philosophy of science, particularly the "life sciences."

It is perhaps not accidental that both Rorty and Hacking are concerned with the history of physical science, mathematics, and philoso-

1. For a treatment of the subject see Dreyfus and Rabinow (1982) pp. 44–79.

phy. What has been missing from their accounts is the category of power, and to a lesser extent (in Hacking's case) society. Hacking's current very interesting work on nineteenth-century statistics does, however, include these categories. Although compelling in its deconstructive force, Rorty's story is less convincing in its refusal to comment on how the epistemological turning came about in Western society—according to Rorty, like Galilean science, it just happened—or in its inability to see knowledge as more than free and edifying conversation. Not unlike Jurgen Habermas, although refusing Habermas's striving for foundationalism, Rorty sees free communication, civilized conversation, as the ultimate goal. As Hacking says: "Perhaps Richard Rorty's . . . central doctrine of conversation will some day seem as linguistic a philosophy as the analysis emanating from Oxford a generation ago" (1984 : 109). The content of the conversation and how the freedom to have it is to come about is, however, beyond the domain of philosophy.

But conversation, between individuals or cultures, is only possible within contexts shaped and constrained by historical, cultural, and political relations and the only partially discursive social practices that constitute them. What is missing from Rorty's account, then, is any discussion of how thought and social practices interconnect. Rorty is helpful in deflating philosophy's claims, but he stops exactly at the point of taking seriously his own insight: to wit, thought is nothing more and nothing less than a historically locatable set of practices. How to do this without reverting to epistemology or to some dubious superstructure/infrastructure device is another question, one Rorty is not alone in not having solved.

Representations and Society

Michel Foucault has offered us some important tools for analyzing thought as a public and social practice. Foucault accepts the main elements of the Nietzschean, Heideggerean account of Western metaphysics and epistemology Rorty has given us, but draws different conclusions from these insights—ones, it seems to me, that are both more consistent and more interesting than Rorty's. We find, for example, many of the same elements that are in Rorty's history of philosophy—the modern subject, representations, order—in Foucault's famous analysis of Velazquez's painting *Las Meninas*. But there are also some major differences. Instead of treating the problem of representations as specific to the history of ideas, Foucault treats it as a more general cultural concern, a problem that was being worked on in many other domains. In *The Order of Things* (1973) and later books, Foucault demonstrates how the problem of correct representations has informed a multitude of social domains and practices, ranging from disputes in botany to proposals for prison reform. The problem of representations for Foucault is not, therefore, one that happened to pop up in philosophy and dominate thinking there for three hundred years. It is linked to the wide range of disparate, but interrelated, social and political practices that constitute the modern world, with its distinctive concerns with order, truth, and the subject. Foucault differs from Rorty, then, in treating philosophical ideas as social practices and not chance twists in a conversation or in philosophy.

But Foucault also disagrees with many Marxist thinkers, who see problems in painting as, by definition, ultimately epiphenomenal to, or expressive of, what was "really" going on in society. This brings us briefly to the problem of ideology. In several places, Foucault suggests that once one sees the problem of the subject, or representations, and of truth as social practices, then the very notion of ideology becomes problematic. He says: "behind the concept of ideology there is a kind of nostalgia for a quasi-transparent form of knowledge, free from all error and illusion" (1980: 117). In this sense, the concept of ideology is close kin to the concept of epistemology.

For Foucault, the modern concept of ideology is characterized by three interrelated qualities: (1) by definition, ideology is opposed to something like "the truth," a false representation as it were; (2) ideology is produced by a subject (individual or collective) in order to hide the truth, and consequently the analyst's task consists in exposing this false representation; and revealing that (3) ideology is secondary to something more real, some infrastructural dimension on which ideology is parasitic. Foucault rejects all three claims.

We have already alluded to the broad lines of a critique of the subject and the search for certainty seen as based on correct representations. Consequently, let us briefly focus on the third point: the question of whether the production of truth is epiphenomenal to something else. He has described his project not as deciding the truth or falsity of claims in history "but in seeing historically how effects of truth are produced within discourses which in themselves are neither true nor false" (131–33). Foucault proposes to study what he calls the regime of truth as an effective component in the constitution of social practices.

Foucault has proposed three working hypotheses: "(1) Truth is to be understood as a system of ordered procedures for the production, regulation, distribution, circulation and operation of statements. (2) Truth is linked in a circular relation with systems of power which produce and sustain it, and to effects of power which it induces and which extend it. (3) This regime is not merely ideological or superstructural; it was a condition of the formation and development of capitalism" (133). We shall explore some of the implications of these working hypotheses in the next three sections of the paper.

As Max Weber, I think, once said, seventeenth-century capitalists were not only economic men who traded and built ships, they also looked at Rembrandt's paintings, drew maps of the world, had marked conceptions of the nature of other peoples, and worried a good deal about their own destiny. These representations were strong and effective forces in what they were and how they acted. Many new possibilities for thought and action are opened up if we follow Rorty and abandon epistemology (or at least see it for what it has been: an important cultural movement in Western society) and follow Foucault in seeing power as productive and permeative of social relations and the production of truth in our current regime of power. Here are some initial conclusions and research strategies that might follow from this discussion of epistemology. I merely list them before moving on to recent discussions in anthropology on how best to describe the other.

1. Epistemology must be seen as a historical event—a distinctive social practice, one among many others, articulated in new ways in seventeenth-century Europe.

2. We do not need a theory of indigenous epistemologies or a new epistemology of the other. We should be attentive to our historical practice of projecting our cultural practices onto the other; at best, the task is to show how and when and through what cultural and institutional means other people started claiming epistemology for their own.

3. We need to anthropologize the West: show how exotic its constitution of reality has been; emphasize those domains most taken for granted as universal (this includes epistemology and economics); make them seem as historically peculiar as possible; show how their claims to truth are linked to social practices and have hence become effective forces in the social world.

4. We must pluralize and diversify our approaches: a basic move against either economic or philosophic hegemony is to diversify centers of resistance: avoid the error of reverse essentializing; Occidentalism is not a remedy for Orientalism.

The Writing of Ethnographic Texts: The Fantasia of the Library

There is a curious time lag as concepts move across disciplinary boundaries. The moment when the historical profession is dis-

covering cultural anthropology in the (unrepresentative) person of
Clifford Geertz is just the moment when Geertz is being questioned in
anthropology (one of the recurrent themes of the Santa Fe seminar
that gave rise to this volume). So, too, anthropologists, or some of
them in any case, are now discovering and being moved to new creation by the infusion of ideas from deconstructionist literary criticism,
now that it has lost its cultural energy in literature departments and
Derrida is discovering politics. Although there are many carriers of
this hybridization (many of those present at the seminar, as well as
James Boon, Stephen Webster, James Siegel, Jean-Paul Dumont, and
Jean Jamin) there is only one "professional," so to speak, in the crowd.
For, whereas all the others mentioned are practicing anthropologists,
James Clifford has created and occupied the role of ex officio scribe
of our scribblings. Geertz, the founding figure, may pause between
monographs to muse on texts, narrative, description, and interpretation. Clifford takes as his natives, as well as his informants, those anthropologists past and present whose work, self-consciously or not,
has been the production of texts, the writing of ethnography. We are
being observed and inscribed.

At first glance James Clifford's work, like that of others in this volume, seems to follow naturally in the wake of Geertz's interpretive
turn. There is, however, a major difference. Geertz (like the other anthropologists) is still directing his efforts to reinvent an anthropological science with the help of textual mediations. The core activity is still
social description of the other, however modified by new conceptions
of discourse, author, or text. The other for Clifford is the anthropological representation of the other. This means that Clifford is simultaneously more firmly in control of his project and more parasitical.
He can invent his questions with few constraints; he must constantly
feed off others' texts.

This new speciality is currently in the process of self-definition.
The first move in legitimating a new approach is to claim it has an object of study, preferably an important one, that has previously escaped
notice. Parallel to Geertz's claim that the Balinese were interpreting
their cock fights as cultural texts all along, Clifford argues that anthropologists have been experimenting with writing forms whether
they knew it or not. The interpretive turn in anthropology has made
its mark (producing a substantial body of work and almost establishing itself as a subspeciality), but it is still not clear whether the
deconstructive-semiotic turn (an admittedly vague label) is a salutary
loosening up, an opening for exciting new work of major import, or a
tactic in the field of cultural politics to be understood primarily in sociological terms. As it is certainly the first and the third, it is worth a
closer examination.

In his essay "Fantasia of the Library" (1977) Michel Foucault plays adroitly with the progression of uses Flaubert made throughout his life of the fable of the temptation of Saint Anthony. Far from being the idle products of a fertile imagination, Flaubert's references to iconography and philology in his seemingly phantasmagoric renderings of the saint's hallucinations were exact. Foucault shows us how Flaubert returned throughout his life to this staging of experience and writing, and used it as an ascetic exercise both to produce and to keep at bay the demons that haunt a writer's world. It was no accident that Flaubert ended his life as a writer with that monstrous collection of commonplaces *Bouvard et Pécuchet*. A constant commentary on other texts, *Bouvard et Pécuchet* can be read as a thorough domestication of textuality into a self-contained exercise of arranging and cataloguing: the fantasia of the library.

For the sake of the argument, let us juxtapose Clifford Geertz's interpretive anthropology to James Clifford's textualist meta-anthropology. If Geertz is still seeking to conjure and capture the demons of exoticism—theater states, shadow plays, cock fights—through his limited use of fictionalized stagings in which they can appear to us, the textualist/deconstructive move runs the risk of inventing ever more clever filing systems for others' texts and of imagining that everyone else in the world is hard at work doing the same thing. Lest the argument run away in directions of its own, I should stress that I am not saying that Clifford's enterprise has up to the present been anything but salutary. The raising of anthropological consciousness about anthropology's own textual mode of operation was long overdue. Despite Geertz's occasional acknowledgements of the ineluctability of fictionalizing, he has never pushed that insight very far. The point seems to have needed a metaposition to bring home its real force. The voice from the campus library has been a salutary one. What I want to do briefly in this section is to return the gaze, to look back at this ethnographer of ethnographers, sitting across the table in a cafe, and, using his own descriptive categories, examine his textual productions.

Clifford's central theme has been the textual construction of anthropological authority. The main literary device employed in ethnographies, "free indirect style," has been well analyzed by Dan Sperber (1982) and need not be rehearsed here. The insight that anthropologists write employing literary conventions, although interesting, is not inherently crisis-provoking. Many now hold that fiction and science are not opposed but complementary terms (De Certeau 1983). Advances have been made in our awareness of the fictional (in the sense of "made," "fabricated") quality of anthropological writing and in the integration of its characteristic modes of production. The self-

consciousness of style, rhetoric, and dialectic in the production of anthropological texts should lead us to a finer awareness of other, more
imaginative, ways to write.

Clifford seems, however, to be saying more than this. Substantively,
he argues that from Malinowski on, anthropological authority has
rested on two textual legs. An experiential "I was there" element establishes the unique authority of the anthropologist; its suppression in
the text establishes the anthropologist's scientific authority.[2] Clifford
shows us this device at work in Geertz's famous cockfight paper: "The
research process is separated from the texts it generates and from the
fictive world they are made to call up. The actuality of discursive situations and individual interlocutors is filtered out. . . . The dialogical,
situational aspects of ethnographic interpretation tend to be banished
from the final representative text. Not entirely banished, of course;
there exist approved topoi for the portrayal of the research process"
(1983:132). Clifford presents Geertz's "appealing fable" as paradigmatic: the anthropologist establishes that he was there and then
disappears from the text.

With his own genre Clifford makes a parallel move. Just as Geertz
makes a bow to self-referentiality (thereby establishing one dimension
of his authority) and then (in the name of science) evades its consequences, so, too, Clifford talks a great deal about the ineluctability of
dialogue (thereby establishing his authority as an "open" one), but his
texts are not themselves dialogic. They are written in a modified free
indirect style. They evoke an "I was there at the anthropology convention" tone, while consistently maintaining a Flaubertean remove. Both
Geertz and Clifford fail to use self-referentiality as anything more
than a device for establishing authority. Clifford's telling reading of
the Balinese cockfight as a panoptic construct makes this point per-
suasively, but he himself makes the same omission on another level.
He reads and classifies, describing intention and establishing a canon;
but his own writing and situation are left unexamined. Pointing out
Clifford's textual stance does not, of course, invalidate his insights
(any more than his reading of Malinowski's textual moves invalidates
the analysis of the Kula). It only situates them. We have moved back
from the tent in the Trobriands filled with natives to the writing desk
in the campus library.[3]

An essential move in establishing disciplinary or subdisciplinary
legitimacy is classification. Clifford proposes four types of anthro-

2. The importance of this double move is one of the central arguments of my *Reflections on Fieldwork in Morocco* (1977).
3. I would like to thank Arjun Appadurai for his help in clarifying this and other
points.

pological writing, which have appeared in roughly chronological order. He organizes his essay "On Ethnographic Authority" (1983a) around this progression, but also asserts that no mode of authority is better than any other. "The modes of authority reviewed in this essay—experiential, interpretive, dialogical, polyphonic—are available to all writers of ethnographic texts, Western and non-Western. None is obsolete, none is pure: there is room for invention within each paradigm" (142). This conclusion goes against the rhetorical grain of Clifford's essay. This tension is important and I shall return to it below.

Clifford's main thesis is that anthropological writing has tended to suppress the dialogic dimension of fieldwork, giving full control of the text to the anthropologist. The bulk of Clifford's work has been devoted to showing ways in which this textual elimination of the dialogical might be remedied by new forms of writing. This leads him to read experiential and interpretive modes of writing as monological, linked in general terms to colonialism. "Interpretive anthropology . . . in its mainstream realist strands . . . does not escape the general strictures of those critics of "colonial" representation who, since 1950, have rejected discourses that portray the cultural realities of other peoples without placing their own reality in jeopardy" (133). It would be easy to read this statement as preferring some "paradigms" to others. It is perfectly possible that Clifford himself is simply ambivalent. However, given his own interpretive choices he clearly does characterize some modes as "emergent" and thereby as temporarily more important. Using a grid of interpretation that highlights the suppression of the dialogic, it is hard not to read the history of anthropological writing as a loose progression toward dialogical and polyphonic textuality.

Having cast the first two modes of ethnographic authority (experiential and realist/interpretive) in largely negative terms, Clifford moves on to a much more enthusiastic portrayal of the next set (dialogic and heteroglossic). He says: "Dialogic and constructivist paradigms tend to disperse or share out ethnographic authority, while narratives of initiation confirm the researcher's special competence. Paradigms of experience and interpretation are yielding to paradigms of discourse, of dialogue and polyphony" (133). The claim that such modes are triumphing is empirically dubious; as Renato Rosaldo says: "The troops are not following." Yet there is clearly considerable interest in such matters.

What is dialogic? Clifford at first seems to be using the term in a literal sense: a text that presents two subjects in discursive exchange. Kevin Dwyer's "rather literal record" (134) of exchanges with a Moroccan farmer is the first example cited of a "dialogic" text. However, a page later, Clifford adds: "To say that an ethnography is composed of discourses and that its different components are dialogically related, is not to say that its textual form should be that of a literal dialogue" (135). Alternate descriptions are given, but no final definition is arrived at. Consequently the genre's defining characteristics remain unclear.

"But if interpretive authority is based on the exclusion of dialogue, the reverse is also true: a purely dialogical authority represses the inescapable fact of textualization," Clifford quickly moves on to remind us (134). This is confirmed by Dwyer's adamant distancing of himself from what he perceives as textualist trends in anthropology. The opposition of interpretive and dialogic is hard to grasp—several pages later Clifford praises the most renowned representative of hermeneutics, Hans Georg Gadamer, whose texts certainly contain no direct dialogues, for aspiring to "radical dialogism" (142). Finally, Clifford asserts that dialogic texts are, after all, texts, merely "representations" of dialogues. The anthropologist retains his or her authority as a constituting subject and representative of the dominant culture. Dialogic texts can be just as staged and controlled as experiential or interpretive texts. The mode offers no textual guarantees.

Finally, beyond dialogic texts, lies heteroglossia: "a carnivalesque arena of diversity." Following Mikhail Bakhtin, Clifford points to Dickens's work as an example of the "polyphonic space" that might serve as a model for us. "Dickens, the actor, oral performer, and polyphonist, is set against Flaubert, the master of authorial control moving Godlike, among the thoughts and feelings of his characters. Ethnography, like the novel, wrestles with these alternatives" (137). If dialogic texts fall prey to the evils of totalizing ethnographic adjustment, then perhaps even more radical heteroglossic ones might not: "Ethnography is invaded by heteroglossia. If accorded an autonomous textual space, transcribed at sufficient length, indigenous statements make sense on terms different from those of the arranging ethnographer. . . . This suggests an alternate textual strategy, a utopia of plural authorship that accords to collaborators, not merely the status of independent enunciators, but that of writers" (140).

But Clifford immediately adds: "quotations are always staged by the quoter . . . a more radical polyphony would only displace ethnographic authority, still confirming, the final, virtuoso orchestration by a single author of all the discourses in his or her text" (139). New forms of writing, new textual experiments would open new possibilities—but guarantee none. Clifford is uneasy about this. He moves on. Temporarily enthusiastic for dialogic, Clifford immediately qualifies his praise. He leads us on to heteroglossia: seduced—for a paragraph—until we see that it too is, *hélas*, writing. Clifford closes his essay by proclaiming: "I have argued that this imposition of coherence on an unruly textual process is now, inescapably a matter of strategic choice" (142).

Clifford's presentation clearly offers a progression even if, by the end of the essay, it is a purely decisionist one. However, Clifford explicitly denies any hierarchy. At first I thought this was mere inconsistency, or ambivalence, or the embodiment of an unresolved but creative tension. I now think that Clifford, like everyone else, is *"dans le vrai."* We are at a discursive moment in which the author's intentions have been eliminated or underplayed in recent critical thought. Rather, we have been led to question the structures and contours of various modes of writing per se. Fredric Jameson has identified various elements of post-modern writing (e.g., its refusal of hierarchy, its flattening of history, its use of images) in a manner that seems to fit Clifford's project quite closely.

From Modernism to Post-Modernism in Anthropology

Fredric Jameson, in his "Postmodernism and Consumer Society" (1983), offers us some useful starting points to situate recent developments in anthropological and meta-anthropological writing. Without seeking a univocal definition of post-modernism, Jameson delimits the scope of the term by proposing a number of key elements: its historical location, its use of pastiche, the importance of images.

Jameson locates post-modernism culturally and historically not just as a stylistic term but as a period marker. By so doing he seeks to isolate and correlate features of cultural production in the 1960s with other social and economic transformations. The establishment of analytic criteria and their correlation with socioeconomic changes is very preliminary in Jameson's account, little more than a place marker. However, it is worth marking the place. Late capitalism is defined by Jameson as the moment when "the last vestiges of Nature which survived on into classical capitalism are at last eliminated: namely the third world and the unconscious. The 60s will then have been the momentous transformational period in which this systemic restructuring takes place on a global scale" (207). This is not the place to defend or criticize Jameson's periodization, which he recognizes as provisional. Let us simply note that it gives us the possibility of discussing changes in representational forms within a context of Western developments that lead forward to the present situation of those writing the descriptions not in a backward-looking mode establishing textual connections with writers in very different contexts, which frequently elide differences. For this reason, let us adopt it as heuristic.

The various post-modernisms forming in the sixties surfaced, at least in part, as a reaction against the earlier modernist movements. Classical modernism, to use an expression that is no longer oxymoronic, arose in the context of high capitalist and bourgeois society and stood against it: "it emerged within the business society of the gilded age as scandalous and offensive to the middle class public— ugly, dissonant, sexually shocking. . . . subversive" (124). Jameson contrasts the subversive modernist turn of the early twentieth century with the flattening, reactive nature of post-modern culture:

Those formerly subversive and embattled styles—Abstract Expressionism; the great modernist poetry of Pound, Eliot or Wallace Stevens; the International Style (Le Corbusier, Frank Lloyd Wright, Mies); Stravinsky; Joyce, Proust and Mann—felt to be scandalous or shocking by our grandparents are, for the generation which arrives at the gate in the 1960's, felt to be the establishment and the enemy—dead, stifling, canonical, the reified monuments one has to destroy to do anything new. This means that there will be as many different forms of postmodernism as there were high modernisms in place, since the former are at least initially specific and local reactions against those models. (111–12)

Jameson, not unlike Habermas (1983), clearly thinks there were important critical elements in modernism. Although they would probably differ on what they were, they would agree that in an important sense the project of modernity is unfinished, and certain of its features (its attempt to be critical, secular, anti-capitalist, rational) are worth strengthening.

I would add that if it arose in the 1960s in part as a reaction to the academic canonization of the great modernist artists, post-modernism, moving quickly, has itself succeeded in entering the academy in the 1980s. It has successfully domesticated and packaged itself through the proliferation of classificatory schemes, the construction of canons, the establishment of hierarchies, blunting of offensive behavior, acquiescence to university norms. Just as there are now art galleries for graffiti in New York, so, too, there are theses being written on graffiti, break dancing, and so on, in the most avant-garde departments. Even the Sorbonne has accepted a thesis on David Bowie.[4]

What is post-modernism? The first element is its historical location as a counter-reaction to modernism. Going beyond the by now "classic"

4. As reported in *Le Nouvel Observateur*, November 16–22, 1984.

definition of Lyotard (1979)—the end of metanarratives—Jameson defines its second element as pastiche. The dictionary definition— "(1) An artistic composition drawn from several sources, (2) a hodge podge"—is not sufficient. Pound, for example, drew from several sources. Jameson is pointing at a use of pastiche that has lost its normative moorings, which sees the jumbling of elements as all there is. Hodge podge is defined as "a jumbled mixture," but it comes from the French *hochepot*, a stew, and therein lies the difference.

Joyce, Hemingway, Woolf, et al. began with the conceit of an interiorized and distinctive subjectivity that both drew from and stood at a distance from normal speech and identity. There was "a linguistic norm in contrast to which the styles of the great modernists" (Jameson 1983: 114) could be attacked or praised, but in either case gauged. But what if this tension between bourgeois normality and the modernists' stylistic limit testing cracked, yielding to a social reality in which we had nothing but "stylistic diversity and heterogeneity" without the assumption (however contestable) of relatively stable identity or linguistic norms? Under such conditions, the contestatory stance of the modernists would lose its force: "All that is left is to imitate dead styles, to speak through the masks and with the voices of the styles in the imaginary museum. But this means that contemporary or postmodernist art is going to be about art itself in a new kind of way; even more, it means that one of its essential messages will involve the necessary failure of art and the aesthetic, the failure of the new, the imprisonment in the past" (115–16). It seems to me that this imprisonment in the past is quite different from historicism. Post-modernism moves beyond the (what now seems to be an almost comforting) estrangement of historicism, which looked, from a distance, at other cultures as wholes. The dialectic of self and other may have produced an alienated relationship, but it was one with definable norms, identities, and relations. Today, beyond estrangement and relativism, lies pastiche.

To exemplify this, Jameson develops an analysis of nostalgia films. Contemporary nostalgia films such as *Chinatown* or *Body Heat* are characterized by a "retrospective styling," dubbed "*la mode rétro*" by French critics. As opposed to traditional historical films which seek to recreate the fiction of another age as other, "*mode rétro*" films seek to evoke a feeling tone through the use of precise artifacts and stylistic devices that blur temporal boundaries. Jameson points out that recent nostalgia films often take place in the present (or, as in the case of *Star Wars*, in the future). A proliferation of metareferences to other representations flattens and empties their contents. One of their chief devices is to draw heavily on older plots: "The allusive and elusive plagiarism of older plots is, of course, also a feature of pastiche" (117). These films function not so much to deny the present but to blur the specificity of the past, to confuse the line between past and present (or future) as distinct periods. What these films do is represent our representations of other eras. "If there is any realism left here, it is a 'realism' which springs from the shock of grasping that confinement and of realizing that, for whatever peculiar reasons, we seem condemned to seek the historical past through our own pop images and stereotypes about that past, which itself remains forever out of reach" (118). This, it seems to me, describes an approach that sees strategic choice of representations of representations as its main problem.

Although Jameson is writing about historical consciousness, the same trend is present in ethnographic writing: interpretive anthropologists work with the problem of representations of others' representations, historians and metacritics of anthropology with the classification, canonization, and "making available" of representations of representations of representations. The historical flattening found in the pastiche of nostalgia films reappears in the meta-ethnographic flattening that makes all the world's cultures practitioners of textuality. The details in these narratives are precise, the images evocative, the neutrality exemplary, and the mode *rétro*.

The final feature of post-modernism for Jameson is "textuality." Drawing on Lacanian ideas about schizophrenia, Jameson points to one of the defining characteristics of the textual movement as the breakdown of the relationship between signifiers: "schizophrenia is an experience of isolated, disconnected, discontinuous material signifiers which fail to link up into a coherent sequence . . . a signifier that has lost its signified has thereby been transformed into an image" (120). Although the use of the term *schizophrenic* obscures more than it illuminates, the point is telling. Once the signifier is freed from a concern with its relation to an external referent it does not float free of any referentiality at all; rather, its referent becomes other texts, other images. For Jameson, post-modern texts (he is talking about Language poets) parallel this move: "Their referents are other images, another text, and the unity of the poem is not in the text at all but outside it in the bound unity of an absent book" (123). We are back at the "Fantasia of the Library," this time not as bitter parody but as celebratory pastiche.

Obviously this does not mean that we can solve the current crisis of representation by fiat. A return to earlier modes of unselfconscious representation is not a coherent position (although the news has not yet arrived in most anthropology departments). But we cannot solve it by ignoring the relations of representational forms and social practices either. If we attempt to eliminate social referentiality, other referents will occupy the voided position. Thus the reply of Dwyer's Moroccan informant (when asked which part of their dialogue had interested him most) that he had not been interested in a single question asked by Dwyer is not troubling as long as other anthropologists read the book and include it in their discourse. But obviously neither Dwyer nor Clifford would be satisfied with that response. Their intentions and their discourse strategies diverge. It is the latter that seem to have gone astray.

Interpretive Communities, Power Relations, Ethics

The young conservatives . . . claim as their own the revelations of a decentering subjectivity, emancipated from the imperatives of work and usefulness, and with this experience they step outside the modern world. . . . They remove into the sphere of the far-away and the archaic the spontaneous powers of imagination, self-experience and emotion.
JURGEN HABERMAS, "Modernity—An Incomplete Project"

A variety of important writing in the past decade has explored the historical relations between world macropolitics and anthropology: The West vs. The Rest; Imperialism; Colonialism; Neo-Colonialism. Work ranging from Talal Asad on colonialism and anthropology to Edward Said on Western discourse and the other have put these questions squarely on the agenda of contemporary debate. However, as Talal Asad points out in his paper for this volume, this by no means implies that these macropolitical economic conditions have been significantly affected by what goes on in anthropological debates. We also now know a good deal about the relations of power and discourse that obtain between the anthropologist and the people with whom he/she works. Both the macro- and microrelations of power and discourse between anthropology and its other are at last open to inquiry. We know some of the questions worth asking and have made asking them part of the discipline's agenda.

The metareflections on the crisis of representation in ethnographic writing indicate a shift away from concentrating on relations with other cultures to a (nonthematized) concern with traditions of representation, and metatraditions of metarepresentations, in our culture. I have been using Clifford's metaposition as a touchstone. He is not talking primarily about relations with the other, except as mediated through his central analytic concern, discursive tropes, and strategies. This has taught us important things. I have claimed, however, that this approach contains an interesting blind spot, a refusal of self-reflection. Fredric Jameson's analysis of post-modern culture was introduced as a kind of anthropological perspective on this cultural development. Right or wrong (more right than wrong in my view), Jameson suggests ways of thinking about the appearance of this new crisis of representation as a historical event with its own specific historical constraints. Said another way, Jameson enables us to see that in important ways not shared by other critical stances (which have their own characteristic blind spots) the post-modernist is blind to her own situation and situatedness because, qua post-modernist, she is committed to a doctrine of partiality and flux for which even such things as one's own situation are so unstable, so without identity, that they cannot serve as objects of sustained reflection.[5] Post-modernist pastiche is both a critical position and a dimension of our contemporary world. Jameson's analysis helps us to establish an understanding of their interconnections, thereby avoiding both nostalgia and the mistake of universalizing or ontologizing a very particular historical situation.

In my opinion, the stakes in recent debates about writing are not directly political in the conventional sense of the term. I have argued elsewhere (1985) that what politics is involved is academic politics, and that this level of politics has not been explored. The work of Pierre Bourdieu is helpful in posing questions about the politics of culture (1984a, b). Bourdieu has taught us to ask in what field of power, and from what position in that field, any given author writes. His new sociology of cultural production does not seek to reduce knowledge to social position or interest per se but, rather, to place all of these variables within the complex constraints—Bourdieu's *habitus*—within which they are produced and received. Bourdieu is particularly attentive to strategies of cultural power that advance through denying their attachment to immediate political ends and thereby accumulate both symbolic capital and "high" structural position.

Bourdieu's work would lead us to suspect that contemporary academic proclamations of anti-colonialism, while admirable, are not the whole story. These proclamations must be seen as political moves within the academic community. Neither Clifford nor any of the rest of us is writing in the late 1950s. His audiences are neither colonial officers nor those working under the aegis of colonial power. Our political field is more familiar: the academy in the 1980s. Hence, though not exactly false, situating the crisis of representation within the context of the rupture of decolonization is, given the way it is handled, basically beside the point. It is true to the extent that anthropology is certainly reflective of the course of larger world events, and specifi-

5. I would like to thank James Faubion for this point.

cally of changing historical relations with the groups it studies. Asserting that new ethnographic writing emerged because of decolonization, however, leaves out precisely those mediations that would make historical sense of the present object of study.

One is led to consider the politics of interpretation in the academy today. Asking whether longer, dispersive, multi-authored texts would yield tenure might seem petty. But those are the dimensions of power relations to which Nietzsche exhorted us to be scrupulously attentive. There can be no doubt of the existence and influence of this type of power relation in the production of texts. We owe these less glamorous, if more immediately constraining, conditions more attention. The taboo against specifying them is much greater than the strictures against denouncing colonialism; an anthropology of anthropology would include them. Just as there was formerly a discursive knot preventing discussion of exactly those fieldwork practices that defined the authority of the anthropologist, which has now been untied (Rabinow 1977), so, too, the micropractices of the academy might well do with some scrutiny.

Another way of posing this problem is to refer to "corridor talk." For many years, anthropologists informally discussed fieldwork experiences among themselves. Gossip about an anthropologist's field experiences was an important component of that person's reputation. But such matters were not, until recently, written about "seriously." It remains in the corridors and faculty clubs. But what cannot be publicly discussed cannot be analyzed or rebutted. Those domains that cannot be analyzed or refuted, and yet are directly central to hierarchy, should not be regarded as innocent or irrelevant. We know that one of the most common tactics of an elite group is to refuse to discuss—to label as vulgar or uninteresting—issues that are uncomfortable for them. When corridor talk about fieldwork becomes discourse, we learn a good deal. Moving the conditions of production of anthropological knowledge out of the domain of gossip—where it remains the property of those around to hear it—into that of knowledge would be a step in the right direction.

My wager is that looking at the conditions under which people are hired, given tenure, published, awarded grants, and feted would repay the effort.[6] How has the "deconstructionist" wave differed from the other major trend in the academy in the past decade—feminism?[7] How are careers made now? How are careers destroyed now? What

6. Martin Finkelstein (1984) presents a valuable summary of some of these issues as seen in the social sciences.

7. These issues are being explored in an important doctoral thesis being written by Deborah Gordon at the University of California, Santa Cruz.

are the boundaries of taste? Who established and who enforces these civilities? Whatever else we know, we certainly know that the material conditions under which the textual movement has flourished must include the university, its micropolitics, its trends. We know that this level of power relations exists, affects us, influences our themes, forms, contents, audiences. We owe these issues attention—if only to establish their relative weight. Then, as with fieldwork, we shall be able to proceed to more global issues.

Stop Making Sense: Dialogue and Identity

Marilyn Strathern, in a very challenging paper (1984), "Dislodging a World View: Challenge and Counter-Challenge in the Relationship Between Feminism and Anthropology," has taken an important step in situating the strategy of recent textualist writing through a comparison with recent work by anthropological feminists. Strathern makes a distinction between feminist anthropology, an anthropological subdiscipline contributing to the discipline's advancement, and an anthropological feminism whose aim is to build a feminist community, one whose premises and goals differ from, and are opposed to, anthropology. In the latter enterprise, difference and conflict—as historical conditions of identity and knowledge—are the valorized terms, not science and harmony.

Strathern reflects on her annoyance when a senior male colleague praised feminist anthropology for enriching the discipline. He said: "Let a thousand flowers bloom." She says: "Indeed it is true in general that feminist critique has enriched anthropology—opened up new understandings of ideology, the construction of symbolic systems, resource management, property concepts, and so on." Anthropology, in its relative openness and eclecticism, has integrated these scientific advances, at first reluctantly, now eagerly. Strathern, drawing on Kuhn's much-used paradigm concept, points out that this is how normal science works. Yet the "let a thousand flowers bloom" tolerance produced a sense of unease; later, Strathern realized that her unease stemmed from a sense that feminists should be laboring in other fields, not adding flowers to anthropology's.

Strathern distances her own practice from the normal science model in two ways. First, she claims that social and natural science are different: "not simply [because] within any one discipline one finds diverse 'schools' (also true in science) but that their premises are constructed competitively in relation to one another." Second, this competition does not turn on epistemological issues alone, but ultimately on political and ethical differences. In his essay, "What Makes an Interpretation Acceptable?" (1980), Stanley Fish makes a similar point (albeit to advance a very different agenda). He argues that all statements are interpretations, and that all appeals to the text, or the facts, are themselves based on interpretations; these interpretations are community affairs and not subjective (or individual) ones—that is, meanings are cultural or socially available, they are not invented ex nihilo by a single interpreter. Finally, all interpretations, most especially those that deny their status as interpretations, are only possible on the basis of other interpretations, whose rules they affirm while announcing their negation.

Fish argues that we never resolve disagreements by an appeal to the facts or the text because "the facts emerge only in the context of some point of view. It follows, then, that disagreements must occur between those who hold (or are held by) different points of view, and what is at stake in a disagreement is the right to specify what the facts can hereafter be said to be. Disagreements are not settled by the facts, but are the means by which the facts are settled" (338). Strathern adroitly demonstrates these points in her contrast of anthropological feminism and experimental anthropologists.

The guiding value of those interested in experimental ethnographic writing, Strathern argues, is dialogic: "the effort is to create a relation with the Other—as in the search for a medium of expression which will offer mutual interpretation, perhaps visualised as a common text, or as something more like a discourse." Feminism, for Strathern, proceeds from the initial and unassimilable fact of domination. The attempt to incorporate feminist understandings into an improved science of anthropology or a new rhetoric of dialogue is taken as a further act of violence. Feminist anthropology is trying to shift discourse, not improve a paradigm: "that is, it alters the nature of the audience, the range of readership and the kinds of interactions between author and reader, and alters the subject matter of conversation in the way it allows others to speak—what is talked about and whom one is talking to." Strathern is not seeking to invent a new synthesis, but to strengthen difference.

The ironies here are exhilarating. Experimentalists (almost all male) are nurturing and optimistic, if just a touch sentimental. Clifford claims to be working from a combination of sixties idealism and eighties irony. Textual radicals seek to work toward establishing relationships, to demonstrate the importance of connection and openness, to advance the possibilities of sharing and mutual understanding, while being fuzzy about power and the realities of socioeconomic constraints. Strathern's anthropological feminist insists upon not losing sight of fundamental differences, power relationships, hierarchical domination. She seeks to articulate a communal identity on the basis of conflict, separation, and antagonism: partially as a defense against the threat of encompassment by a paradigm of love, mutuality, and understanding in which she sees other motives and structures; partially as a device to preserve meaningful difference per se as a distinctive value.

Difference is played out on two levels: between feminists and anthropology and within the feminist community. Facing outward, resistance and nonassimilation are the highest values. Within this new interpretive community, however, the virtues of dialogic relationships have been affirmed. Internally, feminists may disagree and compete; but they do so in relation to one another. "It is precisely because feminist theory does not constitute its past as a 'text' that it cannot be added on or supplant anthropology in any simple way. For if feminists always maintain a divide against the Other, among themselves by contrast they create something indeed much closer to discourse than to text. And the character of this discourse approaches the 'interlocutionary common product' for which the new ethnography aims." While tropes are available for all to use, how they are used makes all the difference.

Ethics and Modernity

The emergence of factions within a once interdicted activity is a sure sign of its having achieved the status of an orthodoxy.
STANLEY FISH, "What Makes an Interpretation Acceptable?"

Recent discussions on the making of ethnographic texts have revealed differences and points of opposition as well as important areas of consensus. To borrow yet another of Geertz's phrases, we can, and have been, vexing each other with profit, the touchstone of interpretive advance. In this last section, through the device of a schematic juxtaposition of the three positions previously outlined, I shall propose my own. Although critical of dimensions of each of these positions, I consider them to be members, if not of an interpretive community, at least of an interpretive federation to which I belong.

Anthropologists, critics, feminists, and critical intellectuals are all concerned with questions of truth and its social location; imagination and formal problems of representation; domination and resistance; the ethical subject and techniques for becoming one. These topics are, however, interpreted in differing fashions; different dangers and different possibilities are picked out; and different hierarchies between these categories are defended.

1. *Interpretive Anthropologists.* Truth and science conceived as interpretive practices are the commanding terms. Both anthropologist and native are seen as engaged in interpreting the meaning of everyday life. Problems of representation are central for both, and are the loci of cultural imagination. Representations are not, however, sui generis; they serve as means for making sense of life worlds (which they are instrumental in constructing) and consequently they differ in their functions. The goals of the anthropologist and the native are distinct. To take one example, science and religion differ as cultural systems in strategy, ethos, and ends. The political and ethical positions are important, if largely implicit, anchors. Weber's twin ideals of science and politics as vocations would, if embodied in a researcher, yield the ethical subject for this position. Conceptually, scientific specification concerning cultural difference is at the heart of the project. The greatest danger, seen from the inside, is the confusion of science and politics. The greatest weakness, seen from the outside, is the historical, political, and experiential cordon sanitaire drawn around interpretive science.

2. *Critics.* The guiding principle is formal. The text is primary. Attentiveness to the tropes and rhetorical devices through which authority is constructed allows the introduction of themes of domination, exclusion, and inequality as subject matter. But they are only material. They are given form by the critic/writer, be she anthropologist or native: "Other tribes, other Scribes." We change ourselves primarily through imaginative constructions. The kind of beings we want to become are open, permeable ones, suspicious of metanarratives; pluralizers. But authorial control seems to blunt self-reflection and the dialogic impulse. The danger: the obliteration of meaningful difference, Weber's museumification of the world. The truth that experience and meaning are mediated representationally can be over-extended to equate experience and meaning with the formal dimension of representation.

3. *Political subjects.* The guiding value is the constitution of a community-based political subjectivity. Anthropological feminists work against an other cast as essentially different and violent. Within the community the search for truth, as well as social and esthetic experimentation are guided by a dialogic desire. The fictive other allows a pluralizing set of differences to appear. The risk is that these enabling fictions of essential difference may become reified, thereby reduplicating the oppressive social forms they were meant to undermine. Strathern puts this point well: "Now if feminism mocks the anthropological pretension of creating a product in some ways jointly authored then anthropology

mocks the pretension that feminists can ever really achieve the separation they desire."

4. *Critical, Cosmopolitan Intellectuals.* I have emphasized the dangers of high interpretive science and the overly sovereign representer, and am excluded from direct participation in the feminist dialogue. Let me propose a critical cosmopolitanism as a fourth figure. The ethical is the guiding value. This is an oppositional position, one suspicious of sovereign powers, universal truths, overly relativized preciousness, local authenticity, moralisms high and low. Understanding is its second value, but an understanding suspicious of its own imperial tendencies. It attempts to be highly attentive to (and respectful of) difference, but is also wary of the tendency to essentialize difference. What we share as a condition of existence, heightened today by our ability, and at times our eagerness, to obliterate one another, is a specificity of historical experience and place, however complex and contestable they might be, and a worldwide macro-interdependency encompassing any local particularity. Whether we like it or not, we are all in this situation. Borrowing a term applied during different epochs to Christians, aristocrats, merchants, Jews, homosexuals, and intellectuals (while changing its meaning), I call the acceptance of this twin valorization *cosmopolitanism.* Let us define cosmopolitanism as an ethos of macro-interdependencies, with an acute consciousness (often forced upon people) of the inescapabilities and particularities of places, characters, historical trajectories, and fates. Although we are all cosmopolitans, *Homo sapiens* has done rather poorly in interpreting this condition. We seem to have trouble with the balancing act, preferring to reify local identities or construct universal ones. We live in-between. The Sophists offer a fictive figure for this slot: eminently Greek, yet often excluded from citizenship in the various poleis; cosmopolitan insider's outsiders of a particular historical and cultural world; not members of a projected universal regime (under God, the imperium, or the laws of reason); devotees of rhetoric and thereby fully aware of its abuses; concerned with the events of the day, but buffered by ironic reserve.

The problematic relations of subjectivity, truth, modernity, and representations have been at the heart of my own work. Feeling that considerations of power and representation were too localized in my earlier work on Morocco, I have chosen a research topic that employs these categories more broadly. Being temperamentally more comfortable in an oppositional stance, I have chosen to study a group of elite

French administrators, colonial officials as well as social reformers, all concerned with urban planning in the 1920s. By "studying up" I find myself in a more comfortable position than I would be were I "giving voice" on behalf of dominated or marginal groups. I have chosen a powerful group of men concerned with issues of politics and form: neither heroes nor villains, they seem to afford me the necessary anthropological distance, being separate enough to prevent an easy identification, yet close enough to afford a charitable, if critical, understanding.

The discipline of modern urbanism was put into practice in the French colonies, particularly in Morocco under Governor-general Hubert Lyautey (1912–25). The colonial architect-planners and the colonial governmental officials who hired them conceived of the cities where they worked as social and esthetic laboratories. These settings offered both groups the opportunity to try out new, large-scale planning concepts and to test the political effectiveness of these plans for application both in the colonies and eventually, they hoped, at home.

Studies of colonialism have until recently been cast almost exclusively in terms of this dialectic of domination, exploitation, and resistance. This dialectic is, and was, an essential one. By itself, however, it neglects at least two major dimensions of the colonial situation: its culture and the political field in which it was set. This has led to a number of surprising consequences; strangely enough the group in the colonies who have received the least attention in historical and sociological studies are the colonists themselves. Fortunately, this picture is beginning to change; the varied systems of social stratification and the cultural complexity of colonial life—as it varied from place to place at different historical periods—is beginning to be understood.

As a more complex view of colonial culture is being articulated, I think we also need a more complex understanding of power in the colonies. The two are connected. Power is frequently understood as force personified: the possession of a single group—the colonialists. This conception is inadequate for a number of reasons. First, the colonists themselves were highly factionalized and stratified. Second, the state (and particularly the colonial state) is something we need to know a great deal more about. Third, the view of power that understands it as a thing, or a possession, or emanating unidirectionally from the top down, or operating primarily through the application of force has been put seriously in question. With less than 20,000 troops, the French, after all, ran Indochina in the 1920s with a degree of control that the Americans with 500,000 some fifty years later never approached. Power entails more than arms, although it certainly does not exclude them.

The work of Michel Foucault on power relations provides us with some helpful analytic tools. Foucault distinguishes between exploitation, domination, and subjection (1982:212). He argues that most analyses of power concentrate almost exclusively on relations of domination and exploitation: who controls whom, and who extracts the fruits of production from the producers. The third term, subjection, focuses on that aspect of a field of power farthest removed from the direct application of force. That dimension of power relations is where the identity of individuals and groups is at stake, and where order in its broadest meaning is taking form. This is the realm in which culture and power are most closely intertwined. Foucault sometimes calls these relations "governmentality," and the term is a helpful one.

Following Foucault, Jacques Donzelot has argued that during the later part of the nineteenth century, a new relational field of great historical import was being constructed: Donzelot (1979) calls it the "social." Specific areas, frequently taken to be outside of politics, such as hygiene, family structure, and sexuality, were being made into targets for state intervention. The social became a demarcated and objectified set of practices partially constructed by, and partially understood through, the emerging methods and institutions of the new social science disciplines. The "social" was a privileged locus for experimentation with new forms of political rationality.

Lyautey's highly sophisticated view of colonization turned on the need to bring social groups into a different field of power relations than had previously existed in the colonies. In his view, this could only be achieved through large-scale social planning, in which city planning played a central role. As he said in a eulogy for his chief planner, Henri Prost: "The art and science of urbanism, so flourishing during the classical age, seems to have suffered a total eclipse since the Second Empire. Urbanism, the art and science of developing human agglomerations, is coming back to life under Prost's hand. Prost is the guardian, in this mechanical age, of 'humanism.' Prost worked not only on things, but on men, different types of men, to whom *la Cité* owes something more than roads, canals, sewers and a transport system" (Marrast, ed. 1960:119). For Lyautey and his architects, then, the new humanism applied itself appropriately not only to things, but to men, and not only to men in general—this was not Le Corbusier's humanism—but to men in different cultural and social circumstances. The problem was to accommodate this diversity. For these architects, planners, and administrators, the task confronting them was how to conceive of and produce a new social *ordonnance*.

This is the reason why the cities of Morocco were of such importance in Lyautey's eyes. They seemed to offer hope, a way to avoid the impasses both of France and of Algeria. Lyautey's famous dictum "A *chantier* [construction site] is worth a battalion" was meant literally. Lyautey feared that if the French were allowed to continue to practice politics as usual, the results would continue to be catastrophic. A directly political solution, however, was not at hand. What was urgently required was a new scientific and strategic social art; only in this way could politics be sublated—and power truly "*ordonné.*"

These men, like so many others in the twentieth century, were trying to escape from politics. This did not mean, however, that they were unconcerned with power relationships. Far from it. Their goal, a kind of technocratic self-colonization, was to develop a new form of power relations where "healthy" social, economic, and cultural relations could unfold. Integral in this scheme was the need to invent a new governmentality through which the (to them) fatally decadent and individualistic tendencies of the French could be reshaped. They constructed and articulated both new representations of a modern order and technologies for its implementation. These representations are modern social facts.

This paper has outlined some of the elements of the discourses and practices of modern representation. The relationship of this analysis to political practice has been only glancingly touched on. What, how, and who might be represented by those holding a similar view of things escapes from our more standard categories of social actors and political rhetoric. In closing, I simply mark the space. Foucault, responding to the charge that by refusing to affiliate himself with an already identified and politically locatable group he forfeited any claims to represent anybody or any values, answered: "Rorty points out that in these analyses I do not appeal to any 'we'—to any of those 'we's' whose consensus, whose values, whose traditions constitute the framework for a thought and define the conditions in which it can be validated. But the problem is, precisely to decide if it is actually suitable to place oneself within a 'we' in order to assert the principles one recognizes and the values one accepts; or if it is not, rather, necessary to make the future formation of a 'we' possible" (1984:385).

I would like to thank Talal Asad, James Faubion, Stephen Foster, Michael Rogin, Marilyn Strathern, and the participants in the Santa Fe seminar. The usual disclaimers apply. Paragraphs of this article have appeared elsewhere.

GEORGE E. MARCUS

Afterword: Ethnographic Writing and Anthropological Careers

If you want to understand what a science is, you should look in the first instance not at its theories or its findings, and certainly not at what its apologists say about it; you should look at what the practitioners of it do.

CLIFFORD GEERTZ, *The Interpretation of Cultures*

The task of the Santa Fe seminar from which these essays emerged was to introduce a literary consciousness to ethnographic practice by showing various ways in which ethnographies can be read and written. What we have said about the enterprise of representing society and culture would not be news in the complex debates of contemporary literary theory, one major thrust of which has been to transform literary criticism into a more encompassing cultural criticism. Fortunately, we did not have to enter too far into the thickets of these often convoluted and technical debates to have a therapeutic effect on anthropological practitioners of ethnography. They are more self-conscious than ever before that they are writers who, as maturing professionals, routinely outgrow the models of ethnography by which they were inducted into anthropology.

The question for the anthropologist is, then, how consequential this literary therapy should be—does it merely add a new critical appreciation of ethnography, which one can take or leave in reading and writing ethnographic accounts, or does it clear the way for reconceptualizing anthropological careers and valorizing innovations in strategies for projects that link fieldwork and writing? History, for example, has long had an internal discourse (the specialty of historiography) that has viewed its method as writing, and a number of recent works (most prominently, White 1973) have sought to give this discourse a distinctly literary cast, as we have tried to do here for a consideration of ethnography. However, the potentially radical influence such liter-

ary therapy might have had on the practice of historians has been contained within the recognition of "a narrative perspective"—one valid
way of understanding historical writing, but hardly more than that.
The coming of a literary consciousness to ethnography promises to be
somewhat more eventful, not only because the salience of writing as
professional activity has never been as much of a commonplace in anthropology as it has been in history, but also because this arrival occurs
at a moment when the larger theoretical project of twentieth-century
social and cultural anthropology is in disarray, leaving disciplinary debates to focus upon and problematize both the textual expressions of
knowledge and the career process that generates them. And in this
literary treatment of ethnography more is at stake than the mere de-
mystification of past dominant conventions of representation. Rather,
such a critique legitimates experimentation and a search for options
in research and writing activity, which would be equal to the claims
and ambitions of the influential interpretive styles of analysis in contemporary anthropological thought.

My intention is thus to view, however schematically, the major concern of the seminar with ethnographic writing in the typical career
context of contemporary anthropologists. A full analysis in this vein
would relate the issues raised in the seminar papers to a detailed ethnographic consideration of the professional culture of anthropology
itself, which Paul Rabinow has called for.

Most of the anthropologists in the seminar presented themselves
as readers of ethnography, and mainly of influential classics rather
than of current, less established, and self-consciously experimental
works. What this persona as readers obscured was the fact that they,
like all professional sociocultural anthropologists, were equally, if not
primarily, writers of ethnography, and accomplished ones at that. All
the anthropologist participants in the seminar had published ethnographic works beyond a dissertation, and were involved in writing
projects quite different from the work that had launched their professional careers. Answers to my casual question "What are you working
on now?" in conversations between seminar sessions revealed a remarkable diversity of projects, all evolving in one way or another from
the intellectual lessons each participant had derived from his initial
experience of ethnographic writing as imposed professional training.

I came to see the papers that were presented and discussed as reflections of their authors' behind-the-scenes evolutions from, and reactions to, their initiatory experiences as ethnographic writers. It is
thus important to understand that the explicit concerns of the seminar's papers with reading past and present ethnographies in terms of
their rhetorical devices and literary construction do not arise pri-

marily either from the stimulation of post-structuralist literary theorists, or from a desire to assume the role of critic as distinct from writer in the genre criticized (although a central claim in contemporary literary theory, expressed by Geoffrey Hartman [1980], among others, is that critical discourse has achieved, or should aspire to, the status of the literature that is the object of criticism). Rather, the impetus for the seminar's readings of ethnography in a literary mode derives most strongly from the predicaments of the participants as active researchers and writers, trained in the anthropological tradition of ethnographic practice and acutely aware of the critiques of its conventions that have been developing since the 1960s. Removing the constrictions on the ways of reading past ethnography, and thus exposing forgotten or unnoticed possibilities in it, is a necessary and natural concomitant to the present experimental moment, which encourages a diversity of strategies and influences in the writing projects of both older and younger anthropologists (see Marcus and Fischer 1986).

Though some of my most valuable insights thus came in effect from the talk between sessions, I do not intend further to reveal this masked side of the seminar by matching participants' current writing projects, as I understand them, against what they have had to say as critical readers of ethnography. Instead, I want to suggest how the current trend of self-conscious experimentation and diversity of writing projects in anthropology might derive from the constitutional experience of producing an ethnographic account in the course of obtaining professional credentials.

Regardless of whether anthropologists ever publish monographs —and many never do—most careers begin with an ethnographic research process that in all its phases involves descriptive-interpretive writing and the applications of techniques for the representation of social and cultural life. Although the initial ethnographic experience serves inaccurately as the actual model of professional craft presumably to be repeated throughout a career, it does shape the cognitive terms in which anthropologists think and speak about their research projects. These are segmented primarily as periods of fieldwork encompassed as ethnographic writing projects. The image or concept of work toward "an ethnography" is very strong indeed in the way anthropologists think about and discuss their career projects, however careers of writing are in fact played out.

Textualization is at the heart of the ethnographic enterprise, both in the field and in university settings. In an important sense, fieldwork is synonymous with the activity of inscribing diverse contexts of oral discourse through field notes and recordings. Unlike historical research (with the exception of oral history), ethnography originates in orality and only makes the transition to writing with difficulty. Much of the critique of dominant conventions of ethnographic realism, as well as alternatives to them, thus arises from reflections on the origins of anthropological knowledge in this primary process of textualization. The ethnographic task as one of inscription, strategies of representing dialogue in ethnographic accounts, and objections to the notion of representation itself were issues that recurred throughout the seminar discussions, especially as they were formulated in the papers by Clifford and Tyler.

The anthropological dissertation, typically a straightforward analytical and descriptive account from fieldwork, is the ethnography that most anthropologists must write. Since the granting of professional credentials has depended on its evaluation, it has tended to be a conservative exercise. It is in turning the dissertation into a published monograph or series of articles that career directions are determined on a number of levels. For one thing, reputations and tenure depend on writing beyond the dissertation. On a more personal level of intellectual development, the transformation of the dissertation, and the textualized field materials on which it is based, into other written versions embodies a reaction to the training model of ethnographic practice. In this transformation, one is freer to take risks and also more subject to intertextuality—that is, writing under the influence of, and with the desire to influence, other writers. Among recent generations of anthropologists, the new "classics," particular ethnographies that come to be received as tokens of an idealized image of what the practice of anthropology should exemplify, derive primarily from writing in reaction to the initiatory training experience.

Affected by the general intellectual mood of the period in which it occurs, the initial experience of producing an account for professional qualification can be personally reconfirmed, quietly modified, strenuously criticized, or even rejected in the varied outcomes of attempts to rewrite the conservative training model of ethnography. The general mood now being reflexive and self-critical, dissertation conventions are perhaps less conservative, but the legitimate array of options in the production of published accounts is also more extensive. Producing an ethnographic account from fieldwork may still occupy its seminal role in inaugurating careers and creating a certain ideological community of shared experience among anthropologists, but it can no longer be so easily understood simply as the definitive model of craft to be repeated in a career of research. In many careers, the kind of text one produces, or fails to produce, following the dissertation is formative of the future writing projects one undertakes. Often as not these depart in interesting ways from dissertation ethnography, especially in the textual uses made of the corpus of field material.

It has probably always been the case that the initial experience of ethnographic writing has been constitutional and experimental in the context of research careers, even among the pioneering exemplars of modern ethnographic practice, such as Malinowski, Evans-Pritchard, and Firth, and certainly for succeeding generations of anthropologists who have continued to regard certain of the former's texts canonically. However, the ethnography forged from a post-dissertation attempt to rewrite material by putting a more personal stamp on it is in many careers a one-of-a-kind phenomenon rather than a standard product. Some distinguished careers have been made by the continual rewriting of original field materials, and it is a common observation that when anthropologists start a second project and thus begin anew, they are rarely able to achieve the freshness and intensity of the projects that inaugurated their careers. Often, the most interesting writers in anthropology are those who, while continuing to invoke ethnographic authority and to work through ethnographic detail in their writing, never try to reproduce the kind of text that they wrote in response to training, but rather attempt to explore lessons gained from that experience, which requires different forms and styles of exposition.

A certain image of the ethnography is powerfully inculcated by initiatory research training and articulated in a professional socializing discourse that speaks around its subject rather than to it (you only know a good ethnography when you read one, despite the widespread sense that there *are* standards). Consequently, the actual diversity and patterning of anthropological careers as to their textual products have been obscured and largely unexamined. The work of the seminar was to unfix, by literary therapy, the narrow frames in which ethnographies have typically been read. This has been by no means a hermetic or naive enterprise, as some may fear, since the concern of much contemporary literary criticism is to expose the historical and political contexts of writing—precisely the dimensions ethnography of an interpretive bent has long been criticized for eliding or skirting. But, beyond this critical function, our questioning of the particular modes of realist description in contemporary anthropology conditions the writing strategies of anthropologists who continue to look primarily to the ethnographic tradition for both limits and possibilities. By criticism of the terms in which ethnography has been received and by alternative readings of exemplary works, we have tried to expose possibilities in past ethnographic writing that make it relevant to the current spirit of experimentation.

Bibliography

ADORNO, THEODOR
 1977   *Aesthetics and Politics*. London: New Left Books.
AGAR, MICHAEL
 1985   *Independents Declared: The Dilemma of Independent Trucking*. Washington, D.C.: Smithsonian Institution.
ALTER, ROBERT
 1981   *The Art of Biblical Narrative*. New York: Basic Books.
 1982   "The Jew Who Didn't Get Away: On the Possibility of an American Jewish Culture." *Judaism* 31:274–86.
ALURISTA [ALBERTO URISTA]
 1976   *Floricanto en Aztlan*. Los Angeles: UCLA Chicano Studies Center.
ANAYA, RUDOLFO
 1975   *Bless Me Ultima*. Berkeley, Calif.: Tonatiuh International.
ANGELOU, MAYA
 1969   *I Know Why the Caged Bird Sings*. New York: Random House.
ARIAS, RON
 1975   *The Road to Tamazunchale*. Reno, Nev.: West Coast Poetry Review.
ARLEN, MICHAEL
 1975   *Passage to Ararat*. New York: Farrar, Straus and Giroux.
ASAD, TALAL
 1980   "Ideology, Class, and the Origin of the Islamic State." *Economy and Society* 9:450–73.
 1983a   "Anthropological Conceptions of Religion: Reflections on Geertz." *Man* 18:237–59.
 1983b   "Notes on Body Pain and Truth in Medieval Christian Ritual." *Economy and Society* 12:287–327.
————, ed.
 1973   *Anthropology and the Colonial Encounter*. London: Ithaca Press.
ATKINSON, JANE
 1982   "Anthropology," *Signs* 8:236–58.
AVRUCH, KEVIN
 1981   *American Immigrants in Israel*. Chicago: University of Chicago Press.

BAHR, DONALD, J. GREGORIO, D. I. LOPEZ, AND A. ALVAREZ
    1974   *Piman Shamanism and Staying Sickness.* Tucson, Ariz.: University of Arizona Press.

BAKHTIN, MIKHAIL
    1965   *Rabelais and His World.* Cambridge, Mass.: MIT Press.
    1981   "Discourse in the Novel." In *The Dialogical Imagination,* edited by Michael Holquist, 259–442. Austin, Tex.: University of Texas Press.

BALANDIER, GEORGES
    1955   *Sociologie actuelle de l'Afrique noire.* Paris: Presses universitaires de la France.
    1957   *L'Afrique ambiguë.* Paris: Plon.

BARAKA, AMIRI
    1984   *The Autobiography of LeRoy Jones.* New York: Freundlich.

BARNES, R. H.
    1984   *Two Crows Denies It: A History of Controversy in Omaha Sociology.* Lincoln, Nebr.: University of Nebraska Press.

BARROW, JOHN
    1801   *Travels in the Interior of Southern Africa in the Years 1797 and 1798.* New York: Johnson Reprint Corp., 1968.

BARTHES, ROLAND
    1977   *Image Music Text.* New York: Hill and Wang.
    1981   *Camera Lucida.* New York: Hill and Wang.
    1984   "Jeunes Chercheurs." In *Le Bruissement de la langue,* 97–103. Paris: Le Seuil.

BATESON, GREGORY
    1936   *Naven: A Survey of the Problems Suggested by a Composite Picture of a Culture of a New Guinea Tribe Drawn From Three Points of View.* Stanford, Calif.: Stanford University Press.

BAUDELAIRE, CHARLES
    1846   "Salon de 1846." In *Oeuvres complètes,* edited by Y. G. le Dantec and Claude Pichois, 605–80. Paris: Edition de la Pléiade, 1954.

BAUMGARTEN, MURRAY
    1982   *City Scriptures: Modern Jewish Writing.* Cambridge, Mass.: Harvard University Press.

BEATTIE, JOHN
    1964   *Other Cultures.* London: Cohen and West.

BEAUJOUR, MICHEL
    1980   *Miroirs d'Encre.* Paris: Le Seuil.
    1981   "Some Paradoxes of Description." *Yale French Studies* 61:27–59.

BEDROSIAN, MARGARET
    1982   "The Other Modernists: Tradition and the Individual Talent in Armenian-American Literature." Ph.D. diss., University of California, Davis.

BENEDICT, RUTH
    1934   *Patterns of Culture.* New York: New American Library.

BENJAMIN, WALTER
  1969   *Illuminations*. New York: Schocken.
  1977   *The Origin of German Tragic Drama*. London: New Left
              Books.
  1978   *Reflections*. Translated by Edmund Jephcott and edited by
              Peter Demetz. New York: Harcourt Press.
BENVENISTE, EMILE
  1966   *Problèmes de linguistique générale*. Paris: Gallimard.
BERGER, HARRY, JR.
  1984   "The Origins of Bucolic Representation: Disenchantment
              and Revision in Theocritus' Seventh *Idyll*." *Classical Antiq-
              uity* 3, no. 1 : 1–39.
BERNSTEIN, MICHAEL ANDRÉ
  1983   "When the Carnival Turns Bitter: Preliminary Reflections
              upon the Abject Hero." *Critical Inquiry* 10, no. 2 : 283–305.
BERNSTEIN, RICHARD J.
  1976   *The Restructuring of Social and Political Theory*. Philadelphia:
              University of Pennsylvania Press.
  1983   *Beyond Objectivism and Relativism: Science, Hermeneutics, and
              Practice*. Philadelphia: University of Pennsylvania Press.
BERTAUX, DANIEL, AND ISABELLE BERTAUX-WIAME
  1981   "Artisanal Bakery in France: How it Lives and Why it Sur-
              vives." In *The Petite Bourgeoisie: Comparative Studies of the
              Uneasy Stratum*, edited by Frank Bechhofer and Brian
              Elliott, pp. 187–205. New York: St. Martin's Press.
BETTELHEIM, BRUNO
  1983   *Freud and Man's Soul*. New York: Alfred A. Knopf.
BIALE, DAVID
  1979   *Gershom Scholem*. Cambridge, Mass.: Harvard University
              Press.
BIOCCA, ETTORE
  1969   *Yanoama: The Narrative of a White Girl Kidnapped by Amazo-
              nian Indians*. New York: E. P. Dutton.
BLOOM, HAROLD
  1973   *The Anxiety of Influence*. New York: Oxford University Press.
  1975a   *A Map of Misreading*. New York: Oxford University Press.
  1975b   *Kabbalah and Criticism*. New York: Seabury.
  1982a   *Agon: Towards a Theory of Revisionism*. New York: Oxford
              University Press.
  1982b   *The Breaking of the Vessels*. Chicago: University of Chicago
              Press.
BLU, KAREN
  1980   *The Lumbee Problem*. Cambridge: Cambridge University
              Press.
BOON, JAMES
  1972   *From Symbolism to Structuralism: Lévi-Strauss in a Literary Tra-
              dition*. New York: Harper and Row.

1977   *The Anthropological Romance of Bali, 1597–1972.* Cambridge: Cambridge University Press.

1982   *Other Tribes Other Scribes.* Ithaca, N.Y.: Cornell University Press.

1983   "Folly, Bali, and Anthropology, or Satire Across Cultures." *Proceedings of the American Ethnological Society,* 156–77.

BOUGAINVILLE, LOUIS DE

1772   *A Voyage Round the World.* Ridgewood, N.J.: Gregg Press, 1967.

BOURDIEU, PIERRE

1977   *Outline of a Theory of Practice.* Cambridge: Cambridge University Press.

1979   *Algeria 1960.* New York: Cambridge University Press.

1984a   *Distinction.* Cambridge, Mass.: Harvard University Press.

1984b   *Homo Academicus.* Paris: Editions de Minuit.

BOWEN, ELENORE SMITH [PSEUD. OF LAURA BOHANNAN]

1954   *Return to Laughter.* New York: Harper and Row.

BOWERS, ALFRED W.

1950   *Mandan Social and Ceremonial Organization.* Chicago: University of Chicago Press.

BRADLEY, DAVID

1984   "Novelist Alice Walker: Telling the Black Woman's Story." *New York Times Magazine,* January, 8, 1984, 25ff.

BRIGGS, JEAN

1970   *Never in Anger.* Cambridge, Mass.: Harvard University Press.

BRODY, HUGH

1982   *Maps and Dreams.* New York: Pantheon.

BROWN, CLAUDE

1965   *Manchild in the Promised Land.* New York: Macmillan Co.

BROWN, NORMAN O.

1969   *Hermes the Thief: The Evolution of a Myth.* New York: Random House.

BRUCE-NOVA, JUAN, ed.

1980   *Chicano Authors: Inquiry by Interview.* Austin, Tex.: University of Texas Press.

1982   *Chicano Poetry.* Austin, Tex.: University of Texas Press.

BRUNER, EDWARD M., ed.

1984   *Text, Play, and Story: The Construction and Reconstruction of Self and Society.* Washington, D.C.: American Ethnological Society.

1985   "Ethnography as Narrative." In *The Anthropology of Experience,* edited by Victor Turner and Edward M. Bruner. Forthcoming.

BURKE, KENNETH

1969   *A Rhetoric of Motives.* Berkeley and Los Angeles: University of California Press.

BURTON, RICHARD F.
    1868   *The Lake Regions of Central Africa: A Picture of Exploration.*
                    New York: Horizon Press, 1961.
CASTANEDA, CARLOS
    1968   *The Teachings of Don Juan.* Berkeley and Los Angeles: Uni-
                    versity of California Press.
CASTRO, MICHAEL
    1983   *Interpreting the Indian: Twentieth Century Poets and the Native
                    American.* Albuquerque, N. Mex.: University of New Mex-
                    ico Press.
CATLIN, GEORGE
    1841   *Letters and Notes on the Manners, Customs, and Conditions of
                    the North American Indians.* 2 vols. New York: Dover Publica-
                    tions, 1973. Citations from vol. 1.
    1867   *O-Kee-Pa: A Religious Ceremony and Other Customs of the
                    Mandan.* New Haven, Conn.: Yale University Press, 1967.
CESARA, MANDA
    1982   *Reflections of a Woman Anthropologist: No Hiding Place.* New
                    York: Academic Press.
CHAGNON, NAPOLEON
    1968   *Yanomamo: The Fierce People.* New York: Holt, Rinehart and
                    Winston.
    1974   *Studying the Yanomamo.* New York: Holt, Rinehart and
                    Winston.
CHAN, JEFFREY PAUL
    1972   "Auntie Tisa Lays Dying." In *Asian American Authors*, edited
                    by Kai-yu Hsu and Helen Palubinskas, 77–85. Boston:
                    Houghton Mifflin Co.
    1974a   "Jackrabbit." In *Yardbird Reader*, vol. 3, edited by Frank
                    Chin and Shawn Hsu Wong, 217–38. Berkeley, Calif.:
                    Yardbird Publication Co.
    1974b   "The Chinese in Haifa." In *Aiiieeeee! An Anthology of Asian-
                    American Writers*, edited by Frank Chin, J. P. Chan, Lawson
                    Fusao Inada, and Shawn Hsu Wong, 11–29. Washington,
                    D.C.: Howard University Press.
CHIN, FRANK
    1970   "Goong Hai Fot Choy." In *19 Necromancers from Now*, edited
                    by Ishmael Reed, 31–54. New York: Doubleday.
    1972a   "Confessions of the Chinatown Cowboy." *Bulletin of Con-
                    cerned Asian Scholars*: 58–70.
    1972b   "Food for All His Dead." In *Asian American Authors*, edited
                    by Kai-yu Hsu and Helen Palubinskas, 48–61. Boston:
                    Houghton Mifflin Co.
    1977   "Riding the Rails with Chickencoop Slim." *Greenfield Re-
                    view* 6, nos. 1 and 2:80–89.
    1981   *The Chickencoop Chinaman and The Year of the Dragon.* Seattle:
                    University of Washington Press.

272   Bibliography

————, and JEFFREY PAUL CHAN
    1972   "Racist Love." In *Seeing through Shuck*, edited by Richard
                Kostelanetz, 65–79. New York: Ballantine Books.
————, JEFFREY PAUL CHAN, LAWSON FUSAO INADA, and SHAWN HSU
WONG, eds.
    1974   *Aiiieeeee! An Anthology of Asian-American Writers.* Washing-
                ton, D.C.: Howard University Press.
CHODOROW, NANCY
    1978   *The Reproduction of Mothering.* Berkeley and Los Angeles:
                University of California Press.
CISNEROS, SANDRA
    1983   *The House on Mango Street.* Houston, Tex.: Arte Publico
                Press.
CLARK, TERRY
    1973   *Prophets and Patrons: The French University and the Emergence
                of the Social Sciences.* Cambridge, Mass.: Harvard University
                Press.
CLEAVER, ELDRIDGE
    1968   *Soul on Ice.* New York: McGraw-Hill.
CLIFFORD, JAMES
    1979   "Naming Names." *Canto: Review of the Arts* 3, no.
                1 : 142–53.
    1980   "Review Essay of Edward Said's *Orientalism.*" *History and
                Theory* 19, no. 2 : 204–23.
    1981   "On Ethnographic Surrealism." *Comparative Studies in So-
                ciety and History* 23, no. 4 : 539–64.
    1982a   *Person and Myth: Maurice Leenhardt in the Melanesian World.*
                Berkeley and Los Angeles: University of California Press.
    1982b   Review of *Nisa: The Life and Words of a !Kung Woman*, by
                Marjorie Shostak. *Times Literary Supplement*, September 17,
                1982.
    1983a   "On Ethnographic Authority." *Representations* 1, no.
                2 : 118–46.
    1983b   "Power and Dialogue in Ethnography: Marcel Griaule's In-
                itiation." In *Observers Observed: Essays on Ethnographic Field-
                work*, edited by George W. Stocking, Jr., 121–56. Madison,
                Wis.: University of Wisconsin Press.
    1985a   "On Ethnographic Self-Fashioning: Conrad and Mali-
                nowski." In *Reconstructing Individualism.* Stanford, Calif.:
                Stanford University Press. Forthcoming.
    1985b   "Histories of the Tribal and the Modern." *Art in America*,
                April 1985, 164–77.
COHN, BERNARD
    1980   "History and Anthropology: The State of Play." *Com-
                parative Studies in Society and History* 22 : 198–221.
    1981   "History and Anthropology: Towards a Rapprochement."
                Journal of Interdisciplinary History 12, no. 2 : 227–52.

COLERIDGE, SAMUEL TAYLOR
  1936   *Miscellaneous Criticism.* Edited by T. M. Raysor. London:
                Constable.
CRAPANZANO, VINCENT
  1973   *The Hamadsha: A Study in Moroccan Ethnopsychiatry.* Berkeley
                and Los Angeles: University of California Press.
  1977   "The Writing of Ethnography." *Dialectical Anthropology*
                2:69–73.
  1980   *Tuhami: Portrait of a Moroccan.* Chicago: University of Chi-
                cago Press.
  1981a   Review of *Meaning and Order in Moroccan Society: Three
                Essays in Cultural Analysis,* by C. Geertz, H. Geertz, and
                L. Rosen. *Economic Development and Cultural Change*
                29:851–60.
  1981b   "The Self, The Third, and Desire." In *Psychosocial Theories
                of the Self,* edited by B. Lee, 179–206. New York and Lon-
                don: Plenum.
  1981c   "Text, Transference, and Indexicality." *Ethos* 9, no.
                2:122–48.
  1985a   *Waiting: The Whites of South Africa.* New York: Random
                House.
———, and VIVIAN GARRISON
  1977   *Case Studies in Possession.* New York: John Wiley and Sons.
CRICK, MALCOLM
  1976   *Explorations in Language and Meaning.* London: Malaby
                Press.
CULLER, JONATHAN
  1975   *Structuralist Poetics.* Ithaca, N.Y.: Cornell University Press.
DARNTON, ROBERT
  1985   "Revolution sans Revolutionaries." *New York Review of
                Books,* January 31, 1985, 21–28.
DAVIS, NATALIE
  1979   "Les Conteurs de Montaillou." *Annales: Economies, Sociétés,
                Civilisations,* no. 1:61–73.
  1981   "The Possibilities of the Past." *Journal of Interdisciplinary
                History* 12, no. 2:267–75.
DE CERTEAU, MICHEL
  1980   "Writing vs. Time: History and Anthropology in the Works
                of Lafitau." *Yale French Studies* 59:37–64.
  1983   "History: Ethics, Science, and Fiction." In *Social Science as
                Moral Inquiry,* edited by Norma Hahn, Robert Bellah, Paul
                Rabinow, and William Sullivan, 173–209. New York: Co-
                lumbia University Press.
DEHOLMES, REBECCA
  1983   "Shabono: Scandal or Superb Social Science." *American An-
                thropologist* 85, no. 3:664–67.

DE LAURETIS, TERESA
1984   *Alice Doesn't: Feminism, Semiotics, Cinema.* Bloomington,
                Ind.: University of Indiana Press.
DELEUZE, GILLES
1962   *Nietzsche and Philosophy.* New York: Columbia University
                Press.
DELGADO, ABELARDO
1982   "Stupid America." In *Chicano Poetry,* edited by Juan Bruce-
                Nova, 30. Austin, Tex.: University of Texas Press.
DELORIA, VINE
1969   *Custer Died for Your Sins.* New York: Macmillan Co.
DE MAN, PAUL
1969   "The Rhetoric of Temporality." In *Interpretation: Theory and
                Practice,* edited by Charles Singleton, 173–209. Baltimore:
                Johns Hopkins University Press.
1979   *Allegories of Reading.* New Haven, Conn.: Yale University
                Press.
DERRIDA, JACQUES
1967   *L'Ecriture et la différence.* Paris: Editions du Seuil.
1972   *Disseminations.* Chicago: University of Chicago Press.
1973   *Speech and Phenomena.* Evanston, Ill.: Northwestern Uni-
                versity Press.
1974   *Of Grammatology.* Baltimore: Johns Hopkins University
                Press.
DIAMOND, STANLEY
1974   *In Search of the Primitive: A Critique of Civilization.* New
                Brunswick, N.J.: E. P. Dutton.
DONNER, FLORINDA
1982   *Shabono: A True Adventure in the Remote and Magical Heart of
                the South American Jungle.* New York: Laurel Books.
DONZELOT, JACQUES
1979   *The Policing of Families.* New York: Pantheon.
DOUGLAS, MARY
1966   *Purity and Danger.* London: Routledge & Kegan Paul.
DREYFUS, HUBERT, and PAUL RABINOW
1982   *Michel Foucault Beyond Structuralism and Hermeneutics.* Chi-
                cago: University of Chicago Press.
DUCHET, MICHELE
1971   *Anthropologie et histoire au siècle des lumières.* Paris: Maspero.
DUMMETT, M.
1981   "Objections to Chomsky." *London Review of Books,* Septem-
                ber 3–16, 1981, 5–6.
DUMONT, JEAN-PAUL
1976   *Under the Rainbow.* Austin, Tex.: University of Texas Press.
1978   *The Headman and I.* Austin, Tex.: University of Texas Press.
DURANT, STEPHEN
1979   "The Nishan Shaman Complex in Cultural Contradiction."
                Signs 5:338–47.

DUVIGNAUD, JEAN
  1970   *Change at Shebika: Report from a North African Village.* New York: Vintage Books.
  1973   *Le Langage perdu: Essai sur la différence anthropologique.* Paris: Presses universitaires de France.

DWYER, KEVIN
  1977   "The Dialogic of Anthropology." *Dialectical Anthropology* 2:143–51.
  1982   *Moroccan Dialogues.* Baltimore: Johns Hopkins University Press.

EAGLETON, TERRY
  1983   *Literary Theory.* Oxford: Oxford University Press.

EISENSTEIN, ELIZABETH I.
  1979   *The Printing Press as an Agent of Change.* Vol. 2. Cambridge: Cambridge University Press.

ELLISON, RALPH
  1952   *Invisible Man.* New York: Random House.

EMPSON, WILLIAM
  1950   *Some Versions of Pastoral.* Norfolk, Conn.: New Directions.

ESTROFF, SUE E.
  1985   *Making it Crazy: An Ethnography of Psychiatric Clients in an American Community.* Berkeley and Los Angeles: University of California Press.

EVANS-PRITCHARD, EDWARD E.
  1940   *The Nuer.* Oxford: Oxford University Press.
  1956   *Nuer Religion.* Oxford: Clarendon Press.
  1976   *Witchcraft, Oracles, and Magic among the Azande.* Oxford: Oxford University Press.
  1981   *A History of Anthropological Thought.* London: Faber and Faber.

EWERS, JOHN C.
  1967   Introduction to *O-Kee-Pa: A Religious Ceremony and Other Customs of the Mandan,* by George Catlin. New Haven, Conn.: Yale University Press.

FABIAN, JOHANNES
  1983   *Time and the Other: How Anthropology Makes Its Object.* New York: Columbia University Press.

FAHIM, HUSSEIN, ed.
  1982   *Indigenous Anthropology in Non-Western Countries.* Durham, N.C.: Carolina Academic Press.

FAIRLEY, BARKER
  1947   *A Study of Goethe.* Oxford: Clarendon Press.

FAVRET-SAADA, JEANNE
  1980   *Deadly Words: Witchcraft in the Bocage.* London: Cambridge University Press.

————, and JOSÉE CONTRERAS
  1981   *Corps pour corps: Enquête sur la sorcellerie dans le bocage.* Paris: Gallimard.

FAY, STEPHEN
    1982   *Beyond Greed*. New York: Viking Press.
FELD, STEVEN
    1982   *Sound and Sentiment: Birds, Weeping, Poetics, and Song in
                    Kaluli Expression*. Philadelphia: University of Pennsylvania
                    Press.
FERNANDEZ, JAMES
    1974   "The Mission of Metaphor in Expressive Culture." *Current
                    Anthropology* 15:119–45.
FINKELSTEIN, MARTIN J.
    1984   *The American Academic Profession: A Synthesis of Social Scien-
                    tific Inquiry Since World War II*. Columbus, Ohio: Ohio State
                    University Press.
FIRTH, RAYMOND
    1936   *We, the Tikopia*. London: Allen and Unwin.
    1966   "Twins, Birds and Vegetables." *Man* 1:1–17.
    ——— et al.
    1977   "Anthropological Research in British Colonies: Some Per-
                    sonal Accounts." *Anthropological Forum* 4, no. 2.
FISCHER, MICHAEL M. J.
    1977   "Interpretive Anthropology." *Reviews in Anthropology*
                    4:391–404.
    1980   *Iran: From Religious Dispute to Revolution*. Cambridge,
                    Mass.: Harvard University Press.
    1982a   *From Interpretive to Critical Anthropologies*. Trabalhos de
                    Ciencias Sociais, Serie Antropologia Social, no. 34, Fun-
                    daçao Universidade de Brasilia.
    1982b   "Portrait of a Mulla: The Autobiography of Aqa Naijafe-
                    Quchani." *Persica* 10:223–57.
    1983   "Imam Khomeini: Four Ways of Understanding." In *Voices
                    of Resurgent Islam*, edited by J. Esposito, 89–108. New York:
                    Oxford University Press.
    1984   "Towards a Third World Politics: Seeing Through Fiction
                    and Film in the Iranian Culture Area." *Knowledge and So-
                    ciety* 5:171–241.
FISH, STANLEY
    1980   "What Makes an Interpretation Acceptable?" In *Is There a
                    Text in This Class?* Cambridge, Mass.: Harvard University
                    Press.
FLETCHER, ANGUS
    1964   *Allegory: The Theory of a Symbolic Mode*. Ithaca, N.Y.: Cornell
                    Univeristy Press.
FONTANIER, PIERRE
    1977   *Les Figures du discours*. Paris: Flammarion.
FOSTER, GEORGE, et al., eds.
    1979   *Long-term Field Research in Social Anthropology*. New York:
                    Academic Press.

FOUCAULT, MICHEL
1973   *The Order of Things*. New York: Vintage Press.
1976   *The Discourse on Language*. In *The Archaeology of Knowledge*,
            215–37. New York: Harper and Row.
1977   "Fantasia of the Library." In *Language, Counter-Memory,
            Practice*, edited by Donald Bouchard, 87–109. Ithaca, N.Y.:
            Cornell University Press.
1978a   *Discipline and Punish*. New York: Pantheon Books.
1978b   *The History of Sexuality: Introduction*. New York: Pantheon
            Books.
1980   "Truth and Power." In *Power/Knowledge*. New York: Pan-
            theon Books.
1982   "The Subject and Power." In Hubert Dreyfus and Paul
            Rabinow, *Michel Foucault Beyond Structuralism and Her-
            meneutics*, 208–26. Chicago: University of Chicago Press.
1984   "Polemics, Politics, and Problemizations." In *The Foucault
            Reader*, edited by Paul Rabinow, 381–90. New York:
            Pantheon.

FREEMAN, DEREK
1983   *Margaret Mead and Samoa: The Making and Unmaking of an
            Anthropological Myth*. Cambridge, Mass.: Harvard Univer-
            sity Press.

FREUD, SIGMUND
1911–13   *The Interpretation of Dreams*. 3rd ed. New York: Macmillan
            Co.

FRYE, NORTHROP
1963   *Fables of Identity: Studies in Poetic Mythology*. New York: Har-
            court Brace Jovanovich.
1971   *Anatomy of Criticism*. Princeton, N.J.: Princeton University
            Press.

FUSSELL, PAUL
1975   *The Great War and Modern Memory*. Oxford: Oxford Uni-
            versity Press.

GADAMER, HANS-GEORG
1960   *Truth and Method*. New York: Seabury.

GALARZA, ERNESTO
1971   *Barrio Boy*. Notre Dame, Ind.: University of Notre Dame
            Press.

GEERTZ, CLIFFORD
1973   *The Interpretation of Cultures*. New York: Basic Books.
1983a   "Slide Show: Evans-Pritchard's African Transparencies."
            Raritan Review, Fall 1983, 62–80.
1983b   *Local Knowledge*. New York: Basic Books.
1983c   "Works and Lives: The Anthropologist as Author," Lec-
            tures delivered at Stanford University, Spring 1983. Forth-
            coming from Stanford University Press in revised and
            expanded form.

GELLEY, ALEXANDER
    1979   "The Represented World: Toward a Phenomenological
                    Theory of Description in the Novel." *Journal of Aesthetics
                    and Art Criticism* 37 : 415–22.

GELLNER, ERNEST
    1959   *Words and Things*. London: Gollancz.
    1969   *Saints of the Atlas*. London: Weidenfeld and Nicolson.
    1970   "Concepts and Society." In *Rationality*, edited by B. R.
                    Wilson, 18–49. Oxford: Basil Blackwell.

GENETTE, GERARD
    1982   *Figures of Literary Discourse*. New York: Columbia University
                    Press.

GIDDENS, ANTHONY
    1979   *Central Problems in Social Theory*. Berkeley and Los Angeles:
                    University of California Press.

GLUCKMAN, MAX
    1973   "The State of Anthropology," *Times Literary Supplement*, 3,
                    August, 1973, 905.

GOETHE, J. W. VON
    1976a   *Italienische Reise*. 2 vols. Frankfurt am Main: Insel Verlag.
    1976b   *Tagebuch der Italienische Reise: 1786*. Frankfurt am Main:
                    Insel Verlag.
    1982   *Italian Journey: 1786–1788*. Translated by W. H. Auden
                    and Elizabeth Mayer. San Francisco: North Point Press.

GOLDEN, MARITA
    1983   *Migrations of the Heart*. New York: Doubleday.

GOODY, JACK
    1977   *The Domestication of the Savage Mind*. Cambridge: Cam-
                    bridge University Press.

GOULD, ERIC, ed.
    1985   *The Sin of the Book: Edmond Jabès*. Lincoln, Neb.: University
                    of Nebraska Press.

GREENBLATT, STEPHEN
    1980   *Renaissance Self-Fashioning: From More to Shakespeare*. Chi-
                    cago: University of Chicago Press.

GREENBURG, BLU
    1981   *On Women and Judaism*. Philadelphia: Jewish Publication
                    Society.

GUSDORF, GEORGES
    1956   "Conditions et limites de l'autobiographie." In *Formen der
                    Selbstdarstellung*, edited by Günther Reichenkrom and
                    Erich Haase. Berlin: Duncker and Humblot.

HABERMAS, JURGEN
    1975   *Legitimation Crisis*. Boston: Beacon Press.
    1983   "Modernity—An Incomplete Project." In *The Anti-Aesthetic
                    Essays on Postmodern Culture*, edited by Hal Foster, 3–15.
                    Port Townsend, Wash.: Bay Press.
    1984   *The Theory of Communicative Action*. Boston: Beacon Press.

HACKING, IAN
　1982　　　　"Language, Truth, and Reason." In *Rationality and Rela-*
　　　　　　　tivism, edited by R. Hollis and S. Lukes, 185–203. Cam-
　　　　　　　bridge, Mass.: MIT Press.
　1984　　　　"Five Parables." In *Philosophy in History*, edited by Richard
　　　　　　　Rorty, J. B. Scheewind, and Quentin Skinner, 103–24.
　　　　　　　Cambridge: Cambridge University Press.
HAMILTON, SIR WILLIAM
　1863　　　　"On the Philosophy of Commonsense." In *The Philosophical*
　　　　　　　Works of Thomas Reid, vol. 2, 186–312. Edinburgh: James
　　　　　　　Thin, 1895.
HANDELMAN, DON
　1979　　　　"Is Naven Ludic? Paradox and the Communication of
　　　　　　　Identity." *Social Analysis* 1, no. 1:177–92.
HANDELMAN, SUSAN
　1982　　　　*The Slayers of Moses: The Emergence of Rabbinic Interpretation
　　　　　　　in Modern Literary Criticism*. Albany: SUNY Press.
HARAWAY, DONNA
　1985　　　　"A Manifesto for Cyborgs: Science, Technology, and So-
　　　　　　　cialist Feminism in the 1980s." *Socialist Review* 15, no.
　　　　　　　2:65–108.
HARRIS, MARVIN
　1968　　　　*The Rise of Anthropological Theory*. New York: Thomas
　　　　　　　Crowell.
HARTMAN, GEOFFREY
　1980　　　　*Criticism in the Wilderness*. New Haven, Conn.: Yale Univer-
　　　　　　　sity Press.
HARTOG, FRANÇOIS
　1980　　　　*Le Miroir d'Hérodote*. Paris: Gallimard.
HESCHEL, SUSAN
　1983　　　　*On Being a Jewish Feminist: A Reader*. New York: Shocken.
HINOJOSA, ROLANDO
　1982　　　　*Rites and Witnesses*. Houston, Tex.: Arte Publico Press.
HINTON, WILLIAM
　1966　　　　*Fanshen: A Documentary of Revolution in a Chinese Village*.
　　　　　　　New York: Alfred A. Knopf.
HOLLANDER, J.
　1959　　　　"Versions, Interpretations, and Performances." In *On
　　　　　　　Translation*, edited by R. A. Brower, 205–31. Cambridge,
　　　　　　　Mass.: Harvard University Press.
HONIGMAN, JOHN J.
　1976　　　　"The Personal Approach in Cultural Anthropological Re-
　　　　　　　search." *Current Anthropology* 16:243–61.
HOOKS, BELL
　1981　　　　*Ain't I a Woman?* Boston: South End Press.
HULL, GLORIA; PATRICIA BELL SCOTT, and BARBARA SMITH, eds.
　1982　　　　*All the Women Are White, All the Men Are Black, but Some of*

Us Are Brave: Black Women's Studies. Old Westbury, Conn.: Feminist Press.

HYMES, DELL, ed.

1974   *Reinventing Anthropology.* New York: Vintage.

IRIGARAY, LUCE

1977   *Ce sexe qui n'en est pas un.* Paris: Editions de Minuit.

IVINS, WILLIAM

1953   *Prints and Visual Communication.* Cambridge, Mass.: MIT Press.

JAEGER, WERNER

1945   *Paideia: The Ideals of Greek Culture.* Translated by Gilbert Highet. Vol. 1. 2nd ed. New York: Oxford University Press.

JAMES, HENRY

1873   "A Roman Holiday." In *Italian Hours*, 136–54. New York: Grove Press, 1959.

JAMESON, FREDRIC

1980   "Marxism and Historicism." *New Literary History*, Spring 1980, 41–73.

1981   *The Political Unconscious: Narrative as a Socially Symbolic Act.* Ithaca, N.Y.: Cornell University Press.

1983   "Postmodernism and Consumer Society." In *The Anti-Aesthetic Essays on Postmodern Culture*, edited by Hal Foster, 111–25. Port Townsend, Wash.: Bay Press.

1984a   "Postmodernism, or The Cultural Logic of Late Capitalism." *New Left Review* 146:53–92.

1984b   "Periodizing the 60s." In *The Sixties Without Apology*, edited by S. Sayers, A. Stephanson, S. Aronwitz, and F. Jameson, 178–215. Minneapolis, Minn.: University of Minnesota Press.

JAMIN, JEAN

1979   "Une Initiation au réel: À propos de Segalen." *Cahiers internationaux de la sociologie* 66:125–39.

1980   "Un Sacré college, ou les apprentis sorciers de la sociologie." *Cahiers internationaux de la sociologie* 68:5–32.

———, ed.

1985   "Le Texte ethnographique." Special issue of *Etudes rurales*, nos. 97–98. Contains essays by M. Leiris, P. Lejeune, P. Rabinow, J. Jamin, F. Zonabend, J. Clifford, J. Lindenfeld.

JEHLEN, MYRA

1981   "Archimedes and the Paradox of Feminist Criticism." *Signs* 6, no. 4:575–601.

KAEL, PAULINE

1984   Film Review of "The Bostonians," *The New Yorker*, August 6, 1984, 68.

KARP, IVAN

1985   "Laughter at Marriage: Subversion in Performance." In *The Transformation of African Marriage*, edited by David

Parkin. London: International African Institute. Forthcoming.

KAUFFMANN, ROBERT LANE
1981 "The Theory of the Essay: Lukács, Adorno, and Benjamin." Ph.D. diss., University of California, San Diego.

KELBER, WERNER
1983 *The Oral and Written Gospel*. Philadelphia: Fortress Press.

KELLER, EVELYN FOX
1985 *Reflections on Gender and Science*. New Haven, Conn.: Yale University Press.

KERMODE, FRANK
1952 *English Pastoral Poetry: From the Beginnings to Marvell*. London: Harrap.

KIM, ELAINE
1982 *Asian-American Literature*. Philadelphia: Temple University Press.

KINGSLEY, MARY
1897 *Travels in West Africa*. London: Macmillan & Co.
1899 *West African Studies*. London: Macmillan & Co.

KINGSTON, MAXINE HONG
1976 *The Warrior Woman: Memoirs of a Girlhood Among Ghosts*. New York: Alfred A. Knopf.
1980 *Chinamen*. New York: Alfred A. Knopf.

KLUCKHOHN, CLYDE
1948 Introduction to *Magic, Science, and Religion* by Bronislaw Malinowski. Garden City, N.J.: Free Press.

KNORR-CETINA, KARIN
1981 *The Manufacture of Knowledge*. Oxford: Pergamon Press.
————, and A. V. CICOUREL
1981 *Advances in Social Theory and Methodology: Toward an Integration of Micro- and Macro-Sociologies*. Boston: Routledge & Kegan Paul.
————, and MICHAEL MULKAY
1983 *Science Observed: Perspectives on the Social Study of Science*. Beverley Hills, Calif.: Sage Publications.

KONNER, MELVIN
1982 *The Tangled Wing: Biological Constraints on the Human Spirit*. New York: Harper and Row.

KRIEGER, SUSAN
1983 *The Mirror Dance: Identity in a Women's Community*. Philadelphia: Temple University Press.

KRISTEVA, JULIA
1980 "Women Can Never Be Defined." In *New French Feminisms*, edited by Elaine Marks and Isabelle de Courtivon, 118–35. Amherst, Mass.: University of Massachusetts Press.

KUHN, ANNETTE
1982 *Women's Pictures: Feminism and Cinema*. London: Routledge & Kegan Paul.

KUKLICK, HENRIKA
  1984   "Tribal Exemplars: Images of Political Authority in British
              Anthropology, 1885–1945." In *History of Anthropology*, vol.
              2, edited by George Stocking, 59–82. Madison, Wis.: Uni-
              versity of Wisconsin Press.
KUNDERA, MILAN
  1984   "The Tragedy of Central Europe." *New York Review of
              Books*, April 26, 1984, 33ff.
LACAN, JACQUES
  1968   *The Language of the Self*. Baltimore: Johns Hopkins Univer-
              sity Press.
  1977   *Ecrits*. New York: Norton.
LACOSTE-DUJARDIN, CAMILLE
  1977   *Dialogue des femmes en ethnologie*. Paris: Maspero.
LAFITAU, JOSEPH FRANÇOIS
  1724   *Moeurs des sauvages ameriquains*. Paris: n.p.
LARCOM, JOAN
  1983   "Following Deacon: the Problem of Ethnographic Re-
              analysis." In *History of Anthropology*, vol. 1, edited by
              George Stocking, 175–95. Madison, Wis.: University of
              Wisconsin Press.
LATOUR, BRUNO
  1984   *Les Microbes: Guerre et paix, suivi des irréductions*. Paris:
              Metailie.
———, and STEVE WOOLGAR
  1979   *Laboratory Life: The Social Construction of Scientific Facts*. Bev-
              erley Hills, Calif.: Sage Publications.
LEACH, EDMUND R.
  1954   *Political Systems of Highland Burma*. London: G. Bell and
              Sons.
  1973   "Ourselves and Others." *Times Literary Supplement*, July 6,
              1973, 771–72.
LECLERC, GERARD
  1972   *Anthropologie et colonialisme: Essai sur l'histoire de l'africanisme*.
              Paris: Fayard.
LEE, RICHARD B.
  1979   *The !Kung San: Men, Women, and Work in a Foraging Society*.
              New York: Cambridge University Press.
———, and IRVEN DEVORE
  1976   *Kalahari Hunter-Gatherers*. Cambridge, Mass.: Harvard
              University Press.
LEIRIS, MICHEL
  1934   *L'Afrique fantôme*. Paris: Gallimard.
  1950   "L'Ethnographe devant le colonialisme." *Les Temps modernes*
              58. Reprinted in *Brisées*, 125–45. Paris: Mercure de France,
              1966.

LEITER, KENNETH
    1980   *A Primer on Ethnomethodology.* Oxford: Oxford University Press.

LEJEUNE, PHILIPPE
    1975   *Le Pacte autobiographique.* Paris: Seuil.

LE ROY LADURIE, EMMANUEL
    1978   *Montaillou: The Promised Land of Error.* New York: George Braziller.

LEVINAS, EMMANUEL
    1963   "To Love the Torah More Than God." *Judaism* 110(2): 216–23.

LÉVI-STRAUSS, CLAUDE
    1975   *Tristes Tropiques.* New York: Atheneum.

LEWES, GEORGE HENRY
    1855   *The Life and Works of Goethe.* London: J. M. Dent.

LIEBERSON, JONATHAN
    1984   Review of *Local Knowledge: Further Essays in Interpretive Anthropology,* by C. Geertz. *New York Review of Books* 31:39–46.

LIENHARDT, GODFREY
    1954   "Modes of Thought." In *The Institutions of Primitive Society,* by E. E. Evans-Pritchard et al., 95–107. Oxford: Basil Blackwell.
    1961   *Divinity and Experience: The Religion of the Dinka.* Oxford: Oxford University Press.

LURIA, A. R., and F. I. YUDOVICH
    1971   *Speech and the Development of Mental Processes in the Child.* London: Penguin Books.

LYOTARD, JEAN FRANÇOIS
    1979   *La Condition postmoderne.* Paris: Editions de Minuit. Translated by Geoff Bennington and Brian Massumi as *The Postmodern Condition: A Report on Knowledge.* Minneapolis, Minn.: University of Minnesota Press, 1984.

MACCORMACK, CAROL, and MARILYN STRATHERN
    1980   *Nature, Culture and Gender.* Cambridge: Cambridge University Press.

MAJNEP, IAN SAEM, and RALPH BULMER
    1977   *Birds of My Kalam Country.* Auckland, N.Z.: Auckland University Press.

MAKKREEL, RUDOLPH
    1975   *Dilthey: Philosopher of Human Sciences.* Princeton, N.J.: Princeton University Press.

MALCOLM, J.
    1982   *Psychoanalysis: The Impossible Profession.* London: Pan Books.

MALCOLM X (WITH ALEX HALEY)
    1965   *The Autobiography of Malcolm X.* New York: Grove Press.

MALINOWSKI, BRONISLAW
1961   *Argonauts of the Western Pacific*. New York: E. P. Dutton.
1967   *A Diary in the Strict Sense of the Term*. New York: Harcourt,
            Brace, & World.
MAQUET, JACQUES
1964   "Objectivity in Anthropology." *Current Anthropology*
            5:47–55.
MARCUS, GEORGE
1980   "Rhetoric and the Ethnographic Genre in Anthropological
            Research." *Current Anthropology* 21:507–10.
———, ed.
1983   *Elites: Ethnographic Issues*. Albuquerque, N. Mex.: Univer-
            sity of New Mexico Press.
———, and DICK CUSHMAN
1982   "Ethnographies as Text." *Annual Review of Anthropology*
            11:25–69.
———, and MICHAEL FISCHER
1986   *Anthropology as Cultural Critique*. Chicago: University of
            Chicago Press.
MARCUS, GREIL
1975   *Mystery Train*. New York: E. P. Dutton.
MARRAST, JEAN, ed.
1960   *L'Oeuvre de Henri Prost: Architecture et urbanisme*. Paris: Im-
            primerie de Compagnonnage.
MARX, KARL
1963   *The Eighteenth Brumaire of Louis Bonaparte*. New York: Inter-
            national Publishing Co.
MATTHEWS, WASHINGTON
1873   *Grammar and Dictionary of the Language of the Hidatsa*. New
            York: Shea's American Linguistics, series 2, no. 1.
MAUSS, MARCEL
1967   *The Gift: Forms and Functions of Exchange in Archiac Societies*.
            New York: Norton.
MAYBURY-LEWIS, DAVID
1965   *The Savage and the Innocent*. Cleveland: World Publishing
            Co.
1967   *Akwe-Shavante Society*. Oxford: Clarendon Press.
MEAD, MARGARET
1923   *Coming of Age in Samoa*. New York: William Morrow.
MEIGS, ANNA
1984   *Food, Sex, and Pollution: A New Guinea Religion*. New Bruns-
            wick, N.J.: Rutgers University Press.
MERNISSI, FATIMA
1984   *Le Maroc raconté par ses femmes*. Rabat: Société marocaine
            des éditeurs réunis.
MICHEL, CHRISTOPH
1976   "Nachwort" in J. W. von Goethe, *Italienische Reise*, vol. 2,
            737. Frankfurt am Main: Insel Verlag.

MINGUS, CHARLES, and NEL KING
    1971   *Beneath the Underdog*. New York: Alfred A. Knopf.
MOMADAY, N. SCOTT
    1968   *The House Made of Dawn*. New York: Harper and Row.
    1969   *The Way To Rainy Mountain*. Albuquerque, N. Mex.: University of New Mexico Press.
    1977   *The Names: A Memoir*. New York: Harper and Row.
MORAGA, CHERRIE
    1983   *Loving in the War Years*. Boston: South End Press.
MULVEY, LAURA
    1975   "Visual Pleasure and Narrative Cinema." *Screen* 16, no. 3:6–18.
MURPHY, ROBERT
    1984   "Requiem for the Kayapo." *New York Times Book Review*, August 12, 1984: 34.
NADER, LAURA
    1969   "Up the Anthropologist—Perspectives Gained from Studying Up." In *Reinventing Anthropology*, edited by Dell Hymes, 284–311. New York: Pantheon.
NEEDHAM, RODNEY
    1970   "The Future of Anthropology: Disintegration or Metamorphosis?" In *Anniversary Contributions to Anthropology*, 34–47. Leiden: Brill.
    1972   *Belief, Language, and Experience*. Oxford: Basil Blackwell.
    1974   *Remarks and Inventions: Skeptical Essays on Kinship*. London: Tavistock Publications.
NEUSNER, JACOB
    1981   *Judaism: The Evidence of the Mishnah*. Chicago: University of Chicago Press.
NILSSON, M. P.
    1949   *History of Greek Religion*. 2nd ed. Oxford: Oxford University Press.
OBEYESEKERE, GANANATH
    1981   *Medusa's Hair*. Berkeley and Los Angeles: University of California Press.
OHNUKI-TIERNEY, EMIKO
    1984   "'Native' Anthropologists." *American Ethnologist* 11, no. 3:584–86.
OLNEY, JAMES
    1972   *Metaphors of Self: The Meaning of Autobiography*. Princeton, N.J.: Princeton University Press.
ONG, WALTER J.
    1967   *The Presence of the Word*. New Haven, Conn.: Yale University Press.
    1971   *Rhetoric, Romance, and Technology: Studies on the Interaction of Expression and Culture*. Ithaca, N.Y.: Cornell University Press.

1977   *Interfaces of the Word.* Ithaca, N.Y.: Cornell University Press.
1982   *Orality and Literacy.* London: Methuen.

ORTNER, SHERRY B.
1974   "Is Female to Male as Nature is to Culture?" In *Women,
              Culture, and Society,* edited by Michele Rosaldo and Louise
              Lamphere, 67–87. Stanford, Calif.: Stanford University
              Press.
1984   "Theory in Anthropology Since the Sixties." *Comparative
              Studies in Society and History* 26, no. 1 : 126–66.

OWENS, CRAIG
1980   "The Allegorical Impulse: Toward a Theory of
              Postmodernism (Part 2)." *October* 13 : 59–80.

OZICK, CYNTHIA
1983   *Art and Ardor.* New York: Alfred A. Knopf.

PARK, MUNGO
1799   *Travels in the Interior Districts of Africa.* London: Black-
              wood's, 1860.

PICCHI, DEBRA
1983   "Shabono: A Visit to A Remote and Magical World in the
              Heart of the South American Jungle." *American Anthropolo-
              gist* 85, no. 3 : 674–75.

PLATO
370 B.C.   *Phaedrus,* translated by Walter Hamilton. Harmondsworth:
              Penguin, 1973.

POCOCK, DAVID
1961   *Social Anthropology.* London and New York: Sheed and
              Ward.

POGGIOLI, RENATO
1975   *The Oaten Flute: Essays on Pastoral Poetry and the Pastoral.*
              Cambridge, Mass.: Harvard University Press.

POLANYI, KARL
1944   *The Great Transformation: The Political and Economic Origins
              of Our Times.* New York: Rinehart and Co.

PORTER, DENIS
1984   "Anthropological Tales: Unprofessional Thoughts on the
              Mead/Freeman Controversy." *Notebooks in Cultural Analysis*
              1 : 15–37.

PRATT, MARY LOUISE
1977   *Toward a Speech Act Theory of Literary Discourse.* Blooming-
              ton, Ind.: Indiana University Press.
1982   "Conventions of Representation: Where Discourse and
              Ideology Meet." In *Contemporary Perceptions of Language:
              Interdisciplinary Dimensions,* edited by Heidi Byrnes, 139–55.
              Georgetown University Roundtable on Language and Lin-
              guistics. Washington, D.C.: Georgetown University Press.
1985   "Scratches on the Face of the Country: What Mr. Barron
              Saw in the Land of the Bushmen." *Critical Inquiry.*
              Forthcoming.

PRELL-FOLDES, RIV-ELLEN
1978   "Coming of Age in Kelton." In *Women in Ritual and Symbolic Roles*, edited by J. Hoch-Smith and A. Spring, 75–99. New York: Plenum.

PRICE, RICHARD
1983   *First-Time: The Historical Vision of an Afro-American People.* Baltimore: Johns Hopkins University Press.

PULLUM, GEOFFREY K.
1984   "The Revenge of the Methodological Moaners." *Natural Language and Linguistic Theory* 1, no. 4, 583–88.

RABINOW, PAUL
1975   *Symbolic Domination: Cultural Form and Historical Change in Morocco.* Chicago: University of Chicago Press.

1977   *Reflections on Fieldwork in Morocco.* Berkeley and Los Angeles: University of California Press.

1985   "Discourse and Power: On the Limits of Ethnographic Texts." *Dialectical Anthropology.* Forthcoming.

RAMPERSAD, ARNOLD
1983   "Biography, Autobiography, and Afro-American Culture." *Yale Review* 73 : 1–16.

RANDALL, FREDERIKA
1984   "Why Scholars Become Storytellers." *New York Times Book Review,* January 29, 1984, 1–2.

REID, THOMAS
1895   *The Philosophical Works of Thomas Reid.* Edinburgh: James Thin.

RICH, ADRIENNE
1976   *Of Woman Born.* New York: Norton.
1979   "Disloyal to Civilization: Feminism, Racism, Gynephobia (1978)." In *On Lies, Secrets, and Silence.* New York: Norton.

RIVERA, TOMAS
1971   *y no se lo trago la tierra (and the earth did not part).* Berkeley, Calif.: Quinto Sol Publications.

ROBERTS, HELEN, ed.
1981   *Doing Feminist Research.* London: Routledge & Kegan Paul.

RODRIGUEZ, RICHARD
1981   *Hunger of Memory.* Boston: David R. Godine.

RORTY, RICHARD
1979   *Philosophy and the Mirror of Nature.* Princeton, N.J.: Princeton University Press.

ROSALDO, MICHELE
1980   "The Use and Abuse of Anthropology: Reflections on Feminism and Cross-Cultural Understanding." *Signs,* 5, no. 3 : 389–417.

———, and LOUISE LAMPHERE, eds.
1974   *Woman, Culture and Society.* Stanford, Calif.: Stanford University Press.

ROSALDO, RENATO

1978   "The Rhetoric of Control: Ilongots Viewed as Natural
               Bandits and Wild Indians." In *The Reversible World: Sym-
               bolic Inversion in Art and Society*, edited by Barbara A. Bab-
               cock, 240–57. Ithaca, N.Y.: Cornell University Press.

1980   *Ilongot Headhunting 1883–1974: A Study in Society and His-
               tory*. Stanford, Calif.: Stanford University Press.

1984   "Grief and a Headhunter's Rage: On the Cultural Force of
               Emotions." In *Text, Play, and Story*, edited by E. Bruner,
               178–95. Seattle: American Ethnological Society.

1985   "Where Objectivity Lies: The Rhetoric of Anthropology."
               MS.

ROSEN, LAWRENCE

1984   Review of *Moroccan Dialogues*, by Kevin Dwyer. *American
               Ethnologist* 11, no. 3:597–98.

RUBIN, GAYLE

1975   "The Traffic in Women: Notes on the 'Political Economy'
               of Sex." In *Towards an Anthropology of Women*, edited by
               Rayna Reiter, 157–210. New York: Monthly Review Press.

RUPP-EISENREICH, BRITTA, ed.

1984   *Histoires de l'anthropologie: XVI–XIX siècles*. Paris:
               Klincksieck.

RUSS, JOANNA

1975   *The Female Man*. New York: Bantam.

SAID, EDWARD

1978   *Orientalism*. New York: Pantheon.

SAHLINS, MARSHALL

1981   *Historical Metaphors and Mythical Realities*. Ann Arbor,
               Mich.: University of Michigan Press.

SALINAS, RAUL R.

1969   "Trip through the Mind Jail." *Entrelineas* 1, no. 1:10–11.

SAMUELSSON, KURT

1961   *Religion and Economic Action*. London: Heinemann.

SAPIR, EDWARD

1966   "Culture, Genuine and Spurious" (1924). In *Culture, Lan-
               guage, and Personality*, 78–119. Berkeley and Los Angeles:
               University of California Press.

SAROYAN, WILLIAM

1961   *Here Comes, There Goes, You Know Who*. New York: Simon
               and Schuster.

SCHNEIDER, DAVID

1972   "What is Kinship All About?" In *Kinship Studies in the Mor-
               gan Centennial Year*, edited by P. Reining, 32–63. Washing-
               ton, D.C.: Anthropological Society of Washington.

1980   *American Kinship*. 2nd ed. Chicago: University of Chicago
               Press.

1984   *A Critique of the Study of Kinship*. Ann Arbor, Mich.: Univer-
               sity of Michigan Press.

SCHOLEM, GERSHOM
    1965   *On the Kabbalah and its Symbolism.* New York: Schocken.
    1971   *The Messianic Idea in Judaism.* New York: Schocken.
SCHOLTE, BOB
    1971   "Discontents in Anthropology." *Social Research* 38, no. 4:777–807.
    1972   "Toward a Reflexive and Critical Anthropology." In *Reinventing Anthropology,* edited by Dell Hymes, 430–57. New York: Pantheon.
    1978   "Critical Anthropology Since Its Reinvention." *Anthropology and Humanism Quarterly* 3, nos. 1, 2:4–17.
SCHOOLCROFT, H. R.
    1851–57   *Historical and Statistical Information Respecting the History, Condition, and Prospects of the Indian Tribes of the United States.* Washington, D.C.: Bureau of Indian Affairs.
SEGALEN, VICTOR
    1978   *Essai sur l'exotisme: Une Esthétique du divers.* Montpellier: Editions Fata Morgana.
SERRES, MICHEL
    1972   *L'Interférence.* Paris: Editions de Minuit.
SHORE, BRADD
    1982   *Sala'ilua: A Samoan Mystery.* New York: Columbia University Press.
SHOSTAK, MARJORIE
    1981   *Nisa: The Life and Words of a !Kung Woman.* Cambridge, Mass.: Harvard University Press.
SILKO, LESLIE MARMON
    1977   *Ceremony.* New York: Viking Press.
SONTAG, SUSAN
    1966   *Against Interpretation.* New York: Farrar, Straus and Giroux.
SPARRMAN, ANDERS
    1785   *Voyage to the Cape of Good Hope.* New York: Johnson Reprint Corp., 1975.
SPERBER, DAN
    1982   "Ethnographie interprétative et anthropologie théorique." In *Le Savoir des anthropologues,* 13–48. Paris: Hermann.
STADE, HANS
    1874   *The Captivity of Hans Stade of Hess in A.D. 1547–1555 Among the Wild Tribes of Eastern Brazil.* London: Hakluyt Society.
STAIGER, EMIL
    1956   *Goethe.* Vol. 2. Zurich: Atlantis Verlag.
STOCK, BRIAN
    1983   *The Implications of Literacy.* Princeton, N.J.: Princeton University Press.
STOCKING, GEORGE
    1968   "Arnold, Tylor, and the Uses of Invention." In *Race, Culture, and Evolution,* 69–90. New York: Free Press.

1983   "The Ethnographer's Magic: Fieldwork in British Anthro-
                pology from Tylor to Malinowski." In *Observers Observed:
                Essays on Ethnographic Fieldwork*, edited by George W.
                Stocking, Jr., 70–120. Madison, Wis.: University of
                Wisconsin Press.

——, ed.
1983   *Observers Observed: Essays on Ethnographic Fieldwork*. Vol. 1
                of *History of Anthropology*. Madison, Wis.: University of
                Wisconsin Press.

STOLLER, PAUL
1984a   "Sound in Songhay Cultural Experience." *American Eth-
                nologist* 12, no. 3:91–112.
1984b   "Eye, Mind and Word in Anthropology." *L'Homme* 24, nos.
                3–4:91–114.

STRATHERN, MARILYN
1984   "Dislodging a World View: Challenge and Counter-
                Challenge in the Relationship Between Feminism and An-
                thropology." Lecture at the Research Center for Women's
                Studies, University of Adelaide, July 4, 1984. Forthcoming
                in *Changing Paradigms: The Impact of Feminist Theory upon the
                World of Scholarship*, edited by Susan Magarey (Sydney:
                Hale and Iremonger); a version will also appear in *Signs*.

TAMBIAH, STANLEY J.
1976   *World Conqueror, World Renouncer*. New York: Cambridge
                University Press.

TARN, NATHANIEL
1975   "Interview with Nathaniel Tarn." *Boundary* 2 4, no. 1:1–34.

TAUSSIG, MICHAEL
1980   *The Devil and Commodity Fetishism in South America*. Chapel
                Hill, N.C.: University of North Carolina Press.
1984   "History as Sorcery." *Representations* 7:87–109.

TEDLOCK, DENNIS
1979   "The Analogical Tradition and the Emergence of a Di-
                alogical Anthropology." *Journal of Anthropological Research*
                35:387–400.
1983   *The Spoken Word and the Work of Interpretation*. Philadelphia:
                University of Pennsylvania Press.

THEAL, GEORGE MCCALL
1897   *History and Ethnography of Africa South of the Zambesi*. Lon-
                don: S. Sonnenschein and Co.
1892–1919   *History of South Africa*. 11 vols. London: George Allen and
                Unwin. Cape Town: C. Struik, 1964.

THOMAS, ELIZABETH MARSHALL
1959   *The Harmless People*. New York: Alfred A. Knopf.

THORNTON, ROBERT J.
1983   "Narrative Ethnography in Africa, 1850–1920." *Man*
                18:502–20.

1984   "Chapters and Verses: Classification as Rhetorical Trope in
                Ethnographic Writing." Paper presented at the School of
                American Research Seminar, "The Making of Ethno-
                graphic Texts," April 1984.

TODOROV, TZVETAN
1973   *The Fantastic.* Cleveland and London: Case Western Re-
                serve Press.
1982   *The Conquest of America: The Question of the Other.* New York:
                Harper and Row, 1984.

TRAWEEK, SHARON
1982   "Uptime, Downtime, Spacetime and Power: An Ethnogra-
                phy of U.S. and Japanese Particle Physics." PhD thesis,
                University of California, Santa Cruz, History of Conscious-
                ness Program.

TURNBULL, COLIN
1962   *The Forest People.* New York: Simon and Schuster.

TURNER, VICTOR
1974   *Dramas, Fields, and Metaphors: Symbolic Action in Human So-
                ciety.* Ithaca, N.Y.: Cornell University Press.

1975   *Revelation and Divination in Ndembu Ritual.* Ithaca, N.Y.:
                Cornell University Press.

——, ed.
1982   *Celebration: Studies in Festivity and Ritual.* Washington, D.C.:
                Smithsonian Institution.

TYLER, STEPHEN A.
1978   *The Said and the Unsaid.* New York: Academic Press.
1981   "Words for Deeds and the Doctrine of the Secret World."
                In *Papers from the Parasession on Language and Behavior,*
                34–57. Proceedings of the Chicago Linguistics Society.
                Chicago: University of Chicago Press.
1984a   "Ethnography, Intertextuality, and the End of Descrip-
                tion." *American Journal of Semiotics.* In press.
1984b   "Postmodern Anthropology." In *Proceedings of the Anthro-
                pological Society,* edited by Phyllis Chock. In press.
1984c   "The Vision Quest in the West or What the Mind's Eye
                Sees." *Journal of Anthropological Research* 40, no. 1:23–40.
1985   "What Laksmayya Wrote: Koya Ethnographic Texts." MS.

VALDEZ, LUIS, and STAN STEINER, eds.
1972   *Aztlan: An Anthology of Mexican-American Literature.* New
                York: Alfred A. Knopf.

VALERO, HELENA
1969   *Yanoama: The Narrative of a White Girl Kidnapped by Amazo-
                nian Indians.* New York: E. P. Dutton.

VAN DER POST, LAURENS
1958   *The Lost World of the Kalahari.* London: Hogarth Press.

VERNANT, JEAN-PIERRE
  1965   *Myth and Thought Among the Greeks.* London: Routledge & Kegan Paul, 1983.

VIELIE, ALAN R.
  1982   *Four Indian Literary Masters: N. Scott Momaday, James Welch, Leslie Marmon Silko, Gerald Vizenor.* Norman, Okla.: University of Oklahoma Press.

VIGIL, EVANGELINA
  1983   "Woman of Her Word: Hispanic Women Write." *Revista Chicano-Riquena* 10:3–4.

VILLARREAL, JOSE ANTONIO
  1959   *Pocho.* New York: Doubleday.
  1974   *The Fifth Horseman.* New York: Doubleday.

VIZENOR, GERALD
  1978a   *Darkness in Saint Louis Bearheart.* Saint Paul, Minn.: Bookslinger.
  1978b   *Wordarrows: Indians and Whites in the New Fur Trade.* Minneapolis, Minn.: University of Minnesota Press.

WAGLEY, CHARLES
  1977   *Welcome of Tears.* New York: Oxford University Press.

WAGNER, ROY
  1979   "The Talk of Koriki: a Daribi Contact Cult." *Social Research* 46, no. 1, 140–65.
  1980   *The Invention of Culture.* Chicago: University of Chicago Press.

WALKER, JAMES
  1917   *The Sun Dance and Other Ceremonies of the Oglala Division of the Teton Sioux.* New York: AMS Press, 1979.
  1982a   *Lakota Belief and Ritual.* Edited by Raymond J. DeMallie and Elaine A. Jahner. Lincoln, Nebr.: University of Nebraska Press.
  1982b   *Lakota Society.* Edited by Raymond J. DeMallie. Lincoln, Nebr.: University of Nebraska Press.
  1983   *Lakota Myth.* Edited by Elaine A. Jahner. Lincoln, Nebr.: University of Nebraska Press.

WALLERSTEIN, IMMANUEL
  1976   *The Modern World System: Capitalist Agriculture and the Origins of the European World-Economy in the Sixteenth Century.* New York: Academic Press.

WASHBURN, WILCOMB E.
  1982   Postscript to *Celebration: Studies in Festivity and Ritual,* edited by Victor Turner, 297–99. Washington, D.C.: Smithsonian Institution.

WEBSTER, STEVEN
  1982   "Dialogue and Fiction in Ethnography." *Dialectical Anthropology* 7, no. 2:91–114.

WEINER, ANNETTE
    1976   *Women of Value, Men of Renown*. Austin, Tex.: University of
        Texas Press.
WEINREICH, MAX
    1980   *History of the Yiddish Language*. Chicago: University of Chi-
        cago Press.
WEINREICH, URIEL
    1968   *Languages in Conflict*. The Hague: Mouton.
    1969   *Conference on Yiddish Dialectology*. The Hague: Mouton.
WELCH, JAMES
    1974   *Winter in the Blood*. New York: Harper and Row.
WHITE, HAYDEN
    1973   *Metahistory*. Baltimore: Johns Hopkins University Press.
    1978   *Tropics of Discourse*. Baltimore: Johns Hopkins University
        Press.
WHITTEN, NORMAN E.
    1978   "Ecological Imagery and Cultural Adaptability: The
        Canelos Quichua of Eastern Equador." *American Anthropol-
        ogist* 80:836–59.
WILLIAMS, RAYMOND
    1966   *Culture and Society: 1780–1950*. New York: Harper and
        Row.
    1973   *The Country and the City*. New York: Oxford University
        Press.
    1981   *Politics and Letters: Interviews with New Left Review*. London:
        New Left Review Editions, Verso.
WILLIS, PAUL
    1981   *Learning to Labour: How Working Class Kids Get Working Class
        Jobs*. New York: Columbia University Press.
WITTIG, MONIQUE
    1975   *The Lesbian Body*. Translated by David LeVay. New York:
        Avon.
    1981   "One is Not Born a Woman." *Feminist Issues*, Winter 1981,
        47–54.
WOLF, ERIC
    1980   "They Divide and Subdivide and Call it Anthropology."
        New York Times, November 30, 1980.
WOLIN, RICHARD
    1982   *Walter Benjamin*. New York: Columbia University Press.
WONG, SHAWN HSU
    1979   *Homebase*. New York: Reed Books.
WOOLF, VIRGINIA
    1936   *Three Guineas*. New York: Harcourt, Brace & World.
YANAGISAKO, SYLVIA
    1979   "Family and Household: The Analysis of Domestic
        Groups." *Annual Review of Anthropology* 8:161–205.

YATES, FRANCIS
    1966   *The Art of Memory*. Chicago: University of Chicago Press.
YERUSHALMI, YOSEF HAYIM
    1982   *Zakhor: Jewish History and the Jewish Memory*. Seattle: University of Washington Press.
ZAMORA, BERNICE
    1976   *Restless Serpents*. Menlo Park, Calif.: Diseños Literarios.
                  (Bound with José Antonio Burciaga, *Restless Serpents*.)

Notes on Contributors

TALAL ASAD teaches in the Department of Sociology and Social Anthropology at the University of Hull, England. He is an editor of *Economy and Society*, and has written extensively on theories of religion, on ideology, and on the relationship of anthropology to colonialism. His present research is centered on medieval Christianity, being a critical-historical investigation of the basic categories underlying Western anthropological conceptions of religion.

JAMES CLIFFORD teaches in the History of Consciousness Program at the University of California, Santa Cruz. He is on the editorial board of *History of Anthropology*, the *American Ethnologist*, and *Cultural Anthropology*. He has written extensively on the history of missionary discourse, travel writing, ethnography, and museums. A collection of his essays on these topics will appear in the near future.

VINCENT CRAPANZANO is a member of the Department of Comparative Literature at Queens College, New York, and the Department of Anthropology at the City University of New York Graduate Center. He has published numerous works on spirit possession (particularly in Morocco), on psychoanalysis, and on the writing and epistemology of ethnography. His most recent ethnographic study is *Waiting: The Whites of South Africa* (1985).

MICHAEL M. J. FISCHER teaches anthropology at Rice University in Houston, Texas. He has written on the Iranian revolution, on theoretical problems in interpretive anthropology, and on modern religious and poetic movements in the Third World. His most recent book, co-authored by George Marcus, is *Anthropology as Cultural Critique* (1986). His recent fieldwork focuses on industrial relations and religious ideology in India.

GEORGE E. MARCUS is chairman of the Department of Anthropology at Rice University and editor of *Cultural Anthropology*. He has published studies of elites in Polynesia and in the United States, and has written on textual strategies in ethnography. His most recent book is *Anthropology as Cultural Critique*, co-authored by Michael Fischer (see above). His current research centers on the invention of ideologies of superiority among upper and middle classes amid visions of decline and decay.

MARY LOUISE PRATT is a member of the Department of Spanish and Portuguese at Stanford University. She has published widely on speech-act theory and discourse analysis. An editor of *Tabloid*, she is actively concerned with popular culture and ideology. Currently she is completing a book on the history, rhetoric, and politics of travel writing, with particular focus on Africa and Latin America from the eighteenth to the twentieth century.

PAUL RABINOW teaches anthropology at the University of California, Berkeley. He has published books on power and symbolism in Morocco, on fieldwork, on interpretive social science, and on Michel Foucault. He is currently completing a study of modern forms of political rationality in France and the French colonies between the two world wars.

RENATO ROSALDO is a member of the Department of Anthropology at Stanford University. He has written widely on the status of history in anthropological work, on discourses of domination in the Philippines, on Mayan and Chicano studies. He is currently finishing a collection of essays on ethnographic rhetorics and strategies, rethinking the role of experience and emotion in cultural interpretation.

STEPHEN A. TYLER teaches anthropology at Rice University. He has written extensively on cognitive and linguistic anthropology. His present work explores the possibilities of a post-modern ethnographic poetics, with special emphasis on oral vs. literate modes and on the writing of indigenous collaborators. He is preparing a new book entitled *What Lakśmayya Wrote: Koya Ethnographic Texts*.

Publications by each contributor are listed in the Bibliography.

Index

Adorno, Theodor, 131, 132, 191
Advances in Social Theory and Methodology, 169n
Aesthetic integration, 125, 132
Africa, 9, 35, 40, 93, 116, 192, 216–17. *See also* Evans-Pritchard, Edward E.; !Kung; Morocco
Afrique fantôme, 13
Afro-Americans, 201, 202–3n, 213–18
Agnon, Shmuel, 232
Akwe-Shavante Society, 31, 40–41
Algeria, 192
Allegory, 67–68, 75, 98–121, 122, 127–28, 132, 198
Allochronic representations, 111
Alphabetic writing, 117
Alter, Robert, 231
Alurista (Alberto Urista), 220
Ambiguity, 135–36
America. *See* United States
American Anthropologist, 28
American Ethnologist, 112
American Immigrants in Israel, 196
Amerindians, 115n, 201, 202n, 211, 212, 224–29. *See also* Mandan Indians; Yanomamo
Anachronism, 83
Anarcho-rationalism, 238
Anaya, Rudolfo, 219, 221
Angelou, Maya, 203n
Anglo-American identity, 229
Anglo-American thought, 166, 167n, 169. *See also* British academics
Anthropology and the Colonial Encounter, 9
Anxiety, ethnic, 197–98, 204–6
Arabic, 158
Archaeology, 4
Archaelogy of Knowledge, 238
Arendt, Hannah, 231
Argonauts of the Western Pacific, 1–2, 27, 37–38
Arias, Ron, 219, 221–22
Aristotle, 133–34, 235

"Arizona Highways," 228
Arlen, Michael, 195, 204–7
Armenian-Americans, 201, 204–7, 218
Arrival stories, 13; by Barrow, 47; by Bougainville, 35, 36–37, 47; by Evans-Pritchard, 39–40; by Firth, 35–36; by Geertz, 69–70; by Malinowski, 37–38; by Maybury-Lewis, 40–41; by Shostak, 42–44, 45, 47
Art, 3, 4, 5–6
Asad, Talal, 9, 97n, 251, 261n; on allegories, 119; on cultural translation, 19, 22, 24, 141–64
Austin, J. L., 144
Authority, 6, 15, 32, 118, 163, 189, 243, 244–47; in "Deep Play," 53, 74, 76, 244; in *Iran*, 192; in *Manners, Customs, and Conditions*, 53, 57, 58, 59–60, 76; in *Montaillou*, 77, 78–81, 82; in *Nuer*, 41, 77, 88–89, 90, 92; in *Roman Carnival*, 53, 68n, 76
Autobiography, 195, 197, 198–233
Autobiography of Malcolm X, 203n
Avruch, Kevin, 196
Azande, 90

Babcock, Barbara, 26n
Baker, Tanya, 164n
Bakhtin, Mikhail, 15, 64n, 67, 246
Balandier, Georges, 8, 9, 14
Balinese cockfight, 53–54, 68–76, 244
Barrio Boy, 219–20, 221
Barrow, John, 46, 47
Barthes, Roland, 1, 12, 105
Barton, Roy-Franklin, 31
Bastian, Adolph, 112
Bateson, Gregory, 192–93
Baudelaire, Charles, 56
Baumgarten, Murray, 198, 231–32
Beattie, John, 142
Beaujour, Michel, 99
Beaver Indians, 115n
Bedrosian, Margaret, 205n, 206, 207

Belief, Language, and Experience, 143
Beneath the Underdog, 202, 213–15
Benedict, Ruth, 3, 4, 102
Benjamin, Walter, 131, 194–95n, 198,
    221; on allegory, 119; on transla-
    tion, 51, 52, 156, 157, 159
Benveniste, Emile, 71
Berbers, Moroccan, 153–55
Berger, Harry, 121n
Bernstein, Michael André, 68n
Bernstein, Richard J., 166n
Bertaux, Daniel, 176n, 177n
Bertaux-Wiame, Isabelle, 176n, 177n
Beyond Greed, 171–72
Beyond Objectivism and Relativism, 166n
Bialik, Chaim Nachman, 198
Bible, 127
Bifocality, 199, 213–18, 233
Biocca, Ettore, 28n
Biographies, 197
Biological anthropology, 4
Birmingham Centre for Contemporary
    Cultural Studies, 23
Blacks, 9, 201, 202–3n, 213–18
Bless Me Ultima, 221
Bloom, Harold, 135, 195n, 231
Boas, Franz, 4, 113
Bogard, Abraham, 55, 60
Bohannan, Laura, 13
Borges, Jorge Luis, 232
Bougainville, Louis de, 35, 36–37, 47
Bourdieu, Pierre, 3, 169, 212, 252
Bouvard et Pécuchet, 243
Bowen, Elenore Smith, 1, 13
Briggs, Jean, 14
British academics, 17–18, 89, 111,
    141–64, 166, 169, 170–71, 174
Brown, Claude, 203n
Bruce-Nova, Juan, 223
Bucher, Henry, 116n
Buddhism, 199
Bulmer, Ralph, 136
Burce, Amy, 97n
Burke, Kenneth, 11, 96
Burton, Richard, 35, 40
Bushmen. *See* !Kung

Canguilhem, Georges, 238
Capitalism, 172–86 passim, 241, 247,
    248
Captives, images as, 38
Captivity of Hans Stade of Hesse, 33–34
Carnival, Roman, 53, 54, 60–68, 75
Castaneda, Carlos, 28, 30
Castaway image, 38
Castro, Michael, 228, 229
Catlin, George, 53–68 passim, 72, 74,
    75, 76

Ceremony, 226–27
Césaire, Aimé, 9
Chagnon, Napoleon, 31
Chan, Jeffrey Paul, 203n, 210, 211–12
Charity, excessive, 143, 146, 149, 150,
    151, 152–53
Chicanos. *See* Mexican-Americans
Chin, Frank, 202, 203n, 210, 211
Chinamen, 212
Chinatown, 211
Chinese-Americans, 201, 203n,
    208–12
Cicourel, Aaron V., 23, 169n
Cisneros, Sandra, 219, 220
Civil rights movement, 203n
Clark, Terry, 11n
Class culture, 178. *See also* Middle class;
    Working class
Cleaver, Eldridge, 203n
Clifford, James, 1–26, 39n, 97n, 233n,
    265; on allegory, 98–121; critique
    of, 242, 243–47, 251, 252, 255; on
    narrative, 32, 100, 106
Cockfight, Balinese, 53–54, 68–76,
    244
Coleridge, Samuel Taylor, 101
Colonialism, 8–9, 10, 40–41, 42,
    252–53, 259–61; !Kung, 46–47,
    48, 49; Nuer and, 91, 93, 96
Colorado Historical Society, 16
Coming of Age in Samoa, 102–3, 217
Communication, vs. representation,
    123–24
Communist Party, 227
"Concepts and Society," 143–56
Context, 6, 151–53
Continental philosophy, 166, 236
Conversation, 236, 239
Cooperation, enthnographic, 126,
    127–28
Cosmopolitanism, 258
Country and the City, 113, 170
Crapanzano, Vincent, 6, 23–24,
    51–76, 97n, 192; and dream-work,
    212; and post-modernism, 136; and
    transference, 208
Crawford, L., 55, 60
Crime and Punishment, 72, 73
Cultural anthropology, 4
Cultural criticism, 3, 23, 233, 262; in
    autobiography, 195, 199, 201–2,
    217–18, 230; and Willis study,
    180–82
Culturalist allegories, 101, 102
Cultural poetics, 3, 12, 16–17, 24, 26,
    125–26. *See also* Poetry, ethnic
    autobiographical
Cultural translation. *See* Translation

Culture, 5–6, 15, 18, 19, 141, 170–71, 178–79
"Culture, Genuine and Spurious," 114
Custer Died for Your Sins, 9

Damas, Léon, 9
Darkness in St. Louis Bearheart, 227–28
Davis, Natalie, 3
Deacon, A. B., 117
de Beauvoir, Simone, 110
de Certeau, Michel, 3, 5
"Deep Play," 68–76
Deep Throat, 68–69
Defense. *See* Justification
Deferred meaning, 194n
DeHolmes, Rebecca B., 28–30
Deictics, 53, 58, 65–66, 75
Delgado, Abelardo, 220–21
Deloria, Vine, 9
De Man, Paul, 100, 110
Der Hovanessian, Diana, 203
Derrida, Jacques, 10, 117–18, 128, 131, 194n, 195n, 229
Descartes, René, 235
Description, 51–76, 81–87, 166, 175; allegory and, 100, 101; and narrative, 28, 32–33, 34–35, 38–39, 41, 45; post-modernism and, 130–31, 137
Devil and Commodity Fetishism in South America, 176n
Dewey, John, 236
Dialectics, negative, 132
Dialogue, 14–15, 175, 244, 245–46; feminism and, 255, 256; in postmodern ethnography, 126, 132, 140
Diamond, Stanley, 9
Dickens, Charles, 246
Diderot, Denis, 12
Dilthey, Wilhelm, 10, 195n
Dinka, 17–18
Discourse, 5, 11–19, 27, 166, 251, 256; cultural translation and, 145–46, 160; post-modernism and, 122–39 passim. *See also* Description; Narrative; Rhetoric
Discourse on Language, 238
"Dislodging a World View," 21n, 254
Dissertations, 265–66
Divinity and Experience, 17–18
Dixon, John, 164n
Domination, 12, 81, 88, 93, 96–97, 255, 261. *See also* Politics/Power
Donner, Florinda, 28–31, 38
Donzelot, Jacques, 260
Douglas, Mary, 3, 160
Dream-work, 208–13
"Dumb Broad," 223

Dumont, Jean-Paul, 14, 31
Durkheim, Emile, 145
Duvignaud, Jean, 3
Dwyer, Kevin, 245, 246, 251

Eagleton, Terry, 5
Ecology: *Montaillou*, 78–79; *Nuer*, 87–88
Elective Affinities, 76
Elementary Forms of the Religious Life, 145
Eliot, George, 114
Ellison, Ralph, 203n
Engels, F., 174
Enlightenment, 147, 224n
Epistemology, 234–41
Essays, modernist, 191–93
Ethics, 122, 126, 131, 136, 232–33, 257, 258
Ethnicity, 22, 84–85, 194–233
"Ethnographe devant le colonialisme," 8
Ethnographic pastoral. *See* Pastoral
Europe, 120, 166, 236. *See also* Colonialism; *individual countries*
Evangelical justification, 59
Evans-Pritchard, Edward E., 90, 142; *Nuer* of, 32, 39–42, 77–78, 83, 85, 87–97, 111–12, 161; *Nuer Religion* of, 90, 149–50, 151
Evocation, 12, 99, 123–39 passim, 185–87, 189, 190
Explanation, 19, 59, 145, 150, 167
Exploitation, 260

Fabian, Johannes, 12, 33, 101–2, 111
Fanshen, 189
"Fantasia of the Library," 243, 250
Faubion, James, 261n
Fay, Stephen, 171–72
Feld, Steven, 200
Feminism, 17, 18, 19–21, 203; Jewish, 232; and *Learning to Labour*, 188; *Nisa* and, 107–8; Strathern on, 254, 255–56, 257–58; Zamora and, 223
Fenellosa, Ernest, 130
Feyerabend, Paul, 238
Fictions, 5, 6–7, 243–44
Fieldwork accounts, 13–14, 27–50, 109, 189, 208, 253, 264; in *Nisa*, 42–46, 106–7, 109; in *Nuer*, 32, 39–42, 88–93, 96
Fifth Horseman, 219
Figurative style, 5n
Films, nostalgia, 249–50
Fingere, 6
First-Time, 7–8
Firth, Raymond, 13, 35–36, 38–39, 41, 150
Fischer, Eric, 233n

Fischer, Michael M. J., 22, 23–24, 97n,
    121n, 190, 194–233
Fish, Stanley, 255, 256
Flaubert, G., 243, 246
Fletcher, Angus, 98n, 100
Floricanto en Aztlan, 220
Foster, Stephen, 261n
Foucault, Michel, 11n, 18n, 81, 195n,
    234; on Flaubert, 243; on literature,
    5; Panopticon of, 92; on power/
    politics, 241, 260, 261; on thought,
    238, 239–40; on truth/falsity, 237,
    238, 240–41
Fournier, Jacques, 78, 79–80, 81, 82,
    88, 93
France, 3, 9, 259
Frankenberg, Ruth, 26n
Freeman, Derek, 102–3
Freud, Sigmund, 195n, 196, 198
Frye, Northrop, 96n–97n, 98n, 102
Functionalism, 141–42, 143–45, 146,
    147–48, 150, 183
Fussell, Paul, 89

Gabon, 116
Gadamer, Hans-Georg, 195n, 197, 246
Galarza, Ernesto, 219–20, 221
Garfinkel, Harold, 23
Geertz, Clifford, 3, 35, 179, 195n, 242,
    243, 256, 262; on Balinese cock-
    fight, 53, 68–76, 244; on Evans-
    Pritchard, 40, 93
Gelley, Alexander, 57–58
Gellner, Ernest, 142, 143–56, 162,
    163–64
Gender. *See* Men; Women
Genres, 6, 27, 188, 189–90
German philosophy, 236
Gevirtz, Susan, 121n
Giddens, Anthony, 166n, 169
Gift, 120
Ginzburg, Carlo, 3
Gluckman, Max, 143
Goethe, Johann Wolfgang von, 53,
    60–68, 69, 75, 76
Golden, Marita, 195, 196, 213, 215–18
Gonzales, Rudolpho "Corky," 220
Gordon, Deborah, 21n, 26n
Gorky, Arshile, 207, 231
Governmentality, 260, 261
Grammatology, 117
Great Transformation, 173–74
Great War and Modern Memory, 89
Greek philosophers, 116, 133–34, 235,
    238
Greenblatt, Stephen, 3
Griaule, Marcel, 9
Guilt, 45–46, 47

Habermas, Jurgen, 125, 239, 248, 251
Hacking, Ian, 234, 237–39
Hall, Stuart, 23
Hamilton, William, 133
Handler, Richard, 121n
Haraway, Donna, 26n
"Harlem Montana," 228
Harmless People, 105
Hartman, Geoffrey, 264
Harvard Kalahari Project, 45, 48, 49,
    105, 110
Hawthorne, N., 66
Hayes, Ira, 225
Headman and I, 31
Heidegger, Martin, 10, 236
Hermeneutics, 10, 166; in "Deep Play,"
    75, 76; in *Learning to Labour*, 177,
    183–85; Rorty on, 236, 238
Hermes, 51, 52–53, 68, 76
Herodotus, 2
Heteroglossia, 246–47
Hidden meaning, 194–95n, 198
Hinojosa, Rolando, 219, 222
Hinton, William, 189
*Historical and Statistical Information Re-
    specting the History, Condition and
    Prospects of the Indian Tribes of the
    United States*, 60
Historical ethnography, 3, 77
History, 3, 6, 8–11, 24, 165–66n, 189,
    262–63; allegories and, 101–2,
    119; and gender, 17–18; *Montaillou*
    and, 77; post-modernism and, 24n,
    249; truth and, 237
Holism, 132–33, 171, 188, 191, 192,
    224
Homebase, 212
House Made of Dawn, 225–26
House on Mango Street, 219
Humanism, 101, 102, 260
Humboldt, Alexander von, 60
Humor, 224–30
Hunger of Memory, 219, 220
Hunt brothers, 172
Hymes, Dell, 9
Hypotyposis, 53, 57–58

"I am Joaquin," 220
Id, 196
Identity, ethnic, 195–96, 197, 201, 211,
    216, 217, 220, 228
Ideology, 240
I Know Why the Caged Bird Sings, 203n
Ilongots, 165–66n
Immigrant novels, 195
Indians. *See* Amerindians
Indigenous ethnographers, 9. *See also*
    Autobiography

Indochina, 259
Inscription, 99, 113, 116, 117, 118
Interdisciplinarity, 3
Interference, 219, 232
Interlinguistics, 195n, 202, 218–20, 223
Interpretive anthropology, 167, 168n, 169, 250, 256–58; Clifford and, 242, 243, 245, 246; Fish on, 255; Geertz and, 53, 75–76, 242, 243, 256; Gellner and, 143–44, 151–52
Inter-references, 195n, 201, 202, 218–23, 230, 232
Intertextuality, 117, 195n, 202, 265
Invisible Man, 203n
Iran, 190
Irony, 111–12, 121, 182–83, 224–30
Israel, 196
Italienische Reise (Italian Journey), 53, 61, 62, 63, 64

Jacobson, Roman, 10
James, Henry, 66, 68n
Jameson, Fredric, 3, 194n, 247–50, 252
Jewish-Americans, 231–32
Justification, 58–59, 123, 125, 145, 150

Kachins, 151–52
Kaluli, 200
Kant, Immanuel, 235–36
Kauffmann, Angelika, 63
Kenny, Maurice, 229
Kim, Elaine, 211
King, Martin Luther, Jr., 196
King Lear, 72, 73
Kingsley, Mary, 35
Kingston, Maxine Hong, 195, 203n, 208–10, 211–12, 213
Kipp, J., 55, 60
Kluckhohn, Clyde, 31
Knorr-Cetina, Karin, 169n, 177, 180, 182
Knowable community, 170
Knowledge, 234–41
Kuhn, Thomas, 3, 234, 254
Kuklick, Henrika, 111
!Kung, 42–49, 98–99, 103–9

Lacan, Jacques, 195n, 250
Lafitau, Joseph François, 101
Lake Regions of Central Africa, 35, 40
Lakota Belief, 15–16, 17
Lakota Myth, 16, 17
Lakota Society, 16, 17
Languages: inequality of, 156–60, 164; sciences of, 4, 10. *See also* Interlinguistics

"Language, Truth, and Reason," 237
"Law of the Conditioned," 133
Leach, Edmund, 3, 142, 151–52
Learning to Labour, 169, 173–88
Leavis, F. R., 142
Leclerc, Gérard, 9
Lee, Richard, 47, 48
Leiris, Michel, 8, 9, 13
Lele, 160–61
Le Roy Ladurie, Emmanuel, 3, 77–88, 93, 94, 95, 97
Levinas, Emanuel, 194, 231
Lévi-Strauss, Claude, 3, 112, 121n, 199–200, 229
Lienhardt, Godfrey, 17–18, 142, 145, 158–59
Linguistics, 4, 10. *See also* Interlinguistics
Linton, Ralph, 141
Literacy, 117, 118
Literary approaches, 3–4, 5–6, 262–63, 266
Literature, 5–6, 138
Logic, 237
Lyautey, Hubert, 259, 260–61
Lyotard, Jean François, 125, 137, 194n, 230, 249

Macro perspectives, 22, 165–93, 251, 258
Majnep, Ian Saem, 136
Malinowski, Bronislaw, 1–2, 3, 13, 27, 29, 37–38, 112; and cultural translation, 141–42; diaries of, 14, 31, 92; narrative-description duality of, 35; and scientific ethnography, 39, 41; and tent, 1–2, 92n
Manchild in the Promised Land, 203n
Mandan Indians, 53, 54–60, 72, 75, 76
Manners, Customs, and Conditions of the North American Indians, 55, 56, 57, 58, 59, 60
Maps and Dreams, 115n
Maquet, Jacques, 9
Marcus, George E., 20, 22, 24, 26n, 97n, 156–93, 262–66
Marin, Louis, 3
Marx, Karl, 207–8
Marxism, 23, 170–87 passim, 240
Massignon, Louis, 199
Master narrative, 24n
Maurs, Guillaume, 86
Maury, Pierre, 86, 87, 95
Mauss, Marcel, 120
Maximilian of Neuwied, Prince, 60
Maybury-Lewis, David, 14, 31, 39, 40–42
Mayhew, Henry, 23

Mead, Margaret, 1, 3, 9, 13, 109; and
　　Coming of Age in Samoa, 102–3, 217;
　　and cultural criticism, 217; and
　　female domains, 18
Meaning, 53–54, 160–63, 187–88
Melanesia, 115n
Melville, Herman, 103
Memory, 163, 197, 198, 201
Men, 18–19; Asian-American, 211–12;
　　Dinka, 17–18
Mendel, Gregor, 238
Ménil, René, 9
Mexican-Americans, 201, 215, 218–23
Micro perspectives, 166–67, 169n, 170,
　　177, 180, 182, 193
Middle class, 174, 175, 176n, 181–86
　　passim, 191–92
Middlemarch, 114
Midwifery, ethnographic, 180, 181
Migrations of the Heart, 195, 215–18
Mingus, Charlie, 202, 213–15
Mitchell, David D., 60
Mixed-genre texts, 188, 189–90
Modernism, 21, 138–39, 168n, 190–
　　93, 194n, 248
"Modes of Thought," 142, 158–59
Momaday, N. Scott, 225–26
Monophony. *See* Univocity/Monophony
Montaillou, 77–87, 88, 93, 95
Montesquieu, C., 2
Montoya, Jose, 218, 223
Morocco, 153–55, 212, 259, 260–61
Mpongwé, 116
Multi-locale ethnography, 171–73, 177
Murphy, Robert, 115
Myth, 200n

Nambikwara, 112
Names, 225
Narayan, Kirin, 97n
Narrative, 24, 28–47, 165n, 171, 172,
　　175, 263; allegory and, 100; Amer-
　　indian talk-story, 224–28; and de-
　　scription, 28, 32–33, 34–35, 38–
　　39, 41, 45; in *Italienische Reise*, 53; in
　　Montaillou, 88; in *Nisa*, 42–45, 47,
　　106; in *Nuer*, 39–40, 41, 88–93, 94
Nationality, 84–85. *See also* Ethnicity
Natural history, 130–31
Navarro, Fats, 214
Naven, 192–193
Needham, Rodney, 5, 143, 164n
Negative dialectics, 132
Négritude movement, 9
Neusner, Jacob, 231
Newspapers, 127
Newsweek, 28

New-York Commercial Advertiser, 55
Nield, Keith, 164n
Nietzsche, Friedrich, 195n, 253
Nigeria, 216–17
Nines, Charles, 15
Nines, Richard, 15
Nisa, 42–46, 98–99, 103–9
Nishan Shaman, 209
Novels, 114, 170, 195
Nuer, 32, 39–42, 77–78, 87–97, 111–
　　12, 161
Nuer Kinship and Marriage, 90
Nuer Religion, 90, 149–50, 151

Obeyesekere, Gananath, 207
Objectivity, 13, 14, 63, 93–95, 237
"Objectivity in Anthropology," 9
Occult, 134, 194n
Odor, 11
Oglalas, 15–16
O-Kee-Pa ceremony, 53, 54–60, 67–68,
　　72, 75
Olson, Charles, 24
"On Ethnographic Authority, 245–47
Ong, Walter J., 10, 11–12, 119, 131
Orality, 115–17, 118, 128, 177, 184–
　　85, 221–22, 264–65
Order of Things, 239
Orientalism, 12
Ortigues, Edmond, 9
Ortiz, Simon, 224
Ortner, Sherry B., 22n
Other Cultures, 142
Otherness, 23, 127–28, 142, 167–68n
Outline of a Theory of Practice, 169
Oxford, 142
Ozick, Cynthia, 232

Pannwitz, Rudolf, 157
Panopticon, 92
Paris, 3
Park, Mungo, 35, 38
Park, Robert, 23
Partiality, 7–8, 18, 24n, 25
Participant-observation, 13, 14, 38, 111,
　　183–84; in Eliot's novels, 114; in
　　Manners, Customs, and Conditions, 57;
　　in *Nuer*, 88, 92; in *Roman Carnival*,
　　66–67
Passage to Ararat, 195, 204–7
Pastiche, 249–50, 252
Pastoral, 96–97, 110, 113–16, 118–19,
　　121n; in *Montaillou*, 86–87, 95,
　　96–97; in *Nuer*, 89, 95, 96–97
Patterns of Culture, 102
Phaedrus, 117
Phenomenology, 75, 166

Philosophy and the Mirror of Nature, 234
Physical anthropology, 4
Picchi, Debra, 30
Pine Ridge Sioux Reservation, 15–16
Plato, 116, 133
Pocho, 219
Pocock, David, 161–62
Poetics, 232. *See also* Cultural poetics
Poetry, ethnic autobiographical, 219, 220–23, 228
Polanyi, Karl, 173–74
Political economy, 165–93, 251. *See also* Capitalism
Political Systems of Highland Burma, 151–52
Politics/Power, 6, 11, 17–18, 24, 166, 239, 251–61 passim; and cultural translation, 152–53, 163, 164; Foucault on, 241, 260, 261; *Montaillou* and, 81, 88, 97; *Nuer* and, 88, 91, 93, 96, 97, 111; rhetoric of, 122, 125. *See also* Colonialism; Feminism; Political economy
Polyphony/Polyvocality, 15, 126, 127, 137, 203, 223, 246; in *Montaillou*, 82; in *Nisa*, 45, 104–6, 109
Positivism, 100, 166, 169, 184
Post-modernism, 21, 22–23, 24, 122–40, 194–233, 247–51, 252
"Postmodernism and Consumer Society," 247–50
Pound, Ezra, 130
Power. *See* Politics/Power
Practice, 166, 169, 170, 177
Pragmatism, 59
Pratt, Mary Louise, 11, 13, 24, 27–50, 97n
Présence Africaine, 9
Price, Richard, 7–8
Prost, Henri, 260
Psychoanalysis, 161, 162, 196, 203, 204, 209, 213–14
Puns, 69

Quintilian, 98n

Rabinow, Paul, 24, 26n, 31, 97n, 164n, 234–61, 263; fieldwork account by, 14, 31, 165n; and Strathern, 21n, 254, 255–56, 257–58
Racism, 202, 211, 214, 215
Radin, Paul, 13
Rampersad, Arnold, 197
Raponda-Walker, Abbé, 116
Realism, 25, 130, 168n, 171, 198, 232, 265; by Catlin, 57–58; De Man and, 100; by Evans-Pritchard, 92; mod-

ernist essay and, 190, 191, 192; in nostalgia films, 250; of post-modernism, 134, 137; Williams on, 169–70, 188, 190; by Willis, 175, 176, 177, 185
Reasoning, 237–38
Redemptive ethnography, 99, 113,165n
Reflections on Fieldwork in Morocco, 31
Reid, Thomas, 137
Reinventing Anthropology, 9
Relativism, 129, 147–48, 155
Religion, 135, 149–50, 153–55
Religion and Economic Action, 143
"Religion of the Dinka," 17–18
Repetitions, 206, 207–8
Representation, 10–11, 19, 77, 123, 168n, 169, 189–93, 234–61; post-modernism and, 128, 129–30, 131; Willis and, 177, 180, 183, 184. *See also* Rhetoric
Research Group on Colonial Discourse, 26n
Restless Serpents, 222, 223
Restructuring of Social and Political Theory, 166n
Return to Laughter, 13
Revolutions, 189–90
Rhetoric, 5, 6, 10–11, 12, 57, 122, 135; allegory and, 100; of irony, 224; of modern essay, 191, 192; in *Montaillou*, 77, 81–87; in *Nuer*, 77, 83, 85, 93–95; political, 122, 125; scientific, 122, 123–25, 130, 136
Ricoeur, Paul, 10
Rites and Witnesses, 222
Rivera, Tomas, 221
Rivet, Paul, 9
Road to Tamazunchale, 221–22
Rodriguez, Richard, 219, 220
Rogin, Michael, 261n
Roman carnival, 53, 54, 60–68, 75
Romanticism, 100, 114, 128, 229
Römische Karneval (Roman Carnival), 61, 62, 63, 67
Rorty, Richard, 234, 235, 236, 237, 238–39, 261
Rosaldo, Michelle, 110–11
Rosaldo, Renato, 12, 23, 24, 77–97, 165–66n, 233n, 245

Sacks, Harvey, 23
Sahlins, Marshall, 208
Said, Edward, 3, 12, 241, 251
Said and the Unsaid, 140n
Salinas, Raul, 202, 222, 223
Salvage ethnography, 112–13, 115, 118, 165n

Samoa, 102–3, 119, 217
Samuelsson, Kurt, 143–44
Sanchez, Ricardo, 218–19
Santayana, George, 78
Sapir, Edward, 3, 4, 10, 114
Saramakas, 7–8
Saroyan, William, 203 n, 204, 205 n
Sartre, Jean-Paul, 128
Saudis, 172
Saussure, Ferdinand de, 10
Savage and the Innocent, 31
Schizophrenia, 250
Schneider, David, 121 n, 179
Scholem, Gershom, 231
Scholte, Bob, 9
Schoolcraft, Henry Rome, 60
Science, 235; art and, 3, 4; interpretive, 257; rhetoric of, 122, 123–25, 130, 136; transcendental, 135
Scientific communities, study of, 3
Scientific ethnography, 39, 41, 104–5, 110–11
Segalen, Victor, 103
Self-fashioning, 23–24
Selves, alternative, 213–18
Semiotics, 3, 11, 166, 195 n
Senghor, Léopold, 9
Senses, 11–13, 131
Serres, Michel, 195 n, 219
Sex (gender). See Men; Women
Sex and Temperament in New Guinea, 217
Sexuality, in Montaillou, 83–84
Shabono, 28–31, 32
Shavante, 41
Shi'ites, 190
Shore, Bradd, 165 n
Shostak, Marjorie, 42–46, 47, 48, 49, 98–99, 103–9, 110
Silko, Leslie Marmon, 213, 226, 227, 229
Silver market, 172
Simple style, 5 n
Snyder, Gary, 229
Social anthropology, 4
Social heredity, 141
Social planning, in colonies, 260–61
Social structure, 93–94; Montaillou, 82–86; Nuer, 88, 93–95
Sociology, 22, 23, 114, 162, 195
Socrates, 116, 117
Soul on Ice, 203 n
Sounds, 11 n, 12–13
South Africa, 192
South Seas, 35–37, 102–3
Sparrman, Anders, 46
Sperber, Dan, 243
Stade, Hans, 33–34, 38

Staiger, Emil, 63
Statistics, 177, 238
Stocking, George, 11 n, 92 n
Strathern, Marilyn, 21 n, 254, 255–56, 257–58, 261 n
Structures of feeling, 3, 112
Studying the Yanomamo, 31
"Stupid America," 220–21
Style, scholarly, 164
Subjection, 260
Subjectivity, 5, 13, 96, 111, 114, 135–36; Catlin and, 57; Geertz and, 70, 73–74; Shostak and, 107, 108
Subversion, 51–76
Sun Dance and Other Ceremonies, 15
Sword, George, 15, 16, 117
Symbolic Domination, 31

Tahiti, 36–37
Talaat Bey, 206
Talmud, 200
Tambiah, Stanley, 199
Tarn, Nathaniel, 12–13
Taussig, Michael, 176–77 n, 178–79, 180
Tedlock, Dennis, 136
Television, 163
Tent, 1–2, 92 n
Textuality, 10, 12, 20–21, 168–73, 190–93, 230, 241–55 passim, 264–66; and allegory, 99, 111, 113, 114–18; post-modernism and, 127, 128, 129, 250; Willis and, 171, 173, 175, 177, 183–88, 190. See also Dialogue; Evocation; Intertextuality; Polyphony/Polyvocality; Representation; Rhetoric
Thomas, Elizabeth Marshall, 48, 105
Thornton, Robert, 97 n
Thought, analysis of, 238, 239–40
Todorov, Tzvetan, 3, 98 n, 201
Transcendence, 99, 123–36 passim
Transference, 203–8
Transcription, 116–17
Translation, 22, 51, 52, 137–38, 141–64
Travels in the Interior Districts of Africa, 35
Travels in West Africa, 35
Travel writing, 11, 28, 33–42 passim
"Trip Through the Mind Jail," 202, 222
Tristes Tropiques, 13, 112, 121 n
Trobriand Cricket, 112
Trobriands, 38, 112
Tropes, 50, 132, 256; arrival, 37, 42–43; Orientalist, 12
Truths, 6, 7, 25, 52–53, 237–38, 240–41, 257

Tuhami, 192, 208, 212
Turnbull, Colin, 1
Turner, Victor, 3, 98, 195 n, 199
Tyler, Stephen A., 1, 12, 24, 97 n,
    195 n, 265; post-modernism of, 21,
    122–140, 194 n; on univocal mean-
    ing, 230
Tylor, E. B., 141
Tyon, Thomas, 15–16
Typee, 103

Under the Rainbow, 31
Unintended consequences, 182–83,
    186, 187
United States: academic political econ-
    omy in, 167 n; ethnicity in, 194–
    233; social thought in, 166, 169
Univocity/Monophony, 5, 15, 126, 132,
    203, 230
Urbanism, 259, 260–61
"Use and Abuse of Anthropology," 110
Utopianism, 127, 128–29, 138–39

Valero, Helena, 28–30, 38
van der Post, Laurens, 48
Vernant, Jean-Pierre, 194
Vico, G., 10, 127
Vigil, Evangelina, 223
Village studies, 189
Villarreal, Jose Antonio, 219
Visualism, 11–12, 57–58, 130–31
Vizenor, Gerald, 202, 224, 227–28

Wagner, Roy, 115 n
Waiting, 192
Walker, Alice, 213
Walker, James, 15–17, 117
Wallerstein, Immanuel, 22 n, 167
Warner, Lloyd, 23
Way to Rainy Mountain, 225
Weber, Max, 143, 144, 241, 257
Weiner, Annette, 20
Weinreich, Max, 195 n, 231

Weinreich, Uriel, 195 n, 231
Welch, James, 202, 228
Welsh ancestry, of Mandans, 55, 59
Wendt, Alfred, 119
Werther, 61
West African Studies, 35
We, the Tikopia, 35–36
"What Makes an Interpretation Accept-
    able," 255
White, Hayden, 3, 26 n, 224 n
Whorf, Benjamin Lee, 10
Whyte, William F., 23
Williams, Raymond, 5–6; on pastoral,
    113–14; on realism, 169–70, 188,
    190; on structures of feeling, 3, 112
Williams, William Carlos, 3
Willis, Paul, 23, 169, 171, 173–88, 190
Winter in the Blood, 228
Wittgenstein, L., 10, 144, 236
Women, 17–19; Dinka, 17; in *Migra-
    tions of the Heart*, 217; *Nisa* and, 99,
    104, 107–8; *Woman Warrior* and,
    209; working class and, 188; Zamora
    and, 223. *See also* Feminism
Woman Warrior, 195, 208–10
Wong, Shawn Hsu, 210, 211–12
Woolf, Virginia, 2
Wordarrows, 227
Working class, 174–88 passim
World system, 22, 165 n, 167
World War I, 120
World War II, 207

Yanagisako, Sylvia, 97 n
Yanoama, 28
Yanomamo, 28–31
Yanomamo: The Fierce People, 31
Yates, Frances, 12
*y no se lo tragó la tierra (and the earth did
    not part)*, 221

Zamora, Bernice, 218, 222, 223

Designer: Sandy Drooker
Compositor: G&S Typesetters, Inc.
Text: 10/12 Baskerville
Display: Baskerville
Printer: Vail-Ballou Press
Binder: Vail-Ballou Press